D0398785

BOOK SALE

FEB 0 1 2006

Marshall McLuhan

Marshall McLuhan
Escape into Understanding
A Biography

W. Terrence Gordon

BasicBooks
A Division of HarperCollins*Publishers*

WEST DES MOINES PUBLIC LIBRARY

Photography credits: M.M. with Pierre Trudeau, reprinted with permission, Mr. F. Lennon/*Toronto Star*; M.M. with Ted Carpenter, reprinted with permission, courtesy Adelaide de Menil. Every reasonable effort has been made to obtain reprint permissions. The publisher will gladly receive information that will help rectify any inadvertent errors or omissions in subsequent editions

Copyright © 1997 by W. Terrence Gordon

Published by BasicBooks,
A Division of HarperCollins Publishers, Inc.

Published by arrangement with
Stoddart Publishing Co. Ltd.

All rights reserved. Printed in the United States of America. No part of this book may be used or reproduced in any manner whatsoever without written permission except in the case of brief quotations embodied in critical articles and reviews. For information address BasicBooks, 10 East 53rd Street, New York, NY 10022-5299.

Designed by Tannice Goddard

ISBN 0-465-00549-7

97 98 99 00 01 RRD 10 9 8 7 6 5 4 3 2 1

Non ridere, non lugere, neque detestari, sed intelligere. (Not to laugh, not to lament, not to curse, but to understand.)

– Spinoza

To high speed change no adjustment is possible. We become spectators only and must escape into understanding.

– Marshall McLuhan to Claude Bissell
8 March 1960

There seems to be a deeply willed ignorance in man. "Sin" might also be defined as lack of "awareness," "resistance to learning," and mankind being "threatened by understanding."

– Marshall McLuhan, conversation with Allen Maruyama
11 January 1972

CONTENTS

ACKNOWLEDGMENTS

I WISH TO THANK the many people who provided valuable help and support at various stages during the writing of this book. In particular, I thank Ruth Anderberg, Don Bastian, Michael Bishop, Patricia DeMéo, Sylvia Gravel (Canadian Conference of Catholic Bishops), Rubin Gorewitz, Bruce Greenfield, Jane Jacobs, Kathy Hutchon Kawasaki, Joe and Ann Marie Keogh, Tom and Jeannine Langan, Bob Logan, Bertrum MacDonald, Matie Molinaro, Henry Schogt, William Sloan, Father Francis Stroud, Jack and Mary Wilson, Natalie Wood, and Frank Zingrone.

Very special thanks must go to the McLuhan family, not only for inviting me to undertake the challenge of doing justice to Marshall McLuhan's life and work, but also for their generous assistance and constant encouragement. In particular, I thank Corinne McLuhan, Eric McLuhan, and Maurice McLuhan.

I could not have written this book without the surrounding and sustaining love and devotion of my family. My wife Theresa was involved in every aspect of the work, from the research to reading the final proofs. No expression of gratitude for her unfailing and selfless help could ever be adequate, but I offer it all the same.

W. T. G.
Bedford, Nova Scotia
June 1997

INTRODUCTION

I FIRST HEARD MARSHALL MCLUHAN speak in a lunch-hour lecture series at Victoria College, University of Toronto, in the mid-1960s, when his *Understanding Media* was bringing him to prominence. My fellow Vic students, along with engineers, pharmacists, lawyers, and faculty from across campus, had come to hear the man some were already labeling "seer," "guru," and "sage." McLuhan had come to warn against labels and teach about hearing.

Tall and straight in regulation tweed, bemused, bristling, and wearing the look of a man with a rich secret, he stepped up to the lectern, appearing not to notice that Alumni Hall was thronged to overflowing. The aftermath of his opening volley made it clear not only that he had noticed, but he had taken dead aim at every head in the room. A hush spread. McLuhan's voice, all caramel vowels, riding a roller coaster of cultured intonation, buffered the shock waves he set up between words and ideas — "utterings . . . outerings . . . outer rings."

Around me, some of the casualties began moaning. But the room was also taking on a lively buzz, and a few faces were lighting up. Including McLuhan's. Having issued his audience the twin challenge of thinking new thoughts and in new ways, he was taking it up *himself*, pursuing the tangents of his own unscripted talk, absorbed, thrusting, questing, communicating above all the sheer excitement of intellectual exploration.

In my first year at Vic, I had met many students "next door" at McLuhan's home college, St. Michael's. Often they would say, "You have Northrop Frye, but *we* have Marshall McLuhan." Once I heard

McLuhan speak, I thought I was beginning to understand that remark. Just beginning.

After reading *Understanding Media*, I turned to *The Mechanical Bride: The Folklore of Industrial Man*, puzzling over both the subtitle and the explanation of it, before giving up and settling for more lectures by McLuhan. I came to crave the mental bruising you could count on him to give.

Later, as graduate students at the University of Toronto, when we were supposed to be busy with more pedestrian work, my friend Tim Rutledge and I spent countless hours discussing McLuhan, poring over his writings, measuring reaction to him. In 1970, I left for a teaching position at the University of Alberta, having glimpsed McLuhan for the last time, driving his big black Oldsmobile Toronado, somewhat erratically, down Charles Street. (Even at the wheel of a car, he could barely stifle his consuming urge to act with daring originality.)

McLuhan was in my thoughts through more than fifteen years of teaching, though he was never the subject of my active writing projects. Then, in 1986, in an expansive mood after completing a book, I made a here's-what-to-do-with-the-rest-of-your-life list that included "McLuhan biography." My prospective subject had died at the end of 1980. When a life of McLuhan appeared in 1989, I crossed that item off, consoling myself that the project list was looking more manageable, with no effort on my part.

In 1994, with McLuhan receiving so much renewed attention in all the media, I proposed a short book on his work to one of my editors, who exclaimed, "He's my all-time favorite!" Focusing on McLuhan again after so long was pure pleasure. Thirty years of thinking, three months of writing, and I had a draft of *McLuhan for Beginners*. I wrote to the McLuhan family to request formal permission to use quotations from McLuhan's books, sending along a copy of my completed manuscript. A couple of weeks later came a telephone call from Corinne, Marshall's widow. Would I be interested in writing the authorized biography? A new adventure began.

I recognized McLuhan as a master thought-provoker from that first lecture at Victoria College. Two years spent amid thousands of archive files, recording interviews with his family, colleagues, and associates, and rereading his work only served to strengthen that opinion. But it was not till Eric McLuhan showed me his father's copy of Ferdinand de Saussure's *Course in Modern Linguistics* that I finally saw the essence and the unique quality of McLuhan's genius.

The book is crammed with reading notes in plain text and McLuhan cipher. They would have remained a mystery to me without my training in linguistics, and had I not spent as many years thinking about Saussure as about McLuhan. McLuhan's scribbles show him diving, like a kingfisher, into treacherous intellectual waters after Saussure's ideas, effortlessly carrying off those that suit his own purpose, breaking them open with audacious thrusts of the mind, and yet without distorting the little-understood coherence of Saussure's thought. The feat is all the more extraordinary when viewed against the background of misreadings of Saussure that mark twentieth-century intellectual history. And this from the man critics were quick to dismiss as a careless scholar.

In constructing the story of McLuhan's life and work, I have relied in the main on private papers of the McLuhan family, interviews with the family, his colleagues, associates, and friends, and above all, the McLuhan papers in the National Archives of Canada. The last include McLuhan's diaries (principally from his student days at the University of Manitoba and Cambridge University in the 1930s and from the final decade of his life), as well as notebooks, correspondence with family, friends, and collaborators numbering many thousands of pages, and draft copies of both his published and unpublished writings.

It may have been the new decade that inspired McLuhan to begin keeping a journal in 1930. The young man writes with a clear perception that his whole life will be shaped by the time he has chronicled the passage of his university years. A faithful diarist from the outset, he devotes a full page and more each day to recording events at home and at the university, along with his reactions, and giving full expression to his hopes and frustrations. Above all, he fills the pages with thoughts inspired by the authors he is reading and in so doing reveals his quickly emerging intellectual prowess.

By 1935, McLuhan had switched over to a five-year diary. The format forbids the expansive commentary typical of the earlier journals, but McLuhan's life was already crowded enough to make a telegraphic style appropriate to the telling. And what his diaries lack from this time is amply compensated for by the rich correspondence he opens with family and friends. Together, the diaries and the correspondence illuminate the life and the work.

Readers interested in consulting sources of information on McLuhan's life, without engaging in full-scale archival research, or in reading his work should be aware of the two companion volumes to the present work: *Who Was Marshall McLuhan?*, edited by Barrington Nevitt and Maurice McLuhan, and *Essential McLuhan*, edited by Eric McLuhan and Frank Zingrone.

Extracts from McLuhan's writings, interspersed with recollections by friends and colleagues, are available in *Marshall McLuhan: The Man and His Message*, edited by George Sanderson and Frank Macdonald. Additional writings about McLuhan's ideas, or inspired by them, are referred to in the bibliography of the present work.

As a professor in four universities beginning in the 1930s, as the driving force of the University of Toronto's Centre for Culture and Technology from 1964, and as a speaker on the international lecture circuit throughout the 1960s and '70s, McLuhan, while delivering his message about the radical transforming power of media, touched the minds not only of three generations of students but also of a huge number of men and women from all walks of life. And he exerted his own transforming power, leaving the indelible memory of his passion for learning as a vital legacy among colleagues, friends, and even the most casual of acquaintances. This is the man I have tried to evoke in the following pages.

ONE

Breaking Ground

1

The Fortunes of Family

The usual grounds are a great way lower down to the south-ward. There fish can be got at all hours, without much risk, and therefore these places are preferred. The choice spots over here among the rocks, however, not only yield the finest variety, but in far greater abundance; so that we often got in a single day what the more timid of the craft could not scrape together in a week. In fact, we made it a matter of desperate speculation — the risk of life standing instead of labor, and courage answering for capital.

—EDGAR ALLAN POE
"A DESCENT INTO THE MAELSTROM"

WILLIAM MCLUHAN, JR., Marshall McLuhan's great-grandfather, was sent to Canada for his own good. Born in Hillsborough, County Down, Ireland, young William loved money but hated work.[1] He showed no interest in the family linen business, little in his beautiful wife, Mary Edith Bradshaw, or their three children, but a great deal in spending freely and consuming spirits with his brother-in-law, James Bradshaw. The McLuhans and the Bradshaws put up passage money to ship their wayward heirs to Canada, in the belief that they would acquire strength of character by being thrown on their own resources. Together with their wives and young families, William Jr. and his drinking companion took their first sobering taste of the New World as they disembarked in Montreal, in the inhospitable spring of 1846.[2]

The voyage had taken its toll. Both families were confined with ship's fever for six months before they could begin their search for a new home. They settled in central Ontario's Simcoe County, near the town of Barrie. Little is known of this period in their lives, except that a fourth son was born to William Jr. and Mary Edith in the year after their arrival from Ireland. Their last child and only daughter was born in 1851.

Whether or not William Jr. fully mended the error of his ways is not clear, but it is certain that he ran out of money. When he sent a distressed appeal to the relatives in Ireland, the situation must have seemed all too familiar. A quick reply informed him that he had already received his full share of the family fortune and that he should buckle down and get to work.

William Jr.'s three eldest were by now able-bodied youths, and the foursome soon secured a logging contract. The benefits that the McLuhans and Bradshaws had hoped life in Canada would bestow on their errant offspring began to take shape in the desired rugged resourcefulness of the sons of William McLuhan, Jr. The firstborn, who had made the journey from Ireland with his parents at age eight, was James Hilliard McLuhan, the grandfather of Marshall McLuhan.

At age twenty-two, James left Simcoe County with his friend John McCollister and headed farther west into the southern Ontario heartland, attracted by the prospect of cheap land near Luther, near the present-day town of Conn. They made the trip on foot, a distance of some sixty miles over a winding course through seven or eight towns and villages. When the road ended, they made their way around bogs, reaching their final destination only with the help of a guide. The friends took little time deciding to buy adjacent properties of two hundred acres each.

As it happened, two other men were interested in acquiring the same land. Mounted on horseback, they scoffed at the foot-weary young hopefuls and set off for Guelph, forty miles to the south, to stake their claims. It was evening, and James reckoned that an overnight walk to Guelph would give them an advantage over their rivals, who would need to attend to their horses. James and John entered the Land Office as it opened at eight o'clock the next morning and registered their claims just as the pair on horseback rode up.

The young men made their way to Toronto and from there returned home on the Northern Railroad.

It took another year of work to earn the money they needed and to equip themselves for starting their new life in Luther. They made the trek with two wagons and two teams of oxen. Soon they were clearing their land. James built a house of pine logs, a handsome barn with dovetailed corners, and a granary large enough for three thousand bushels. The barn, later moved onto a foundation, is now well into its second century and still stands sturdily.

James McLuhan became a pillar of his community. He served at various times as deputy reeve, reeve, justice of the peace, and township clerk. His initiatives and organizational skills were responsible for the building of gravel roads, the establishment of a butter and cheese company, and the launching of local telephone service.

In 1874 he married Margaret Grieve, who had also come to Canada with her parents as a child — in her case from Scotland. Ten years James's junior, Margaret bore him nine children, the fourth child and second son being Herbert Ernest, the father of Marshall McLuhan.

In 1907, at age seventy, James McLuhan pulled up roots and moved with his family to Mannville, in the newly created province of Alberta. Perhaps he wanted to relive the challenge of his beginnings at Luther. In any case, it was there that Herbert would meet and marry Elsie Hall, and their first son, Marshall, would be born.

The biographical sketch of James McLuhan written by his granddaughter, Mrs. Doris Shebeck of Carmichael, California, shows certain similarities between James and his famous grandson. His love of dancing was apparently matched only by his skill, ranging over the polka, quadrille, step dancing, the shuffle, and more. When he could find a partner with energy to match his own, he would dance through his whole repertoire. Even at seventy, he could step with the best of them.

He was also known as a man of exceptional intellect and congenial personality. He always maintained a keen interest not only in his community but in the world at large. In spite of the demands of business, he read widely, enjoyed good music, and showed an intense curiosity about astronomy. In the final years of his life, he delved into Swedenborgian philosophy. Marshall McLuhan was only eight years old when a stroke felled his grandfather. Had James McLuhan lived longer, his grandson might have found in him a kindred spirit.

James McLuhan's pursuit of intellectual matters provided him with a convenient strategy to use whenever the local Methodist minister came by to inquire if he planned to attend church. The reply would involve a rambling discourse amid the abstractions of obscure sects, leaving nothing clearly understood except that McLuhan would not be joining the congregation. But James's wife Margaret was a deeply spiritual person. It was from her that their son Herbert acquired a great interest in the church, which was to become an anchor in the lives of his own sons, Marshall and Maurice.

THE HALL FAMILY HOMESTEAD sat beside the Annapolis River, on a road branching from the old post road to Greenwood, some two miles east of Kingston Station in Nova Scotia's Annapolis Valley. It was a typical farm home of the nineteenth century, with a large house and several barns and sheds. Poplars, like towering sentinels, flanked the long lane running from the road to the house. Years before, the property had been occupied by Acadian settlers. A large apple tree on the grounds was always referred to as the "Old French Tree."

When Henry Selden Hall married Margaret Marshall, an addition was made to the house, and it was here that Elsie Naomi was born on 10 January 1889, and her brother Ernest Raymond on 19 September 1890. Later, Henry Selden bought a property at North Kingston, on the back road running along the foot of the North Mountain. Here the farms stretched away from the road and up the slope of the mountain onto more level ground.

Elsie and Ray were raised in the Baptist faith. Before sitting down to breakfast, the family would gather in a circle in the kitchen while Henry Selden read a chapter of Scripture. Then, with everyone kneeling, he would pray aloud. No matter how pressing the chores of the day might be, family worship took priority.

The years at North Kingston brought changes to everyone in the family, but especially to Elsie, who thrived on the considerable attention paid to her by the Hall aunts. Encouraged by them, she did more visiting at Grandpa Hall's than anywhere else. Elsie was an excellent student and relished lining up at the front of the room in grade-school question-and-answer competitions. Making a game of learning appealed to her strong desire to excel, and she took "head of the class" as a great honor to be defended zealously. Elsie invariably stood first when report cards were issued. She also excelled at music, taking singing and organ lessons at home from William Brown, a distant cousin of her father. As she blossomed into a young woman, her lively personality and natural talents — combined with an elegance that was both inborn and cultivated — gave the tall, fair-skinned, dark-eyed Elsie Hall a dramatic presence that would later take her to the stage.

Four generations of his family had lived in Nova Scotia when, in 1905, the pioneering spirit infected Henry Selden Hall. He had transplanted the family once again — from North Kingston to Middleton, Nova Scotia — but he was becoming restless for yet another move. The West and its opportunities were much in the news, so he joined the Harvest Excursions, trekking three thousand miles west to Saskatchewan, where he worked for a time in the wheat fields during the late summer.[3] He returned home full of enthusiasm for the West, fixated on the idea of returning as soon as possible to get homestead land. At once he set about plans to wind up his farm operation in Middleton.

Margaret Hall doubted the wisdom of leaving Nova Scotia, their families, their friends. But Henry Selden would not be dissuaded, and before long, he had made all his arrangements for the move. He loaded lumber, beds, chairs, tables, tools, three horses, a cow, a heifer, and the organ from the front parlor into a boxcar bound for Alberta. He also packed the kitchen range and a small box-stove for heat along the way. In a blinding snowstorm on 17 March 1906, the Halls said their farewells and left — without Elsie.

Margaret Hall's protests against the move had proved ineffectual, but her daughter was having her own way. She remained in Nova Scotia to teach school at East Margaretville. Elsie had earned her teaching certificate from Acadia University in Wolfville, Nova Scotia. Among the faculty members there was Miss Josephine L. Goodspeed, who had trained at Boston's Emerson College of Oratory and brought much of that institution's program with her.

Elocution, in the Emerson tradition, was a fine and complex art, involving far more than techniques of voice control and public speaking. Miss Goodspeed taught her students to express "by means of the body, the face, and the voice, the various emotions of the soul."[4] Elocution promoted personal development through the awakening of latent powers and literary appreciation through the acquisition of interpretive skills. In this respect, Elsie's grounding in the elocutionary craft, later honed to perfection during her early years in Winnipeg (and absorbed by both her sons at that time), converged with the performance-based aspect of literary New Criticism that her son Marshall would learn at Cambridge University. The parallel did not end there, for the Course of Study in Elocution at Acadia sought to offer students powers for the true expression of thought and emotion and to encourage independent thinking. The syllabus speaks of students "developing their originality," the course "enabling them to speak with conviction and in a pleasing manner, upon any subject in which they may be interested," the method aiming "to arouse and keep the imagination active while speaking."[5] These were skills that Elsie cultivated and passed on to her sons.

The Halls arrived in Alberta on 3 April 1906. Henry soon found two parcels of land to rent, six miles south of the town of Mannville, where he could put in a spring crop. The family moved into a log cabin on a homestead, near Minburn, prepared to endure hardships in the belief that they would be wealthy landowners within a few years. During their first summer, Margaret Hall ran a sort of private school to bring the family a modest extra income.

For reasons she never disclosed, Elsie had a change of heart about remaining in Nova Scotia and joined the family in 1908. That year she became the teacher at the school in Creighton, Alberta, boarding with a family that had arrived soon after hers: the family of James Hilliard McLuhan, whose son Herbert had already staked his own land claim by the time Elsie arrived as a lodger.

Ten years Elsie's senior, the tall, affable, and engaging Herbert inevitably became the center of her social life. The high-spirited nature they shared drew them together. Despite Elsie's vitality and charms, there had been few young men in her life, and no one quite like Herbert. On New Year's Eve day 1909, Elsie Hall and Herbert McLuhan were married in the front parlor of the Hall family home in Minburn.

THE VISION OF PROSPERITY that had drawn the McLuhans and the Halls to Alberta took the newlyweds out onto the frozen prairie, where Herbert aimed to see his homestead grow. It kept them there less than a year. Elsie was dissatisfied and was looking for a broader stage for her own ambitions. Looking back, at age eighty-two, on their move to Alberta's capital city of Edmonton, Herbert would say to his elder son, "Your mother played her part in the plan."[6] In fact, it *was* Elsie's plan, if not an outright ultimatum.

The move to Edmonton held great promise. The city was growing at a frenzied pace. The construction of the Canadian Pacific Railway in 1883 had bypassed Edmonton in favor of Calgary, two hundred miles to the south, but Edmonton's location on the North Saskatchewan River proved to be its strength. Even without the CPR main line, it had become the provincial capital when Alberta was created in 1905. As the service center for a vast agricultural region beginning to surge with development, the city was about to enjoy its first golden time as Elsie and Herbert arrived.

Optimism abounded. There were fortunes to be made. Though he could be easygoing to the point of apathy, Herbert McLuhan caught the spirit and went into the real estate business. If he had any regrets about selling land instead of tilling it, there was scarcely a moment to express them. Herbert was prospering, and Elsie was pregnant. Herbert Marshall McLuhan was born on 21 July 1911. The proud parents sent out announcements heralding the birth with the saying, "Unto us a child is born, unto us a son is given."[7]

Two years later, Edmonton was still in the grip of feverish growth, and Elsie was pregnant again. Though she was far from enthusiastic about having conceived a second child, in later years, Herbert claimed that prior to his marriage he had heard a voice saying of Elsie: "This woman will give you two sons."[8] A second son was indeed born to the McLuhans on 9 August 1913 and christened Maurice Raymond.

With the outbreak of World War I, Herbert's real estate business collapsed overnight and within a year he was an enlisted man. He had served one year when he succumbed to an outbreak of influenza that prevented him from accompanying his battalion overseas. On being discharged, he moved his young family to the Manitoba capital of Winnipeg and took a job selling insurance with the North American

Life Assurance Company. Without knowing it, he moved Elsie one step closer to the beginning of a long and varied dramatic career.

MAURICE MCLUHAN (NICKNAMED "RED" for his flaming shock of hair) retains memories of his older brother from the time they were three and five. Red pondered their Sunday school lessons as he played with the family kitten and asked, "Do you think we can take her into Heaven?" Marshall was confident, reassuring, authoritative: "Sure, just tuck her under your arm and say the Lord's Prayer as you go through the gates."

As a youngster, Marshall was always quiet and retiring, to the point of being antisocial. He had a great love of animals. "Rags," an Airedale-collie, was an integral and devotedly cared for member of the family.

In his earliest days at public school, Marshall showed no promise as a future scholar. His report cards indicate marks ranging as low as 20 percent for spelling in grade three, borderline failures in other subjects, and few, other than in reading, distinguished achievements. At the end of grade six, he failed his year. But Elsie, engaged at the time in supply teaching, prevailed on the teacher and the school principal to give him a chance in grade seven. The probation was a success and more. Miss Muir proved to be the inspiration Marshall needed, kindling the interest in English literature that would anchor his career. He put scholastic failure behind him, but indulged himself in quirky spellings throughout his life.

From the age of ten, Marshall delivered newspapers. His route consisted of about a hundred papers each day. The experience was encouraged by Elsie to develop discipline and a sense of responsibility. Keen on the prizes offered to paperboys for enlisting new subscribers, but too self-effacing to be assured of success, Marshall would regularly thrust Red forward to make a sales pitch.

As he moved into his early teens, Marshall began to shed his retiring nature. He and Red played baseball, and it was Marshall who formed a team from among the boys of the neighborhood, reserving the coveted position of pitcher for himself. As the organizer of a local hockey team, Marshall decided that he would play at center. Elsie's dynamism and motivation were beginning to show in him. He and

Red played whatever sports were current, including tennis and ping-pong, two favorites at which Marshall excelled.

At age twelve, he became active in the Boy Scouts, participating for two years and earning his King's Scout. Scoutmaster Charles A. Hill recognized his competence and invariably, when guests were present, directed questions relating to scouting Marshall's way, confident that he would have the answers.

Marshall had answers for Red on any number of topics and regularly treated him as a captive audience of one. Having discovered an obscure book on the subject of determinism, Marshall illuminated the subject for his brother: "You see this fly? How it moves? Well, if it lifted the other leg instead, the whole universe would come to an end."

Elsie organized her sons' free hours — concerts and plays in the winter, picnics in the summer — until Marshall refused to have so much of his time planned for him. Till the end of their public school days, Marshall and Red spent summer vacations on the farm at Elm Creek, some twenty-five miles south of Winnipeg, Manitoba, where their grandfather Hall had relocated. These extended visits served to get the boys off the Winnipeg streets for the summer and provided an introduction to the world of farm animals and the vastness of the prairies.

During the summer that Marshall turned twelve, Elsie took her sons to Vancouver Island, where her brother Ray was assistant superintendent on a federal experimental farm, north of Victoria, on the edge of the town of Saanich. The stay proved to be an enriching experience for Marshall. Gertrude Straight, the daughter of the superintendent, was keenly interested in English literature. She and Marshall spent many hours discussing novels and reading poetry aloud. Mountain vistas, a strange sight for a prairie boy, and the Pacific seascapes exerted an enduring influence that first showed itself soon after the family returned to Winnipeg. Marshall loved to build things; he had already built a crystal set fitted with earphones that he and Red could separate as they went to bed, so that each could listen as they fell asleep. Now Marshall turned his hand to building model sailboats, and it became his great enthusiasm. He built one after another, each larger than the last, taking them to Victoria Beach on Lake Winnipeg during holidays.

Elsie's interest in elocution was rekindled and channeled in

Winnipeg under the direction of Alice Leone Mitchell, who, like Miss Goodspeed, had trained at the Emerson College of Oratory. An absorbing interest soon grew into a vocation. Elsie's talent and flair as a dramatic artist put her ability to perform before audiences far above those of the average elocutionist. From Elsie, Marshall and Red spontaneously acquired skills that would serve them well throughout their lifetimes at the lectern and in the pulpit.[9]

With verve and determination, Elsie prepared to make her debut as a traveling performer. Brochures with her photograph were printed, announcing "Elsie McLuhan, Reader and Impersonator." She did all her own organization and scheduling, arranging tours from Winnipeg to Halifax and Winnipeg to Victoria in alternate years. Using an instrumentalist or a choir to punctuate her performances, she would make a change of outfit between numbers. Her clear and forceful voice served her well on the stage as she performed an astonishingly vast repertoire, ranging over the dramatic, the lyric, the inspirational, and the humorous.[10]

WHEN HE WAS SEVENTEEN, Marshall acquired blueprints for a sailboat[11] and enlisted friends Bill Jones and Tom Easterbrook to help build the fourteen-footer. Using a neighbor's garage, they set to work measuring, cutting, planing, and sanding, resorting to outside expertise only when the complexities of the spoon-shaped bow proved to be beyond them. In landlocked Winnipeg, they even managed to find a hundred square feet of silk Egyptian sailcloth to ensure the lightness of the craft and improve its performance.

Completed with loving attention to detail, it was loaded on a wagon and trundled to the Fort Rouge shore of the Red River. The steady breeze off the prairie and the welcome of Winnipeg sailors greeted them. With the launching ceremony complete, *The Lark* slipped into the water and sprang enough leaks to sink within minutes. But by the time the salvage operation was over, water was already beginning to swell the new wood, sealing the seams of the hull. Nature eventually completed her work well enough to make the boat usable. Only a little corking and putty was required by way of repairs.

Though an occasional leak could mar an otherwise peaceful

excursion, the craft was to give years of service and countless happy hours to Marshall and his friends. Red, Elsie, and Herbert would also enjoy the river cruises. Sailing became a passion with Marshall — a passion with a dimension he recognized as spiritual when he reflected on it some years later from the vantage point of Cambridge.[12] There he would find satisfaction of a different kind in team rowing. And even in Toronto, more than twenty years after his days of hoisting sail under the Manitoba sky, given the chance to hear the snap of canvas catching wind, to feel its tug, and water slapping the hull beneath his feet, he would become a sailor again.

Waves on the Red River never reached more than a foot and a half in height,[13] but Marshall would identify throughout his adult life with the sailor who survived the most harrowing of adventures in Edgar Allan Poe's story "A Descent into the Maelstrom."

Poe tells the story of a fisherman caught in a dreaded whirlpool of the Arctic Ocean, known as the Maelstrom, off the northwest coast of Norway. For years the man and his two brothers shunned safe fishing grounds in favor of a more bountiful spot they could reach only by timing their run past the deadly cyclone of water, with its power to suck down boats, trees, whales . . . even the largest of ships. Ahead or behind the time of the slack waters, the bold brothers could be drawn to their doom in the ocean's great funnel. Twice they were stranded beyond the Maelstrom and obliged to stay at anchor overnight. Becalmed on their fishing ground another time, they starved for a week before they could make for home.

After years of calculated risk, they are returning to port once again when the fiercest hurricane of the century bears down on them, leaving them helpless and driven straight for the black, spinning waters. One of the trio perishes at once, carried overboard with the broken mast to which he had lashed himself for safety, and the other two descend into the whirling waters with their vessel. Amid the chaos, one brother sees both horror and magnificence. From his observations as to which objects descend most quickly to their destruction, on the craggy rocks at the bottom of the vortex, he detects a pattern that gives him hope and the clue for a survival strategy.

Unable to make his brother understand what must be done, he jumps overboard alone, lashed to the barrel that will keep him from descending further into the watery spiral. The other, preferring the apparent security of clinging to a ring-bolt on their ship, perishes with it.

When the Maelstrom finally slackens, the hurricane, still raging, carries the surviving brother down the coast, where fishermen pluck him from the sea. Speechless, at first, from the horror he has endured, he is finally able to tell his rescuers what befell him and how he understood the way to escape, only to be greeted with disbelief. Recounting his story to the traveler who is Poe, while showing the scene of it from the heights of a great cliff, he describes himself as broken in body and soul. And he no longer expects anyone to believe his story.

Beginning with a 1946 article entitled "Footprints in the Sands of Crime,"[14] Marshall McLuhan would evoke the story of the Maelstrom many times in his writing and teaching. It figures prominently in the preface to *The Mechanical Bride*, with an explicit statement of its place and importance in the McLuhan method: "Poe's sailor saved himself by studying the action of the whirlpool and by cooperating with it. The present book likewise makes few attempts to attack the very considerable currents and pressures set up around us today by the mechanical agencies of the press, radio, movies, and advertising. It does attempt to set the reader at the center of the revolving picture created by these affairs where he may observe the action that is in progress and in which everybody is involved."[15]

The words might just as well be McLuhan's when Poe's survivor says: "I became obsessed with the keenest curiosity about the whirl itself. I positively felt a *wish* to explore its depths, even at the sacrifice I was going to make; and my principal grief was that I should never be able to tell my old companions on shore about the mysteries I should see."[16]

Like Poe's sailor, McLuhan came to the place of seeking amusement through rational detachment in surveying new environments that threatened the cultural values he cherished. And like the solitary figure in the tale, he would be greeted with skepticism for his explanation of how to escape the maelstrom of the electronic age. But that was years ahead of him as he sailed *The Lark* on the Red River in the carefree summer of 1928.

2

Intellectual Seeds

> "What do you intend to do when you grow up, Mr. McLuhan?"
> Me: "As Dr. Johnson when at the age of three months once
> answered Joseph Addison 'Outside of being a great and influ-
> ential man, sir, I have not the faintest idea,' I too with him can
> say I have not the faintest idea."
>
> –*Marshall McLuhan's diary,*
> *10 January 1930*

THE MANUAL SKILL OF young Marshall the boat-builder seemed to
dictate a career. And the company of practical-minded friends exerted
its influence. Marshall joined them in enrolling in the engineering
program at the University of Manitoba in Winnipeg in the fall of
1928. Before he had completed a year, however, he discovered that he
was not in his element. Then, as he worked at a summer job among
engineers, the misguided choice was confirmed. Some of his coworkers
simply ignored Marshall, as he spent every free moment reading,
while others resented the presence of the lean, self-absorbed six-
footer. But when he tried to turn their conversations away from sex
to English literature, they saw his passionate commitment to the
subject and suggested that here was his true calling. He needed little
persuading. In the fall of 1929, he switched to a four-year Bachelor of
Arts program that would focus on English, history, and philosophy.[1]
   The excitement of setting out on his intellectual odyssey was

dampened as soon as Marshall saw how vast a job it would be to master the domain he wanted to stake out. And nothing less than mastery would satisfy him. He set his own program of reading, developed his own uses for what he read. "I have to read outside the course to maintain interest," he confided to his diary.[2] Thomas Carlyle was an early favorite, because of his bold, innovative language. His gauge of self-worth came from reading Carlyle's biography: the exercise made him feel hopeless and incompetent.[3] After Carlyle, Thomas Macaulay[4] and Samuel Johnson would beckon him to the heights of greatness. Later still, Trevelyan, Boswell, Thackeray, and Shakespeare. Self-doubt began to give way to a sense of mission: "If it be not within the precincts of literature, it will be executed at least by the pen."[5] At the same time, he was mature enough to assess his interests in English literature as immature, but he believed they were developing along the line they would ultimately follow.[6]

Marshall was already indulging a taste for rubbing ideas together, and the impetus was not restricted to literary sources. Of his studies in astronomy and geology, he noted in his diary: "I never study them but that a dozen ideas of probable cycles of man's creation, fall, salvation or condemnation, strike me."[7] This reference to cycles comes five years before Marshall discovered James Joyce and Giambattista Vico's cyclical theory of history. To round out his psychology course, he explored psychic research, but cautiously, because he assessed himself as "susceptible and imaginative"[8] and wished to avoid the dangers of the subject. When his parents entertained Miss James, an English visitor, Marshall discovered that she was deeply involved with psychic matters. He pondered their discussion, concluding in his diary that the power of the mediums was beyond their own understanding, and that there is nothing spiritual in those powers.[9]

By the spring of 1930, Marshall congratulated himself that he was meeting an intellectual standard set by the great minds whose ideas he had discovered largely on his own. He was less sure that any congratulations were in order for his professors. One made Latin "twice as dry as necessary," and at the hands of another the gems of English literature were "degraded to the dust."[10] Others showed their inadequacies: "A little discussion with a prof [after class] often shows you that their reading has not been all-embracing even of the great things.

It makes you feel that some time and some good work would soon place you far beyond them."[11]

Far beyond them meant beyond the university, and that was where Marshall believed the call to greatness would lead.[12] In his first year, he was already entertaining thoughts of graduate work, but not of a life in the ivory tower. In fact, he looked forward to the day when he would "possess the correct phraseology" to explain why he planned to avoid the ranks of the academics, though he was already well able to give the gist of the explanation: "great creative or even critical work never comes from them."[13] At most, teaching would be temporary; at best, it would be a catalyst: "Perhaps teaching until I found myself would be better than even a good job without time or associations suitable to finding myself."[14] In spite of his lack of enthusiasm for a life in the professoriate, the young McLuhan often made thoughtful observations on pedagogical matters. Noting that one instructor's exuberant style had an oppressive effect, he concluded that the most effective enthusiasm in intellectual matters is "cool, deliberate, and using to exuberance only occasionally."[15]

The university year was too short for Marshall and the summer too long,[16] so he set himself a program of study once again: Macaulay on Johnson, Boswell on Johnson, a survey and assessment of modern commentaries on Johnson, more Macaulay.[17] This was no casual summer project; Marshall put the full scholarly apparatus into operation, preparing a complete index of literary references in Macaulay's essays,[18] and making note of particularly striking statements and descriptions.[19] This, and other readings — Charles Lamb's essays,[20] Shakespeare, Matthew Arnold, G. K. Chesterton[21] — were labors of love, and they filled the long hours on those days when he was not called to report for work at his summer job in the 1930 Winnipeg mosquito campaign.

Concerned that he weighed only 136 pounds, he had taken the job to build up his physique. The work was demanding, draining more than invigorating, even if it afforded occasional opportunities for unscheduled diversions.[22] The oil used as an insecticide irritated his eyes. His stomach, sensitive at the best of times, turned at the sickly sweet odor. The reluctant prairie spring brought some days so cold that he had to move about constantly to keep warm. On others the heat was exhausting. On May 23 it snowed. The next day he was sailing his beloved boat on the Red River. Just as he had the summer before, Marshall set himself the task of elevating the level of conversation among the workers by steering it to the classics of English literature.[23] By the middle of June, his duties had been changed, and he was walking twenty miles a day, scouting prospective sites for the work crews.[24] By the middle of July, there were still enough mosquitos to keep the campaign open. By the end of the summer, he still weighed 136 pounds.

Having rescued himself from months of lethal boredom by self-directed reading, Marshall returned to university in September to find that he might have to do so again. His hopes for plunging into a stimulating study of Milton were disappointed at the first lecture in English, where the professor "talked steadily for an hour concerning the man and his work without giving me a new thing."[25] There was, at least, a small satisfaction in being able to answer the boring professor's first question of the year. When he asked the meaning of "imprimatur," Marshall alone knew.[26] His habit of making lists of new words was paying off.[27]

He could tolerate boredom, but not superficiality. He railed against a "shallow, surface-scratching" lecturer and the undiscerning students who could only "stare and gasp at his erudition."[28] He tried to hide his impatience, but often failed. The attitudes that Marshall observed in some of his teachers disappointed him as much as their teachings. When he asked if the New Testament had made any contribution to philosophy, the professor replied that he had not read it, but felt safe in answering "no."[29] From another instructor who had been quick to repeat the received opinion of Macaulay, Marshall elicited the confession that he had never read the great author's History of England.[30]

Occasionally, Marshall's high expectations of his professors were met — even surpassed. He often disagreed with much, if not most, of what history professor Noel Fieldhouse had to say, but his lectures stimulated mental effort of the kind that galvanized Marshall.[31] To distract himself from the far commoner disappointments, he threw himself into writing his first article for publication in the University of Manitoba student newspaper, choosing Macaulay as his subject.

The subject was pure pleasure, the young writer inspired. He saw his responsibility to write carefully, but was sufficiently informed to proceed quickly . . . "Albeit my pen seems palsied. My mind is ever too far ahead of it."[32] By the time he had written the piece and taken pains over revisions, the first flush of enthusiasm had long since passed. His early confidence that the article would be printed gave way to much doubt.[33] It needn't have. Grabbing a copy of the *Manitoban* on 28 October 1930, Marshall was astonished to find that he had not only broken into print but been given pride of place. He had convinced himself that the Macaulay piece was "not up to much," but his peers thought otherwise: "Many glances are now thrown my way that never were before."[34] He was offered the position of associate editor of the *Manitoban* and recognized the benefit that the experience would offer, the connections it would provide. But he turned it down, because of the inevitable sacrifice of time required, and because editorial work seemed as unlikely a part of his future as university teaching.[35]

To be able to savor success over the Macaulay essay brought Marshall a welcome distraction from the tensions of home life. It may have brought the first glimmer of hope that he could fulfill his ambitions in spite of disruption and stress. The sustained and complete quiet he longed for, the harmonious atmosphere that would allow him to luxuriate in his studies, were not to be found in the house at 507 Gertrude Avenue.[36] The problem was Elsie; the problem was Herbert; the problem was their marriage. Marshall assigned the blame democratically: "An utter lack of judgement and experience on both sides is evident."[37]

Perhaps the blame went back even further, to Elsie's father. Henry Selden Hall was an explosive man. His family could confide nothing to him for fear of a violent outburst. In spite of his Christian convictions, he was brutal toward hired hands. He had good stock in the barn, and a finer barn than a house. His animals were his pride and joy, but if a horse misbehaved, he did not hesitate to take a chain to it. When evidence came to light for tuberculosis in cattle in the community, he flared into an uncontrollable rage and shot his entire prize-winning herd, without any indication that they had succumbed to the disease.

He was physically abusive toward his daughter, which colored her attitude and her relations to men for life. Frustrated from the earliest days of her marriage to discover that Herbert's charisma was both his strength and his weakness, Elsie's irritation with him fed on itself, for he consistently failed to respond in kind when she displayed the volatile behavior she had learned — and learned to face — from her father. Later, her younger son, Maurice, would also give in to her verbal attacks and fits of temper. It was only in her elder son, Marshall, that she found a line of resistance, and it earned him her respect.

Herbert did not inherit James McLuhan's penchant for intellectual matters, or at least not enough to suit Elsie. The handsome, well-built six-footer was an inveterate socializer and played the fiddle at local schoolhouse dances. Adaptability and congeniality were his strong suits, but neither these nor any of his other qualities compensated in his wife's eyes for his lack of motivation. Elsie also took a dim view of many of Herbert's relatives. She did not hesitate to ask them to leave the house after the briefest of visits. As a result, the McLuhan family came to regard the Halls as "plootey," a combination of *plutocratic* and *snooty*.

Driven, restless, and every bit as impatient as her father, Elsie generated the turmoil in the McLuhan household. Dissatisfied with her lot in life, her husband's lack of ambition — and perhaps with herself — she made him and her elder son the targets of frequent attacks. Herbert, calm by nature, remained so no matter how explosive his wife became or how unpredictable her behavior. Marshall interpreted this as indifference and wished that his father would "snap out of it."[38] He managed, at times, to inure himself, even to sublimate the chaos into caricature: "Grandma was grumpy, Dad was dopey, Red was ranting, I was irritated. Didn't get much done." An impossible situation was frustrating an impossible goal: "That which I should like to accomplish could only be done by 24 hours of solid concentration every day."[39]

With Elsie away performing on her birthday in 1930, it was Marshall who made a wish: "May we as a family have a happier and more united life in the coming years."[40] Nearly three months later, as she was completing her tour of eastern Canada, he seemed to have little confidence that the wish could come true: "Well, poor Mother will be home one week from today. I note it sadly that we have got on very well without her. I doubt if we could get on as well without Dad, but certainly we can't get along with both."[41] It proved to be a welcome relief when the time came for her next tour.

There was little domestic quiet even when Elsie was between eruptions. She put much of her earnings from her successful performance tours into home improvements, and the house often looked like a construction site — carpentry, painting, plumbing, wallpapering and furniture-shifting seemed to go on without end. A new icebox would arrive, then a Persian rug, then a washing machine. Scholarly concentration was next to impossible. Social gatherings were frequent — too frequent to suit Marshall.[42] And Elsie did not even have to be home to cause upheaval: "What mental discomfort Mother's foolish [holiday] plans and telegrams have caused me."[43]

She regularly returned from her tours in good health and good spirits, still basking in the acclaim she had garnered.[44] But soon storm clouds would darken the domestic sky. Marshall stood his ground in the face of maternal rage and viewed the confrontations as useful training for future debates.[45] He never wished to hurt her feelings, and he pitied her for her instability. His diary note for 1 December 1930 reads: "Mother has not many strong anchors and certainly no sea anchor. When the billows rage and hiss she knows no means to escape or palliate their wrath." He recognized that his mother's was a self-made and self-perpetuating hell.[46] In spite of Marshall's powerful insights into Elsie's character, he despaired of ever fully understanding her: "I cannot figure Mother out. No one else has been able to either. Herself least of all."[47] At the same time, he knew he had learned enough to be cautious in the search for a mate[48] — a search Elsie encouraged him to keep in mind by bringing home young women.

His most extensive meditation on Elsie, from his diary entry of 10 March 1930, offers not only a psychological portrait of the lady but draws together his thoughts on marriage, faith, and the fortunes of family. He readily acknowledges that she is a remarkable woman, but "violent in procedure" and given to overdoing everything. Ostentatious and without continuity, she could be superficial, and Marshall notes that her influence on him and his brother has been "not entirely for the good." In the midst of these observations, he turns to a self-assessment, alternately seeing and overlooking the qualities he shares with Elsie: "I must, must, must attain worldly success to a real degree. It seems inconsistent I know to wish for such things and yet have your trust in God. However, I believe that He meant us all to achieve as much happiness on this earth as we could. My temperament could never be happy, nor give happiness to those who must one day be dependent upon me and my friends, if abject poverty were to be my lot. It has been the fate of both sides of the family."

Marshall was proud of his mother and the success she enjoyed in her career, and in spite of all the upheavals, he shared many pleasant times with Elsie, Herbert, and Red. They attended movies, concerts, recitals, vaudeville shows, and plays. Elsie sailed with Marshall and golfed with Red. And Elsie and Herbert were capable of enjoying an evening out dancing. Elsie showed her love for her sons through her generosity to them. But the gift Marshall treasured most, and received so rarely, was that of uninterrupted hours that could be given to reflection.[49]

Marshall adored his Aunt Ethel, Herbert's sister. A spirited and independent woman, she enjoyed a flourishing practice as a chiropractor in Lynchburg, Virginia. Her visits prompted reflections in which he repaid Elsie in kind for her harsh judgments: "[Aunt Ethel] has spent her whole life in bolstering up other people and especially her brothers and sisters. One could never be otherwise than happy where she is and it is my exquisitely keen regret that I had not such a person for my mother. One who would have softened rather than developed my nature and inherent harshness and weaknesses. I have never known what it was to have a mother, and Mother maintains that I have never had a 'man' for my father. In the latter regard, I am not of her persuasion, though Dad's several incapacities are palpable."[50]

Marshall could overlook the incapacities. He enjoyed his father's company, for they both enjoyed endless talk. Whether they began in the early evening or after midnight, three-hour conversations were common. Marshall read aloud from the latest author to have captured his attention, while Herbert and Red listened respectfully. Herbert's preferences in reading had always run to the Winnipeg newspapers and English magazines. His elder son's growing erudition opened new vistas for him. The style of presentation that Marshall put to use in their bull sessions had its effect, though he apparently gave himself no credit for this. Of an evening spent reading aloud passages from Macaulay to Herbert and Red, he commented: "Poor Dad is fairly haunted by them. I fear that it is because he is not sufficiently occupied with other things."[51] Before long, however, Herbert was occupying himself with readings in economics and psychology suggested by Marshall. He became an avid amateur of psychology, attending lectures by visiting psychologists and using his newfound knowledge in his insurance work.

Occasionally there were heart-to-heart talks about family matters, but more often Marshall steered the discussions to literature, metaphysics, psychology — weighing and probing ideas from his day's lectures. When Herbert introduced a topic, Marshall could be counted on for an animated response and a forceful opinion.[52] It mattered little if they saw eye to eye; these were intellectual disputes, not confrontations of the type in which Elsie trapped Marshall. They talked simply for the satisfaction of exchanging ideas: "We have some great discussions, Dad and I. It hinders free conversation for Grandma or Mother to be present."[53] Their evenings would often end with a singsong around the piano, particularly following evening church services, when they returned home accompanied by friends.[54]

When the long-awaited spring arrived in Winnipeg, Marshall, Red, and Herbert hauled tools and books down to the river. With the boat's rigging repaired, hull painted, and gaff varnished, the trio would spend long, lazy hours absorbed in reading. The give and take of ideas continued. Marshall dominated, without always reducing his father and brother to a mesmerized audience. Herbert even proved to be an inspiration to Marshall in a scheme to work out the moral and social laws "governing humanity, using psychology and metaphysics to throw new light on some of Christ's sayings.[55] "It was Dad's idea, but he has not bothered to carry it far enough." To this private reproach, Marshall added the comment that his father was "prone to be too communicative," concluding with an observation that could hardly be further from the famous McLuhan probes of the 1960s: "These things demand elaboration before communication."[56]

Herbert's idea absorbed Marshall for months, and they pursued it together. They found a passage in a Macaulay essay on Southey's colloquies dealing with laws in the precise sense that they had been trying to develop. Marshall took it as a vindication of their efforts *and* of Macaulay.[57] Gratifying support for their notion continued to emerge: "I was much surprised to find in Aldous Huxley the very theory that Dad and I had worked out."[58]

In the spring of 1931, Herbert lost his position as assistant manager at the North American Life Assurance Company, receiving a demotion to salesman,[59] and it appeared, for the first time since Elsie had begun her career as a monologist, that her concerts would not assure her financial independence for the year ahead.[60] Canada was in the depths of the Great Depression, but Marshall was confident that hardship would not befall the family. At the same time, he began to look at his father as Elsie had for years: "I have found myself subject to a growing tendency to criticize Dad lately. His faults become very firmly impressed on anyone who is vitally interested in anything. His troubles largely spring from a lack of education. He is slow, and careless of time, clothes, and ideas. Lack of aim in anything whatsoever might sum him up."[61] The restless, driving ambition of "H.S.,"[62] so utterly lacking in Herbert, surfaces in this judgment of him by his son. There are few references to Herbert in Marshall's diaries after this time, and none to the moral and social laws that father and son had worked out.

The young McLuhan reflected on the satisfaction and pride that one could take in the success of a brother, son, or friend.[63] And years later, he would work out the laws of media with his firstborn, Eric, taking pride in his son and supreme satisfaction in their collaboration. But in 1931, as his father's "incapacities" became more palpable to Marshall than ever before, more difficult to overlook, the vitality of their relationship weakened. He kept his distance from both the turbulent and the nurturing aspects of family life in reflecting on "the cruel fate that ever mated Elsie Hall and Herb McLuhan."[64]

THOUGH HE MAINTAINED A distance from his family, Marshall felt no estrangement in his religious beliefs. Faith in God had been nurtured in their children by both the Halls and the McLuhans. The families, both Baptists, practiced a religion of faith, hope, and charity that varied little from one generation to the next, though Marshall would hold his own opinions on everything from the practitioners to the pastors, from predestination to Pentecost.

Years of religious training from earliest childhood produced reflexes in Marshall. If it was Sunday morning, he was in Bible class at Winnipeg's Nassau Baptist Church, even in his university years. If a friend confided a personal problem, he prayed for him.[65] There were reflexes of language, too: "with God's help . . .," "may a loving God . . .," "I pray God that . . ." Unless these phrases are understood as spontaneous and unselfconscious, they give the McLuhan diaries of his university years a tone of affected piety. To read beyond the phrases is to see that he was not capable of affectation.

Bible classes were not always up to Marshall's high expectations of spiritual nourishment combined with enlightening insights. His own systematic study of the Scriptures[66] often covered more ground and more intensively. Yet for many years he rarely missed a Bible class, even though he found a succession of teachers had little more to offer than "feeble, faltering, immature, disjointed utterances."[67] In one he would find a disappointing outlook; another would prove unequal to the task of initiating discussion — or perhaps unequal to keeping up in a discussion launched by the enthusiastic Marshall.[68] Occasionally, an intellectual gem would flash, rewarding him for his faithful attendance, as when he learned that Joseph's "coat of many colors" was a mistranslation from the Hebrew of "coat of long sleeves."[69]

At the beginning of 1930, Marshall had recognized that his views on religion were changing, and he speculated that they would become "broad and not radical," noting that it was the most futile of subjects to debate.[70] Futile or not, religion stimulated discussion with cut and thrust, an opportunity Marshall could never resist. A friend craving support for his views on true Christianity found them vivisected, condemned as impractical. "There is a little devil in me that finds holes in everything he suggests," Marshall observed without remorse.[71] Religion required as much rigorous reflection as any other subject.

Years before he would refer to himself as an "intellectual thug,"[72] Marshall was something of a religious thug, capable of taking on several opponents at once. A lunch hour at the university found him with four or five classmates he knew only casually. The science students among them were discussing evolution. It was enough to set Marshall off: "I whaled into them on the matter of 'laws' and God's identity."[73] He took a few jabs at their dogmatism, and they were soon defenseless. A "tall and angelic person"[74] of the evangelical persuasion stepped into the ring but misjudged the strength and endurance of his opponent. "I had all the talking I wanted by three o'clock," Marshall noted with satisfaction.[75]

His habit of reading the Bible and secular literature at the same sitting, formed in his undergraduate days, stayed with him throughout his life.[76] He drew the readings together. When he discovered Jerome K. Jerome's play *The Passing of the Third Floor Back*, he took the character called "The Stranger" to be an imitation of Christ.[77] Plato's views on justice inspired further reflection on God's laws and the idea that the difference between justice and injustice was one of degree rather than kind.[78] He was beginning to see the centuries of literary tradition in relation to each other and the whole of literature in relation to religion.

While Bible classes often disappointed Marshall, sermons could exasperate him altogether: "I was disgusted by a sermon that could have been preached to a 14th century audience without causing offence to their narrowed orthodox minds. It was nothing less than a rant upon the futile and childish subject of Foreknowledge, Predestation, Election, Justification and Glorification."[79] Literature provided an antidote: "Home and read Dr. Faustus, which is to my mind a notable production, the offspring of real genius."[80] Literature provided an alternative: "Up and breakfast but not to church. I sat down and read through Thackeray's lectures on Charity and Humor. It contains more solid lay philosophy than you could pick up from an army of clergymen."[81] It was an alternative that eventually led Marshall away from the Baptist church, but not away from Christianity. Quite the contrary. As he surveyed the great figures of the past, a sense of his own unworthiness impressed itself on him: "As long as the example of Jesus Christ stands before us, let everyone be ashamed of even a moment of self-complacency."[82]

Marshall's continued reflections led him to the conclusion that the uniqueness and dynamism of the Christian faith sprang from Pentecost. At the same time, he noted that the materialism of Western culture was the cause of a general neglect of Pentecost and a stumbling block to the fullness of the Christian experience, a fullness that he prayed he might discover. His commitment to intellectual inquiry was already reconciled with the demands of faith: "I am of a critical and inquiring nature but the true Christian experience, reception of the Holy Ghost is a fact that transcends analysis. Once filled with this miraculous spirit one may or may not give up one's ideals and plans; but whichever happens, there is never a regret. There is absolutely nothing that can disturb the calm poise yet fiery conviction and the noble spirit of service that is the happy lot of the true Christian."[83] *Calm* poise, *fiery* conviction; the paradoxical terms are reconciled. Pentecost is a sort of maelstrom that requires none of the detachment by which Poe's sailor rescued himself, for there is no reason to seek a way out. Marshall viewed materialism too as a maelstrom isolating and entrapping the human spirit, and yet a condition from which even the faithful refuse — and fear — to seek the escape offered by Pentecost.[84]

He read selections from Buddhism and Hinduism and found the teachings to compare very favorably with those of Christianity. But Christianity was set apart for him. "The thing that raises it ineffably above everything else, is Pentecost. After that experience all things past, present, and future are settled in the mind. Casuistry, ethics, doctrine, race and all are transcended."[85]

AT AGE EIGHTEEN MARSHALL sought out his male friends when he wanted good conversation. He could not appreciate a female viewpoint and put this down to having no sisters. But there was more to life than good conversation, and at times he felt "starved for female company." He was thrilled to cut a fine figure on the dance floor. An afternoon of sailing with a young lady was always an occasion to look forward to. A church service could bring a "vision of delight" among the girls in the choir. There were parties, concerts, hockey games, and theater to enjoy in the company of Babe, Mildred, Peggy, Dorothy, Gwen, Isabelle . . . Though it was hardly necessary, Elsie drew interesting young women to Marshall's attention and brought them home to meet her son.[86]

Marshall tried to impose strict discipline on his social life: "I have five invitations for the next four nights. I have refused them all on various pretexts, save that I am going to see H.M.S. Pinafore. As I sit at home revolving ideas and living in the past with Addison and Pope, I have never a qualm in refusing an invite that would make too many evenings out in a week."[87] He believed as a first principle that it was a mistake to focus all his attention on one girl. As a matter of second principle, he turned down invitations in order to avoid such a mistake. At times, the second had to be forsaken, but this could easily be rationalized in the name of the first: "There is a danger in avoiding female company, as I have done of late. The charms of the first 'lovely one' you meet penetrate the rusty armour of sophistication and prepare the way for Cupid's shaft."[88]

Though he speculated that he would not marry until age thirty, Marshall was already giving thought at eighteen to the qualities of a perfect wife.[89] Intellectual ability topped the list: "Speaking of last night [a party with dancing till 2:15 a.m.] I may say that I was brought to the realization more than ever that my wife must be one with keen interest along literary lines or at least intellectual lines. Otherwise my friends would never suit her nor, her friends me."[90] A shallow mate would be as intolerable as a superficial professor. Yet intellect alone could not be enough.[91] If he felt the charms and attractions of some of his female acquaintances without understanding them, he knew, nevertheless, that his lifetime companion must be "sincere and noble."[92] He would use these words again to describe Marjorie Norris, soon after they met in the winter of 1931.

The Norris family were the guests of the McLuhans on 6 January that year — an evening when Marshall was puzzled by his mother's effusive behavior.[93] But the puzzle was so quickly overshadowed by the presence of Marjorie as to be forgotten. Eleven days later she was his date for a party at the home of his good chum Bill Jones. The dancing was a pleasure; being with Marjorie was pure enchantment. A second-generation Canadian, her looks bespoke the Irish blood that flowed in the veins of the Norrises and the McLuhans alike. With her round and pleasant face, high forehead, chestnut hair, and lively brown eyes, she was as attractive in appearance as she was engaging in personality.[94] Like Marshall, she was serious but animated, reflective but whimsical. They spoke of many subjects that evening. Marshall was delighted not only with Marjorie but with Macaulay's gem of wisdom: "the greatest use of conversational powers is to put them forth in a tête-à-tête."[95] Apparently it would not always be necessary to hunt up Bill and Tom and Al for a good talk. It *would* be necessary, however, to remind himself of his first principle for socializing with the fair sex. The trouble was, the principle did not take into account matters of the heart.

The evening after his first date with Marjorie, Marshall was off to Knox Church with Herbert and friends Bill Jones and Tom Easterbrook. He found the music splendid, the sermon good, "but entirely ravishing was Miss Gwen Wookey."[96] If the charms and attractions of Marjorie Norris were many and complex, Marshall had recognized for some time that Gwen Wookey projected mainly sex appeal. He was torn between the desire to see more of Gwen and the determination to resist in the name of his calling to scholarship. One thing was clear: "It looks like curtains for Babe, for I prefer either Marjorie or Gwen to her."[97] In spite of the dilemma, he took satisfaction in sensing that "the world is not so empty of the truly noble type of girl."[98] He invited Gwen to dances and hockey games but soon began to find it necessary to resist her spell: "If I forego the pleasure of her company for a few days more, the potency of her charms will have considerably diminished."[99] A few weeks later, they were out dancing again, and their time together was turning Marshall to self-assessment: "I made a number of witty (?) [MM's brackets] remarks as usual, most of which in retrospect seem cheap and foolish, but which unfortunately are past recall."[100]

Marshall indulged in much self-scrutiny throughout his undergraduate years. He found himself lacking in "any particularly fine qualities."[101] Returning from an evening out, he could feel that he had been hypocritical or worry that his friends had thought him "a cheap jazz hound."[102] He believed he would never win popularity for his social affability alone, counting instead on the knowledge he would acquire to attract a circle of intellects around him.[103] He recognized that his self-consciousness could be misinterpreted as conceitedness.[104] Such assessments of himself, as a social creature, could give way, when least expected, to even more serious intellectual self-doubt: "I often have moments when perfectly at ease that everything I am doing and thinking and hoping are hopelessly futile and childish."[105] Least expected of all was the transformation of his self-image when he fell in love with Marjorie Norris. That would still be a year and a half away as they first sailed together on the Red River on a soft summer afternoon in 1931.[106]

In the meantime, there were parties, concerts, hockey games, and theater to enjoy in the company of Gwen, Peggy . . . The circle of young women in his life was growing smaller, and Marjorie was occupying a larger place in it, but Marshall was still practicing his first law of socialization and getting the benefit of immunity from Cupid's shaft. Besides, Marjorie had a steady boyfriend.

In late August 1931, as was her custom each summer by now, Elsie rented a cottage at Victoria Beach on Lake Winnipeg. An idyllic spot, heavily treed, with sandy walks lacing the woods, it was accessible only by rail.[107] Though it was, for Marshall, a vast improvement over the summer vacations they had spent shuttling to and from crowded city parks on streetcars when he and Red were younger, he made a ritual protest over going. Elsie was astute enough to ask Marjorie to join them for a few days. She accepted. There were walks and picnics, bonfires and singsongs — long, lazy, lovely hours that must have reconciled Marshall to the holiday. On Marjorie's last day, he escorted her to the train that would take her home and spent most of the day regretting her departure, noting that "my susceptibility to female charms is directly proportional to the duration of my exposure to them."[108] The three days with Marjorie had been "rather dangerous."[109]

MARSHALL BEGAN THE THIRD year of his B.A. program with fewer complaints than in previous years. It was not resignation but inspiration. He had already caught a vision of the intellectual excitement that lay ahead of him in graduate studies. Now he needed to settle into the work that would let him put the University of Manitoba behind him. The vision, arising from his massive summer reading projects, had begun to take shape during his first and second years. He knew he wanted to get a graduate degree in England and was already studying the Oxford calendar when one of his English professors urged him to think instead of Cambridge, because of the growing reputation of the university's English department.[110]

And Noel Fieldhouse, once again, offered Marshall the most appealing model of the questing mind in action. It was less than a year since Marshall had declared that he would shun the academic life when he noted, speaking of Fieldhouse, "I constantly keep before me . . . the fact that I will likely be teaching one day and I am continually observing and criticising the methods of others. I believe that if a man is coolly, deliberately, and reasonably interested in his subject, and above all is a master of it, he need not worry much about method."[111]

He also observed the reasons for Fieldhouse's popularity and found in those observations a principle that would remain with him throughout his career as a scholar and teacher: "It is in relating the past to the present, making the past alive and the present historical, by taking in many outside topics and relating them to the subject. If I am ever an English lecturer I vow I shall be no mediocre one . . . I shall give my very best and let it go at that."[112]

The credit for the intellectual seeds planted in Marshall's mind in Manitoba days does not belong to Fieldhouse alone. From other professors such as Rupert Lodge and Robert Marshall, from his wide reading, and from discussion with friends and classmates, Marshall retained many ideas that eventually became part of his thinking, his writing, and his personal credo. Some of these ideas were for projects that never materialized.[113] Some were for intellectual strategies: "I like to argue against fact (for fun). It is quite easy to make a strong case against anyone, especially if you know the whole case (for good and against bad) while your opponent knows only one side, no matter how well."[114] Of an illuminating lecture in economics he noted: "Overproduction results in a fierce attack on the pocket of the individual. The appeal is always to some powerful feeling in man: fear, pride, sex, wealth, ambition, etc. Fifty years hence, if they have not proceded to more absurd extremes, a volume of 1930 slogans and advertising tricks would make more interesting reading than anything that has appeared in this generation."[115] Such a volume would materialize twenty years later as his first book, *The Mechanical Bride*.

Critical thinking was part of Marshall's mind-set from the beginning of his studies: "I have begun to question the right Plato has to the title of Philosopher . . . [I] would concede to him the title of social idealist rather than that of a philosopher in the sense that Spinoza measures up to it."[116]

In the summer before they had begun their third year, Marshall and his friend Tom Easterbrook were on a reading binge. Tom was anxious to pass on a little book by Chesterton, *What's Wrong with the World?* Marshall knew already that he would enjoy it. In fact, it set him on the road to one of his life's greatest turning points, his conversion to Catholicism. He recorded an early reaction to the work, where it is possible to detect Chesterton's formative influence on the McLuhan method of probe and juxtaposition: "It seems to me that G.K.'s words are most valuable when he hangs them on some subject that would seem to admit of no extraneous discussion. No matter what, G.K. had [something] to say on any subject however irrelevant in such a manner as to make the connection at once obvious and important. Few writers, yes I can say, no other writer, has ever before been able to arouse my enthusiasm for ideas as has G.K."[117]

Marshall excelled at essay writing but often disappointed himself in exam results.[118] He set and followed review schedules calling for up to 150 hours of study, with the result that he was frequently overprepared. He vowed to recall forever one such occasion with fasting and mourning, commenting wryly that it had given him the material to write "*How to Lose a Scholarship*: All one need do is to master the work so completely that you are unable to tell the examiners about it in the two hours at your disposal. It helps to leave out one of the four required questions."[119]

Such times led him to reflect on the university system: "At a Manitoba examination it is well nigh impossible to get a high mark if one has a subject up properly. By that I mean if the best outside sources have been consulted. A richly stored mind is anything but an asset in a two-hour examination."[120] In the private forum of his diary, he advocated small classes, no exams, and mandatory summer reading, identifying at the same time the chief shortcoming of his undergraduate education: "The best and most formative years of an English student's life are spent in examining the peaks of English literature. There is no laboring up the slope to these peaks. They are conveniently sawed off and laid before the student and in 99% of the cases at least there is not the slightest appreciation gained of the great intellectual and artistic genius of the author."[121]

Marshall was moving toward an answer to his own question when he had wondered "what I should like to be or where I should like to climb to."[122] England beckoned, and when Marshall allowed himself to bask in the thrill of the intellectual challenges awaiting him there, he could take leave of his syntax: "How I long to get across to that wee island, to talk with the living, to visit, read, absorb, and revere the past, places, the books, the spirit of the great past, and the aspirations for the future."[123] In order to get there, he would need a scholarship, and that seemed doubtful, unless his final grades for third and fourth year improved dramatically, so he settled down to work. But just in case the scholarship did not materialize, he and Tom Easterbrook set out for a visit to England in the summer of 1932.

The trip began inauspiciously when the boys arrived in Montreal after a three-day train trip and were promptly fleeced. They fell in with a man who introduced himself as the son of an English nobleman. Believing his tangled story of misfortune, they agreed to lend him money from the little they had, on the assurance that his father would repay them when they arrived in England. If the innocents had second thoughts, it was too late; they had taken working passage on a cattle boat, and it was time to sail. The heavy seas of the north Atlantic added to the misery of attending to the animals, and the living hell of their days and nights aboard the steamer was enough to put every thought but survival out of their minds.[124]

But the young men put the gut-wrenching crossing behind them the minute they stepped ashore in England. The pages of Macaulay and Johnson, Thackeray and Shakespeare, came alive for Marshall. He and Tom bought a pair of old bicycles, and for three months they toured the country, feasting on the civilizing influence of cultural monuments and the visible roots of England's traditions, breathing an atmosphere that could never have been conjured in the imaginations of two boys from the Canadian prairies. They had so little money that they took turns going in to sights charging admission, but it didn't matter. Extraordinary measures of economy were required for food, broken crackers becoming a staple item. Against all odds, they did locate the father of the fellow who had benefited from their generosity in Montreal. He honored his son's debt and cursed him in the presence of Marshall and Tom. Marshall's head was teeming with more images than he could sort out as the time drew near to return home, but he was clear on one thought: before long he would be back in England as a graduate student.[125]

The incentive to finish his B.A. with distinguished results was now stronger than ever and sustained Marshall throughout his final year. He graduated in the spring of 1933, winning the University Gold Medal in Arts and Science. His English professors wanted him to do graduate work in English, while his history and philosophy professors hoped that he would stay on to work with them.[126] It was a season of triumph. And it was the season of love.

THEY WALKED ALONG the riverbank on a Sunday evening in April, carefree and lost in the thrill of being together. Chatter, laughter, an embrace, their first kiss. Marshall felt his heart loop and crash, heard himself saying everything but what he wanted to say.[127] The eloquence of the diary entries he had written about Marjorie, written for her, written to her, could not be summoned in her presence.

The love that flourished that spring had already blossomed in the deep of winter, precipitating crisis and confusion for Marshall. In spite of an earlier decision not to resort to pen-and-ink therapy, he had composed thirteen pages on the matter, to mitigate "the chaos of my mind and feelings."[128] Liberation from negative thoughts about himself, a surge of noble sentiments, his emotional intensity for the first time lifting him to love instead of plunging him into dispute — it was thrilling, and disorienting.

When Marshall had returned from England in the fall of 1932, he was powerfully attracted to Marjorie but reacted negatively at first in the face of Elsie's "perpetual adulation and encouragement"[129] to him to court Marjorie, who herself offered discouragement by her apparent indifference. Vanity exacted its toll and kept him from becoming her suitor. If, as he suspected, she was not really enthusiastic toward her steady, Jimmy Munroe, this was small consolation, much less encouragement. Jimmy was a presence so disagreeable to Marshall that he could scarcely enjoy Marjorie's company even when they were alone. When they went out as a foursome, with Marjorie as Jimmy's date, Marshall was a "seething cauldron of unutterable misery."[130] Then Marjorie invited Marshall to a dance, and "all the tender of my soul was ablaze."[131] Suddenly they were dating regularly: skating, attending movies and plays. When they were apart, Marshall was love's fool, absorbed in writing poems and dreaming away the hours he had always hoarded for reading and study.

Over and over he sketched a verbal portrait of her in his mind, till the words compelled themselves to paper. A delicately molded mind and heart, a physical beauty the exact counterpart of her inner loveliness, gentleness, a rounded character, much feeling, much power and drive, much ambition, much self-respect, Irish fancy and wistfulness, a love of idleness but a great capacity for work, a love of fun and adventure, fine intelligence, a quick and logical mind, a strong desire for knowledge, and a true sensitivity — these were the qualities that made Marshall say of Marjorie: "The moment you meet her you are aware of the presence of one than whom Shakespeare conceived nothing superior."[132]

Knowing her, he felt, was an education "such as neither my home nor my reading could ever have supplied."[133] Under her influence, his behavior was changing. The shyness and fearfulness that isolated him from people, the overbearing ways and confidence that masked his fears, began to disappear. These transformations were underway as soon as he stopped restraining the love he felt for Marjorie, as soon as he saw his own onesidedness and harshness in the mirror of her feminine wholeness and sympathy. His independent spirit had always made him a detached observer, seeking to understand. At the same time, it created a powerful desire for the intimacy of someone who could understand him. Marjorie did.

Marshall was euphoric enough to begin thinking about marriage, but was troubled immediately by the obstacles he saw. Marjorie was a medical student, committed, like him, to the years of study and training ahead. "Misguided ambition"[134] on the part of Marjorie's mother had steered her in this direction. But there was an even more serious problem: Marjorie was two years his senior. With his own prospects for finding a position after graduate studies at least four years away, it seemed like a cruel and hopeless situation to the ardent Marshall. He spoke in his diary of the "absolute certainty that she shall never be

my wife."[135] Influenced perhaps by the material expectations that so
possessed Elsie, and echoing worries he had expressed about providing
for a wife and family well before Marjorie had come on the scene,
Marshall saw no answer as he asked himself how he could build his
future plans and put all his hopes "in one who should even now be in
a beautiful home of her own?"[136]

He thought of looking for a job immediately, but the Depression
put it out of the question. Besides, he knew that an early marriage
would amount to stunting both their lives. There was nothing to do
but regret that he was not four years older. Yet in moments when the
sheer force of love overwhelmed him, regret and worry and doubt
were banished. Months before that heady April evening, Marshall had
written of his gratitude to Marjorie for her understanding, her
thoughtfulness, and her selflessness, confidently intending to read his
thanks aloud to her when they were man and wife. He loved her for
the sake of love, with all the intensity he was capable of, without
reserve, challenging himself to become worthy of her love, wondering
if he could, for it seemed to him that the unselfish nature he so
admired in her could never become part of his own.

The enchanted spring of 1933 gave way to the uncounted days of
summer. In July, Marshall discovered his diary entry of two years
earlier, written when he and Marjorie had gone sailing for the first
time. The very sight of her name there made his heart leap, and he
noted, "I tremble to think with what experience I may read this two
years hence."[137]

Two years hence, Marshall would be doing graduate work in
England, as he had originally planned (and he would have been very
surprised to be able to look ahead to his relationship with Marjorie at
that time), but for the moment, those plans were deferred, and he
enrolled for an M.A. in English at the University of Manitoba. He was
relishing the thought of undertaking a thesis on George Meredith. At
last, a project of substance and scope would challenge him to make
full use of his boundless intellectual energy and prodigious background reading.

It was no doubt still with thoughts of Marjorie that Marshall prepared an article for the *Manitoban* in November 1933[138] on George
Meredith as a feminist. He wrote: "He typifies the two things which

really make the Victorian age itself — the cheapness and narrowness of its conscious formulae; the richness and humanity of its unconscious tradition[139] . . . While the petty conscious Meredith was fretting about the benevolent enslavement of women by men, and urging uniform education of both sexes, the great unconscious Meredith was painting [women] for what they are, the rulers of the world."

As Marshall worked on the Meredith thesis, the prospect arose of an IODE War Memorial scholarship to take him to Cambridge. He pinned his hopes on it, with no thought of the complication he had caused for himself by outshining his professors. Among these was one of the adjudicators for the award, A. J. Perry, whose classroom authority Marshall had frequently undercut with superior knowledge from his own wide reading. Herbert McLuhan paid a visit to Perry, then head of the English department. He wanted the professor to know how much his son enjoyed his classes. Perry raised his eyebrows. He wanted the professor to know what a high regard his son had for him. Perry listened attentively. Herbert was doing what he did best, selling an idea. It was a day when even Elsie might have been proud of him. Marshall won the scholarship on the strength of Herbert's intervention and was able to renew it on the strength of his own achievements.[140]

Marshall easily met the deadline for completing his M.A. thesis, dealing with Meredith as a poet and dramatic novelist, and was awarded the degree in the spring of 1934.[141] With all the vigor and assurance that was already his trademark, he said of Meredith that he could not be placed.[142] (It was a remark that would later come spontaneously to commentators on the work of Marshall McLuhan.) Expanding on that observation, he noted: "[Meredith] has no derivation and no tendency; and yet he bridges the gap between the eighteenth century and the twentieth century as though the Victorian era had never been."[143] This remark also applies to the later McLuhan, whose objective was to bridge the gap between the nineteenth century and the twenty-first, but *not* as though the intervening era had never been. McLuhan's was the twentieth century, and he remained rooted in it as surely as Meredith had escaped his.

3

England's Green and Pleasant Land

Rise regularly at 8. How I love the reappearance of green.
How much green there is in England.
                              –Marshall McLuhan's diary,
                                          3 May 1935

In early October 1934, Marshall arrived in Cambridge, taking up residence in Magrath Avenue at the home of the newly retired porter from Trinity Hall, where he was enrolled. The bright, airy surroundings augured well: a spacious room with dormer windows, light wallpaper, gray-and-red wool rug, fireplace with white mantel, and a cabinet fashioned from the center section of a rowboat. Magrath Avenue was at some distance from the university, a blind street, and free of surrounding laneways, so Marshall knew he would enjoy privacy and tranquillity.[1]

O. H. Wansborough-Jones, a fellow of Trinity Hall and Marshall's overseer, or formal tutor, informed Elsie that her son had arrived, noting: "As far as I could see, he was quite pleased with himself."[2] And with what he was discovering of Cambridge. Wansborough-Jones, history lecturer Charles William Crawley, who served as Marshall's personal tutor, and English lecturer Lionel Elvin, his study tutor, all in their thirties, were to make a strong impression on him. Less noteworthy were the handful of fellow students he met at first hall "sitting all dead quiet. There were as many waiters. Well, first a plate with a slice of melon (everything is served on dinner plates), a piece of bread (no butter) beside it — then a bit of fish — then fricaseéd chicken, potatoes and cauliflower, then apricot tart and cream — I took no ale (it being extra Odams tells me). So we arose scarcely having murmured and departed into the night."[3]

Departing into the night became one of the charms of Cambridge for Marshall. Narrow, gas-lit streets, great bells sounding solemnly in the darkness, men camped over beer mugs at The Red Cow and The Mitre, students lounging over tea in small shops. The cost of lingering to savor such scenes was six shillings, six pence, the fine levied against any student returning to lodgings past ten o'clock, when the proctors made their rounds checking to see that doors *and* windows were locked. But for Marshall there was more excitement in anticipating the intellectual adventure about to start than in the thought of illicit nighttime prowls.

Before lectures had even begun, he obtained copies of all the English tripos examinations from the preceding year. Exams had been the bane of his existence at Manitoba, but he sensed already that at Cambridge they might prove inspirational. Marshall was delighted to find that the questions challenged the candidate to think and to synthesize a program of wide reading. "I shall have a first or burst," he declared, "but there is a huge deal of work — exciting, joyous work ahead of me."[4]

Within a week of his arrival, he was sending home letters complete with British turns of phrase: "a snap in cap and gown," "[My landlord] Mr. Odams has looked me up a good bike," "travelling in the long vac."[5] Elsie and the family may or may not have taken notice of these stylistic innovations, but Cambridge was taking notice of Marshall's wit. After the first meeting of the term for the Hesperides, the Trinity Hall Literary Society, he was invited back to the rooms of a senior student along with others.[6] The occasion more than made up for the dreary dinner that had initiated him into social life at the university. "They are honors men doing their course in three years. In this place, stimulating or not — well after half an hour they were writing down my *bons mots* for the College magazine — pray for me or I shall disintegrate with conceit."[7]

Fellow students and faculty alike recognized the depth of his background preparation, and Marshall must have begun wondering why

Cambridge had refused to admit him directly to graduate studies in spite of his two degrees from Manitoba. But Lionel Elvin opined at their first meeting that Marshall would need only a year to pass the B.A. before moving on to an M.Litt. or Ph.D.[8] At the same meeting, Marshall took the measure of Elvin and pronounced him "obviously able, keen, and informed."[9] By mid-October he had written his first essay for him and reported that it was well received. "Of course I disagreed very profoundly with Elvin's view."[10] Neither Elvin nor anyone else, it seemed, had taken as much trouble as Marshall to master the philosophy of G. K. Chesterton. "It is a social (not faddish) philosophy based on a completely adequate religion."[11] This observation provided Marshall with a ready explanation for the neglect of Chesterton. "Cambridge and Oxford are cliquish rather than social in their thought and are the birthplaces and spawning ground of every sort of fad."[12] Disagreeing with his tutor in his first essay produced no friction between them, and Marshall predicted confidently that they would get along very well.

It was still the first week of term, and Marshall was sampling lectures to decide on his courses. But he was already in thrall to Mansfield Forbes. Calling Forbes's introductory lecture on poetry in the age of Pope and Wordsworth "the biggest intellectual treat of my life,"[13] he described how it had ranged over D. H. Lawrence, John Galsworthy, T. S. Eliot, William Cowper, and Robert Burns. Enthusiastic about his subject to the point of near incoherence, Forbes appeared to be intent on crushing all of English literature into a single lecture, but made a point of telling his audience otherwise. Alluding explicitly to his fellow lecturers, Forbes said that "they set out to cover ground — I shall cover no ground — I shall teach you to dig in the most fertile parts."[14] It was a remark Marshall was never to forget, a stimulus to his own method of studying and teaching for over forty years.

He was mildly mystified to find that, in spite of the variety in their teaching styles, so many of the English lecturers read poetry aloud in the same manner — "doggedly determined to weigh scrupulously each syllable and without any transitions of manner to suit the poem."[15] He was not sure that such a technique could be justified; he found Elsie's reading style decidedly superior and told her so.[16] When Forbes lectured on the topic of oral delivery, Marshall took massive notes and distilled powerful insights to offer Elsie for an address she planned on the subject of elocution: "Point out that excellence therein is as far removed from the flowers and intonations of rhetorical oratory (with its narrow compass of tones and showy emphasis) as is excellence in poetry (with its organic relation or inter-dependence *between content and tone and material patterns*) with the easy swing of doggerel."[17] He counseled the use of Forbes's terminology: "Forbes believes that nearly all faults in the reading of poetry proceed from '*pathological* (i.e., a mania for) *acceleration*.' Use that phrase. He is wrong of course, in his emphasis."[18]

The stimulation of Cambridge kept Marshall writing home nearly every day. Elsie had by now made a permanent move to Toronto — a new base for a new venture in teaching drama and directing theatrical productions — and was living in a rooming house on Selby Street with Red. Herbert had talked of joining them later, but these were empty words, spoken for the sake of appearances. In all likelihood, he and Elsie had agreed to a permanent separation before she and Red left Winnipeg. The idea for such an arrangement had almost certainly come from Elsie. Confident that the next chapter in her life held great promise, she was equally sure that it was time to close the one in which she had felt nothing but frustration with her husband's lack-luster career.[19]

Marshall cautioned the family that he might have to begin rationing mail, but bombarded them instead with letters, photos, postcards, maps, and guides. He was able to report the best digestion he had enjoyed in years — a testimonial perhaps to the meals he prepared for himself at Magrath Avenue. The culinary adventures at Trinity Hall, innovations to his diet such as rabbit that he mistook for veal, he was able to take in stride, and even boast of. He was also sleeping well and free of stress-induced fatigue. These things he took as signs that he was on his way to becoming "preposterously healthy."[20] For good measure, he planned to join the rowing team, to restore himself to top physical condition, and in the hope of putting on weight.

Though Marshall did not feel the descending autumn chill as early as his classmates, he soon cultivated the habit of eating in front of a fire — a ritual that was to give him great pleasure throughout his life.

Another lifelong penchant — for beefsteak — settled on him at the same time.[21]

Before Marshall's crowded first month at Cambridge had ended, the Trinity Hall boat club was training new crewmen, and he found himself at the oar of an "eight."[22] Marshall's crew scoffed, as they set off, at the inept maneuvers of another team, then quickly fell into the grip of "agonizing uncoordination"[23] themselves. Regretting their laughter, they spent the afternoon rowing up and down the Cam with their racer in a pronounced tilt. By their second outing, the team was already showing improved skills, and Marshall was able to declare it a pleasant occasion. He enjoyed the shift from mental strain in solitude to physical strain in a team effort, and he considered his rowing career officially under way when he bought the heavy, white Trinity Hall sweater he was required to wear when out with the crew.

By now, Red was enrolled in a B.A. program at the University of Toronto, and Marshall was more than ready to pass along those study strategies that had served him well at Manitoba: "You have got the most needful thing — namely an incipient perception of the nature of mental growth — once you feel your thoughts on the move, don't worry about the tempo or pace of University standards — you have a life time ahead of you . . . Go to the Brittanica (not merely the dictionary) and carefully look up everything not only the first time you read it but the second."[24] The works of Chesterton loom large in Marshall's counsels to his brother as "the writings of a thinker and a poet with a serious and comprehensive belief about the nature of life."[25] There are also the first references to treatises on Roman Catholicism: "Now concerning your intention to read further concerning Catholic ideas respecting images and doctrine — you need go no further than the succinct and admirable little volume by Father Darcy entitled *Catholicism*."[26] Marshall was ready and eager to open large perspectives for Red: "It is useful broadly to distinguish Plato and Aristotle as tending towards Buddhism and Christianity respectively . . . Aristotle heartily accepts the senses just as Browning did . . . that is why great Aquinas accepted Aristotle into Christian theology."[27] To this he added evaluation of various editions of scholarly works in literature and philosophy, endless references, and advice on everything from clothing to which friends should be avoided.[28]

Warm weather settled over the campus in late October, when Marshall lunched for the first time at the home of the congenial Crawley, his personal tutor. They ate in the garden with its low wall overlooking the Backs and the playing fields of St. John's. Cambridge continued to weave its spell over Marshall as he gazed at walnut trees, quince, and century elms, the broad expanse of lawn, still as green as at midsummer, and the roses promising to bloom till Christmas. He found Crawley frank and attentive in just the right measure and enjoyed meeting his family, but noted too that "conversation seldom expands among Englishmen."[29]

Marshall heard the legendary Shakespearean scholar Dover Wilson lecture on 2 November 1934. Ever alert to physiognomy and its portents, he sketched Wilson verbally for Elsie and the family: "He is tall and shamefully stooped (about 50 years old) — has a large head and face and neck, on a pigeon chest which only criminal indifference to his body could have left so undeveloped. His feature[s] are loosely strung together, suggesting that they were selected and arranged with the same rigorous eye to light and symmetry as the critical footnotes on one of his pages! The effect is soullessly bookish."[30] As a model for McLuhan the professor-in-training, Wilson repelled. "His manner of delivery is harsh, emphatic, and unnecessarily impatient in irrelevant matters. When he has to mention American and German professors, his gorge fairly rises and one wishes one had an umbrella."[31] Though Marshall conceded the intellectual excellence of Wilson's talk and was absorbed by the thesis that Shakespeare never intended his audience to resolve the conundrums of Hamlet's character and disposition, he said of the evening, "I went to see, I stayed to listen — and, remain unconverted."[32]

Sir Arthur Quiller-Couch,[33] at age seventy-one the oldest member of the English faculty when Marshall arrived at Cambridge, made an entirely different impression. Small of stature, yet a compelling presence, undiminished by a voice beginning to quaver with age, free of the mannerisms of the cadaverous Wilson, immaculately attired, with boots polished beyond anything lethal, "Q," as he was known among the students, came to address a group assembled informally in a common room on the very subject Marshall could claim to be his own — George Meredith.[34]

The brilliant presentation plunged him back into every detail of Meredith's work that he had grappled with in writing his master's thesis at Manitoba. Quiller-Couch brought his remarks to a close and invited questions. No spontaneous hand went up. Marshall hesitated a moment and ventured: "Yes, I have two questions." Sensing the questioner's engagement and the intensity of the discussion to follow, Quiller-Couch walked over to the "freshman" and asked, "Young gentleman, what is your name?"[35] If he was "Marshall" to most, "Mars" to Red alone, "Mac" and "Marsh" to only a few in later life, he was "McLuhan" to his new classmates and fellow scullers at Cambridge, but "Mr. McLuhan" to Sir Arthur Quiller-Couch that night. Being in Cambridge felt like a homecoming to "Marshall" from his first days there, but it was also the birthplace of "McLuhan."

It was "McLuhan" who sat an exam on Thomas Peacock, the nineteenth-century English novelist and poet, for the Latham Prize — a long and grueling ordeal.[36] Unlike the English tripos examinations he had already consulted, it demanded fact upon fact and much quoting from memory of Peacock's work. He felt his preparation had been too hasty, regretted spending the evening before the exam listening to Dover Wilson, but took solace in having at least acquainted himself with the writer who exercised the most far-reaching effect on Meredith.[37]

Within a week the results were posted: McLuhan took the prize.[38] He had underestimated how well his capacity for memorization served him. It was a legacy from Elsie, refined by the techniques he had learned from her as she prepared the repertoire for her stage performances. He announced the win in a letter to the family with a touch of modesty and considerable anticipation of the next term's competition, as well as his hopes and plans to "pick off a few such prizes."[39] Then he would be able to bask in the scholarly leisure he needed for the article on G. K. Chesterton he was already planning, "which will be a knockout when complete."[40] Balancing admiration for his own promise with self-assessment, McLuhan conceded that excessive enthusiasm for Chesterton had distorted his judgment, concluding: "I shall no doubt be much the better for getting it off my chest."[41]

The velvety dampness of November in Cambridge was a treat to McLuhan when he thought about winter descending on Winnipeg. It was also a reminder that brought him back from musings on prizes and publications to the main work ahead of him — preparing for examinations. In spite of his self-assurance and the confident prediction Elvin had made so quickly, he was gritting his teeth at the thought of facing exams at the end of just one year. There was a risk: achieving less than first-class honors could keep him out of the Cambridge Ph.D. program. A month at the university had been enough to convince him that its advantages made going to America for the doctorate look ridiculous.[42] Another month eased his worries. McLuhan learned that his IODE War Memorial Post-Graduate Overseas Scholarship would be renewed for 1935.[43]

As THE BUSY FALL term drew toward its close, McLuhan continued training and competing with his rowing team, grew anxious about the pace Elsie was keeping up in her work, and began thinking about Christmas: "I have been able to discover nothing for Marjorie except a bracelet that is too expensive."[44] Daytime temperatures to sixty degrees continued throughout the first week of December, and McLuhan lit no fire in his room for days on end. If the comfortable weather made it difficult to think about Christmas, it had made the term's studies easier. These had been devoted mainly to the first half of the seventeenth century, described by McLuhan as "a strange period to me . . . It is a rich, various, courtly, learned, mellow, rural-loving period, and quite the most civilized in English history."[45]

Not surprisingly, he had also gone far beyond pastorals and idylls: "Of late I have been wayfaring among the work of T. S. Eliot."[46] He had no plans to write about Eliot — yet — and, this time, no apologies to make for distorted judgment born of excessive enthusiasm. He saw in Eliot "the character of greatness," and pinpointed the essence of his works: "They transform and diffuse and recoalesce the commonest every day occurrences of twentieth century city life."[47] And he identified with him personally: "Now there is something ineffably exciting in reading a man, a genius and a poet, who has by the same stages, in face of the same circumstances, (he is an American) come to the same point of view concerning the nature of religion and Christianity, the interpretation of history, and the value of industrialism."[48] Eliot's *Thoughts After Lambeth* moved McLuhan to call him "the greatest English-speaking poet and the clearest-headed critic of literature writing in our time."[49] He found Eliot's worldview courageous, realistic, and honest by comparison with those of others, like H. G. Wells, who conjured vulgar utopias. Eliot, McLuhan made a point of telling Elsie, was an Anglo-Catholic.

Eliot's poetry, his "uncanny capacity to hang all the terror of eternity on a common phrase,"[50] prompted spiritual reflection in McLuhan — and a practical thought. Modern poetry could become a stepping-stone in Elsie's career. With lines written out from Eliot's "Triumphal March," he presented the idea to her. McLuhan doubted that Eliot was for Ontario audiences, but he saw an opportunity in England: catering to the demand for poetry reading in the cultured circles of English society. "You could take the London élite by storm,"[51] he declared. He saw an "amazing opportunity"[52] for her to "break with the outworn idea of an elocutionist as a pre-movie entertainer"[53] by working up a completely new repertoire. So confident was he in her abilities that he predicted an open door for her at the BBC after a few public readings.

Knowing she had no time for study, he lectured her on the essentials of Eliot. To drive the lesson home, he contrasted Eliot to Elsie's long-time favorite author, Robert Browning. "You see, he is using different rhythms than you are accustomed to. But, they are not used as arbitrarily as Browning's and they are not as hard. Moreover his poems, like Browning's, use the method of dramatic monologue with its swift ranging over every sort of experience. But Eliot's 'consciousness' is not that of a lover, a count, or a distinct individual — it is *impersonal* and universal and instead of ranging over *individual* associations he ranges over all history and all modern society, but with a miraculous relevance and effectiveness."[54]

Elsie had nurtured hopes of visiting England even before her son's departure for Cambridge. Now McLuhan had a plan that could not only bring her over but keep her there. At first glance it was compelling; at second glance it was overwhelming, for it seemed clear that he had no thought of remaining in England once his studies were completed. If she shared his confidence over a new career opening up, she must have also foreseen it leaving her stranded far from home and family. Feeling some need for caution, where her son felt only his habitual exuberance in the face of a new idea, she nevertheless asked him to sound out the prospects of engagements for her.[55]

McLuhan was reading Ezra Pound, Hilaire Belloc, Ernest Hemingway, and James Joyce — the last "very slowly."[56] After a few weeks of self-instruction in French, he tackled Jacques Maritain and the essays of Montaigne.[57] He argued every conceivable topic with Elvin, who continued to be pleased with McLuhan's papers. In fact, McLuhan was beginning to feel less pressure at the university but more from within himself. He learned that he would be allowed to credit his second year of undergraduate work toward the residence requirement for the Ph.D. It meant he could defer writing exams for the B.A. till the spring of 1936, after which he would need to spend only one more year on campus. Then he would be free to return to Canada to complete his thesis. The prospect of a freedom so remote could not counter his mounting sense of futility over attaining his goals — goals he was scarcely aware of setting: "I have an exact knowledge of nothing. When I really get a grip on English I shall be in a position to understand other arts more readily. My mind is a ferment these days — boiling with new ideas and experience. I must keep it so for years, if I am to be worth anything as an educator."[58]

The same antidote to frustration that had always come so easily to Elsie came to McLuhan: work. His mind seethed with ideas for the Chesterton article. He was already using the procedure he would retain till the end of his career — reading far beyond Chesterton, scribbling out thoughts inspired from a hundred sources, rubbing ideas together. Like every project McLuhan would undertake, it was a voyage, a hunt, a challenge. The impatience of youth did not prevent him from saying, "the longer it waits, the better it will be,"[59] and this in spite of an ulterior motive that favored despatch: "To be quite frank, I hope to use it as a means of meeting GK."[60]

He had heard Chesterton on the radio, sounding "like a wheezy old Colonel,"[61] reminding him of no one so much as his Winnipeg scout-master, Charles A. Hill. But Chesterton's on-air persona did not diminish McLuhan's resolve to meet his hero. Nor did a remark from Mansfield Forbes: "You have seen him, haven't you? Why he isn't adult."[62] Whatever reply McLuhan may have made to Forbes, in writing to Elsie he noted simply that "Forbes is of course a 'broad-minded' modern sceptic who has put his shirt on psychoanalysis. Personally I would prefer the hickory bush."[63]

McLuhan was an avid reader of *G.K.'s Weekly*. Long before he was to examine radio as a medium, he noted Chesterton's remark that the internationalization of radio had come about just as the nations had nothing to say to each other.[64] As for the effects of the medium, a key McLuhan topic in years to come, he told Elsie that many of his class-mates had radios in their rooms, but that they themselves recognized this would keep them from achieving first-class honors in their studies.[65]

As HIS SECOND TERM began in January 1935, it was a skeptical and critical McLuhan who reported home on his course in the philosophy of rhetoric with I. A. Richards. *Practical Criticism: A Study of Literary Judgment* (1929) had sent shock waves through Cambridge, showing students their dismal and incoherent critical responses to a selection of unsigned poems,[66] and shaming the faculty who had prepared them for the task so poorly. Now Richards was repeating the experiment by asking students for their criticism of prose extracts. McLuhan had read *Practical Criticism* and saw what could counter its damning evidence. "I have some doubts about the method of giving *one* poem of any person as a test. A really cultivated taste might hit the nail most all the time, but uncultivated people can enjoy many things in a *volume* by one writer where the merits of his craft and ideas and feelings are permitted to permeate the consciousness from a 1000 different angles."[67] *Ideas, feelings, different angles*. Here are some of Richards's key words in an argument subverting his own procedure.

McLuhan's skepticism gave way to outright repugnance in the face of Richards's atheism. "Richards is a humanist who regards all experience as *relative* to certain conditions of life. There are no permanent, ultimate, qualities such as Good, Love, Hope, etc., and yet he wishes to discover objective, ultimate[ly] permanent standards of criticism. He wants to discover those standards (what a hope!) in order to establish intellectualist culture as the only religion worthy [of] a rational being . . . When I see how people swallow such ghastly atheistic nonsense, I could join a bomb-hurling society."[68]

But Richards was allowing McLuhan to assemble the powerful analytical tools he needed for exploring the linguistic complexity and conceptual opaqueness of the modernist poetry he found so compelling. As John Paul Russo describes it in his critical biography of Richards, "The Richardsian method, analyzing the poet's sense, imagery and metaphor, rhythm, form, intention, attitude, and irony, was fully prepared to handle compression, ambiguity, self-referentiality, obscurity, and allusiveness."[69] From Richards, McLuhan learned how a poem works, learned it through a method calling for the same analytical turn of mind, the same curiosity, that had steered him at first to the engineering faculty at the University of Manitoba. Richards taught that poetry "remains unintelligible so long as we separate words from their meanings and treat them as mere signs fitted into a sensory pattern."[70] This was a fundamental principle from which McLuhan developed his later observations and teachings on symbolism, patterns, cliché, archetype, and closure.

Richards's approach was also performance-based and opened new perspectives for McLuhan on principles of elocution — diction, delivery, intonation — that he had picked up over so many years of listening to Elsie rehearse her programs. And long before "McLuhan" became synonymous with "media," he heard the message running through all of Richards's work about the power, the pervasiveness, the subtlety, the complexity, the interaction of media — and their effects.[71]

Richards read McLuhan's anonymous comments on a prose passage aloud to the philosophy of rhetoric class, giving his seal of approval. McLuhan reported the praise he had earned with only mild satisfaction, adding: "He reads many, and much fun we have at the expense of various unknowns."[72]

The influence of Richards, Forbes, Quiller-Couch, and others with whom McLuhan would come in contact over two years in Cambridge was powerful, and powerfully augmented by the minds he met only through their written work. These influences met, complemented each other, and produced a synergetic effect. As he later remembered: "Part of the excitement in reading Maritain was the awareness that he was saying something new about something very old, so that there was the excitement of discovery and of sharing this discovery with one's contemporaries. I discovered Maritain simultaneously with the work of I. A. Richards, and T. S. Eliot, and Ezra Pound, and James Joyce, and Wyndham Lewis. All of these people seem to relate to each other in many different ways, and each seems to enrich the other. Along with the works of contemporary painters and ballet and the world of Sergei Eisenstein and music, one had the experience of a very rich new culture, in which the great intellectual Maritain was a notable ornament. Maritain helped to complete the vortex of significant components in a single luminous logos of our time."[73]

THE ROWING CLUB REMAINED active throughout the winter term. With a training diet consisting of fish, mutton, Brussels sprouts, fruit dessert, and poached eggs on toast washed down by a pint of beer,[74] McLuhan's six-foot frame carried 151 pounds for the first time in his life — to his own disbelief. The weather continued in what he described as "preternatural pleasantness,"[75] but he and his team rowed even when January and February brought the occasional heavy winds blowing up the Cam. With some satisfaction, he noted: "our crew is best in a gale."[76]

He unwrapped a fawn-colored scarf with a cross pattern in black from Marjorie and reckoned it was the fourteenth one she had sent.[77] No record is available of McLuhan's correspondence with Marjorie during the Cambridge years; how often he may have made time to write to her is unknown. But Marjorie loaded the mails enough for McLuhan to occasionally receive three of her letters in one day.[78] Writing to Elsie in February of 1935, he noted that the Norrises "have been buying wedding gifts at a frightful rate for some months past."[79] Of this development he said only: "you must simply reconcile yourself to the idea of Marjorie as a daughter-in-law. It is the *least* you can do in return for a plethora of gifts."[80] He had no time for a more serious remark and may have had no time to be seriously in love. McLuhan recorded no disquiet over enforced separation from Marjorie. But spring was not far away, and Marjorie was planning a summer visit to Cambridge.

Meanwhile, an intellectual dissatisfaction was beginning to gnaw at him: "Each day the private sense of incompleteness due to not having Greek and Latin grows in me. It is hard for one like me, so deeply interested in the roots and beginnings of things, to be without means of access to the fount and reservoir of our own civilization."[81] His thoughts were so crowded, it seemed there was little room among them for Marjorie, and his reflections on the future focused only on his career: "How rapidly my ideas have been shifting and rearranging themselves to make room for others! My difficulty is to keep up with myself. I can see that I would perhaps have done better to have taken History to teach, not only because my faculty is scarcely literary, but because English Literature is a foreign literature, more alien to America and Canada every day."[82]

McLuhan took counsel with L. J. Potts, the head of the board of postgraduate studies, about his plans for continuing on to the Ph.D. Potts ventured the opinion that McLuhan would be able to earn his M.A. credit for one year's research. It was on Potts's recommendation that he decided finally to postpone his tripos examinations till the end of his second year.[83] In preparing for those exams, McLuhan was also laying the foundation for his doctoral work. He was already giving full rein to the synthesizing impulses that would produce his dissertation on sixteenth-century satirist and pamphleteer Thomas Nashe when he wrote: "Plato was, of course, a Puritan in his artistic views, and his philosophy when fully developed as by the 15th century Augustinian monks (of whom Luther was one) leads definitely to the Calvinist position."[84]

The parade of stimulating lecturers continued. McLuhan went to hear A. E. Housman speak on the *Odes* of Horace and found that his slight frame belied "his soul's immensity."[85] He had a smallish but high head (always a good omen for McLuhan), "a smooth sweep of pale delicate-skinned cheek — a white (not wide) moustache."[86] For Elsie's benefit he noted that Housman spoke "quietly with remarkable clarity of tone and precision of phrase."[87] His reputation for "dry ruthless scholarship,"[88] and the same sort of scrupulous attention to textual analysis that McLuhan was learning from I. A. Richards, made Housman's lecture a must.

Of F. R. Leavis, McLuhan had less to say. By the time McLuhan had arrived in Cambridge, Leavis was devoting most of his time to editing the literary journal *Scrutiny*. Having clashed with Quiller-Couch and lost his appointment as assistant lecturer in the university's financial crisis of 1931, Leavis was in the hiatus before his reappointment at the level of full lecturer and was keeping a low profile on the campus, serving only as a tutor. He hosted an open house for his students on Friday afternoons, and it was there that McLuhan met him and his wife, Q. D. Leavis. The Leavises were former students of Richards and inevitably compounded his influence on McLuhan, though one might hardly suspect this from his description of F.R., on first meeting him, as "an uncompromising idealist, tactless, impatient, vain, and affected."[89] The occasion was one of the Friday afternoon meetings, where McLuhan found himself "soon in argument with a nest of Communists."[90]

McLuhan found his time "telescoped, annihilated."[91] Despite this, bouts of discouragement, and self-induced pressure, McLuhan was very much in control. Throughout the university year he was completing, he had been intellectually excited but emotionally serene. Away from Elsie and their abrasive confrontations, his harsh judgments of her rapidly faded from his memory. Their exchange of letters during his Cambridge sojourn gives the sense of a calmer mother and a maturing son growing closer together, despite — or perhaps because of — the thousands of miles between them.

The subject of religion and faith came up in various ways. McLuhan had been profoundly impressed by Sir Jacob Epstein's recently unveiled statue of Christ (known as *Ecce Homo* and *Behold the Man*) and wrote about it at length in a passage that sounds at first like familiar counsel from the later McLuhan on the subject of media effects: "The intense and terrible nature of the expression strikes first (after the early novelty and grotesqueness has been surmounted). The body is puny and passive. All attention is directed to the face, to the eyes, the mouth, and chin. The head is very broad and low, the eyes strained with indescribable anguish and meaning — the nose long and powerful, the lips heavy and protuberant, the chin as broad as the chest, calmly asserting that 'all things are given unto me.' The low, broad head expresses limitless power and practical intensity. The mouth is not simply revolting, as it would be in the face of a man. But set in a face of such unbelievable power and profundity, it is a voluminous commentary on the text 'tempted in all things as we were' . . . set this great interpretation beside the figure of Buddha. Those idols of a philosopher-god, who treated the flesh as a disease to be exterminated, display a hideous hill of flesh surmounted by an expression of sickly placidity. I do not believe that Epstein has done justice to his subject; but merely audacity and unfeeling agnosticism could not produce such a deeply stirring figure. It is worth all the sermons preached since the sermon on the mount. It should be enough to erect each several hair upon the heads of infinite clergymen and Christians who have 'offered their complacency to Christ.'"[92]

McLuhan was reevaluating what he had learned from the man he considered to be the best among his professors at Manitoba: "[Rupert] Lodge is a decided Platonist, and I learned [to think] that way as long as I was trying to interpret Christianity in terms of comparative religion. Having perceived the sterility of that process, I now realize that Aristotle is the soundest basis for Christian doctrine."[93] In such reflections, McLuhan was stimulated by those around him. Guy Turgeon, a Canadian studying Natural Sciences at Cambridge, came by Magrath Avenue to lunch with him, and their talk ranged over countless subjects. His guest was still there at seven o'clock, so McLuhan asked him to stay to tea. Turgeon was a devout Catholic with a keen interest in theology and history, and McLuhan was prepared to ply his visitor with food and drink till he had mined his knowledge.[94]

Another personal influence at this time, stronger than Turgeon's, came from the Willisons — Ted and Kath. McLuhan had taken the trouble to get figures on the circulation of *G.K.'s Weekly*; on discovering that his subscription and the Willisons' were among only three in all of Cambridge, he contacted them. Staunch Catholics, warm-hearted and cultivated, the couple welcomed McLuhan into their home for many visits. He attended mass with the Willisons and enjoyed fireside chats and dinners with them.[95] They not only were instrumental, in their own decisive but unobtrusive way, in moving McLuhan toward conversion, but were also able to help him see past his own comment to Elsie: "The average Englishman moves at a level of taste and feeling which often make me think that he has not only made the industrial revolution but deserves it."[96]

As for Chesterton himself, McLuhan finally set eyes on him in June 1935. Ted Willison was the organizer of the Cambridge chapter of the Distributist League,[97] had all of Chesterton's books, and kept a framed picture of him hanging in his study. He was so thoroughly familiar with the great man's ideas that he and McLuhan talked for hours without exhausting the subject or themselves. McLuhan traveled to London with the Willisons to hear Chesterton speak to the Distributist League.

McLuhan's account of the evening began: "I was not prepared for his quick, light-blue eye, or the refinement and definition of his features."[98] Chesterton reminded McLuhan of a corpulent version of Canadian prime minister Richard Bedford Bennett, "6 feet 2 or 3 and much thicker (at the equator) tha[n] he is at the shoulders, or elsewhere."[99] Chesterton exuded magnanimity, humor, tolerance, and what McLuhan called "significant dignity to the necessity which nature has laid upon him."[100] Having addressed the meeting at several points during the evening, Chesterton prepared to leave. "He announced that he had conquered the morbid desire to fling himself through the emergency exit and would content himself with breaking several stairs as he departed in the usual manner. He urged us to go on with our songs and recitations (which we did) and hoped that his departure would occasion only a geographical deficiency (which it did)."[101] The evening was just the nudge McLuhan needed to complete the article he would entitle "G.K. Chesterton: A Practical Mystic."

Nearly forty years later, McLuhan said: "I know every word of him: he's responsible for bringing me into the church. He writes by paradox — that makes him hard to read (or hard on the reader)."[102] Chesterton and St. Thomas Aquinas, he said, were his two biggest influences. He loved Chesterton's rhetorical flourishes, imbibed his playfulness, turned his impulse to try out new combinations of ideas into the hallmark of the McLuhan method. Superficially, at least, Aquinas appears to be so very different from Chesterton, except that both are rhetoricians, and both were converts to Catholicism.

Within a year of arriving in Cambridge, McLuhan was well on the way to his own conversion. It was not a Damascus-road experience. The seeds had been planted with the agnosticism that had settled on him in spite of himself during his University of Manitoba years, a condition he recognized and acknowledged only under the salutary dislocating effect of Cambridge.[103]

Elsie was alarmed. Apparently she gave him a subtle reminder of his grandfather James McLuhan's preoccupation in his final years with Swedenborgianism, and of his uncle Roy's (Herbert's youngest brother) conversion to the Jehovah's Witnesses. Less subtle was Elsie's reference to what she regarded as her son's "religion-hunting" tendency.[104] His massive missive in reply made it clear how much thought he had already given to the subject, not only as a personal matter, but in its consequences for his future as an academic, and for his prospective marriage to Marjorie.

McLuhan acknowledged his capacity for enthusiasm but described himself as weak in *religious* enthusiasm: "The very definition of an enthusiast is that he has seized a truth which he cannot, and would not if he could, relate to other truths of life . . . I have some elements of enthusiasm which have been more than occupied in hero-worship — e.g. Macaulay and Chesterton. Them days is gone forever, but I shall always think that my selection of heroes was fortunate. Both were calculated to suppress effectively any tendency I had towards harping on *one* truth at a time."[105]

He assured Elsie that any formal step he took toward embracing Catholicism would be considered gravely, predicting that it could take years, because he was not educated for it. But he had already learned enough about the faith to speak categorically and to contrast it with others, writing to Elsie: "The Catholic religion is the only religion — all sects are derivative. Buddhism and similar oriental philosophies are mythologies, and mythologies are not religions in any sense. They have no covenants and no sacraments and no theology . . . Now the Catholic religion as you may be able to check in your own experience of it is alone in blessing and employing all those merely human faculties which produce games and philosophy, and poetry and music and mirth and fellowship with a very fleshy basis."[106] As for the contrast between Catholicism and Protestantism, McLuhan continued: "Catholic culture produced Don Quixote and St. Francis and Rabelais . . . Everything that is especially hateful and devilish and inhuman about the conditions and strains of modern industrial society is not only Protestant in origin, but it is their boast (!) to have originated it."[107]

Elsie had inquired as to the effect conversion might have on his prospects for an academic career, to which he replied: "The Provincial U.'s would be indifferent, religion being at such an ebb in our land . . .

However I will not be a Catholic when I come to apply for posts."[108]

Inevitably, McLuhan reverted to the writings of Chesterton, noting that they had not actually convinced or convicted him of any religious truth. "He opened my eyes to European culture and encouraged me to know it more closely. He taught me the reasons for all that in me was simply blind anger and misery . . . He remained an Anglo-Catholic as long as he could [before converting to Roman Catholicism] . . . His wife became a Catholic a few years later."[109]

As for Marjorie, McLuhan described her as agnostic and believed that she would likely follow his lead in converting. "In any case, her reactions to Protestant morals and the dull dead daylight of Protestant rationalism which ruinously bathes every object from a beer parlour to a gasoline station, are my reactions," he wrote to Elsie. "You see my 'religion-hunting' began with a rather priggish 'culture-hunting.' I simply couldn't believe that men had to live in the mean, mechanical, joyless, rootless fashion that I saw in Winnipeg. And when I began to read English literature, I knew that it was quite unnecessary for them so to live. You will remember my deep personal enjoyment of 'Tom Brown's Schooldays' in grade 8. It brought me in contact with things for which I was starved — things which have since disappeared from England. All my Anglo-mania was really a recognition of things missing from our lives which I felt to be indispensable. It was a long time before I finally perceived that the character of every society, its food, clothing, arts, and amusements are ultimately determined by its religion — It was longer still before I could believe that religion was as great and joyful as these things which it creates — or destroys."[110]

McLuhan addressed every point that Elsie had raised directly: "When you suggest that 'a life of service' is superior to membership in the Church, you say only what every Protestant conscious of exclusion from that membership says. It implies that the map of the universe was not radically altered by the Incarnation and the Resurrection."[111]

England had given McLuhan a vantage point for evaluating the North American attitude toward religious dedication. "The Americans serve 'service.' Like the rest of the world they have smothered man in men and set up the means as an end. It does not speak so well for your discrimination as for your affectionate fears that you should confuse my position with the evangelicism of which you have had experience. Nor do I believe that I am being unfair to Red in pointing out to him that there is an alternative which if he does not honestly face now he cannot but regret when increasing knowledge of that alternative and bitter experience with his present sect shall have mingled in later years."[112] Elsie's fear was that Red might be swayed from his decision to enter the United Church ministry.

The measure of how powerful his convictions were becomes clear from a later letter to Elsie, stating: "Had I come into contact with the Catholic Thing, the Faith, 5 years ago, I would have become a priest, I believe."[113] To assuage Elsie's concerns, McLuhan replied: "I quite realise Red's difficulty — but I am far from increasing it by criticising *now*, before he has even begun his 'theology' courses. I don't pretend to superior reasoning powers in these matters. I simply *know* of certain *things* which I didn't know two years ago and which you have never had an opportunity to know."[114]

It was midsummer, and for want of money, Marjorie had decided to delay her visit till the following year. McLuhan was disappointed *and* relieved, could even call the situation "quite satisfactory."[115] He was short of money himself for the traveling he and Marjorie planned to do. Above all, he was focused on his work. Surely by the following summer he would have more money, and with his exams behind him, be able to feel more justified about taking a vacation.[116]

"An unpleasantly unsettled state of mind" overshadowed whatever disappointment he felt over Marjorie's change of plans.[117] What lay beyond Cambridge, he wondered? Of returning to the University of Manitoba to teach he said, "I would go there like a shot, I'm afraid, if I got the chance. I could not endure the thought of spending my life there, but until these times are past . . . [McLuhan's ellipsis]."[118] But he felt no confidence that *any* job prospects would open, and he worried over the strain that Elsie's generous support of him placed on her finances. A bank balance of £6, as the university term closed, did not help to ease his mind.[119]

McLuhan drew optimism from examining his highly motivated state: "I am ready to work partly because my studies have equipped me for some jobs, and partly because I am eager for some mundane experience simply that I may use it as a weapon to call the bluff of the 'practical,' 'no-nonsense' cads and grafters who have put us where we are. If ever

there was a red-hot revolutionist c'est moi at this moment."[120] Perhaps
this fervor had been inspired in some measure by his brief encounter
with the Distributists. Certainly the great shadow of Chesterton
loomed as McLuhan said, in the same breath: "If I felt no vocation in
this direction, I could think of no more pleasing alternative than to
take a 30 acre orchard-dairy farm in the Maritimes."[121]

It is just as certain that the remark came easily, and with no serious
reflection on the generations of Halls who had worked the land of the
Annapolis Valley, or the patch of prairie abandoned by Herbert
McLuhan. Yet there was much thought in McLuhan's comment on
the return he had made and was making, in his own fashion, to the life
of earlier generations, not of the Halls and the McLuhans, but the
family of mankind: "An innate distaste for spiritual perversion and
incontinence would have kept me neutrally agnostic forever unless
there had come opportunities for knowledge of things utterly alien to
the culture — the grim product of life-denying other worldliness —
that you know I hated from the time I turned from our pavements and
wheels to boats and sails."[122]

WHEN THE SPRING TERM ended, McLuhan remained in Cambridge
until the end of June 1935, meeting then with his Winnipeg friend
Stewart Robb, a student at Oxford, and sailing from Harwich for
Belgium. The objective of the continental excursion was to improve
his French in preparation for the compulsory exam he would write the
following spring. After two weeks in Brussels and Bruges, McLuhan
continued on to France and stayed with the Devin family in
Boulogne-sur-Mer. The family boarded foreigners studying French.
Here McLuhan met a number of Americans, fellow students with
whom he took two weeks of French classes. By the end of July, he was
back in Cambridge and still preoccupied with mastering French, but
spending more time immersed in Joyce and Hemingway than in
Montaigne. Beginning his second year, McLuhan moved to rooms at
Trinity Hall that gave him "infinite content. Certainly I have no right
to be as fortunate and happy — but shall probably have enough of
thin times hereafter to level up, so that I shall die neither more nor
less felicitous than common men."[123]

In January of 1936, his Chesterton article appeared in *The Dalhousie Review*, challenging readers, even those critics who belittled Chesterton as nothing more than a showman, to recognize and understand the paradox that made him, in McLuhan's phrase, a practical mystic. The Chesterton who had for thirty years been "examining current fashion and fatalism," who "fears lest certain infinitely valuable things, such as the family and personal liberty, should perish," is evoked in McLuhan's opening paragraph and evokes the McLuhan who would do the same for another thirty years and more.[124]

Identifying Chesterton with the true mystics who reveal mysteries rather than hiding them, McLuhan again anticipates the basis of his own eventual approach to media in saying: "The mysteries revealed by Mr. Chesterton are the daily miracles of sense and consciousness." The inexpressible value of existence that Chesterton found "superior to any arguments for optimism or pessimism" was transformed in McLuhan's work, beginning with *The Mechanical Bride*, into the suspended judgment that so confounded and perplexed his commentators. Applying to Chesterton the words Jacques Maritain spoke of Arthur Rimbaud ("The Eucharistic passion which he finds in the heart of life"), McLuhan notes that Chesterton transcended poetry.[125] McLuhan quotes Chesterton saying of one of his own literary creations that he "had somehow made a giant stride from babyhood to manhood, and missed that crisis in youth when most of us grow old," words that McLuhan transfers to Chesterton himself.[126] They are equally transferable to McLuhan.

From his "more than ordinary awareness and freshness of perception," McLuhan states, Chesterton derived his "extraordinarily strong sense of fact," a sense that McLuhan too possessed and derived from the same source.[127] For Chesterton, that sense of fact necessitated the humility McLuhan calls "the very condition of honest art and all philosophy."[128] If McLuhan managed in 1936 to convince his readers that Chesterton was humble, he had more difficulty in successfully projecting such an image of himself in years to come, when he assumed the transformed mantle of Chesterton in becoming a media analyst.

But few commentators would deny McLuhan's originality — a quality he identified in Chesterton, adding an important qualifier that serves incidentally to characterize his own work, whether in literary analysis or media, throughout his career: "In short, he is original in the only possible sense, because he considers everything in relation to its origins."[129] In his teachings McLuhan was to emulate the Chesterton who "consciously causes a clash between appearances in order to attract attention to a real truth transcending such a conflict."[130] Those who were willing to grant McLuhan the expansive method of inquiry he required could say of him, as he said of Chesterton: "There is no hint or hue of meaning amidst the dizziest crags of thought that is safe from his swift, darting, pursuit."[131]

McLuhan rises to the defense of Chesterton against those who saw him as a medievalist (a charge later leveled at McLuhan):[132] "The merest reference to anything prior to the Reformation starts a clock-work process in the minds of the nineteenth century journalists who still write most of our papers."[133] Anticipating the historical sweep of his thesis on Thomas Nashe, McLuhan speaks of "the conspiracy . . . to ignore history, which in practice meant the middle ages," noting that it "had not generally been found out when Mr. Chesterton began to write."[134]

McLuhan never defended his own style, though he might have done so with the very words he applies to Chesterton: "In fact, that he turns a few cart-wheels out of sheer good spirits by way of enlivening his pages has annoyed a certain type of person, and is sure to puzzle a lazy or fatigued mind. Such, for instance, is his unparalleled power of making verbal coincidences really coincide."[135] Any McLuhan critic unwilling to concede this point would still need to admit a parallel between Chesterton and McLuhan along the lines the latter describes in the former, saying: "The fact is that Mr. Chesterton has always that additional human energy and intellectual power which constitute humour."[136] As for the intellectual power to "focus a vast range of material into a narrow compass,"[137] a quality McLuhan so admires in Chesterton, it proves to be an admirable (or bewildering — according to one's taste) trait of the later McLuhan.

Chesterton's "great labour of synthesis and reconstruction"[138] was McLuhan's own, focusing on the present and the past "because he is concerned lest our future steps be blindly taken."[139] McLuhan stresses the continuity of Chesterton's ideas as much as he would leave it unspoken for his own work, and characterizes the contrast between

Chesterton's alleged vice of alliteration as "something quite different from a Swinburne lulling the mind by alliterating woolly caterpillar words,"[140] maintaining that in Chesterton's hands the device was "of a piece with the rigorous clarity of his thought."[141] Chesterton's enthusiasm for the detective story, shared by McLuhan, was, the latter explains, "based upon the poetry of fact which Mr. Chesterton has explained so well."[142] McLuhan closes his Chesterton article with an observation recognized, even in his lifetime, as pertaining to himself: "He has become a legend while he yet lives. Nobody could wish him otherwise than as he is."[143]

In Toronto, Elsie approached Father Gerald Phelan, at St. Michael's College, about the prospects for a position for her son, after learning from him that he had received a letter from Phelan expressing his appreciation of the Chesterton article in *The Dalhousie Review*. McLuhan had not expected this initiative. "Regarding your use of Phelan on my behalf, I am of course not exactly elated. But there was nothing disreputable in the proceeding."[144] The immediacy of Elsie's gesture prompted him to reflect on his character and behavior, and in so doing he unintentionally sketched both similarities and differences between mother and son. "I think there is latent in my mind a fear to exert myself fully on *any* occasion, lest I should have to admit the result to be my *best*; and the best not good enough. I have a strong sense of superiority that is utterly incommensurate with my abilities — by superiority I mean superior *ability to do*, not superiority of personal value."[145]

MIDWAY THROUGH HIS second year at Cambridge, McLuhan began his search for a job. Introducing himself as "one of the products of some of the leanest years of the Manitoba English Department,"[146] he wrote to E. K. Brown, then chairing the same department. "[My] last year was somewhat relieved by the presence of Dr. Wheeler, but I had directed my energies to philosophy, and did my best work for Professor Lodge . . . I don't think the thought of any position would have occurred to me as soon as this but for the shock of the suicide of a near friend of mine — a splendid fellow — who found idleness and dependence intolerable . . . and eight years at University is long enough to be a weight on the family . . . Frankly, I am quite keen about teaching, although until I came to the Cambridge English School, my principal qualification was a boundless enthusiasm for great books, great events, and great men. Dr. Richards and Dr. Leavis have proved to be a useful supplement and corrective to that attitude . . . I have been advised, and feel personally the desire for some practical teaching experience before undertaking any research. I should be very happy indeed to work under you and Dr. Wheeler."[147] It was not to be.

Gertrude Stein came to lecture at Cambridge. McLuhan listened, unimpressed. He sat impatiently through a monotonous hour, satisfied by the end of her talk only because he had found just the right way to open the question period. What, he asked, did she, as an author concerned with the subject of time, think of Wyndham Lewis's treatment of it? If he already knew of the dismissive remarks Lewis had made on Stein's writing techniques, he did not let on. McLuhan's probe touched a raw nerve. She drew up her great bulk and launched a tirade, growling out a question of her own for McLuhan: "What are people like you doing here at Cambridge?"[148]

Earlier, at the beginning of what was to be a highly successful lecture tour in America, Stein had taken a question from a reporter marveling at lucid talk from such an obscure writer. Why didn't she write the way she spoke? "Why don't you read the way I write?" she responded.[149] Much later, McLuhan found himself in a similar position to Stein: "I have been asked, 'Why is it your letters to newspapers are simple and clear and your books are so difficult?' In writing to newspapers, I am expounding my thoughts. In my books, I am not expounding or making exposition — I am making exploration . . . I am an explorer, not an explainer. It never occurs to people that you might use the printed word for exploration."[150] McLuhan used the technology of language, an extension of thought, to form new perceptions, instead of rehearsing old ideas. From any domain of thought where the *hear* in *rehearsing* had been muffled, he needed to escape and explore new frontiers. It was his bond with James Joyce. It was also Stein's bond with Joyce, but he had sunk as low in her opinion as the nameless student she berated in Cambridge in 1936.

WHEN THE MAGIC AND majesty of English spring burst on Cambridge, it found McLuhan reading Wyndham Lewis and worrying for the first time about the war clouds darkening Europe.[151] He also learned that he had not been successful in his bid for a National Fellowship.[152] It meant that staying on at Cambridge would be out of the question, if his search for a teaching job failed. On the same day, he suddenly discovered that it was the deadline for submitting his English tripos paper. For this he had reprised George Meredith and the subject of comedy, but by now he was thoroughly weary of the topic. "My brain seems to be softening," he thought.[153] Evidently not: he obtained a twenty-four-hour extension and submitted his five-thousand-word paper by 7:00 p.m. the next day.[154]

The Cam was glorious, but neither its sparkling waters, the virgin greenery cradling the river, nor the rhythm of oars could lift McLuhan out of his leaden mood. He pondered his two Cambridge undergraduate years ending and wished he had them to do over. From the point of view of study, he felt he had made little use of them. He also felt sullen enough to absolve himself from full blame. "I have not yet recovered from Manitoba U," he noted.[155]

A letter arrived from Marjorie. Having earlier entertained the thought of spending a full year in England, she now announced that she would not be coming at all. The Norrises had scotched their daughter's plan for a year abroad, and she was unwilling to spend money on a short stay.[156] But within a month, she had changed her mind: "Marjorie now threatens to come! May be on her way," he wrote in his diary on 7 June 1936. Two years later, rereading his diary entry for the day, McLuhan would add a note, ruefully admitting that Marjorie's change of heart had been prompted by "a silly 'ultimatum' I sent her, which of course I had not expected would produce results but merely smoothe my exit."[157] He had imagined his message saying "Come for a visit or else" would be a tidy way to break off with Marjorie, but the ploy had backfired.

Midsummer's eve was very warm, humid, and green. McLuhan knew by now that Marjorie had sailed from Canada and was scheduled to dock in Liverpool the same day. An unusually strong electrical storm broke over Cambridge, and he was unable to get word to or from her. Perhaps just as well, for all he had to say was "Damn the day of Marjorie's arrival!"[158] The next day, oppressive heat and humidity again brought the roll of thunder and lightning crackling through the Cambridge sky by evening. Marjorie neither arrived nor telephoned. McLuhan guessed that she thought him "a blackguard for not being at the boat."[159] He was reading Hopkins, Eliot, and Pound. By the time the storm had cleared the following morning, he was feeling "blood[y]-minded about Marjorie"[160] and reading Wyndham Lewis's *The Art of Being Ruled.*

His exams were over and the results were announced. McLuhan earned second-class honors, sufficient standing for him to gain admission to the Cambridge graduate program.[161] "I am now a BA Cantab,"[162] he wrote to Elsie, describing the graduation ceremony. "We were presented in batches of four — holding a finger of the praelector's right hand with our right hand — to the vice chancellor, in Latin. Then our names were read out separately and we knelt before the vice chancellor's chair with hands held prayerwise. He laid his hands on mine and received me into the University in the name of the Father, Son, and Holy Ghost — a relic of medieval barbarism![163]

McLuhan took no satisfaction in his new status, describing himself on his graduation day as surfeited with uncertainty and vagueness. The statement merited four exclamation marks.[164] He was chafing at the bit to make his mark on the world. And Marjorie had not turned up yet.

But a letter had. It was from the University of Wisconsin, offering him a position in the English department. It lifted the cloud of unknowing for McLuhan. Now he could contemplate Marjorie's visit and a trip to the Lake District with satisfaction and the assurance that a contract for the Wisconsin position would be awaiting him on his return. He announced the bright future to Elsie: "I certainly don't want to cost you another penny. I have plenty of ideas for articles and will write one per quarter from now on."[165]

"No Marjorie," he wrote in his diary on 2 July, mentioning her there for the first time in ten days. But the next day, he was enraged to receive a telegram from her saying she was not coming to Cambridge. On landing in England she had gone directly to the home of her uncle Albert in Belfast. McLuhan telephoned that evening, but she was not in, and he was not in later to answer her return call.[166] When they finally spoke, briefly, on the telephone the next day, McLuhan decided to take the overnight steamer to Belfast.[167]

Marjorie and her uncle met McLuhan at the dock, and the threesome began their sightseeing at once.[168] They investigated every corner of James Joyce's world, beginning with Dublin's Phoenix Park. It was more than a week later that McLuhan took Marjorie to Howth Castle for the day, and they sat on the grassy cliffside, alone together for the first time.[169] There was no hope of saying everything they thought and felt about the two years they had been apart, no need to say what changes time had brought, no need to say what the moment so clearly showed each of them. They agreed to meet in London, and the next day McLuhan returned to Cambridge.[170]

Before the month was out they made their rendezvous, enjoying the sights of London, candlelit dinners in Soho, an excursion to Windsor. McLuhan recorded a "perfect day with Marj on bike via Ripley, Ockham, Wesley," but said nothing of their farewells to each other.[171] Less than a month later, he was at sea, bound for Canada. It was Marjorie's birthday, and he wondered if she too was crossing the Atlantic.[172] She would be returning home to Winnipeg; he was on his way to Toronto for a visit with Elsie before setting out for Wisconsin.[173]

Looking back on his Cambridge studies after more than forty years, McLuhan would comment on the unexpected advantages they had conferred. Encountering Richards (whom he put first in acknowledging his formative influences, both at the time and later),[174] Chesterton, Quiller-Couch, Forbes, Leavis, and others had generated more than *darshan*, more than ideas: "Seen at a distance, famous people acquire a quite unreal and discouraging character. Seen close up, the quite human limitations and foibles of such people can be the greatest possible stimulus to self-assertion."[175] From figures surrounded by a cult of greatness ("a very debilitating and inhibiting thing"),[176] McLuhan learned to think in terms of environments that needed, above all, to be understood, to be controlled, to be broken through — not broken into — particularly if they were nothing more than cults. And he learned to do this with what he called a "bland acceptance of the contemporary world as a scene,"[177] an acceptance his future critics were to misinterpret as endorsement.

The detachment of Cambridge from the world of commerce, he noted, freed it from the need to react against commercialism, or to expend energy in raising a bulwark of moral defense against it. He was speaking not only of Cambridge but of his own writings, such as *The Mechanical Bride* and *Culture Is Our Business*, in saying: "The same energies could be more usefully spent in seeking to discover the shape and tendencies of the age."[178] In the same context, he noted that "the training of perception has been the aim and boast of many educators at Cambridge in this century." There could be no more succinct statement of his own aims, as he left Cambridge to begin a teaching career, than "the training of perception."

TWO

Dagwood's America

4

A Professor in Spite of Himself

I am sorry that you cannot find work in Canada, but as nothing seems to be available for you here, we cannot object to you going to the States for a little.

–Miss W. Gordon,
National Educational Secretary, IODE,
to Marshall McLuhan, 31 July 1936

I am going to tear the hide right off Canada some day and rub salt into it.

–Marshall McLuhan
to Elsie McLuhan, 28 June 1936

In the analytical terms McLuhan would later use, the United States favors *figure* to the exclusion of *ground*; Canada favors *ground* to the exclusion of *figure*. McLuhan, whose personality and patterns of thought made him a figure inseparable from ground, spent much of the 1960s and '70s shuttling between his native land and its southern neighbor. By then he was the pioneer of media analysis, commanding attention and interest in both countries and on the world stage. But in 1936, his options were teaching English in Wisconsin, unemployment, or turning his life in a new direction.

To be jobless after eight years of university study was unthinkable, and the memory of hardships suffered by those around them during the worst of the Depression years in Winnipeg, hardships that the McLuhans themselves managed to escape, was still too vivid.

Cambridge, on the other hand, had made him forget his brash vow at Manitoba to shun the academic life. That left the University of Wisconsin, not as an option but as a necessity.

"My life in Canada will be a continual discontent," he had written, "my task as a teacher will be to shake others from their complacency — how is it possible to contemplate the products of English life (i.e. Literature) without criticising our own sterility?"[1] His life in Canada was still eight years away as McLuhan signed students into his classes for the fall term, but he would feel the beginnings of continual discontent much sooner.

He had arrived in Madison without recording the event, five days before writing in his diary: "Don't mind things here at all."[2] He felt "pleasantly cynical,"[3] an unaccustomed feeling for McLuhan. About what, he did not say. And he bought a wristwatch and recorded the purchase, eschewing his long-preferred spelling of "bot" in favor of "bought,"[4] perhaps as a concession to his new professorial persona.

On the first day of classes, he asked his students to write impromptu compositions. Sitting down to inspect the results the same evening, he commented: "It is heartbreaking to read some of them."[5] The level of expression in the papers spread before him was "not contemptible" but grim enough to jar him out of his comfortable cynicism of the previous day.[6] The moment was not ripe for tackling literary appreciation through anything so daring as I. A. Richards's "protocols" or launching eagerly prepared salvos against North American sterility. Shaking his students out of complacency would have to wait while the young professor taught them fundamentals of language. It was McLuhan who was shaken.

Though he had not yet received his first paycheck, he bought a briefcase and beefsteak, and armed himself for more grading with the finest red pencils money could buy. For his own edification, and in the hope of finding the key to teaching freshman composition, he delved into H. L. Mencken's *The American Language*. After two days of the illumination provided by Mencken's engaging brand of scholarship, McLuhan could say he was feeling "vurry American." He also said he despised Canada.[7] For England, he felt a bit of nostalgia, especially as temperatures dropped to near freezing in October, the same month when he had lunched with the Crawleys in their sunny Cambridge garden, two years earlier.[8]

A casual letter from Marjorie arrived, followed by silence, till she summoned the courage to write again a month later and broach the subject of their changed relationship. McLuhan answered the same day, expressing the hope that they could keep on writing to one another out of respect and affection.[9] Letters were just as important as love.

Though he spoke of "rather discouraging" staffing matters at the university,[10] McLuhan was quick to strike up acquaintances and soon made satisfying contacts with his English department colleagues. He became fast friends with three other young instructors — John Pick, Kenneth Cameron, and Morton Bloomfield — meeting them of an evening for freewheeling discussions over beer, for study sessions, or for reading poetry aloud. Senior members of the department, among them Ruth Wallerstein, Madeleine Doran, and Helen C. White, were "much impressed not only by his brilliance of mind, but by the breadth of his interests and of his contacts with what was going forward in England and in this country."[11] McLuhan was, in their eyes, "keen and resourceful, ready to share an unusual background. He is enthusiastic and a hard worker."[12]

He admitted freely that he hated grading papers, but said at the same time that he felt very much for the students. At least one student must have felt something for *him*, since she confessed in a footnote that she thought he looked just like movie actor Frederick March.[13] Parsing sentences was something of a novelty for him, and the carefully prepared lessons that earned him praise from his students were as much for himself as for them. When he was not "cracking up grammar"[14] for his classes, he was taking a German course. He found time to rediscover the great joys of Shakespeare, and he and Bloomfield studied philology together. In many respects, McLuhan's new life seemed like a pleasant extension of the best of his days at Cambridge. After less than two months, he could say: "I think my head has never worked so well as since I came to Madison."[15]

McLuhan made contact, once again, with Father Gerald Phelan at St. Michael's College, and told him that he wished to become a Catholic. Visiting Elsie in Toronto over the Christmas holidays, he had several meetings with Phelan, who put questions to him about his faith and satisfied himself that McLuhan could be a candidate for reception into the Church.

Once the second term was under way, with Wisconsin in the grip of winter, McLuhan found himself both settled and unsettled. There were long evenings for reading — Joyce's *Ulysses*, Wyndham Lewis's *Tarr*, Ezra Pound's *ABC of Reading*, C. K. Ogden and I. A. Richards's *The Meaning of Meaning*, Karl Adam's *Spirit of Catholicism*. Perhaps the evenings were too long. Suddenly, he felt as though he had been in America far longer than four months, long enough to have accomplished more than he had: "Might have been finishing my Cambridge Ph.D. here at Madison, had I some guts."[16] *Finishing*. The word shows at once how slowly time was passing and how quickly McLuhan believed he could work.

His $93 monthly paycheck seemed like a handsome income, but teaching composition was a job, not a career.[17] He knew the future would take him — would have to take him — elsewhere. If he despised Canada, he was also "beginning to feel 'up against' America once more."[18] The problem was not just *where* to be but *what* he had not yet become: "I am a set of partially developed and isolated fragments."[19] No ground, no figure.

There were dinners with colleagues who welcomed McLuhan into their homes, discussions as satisfying as the best of those he had enjoyed in Cambridge, efforts to arrange for Elsie to perform in Madison, and hours given to "scratching off some dialogue,"[20] an activity that he found to be "a congenial vehicle for ideas."[21] He was also taking instruction from Father John Kutchera and attending Sunday mass. He missed the benefits of rowing and took little physical exercise apart from skating. As the winter wore on, he suffered from nervous indigestion for the first time in a year.[22] On the best and the worst of days, he turned to his books.

It was in Madison that McLuhan finished reading his way to conversion through the works of Catholic and Protestant writers alike, grappling with their thought, evaluating constantly, forming his ideas of God and faith as much through what he discarded as from what he retained. In the midst of his reflections, he addressed a letter to Red, discussing *Moral Values and the Idea of God*, by W. R. Sorley, whose "idea of perfection is a state of dullness (like an English Sunday) where the mind asks no questions because it is in harmony with nature."[23] Asking no questions was itself a form of spiritual death to McLuhan, and he believed that Sorley had failed to ask the most important one: "He does not consider what knowledge and what graces or helps the mind and soul would require (and once had) if the discord between man and nature were to be resolved. The direct intuition of God which the mind once enjoyed was much more than a dull contemplation of 'law' in nature."[24]

McLuhan had his own question: "What does Sorley mean by 'law' as an 'explanation' of reality?"[25] And his own answer: "To explain is to unfold. To explain reality is to unfold what he calls 'the ground of everything which is real' (p.500) which is God. So to explain is to reveal or expose God. And the philosopher is a sort of detective working on natural clues. But he is a detective who (in most cases) refuses to listen to any account (revealed truth) of the crime which has been committed. He doesn't know that the criminal and the victim were the same person (Adam) nor that the offense has been committed against a person he doesn't know about (God) . . . The fact that even in our disordered lives we have innumerable intimations of an order from which we have fallen is evidence of a mind and a being *above* the natural order *we* perceive. But the order in the universe (as well as its 'purpose') depends upon its being held in position, so to speak, by God's will and intelligence. God is independent of the universe . . . but he is also immanent in it in the sense that its order and life depends from Him."[26]

Stressing Sorley's error in "steering away from the fact of *sin* and merely thinking of *imperfection*,"[27] McLuhan implicitly pointed Red toward Catholicism by recommending Jacques Maritain's *Introduction to Philosophy*. His self-proselytizing, for the better part of three years, had been more explicit. And he scrutinized himself as carefully as he had Sorley's thought: "I realise more and more that I am 'grown up' and that I need look for no miracle to happen now! What I am now, I must be, more or less, for the rest of my life, and it gives me a queer feeling of hopelessness to think that all those large dreams of the powers and talents which I was to possess at this time for the bedazzlement of men and perhaps the 'bedazzlement of Heaven with high astounding terms' are just a chimerical blank. I have no affection for the world. I cannot be sure whether my present indifference to its objectives and pleasures is genuinely grounded in the love of God or

merely in the despair of myself. At least I can say this, that my dissatisfaction is so deep that I cannot imagine anyone in history or anyone
alive who I would choose to be (saints excepted, because they weren't
trying to collect from life) rather than myself."[28]

Five thousand miles from Cambridge, with his Chesterton article
in print, McLuhan was not, as he had expected, better off for having
worked it out of his system. "My malady is of the marrow. It is a
hunger in the bone for something which cannot be satisfied by flesh
and blood."[29] In Winnipeg, McLuhan's prayers, as he realized only
much later, had been for conversion; at Cambridge, his reading of
philosophy and Church history, his friendship with the Willisons, and
the ever-strengthening influence of Chesterton drew him closer to
it.[30] In Madison, a simple question finally made the process complete.

A student, whose name McLuhan could not later recall, recognized
the depth of understanding that he revealed in talking about
Catholicism and asked him, "Why aren't you in the Church?" He had
no answer. The same afternoon, McLuhan was baptized by the
Newman chaplain, who already knew him well and exempted him
from instruction and catechism.[31] That evening, he was received into
the Church, sponsored by his teaching colleague and friend John
Pick; the next day he took first communion at the College chapel.[32] It
was Holy Thursday, 25 March 1937. McLuhan never failed to mark
the anniversary of the event in his diary. He had spent the evening of
his reception into the Church with Pick and other friends in a "strenuous and heated discussion"[33] of Aldous Huxley's writings. Later, it
struck him as very appropriate that their conversation had centered on
the ideas of a celebrated agnostic at that time. Huxley never occupied
McLuhan's thought again.

Despite the fact that McLuhan read so much of his way to conversion, he found no contradiction in saying "I came in[to the Church]
on my knees. That is the only way in."[34] Like all his reading, the
massive study McLuhan made of Catholicism before taking the step
of conversion was simply background that led him decisively neither
to concepts nor precepts but to percepts: "You don't come into the
Church through ideas and concepts."[35] Catholicism for McLuhan
meant "complete intellectual freedom to examine any and all phenomena with the absolute assurance of their intelligibility."[36] When

he looked back on nearly forty years in the Church, McLuhan could say that "belief in God alters existence . . . making it mystical and converting a leaden uninspired human into something lyrically super-human."[37]

Though difficult to detect in McLuhan's publications, the connection between his faith and his media studies emerges clearly in his correspondence and his private papers. It proves to be wholly unlike the bizarre mix, confected by Jonathan Miller in his critical study, *McLuhan*, of a convert's "Catholic piety" and the transmuted legacy of "severe Agrarian partialities" from F. R. Leavis.[38] McLuhan's own account, from a letter written in 1973, runs as follows: "At one time, when I was first becoming interested in the Catholic Church, I studied the entire work of G. K. Chesterton and the entire group from the pre-Raphaelites and Cardinal Newman through to Christopher Dawson and Eric Gill. All of this really is involved in my media study, but doesn't appear at all."[39]

McLuhan expanded on the faith-technology connection at both the personal and historical level: "I even became a Catholic by studying the Renaissance. I mean that my historical studies were all on that period, and I became aware that the Church had been destroyed or dismembered at that time by this crazy accident in technology [of print] . . . The whole of medieval culture was oral because they read — everything aloud to themselves. They could not see the text until they said it, like shorthand today . . . Luther and the first Protestants were all still Schoolmen . . . they carried over the scholastic disputation into the new visual culture. They were still oral men, but they were using the new technique of printing to strengthen and intensify their differences with Rome and with one another."[40]

AFTER HIS CONVERSION, McLuhan became partial to numbers divisible by three (the Trinity) and remained so all his life.[41] He also avoided 13, but on the thirteenth of April 1937, as the academic year began drawing to a close at the University of Wisconsin, he mailed away an application for a teaching position at a Catholic school, Saint Louis University. The Jesuit fathers who administered the university received a supporting letter from Father Phelan in Toronto. Within a

week, McLuhan had a reply, asking what salary he wished to receive.
A mere eleven days after he had applied for the position, his appointment as instructor in the English department was confirmed. It was
Elsie who had been apprehensive about her son's career if he converted
to Catholicism, Elsie to whom he had said he would not be a Catholic
when he came to apply for positions — and yet it was Elsie who had
made the first contact with Father Phelan that led both to McLuhan's
conversion and support for his Saint Louis appointment.

There was a long summer to enjoy before he would have to set out
for Missouri. First came a letter from Marjorie, described by McLuhan
as the "coup de grace."[42] They had redefined their relationship, and
nothing more remained of it than a correspondence between friends.
But now it was Marjorie who looked for an "exit" without taking any
measure as dramatic or rash as the ultimatum McLuhan had sent her
from Cambridge the year before. She did not wish even to continue
their correspondence. He felt wretched, but also took a dispassionate
(if oblique) analytical view of the situation, saying that he could not
"see any essential avoidable circumstance."[43]

A month later, he was vacationing with Elsie on Vancouver Island,
where they had spent such a memorable summer more than a decade
earlier. It was late June when he joined her in the oceanside town of
Sidney, some fifteen miles north of Victoria, for a stay of nearly two
months. In August, Elsie gave a concert at Johnson's Canyon,[44] their
tranquil holiday drew to a close, and they left for Winnipeg. Three
years had gone by since Elsie had relocated in Toronto; three years
during which she had not seen Herbert. She spoke with him for an
hour between trains before heading east again.[45] Her son stayed over
in Winnipeg for three weeks, leaving for St. Louis on 9 September to
take up his new position.

THOUGH THE WINTER MONTHS in Madison had driven McLuhan to self-
reproach over not making any visible progress on his Ph.D., the
compulsion to read far beyond the bounds of any one topic always
won the day. The interminable sessions with Bloomfield, Cameron,
and Pick were too urgent, too vital for the discovery of new ideas that
surged out of good talk, to be sacrificed to the dreary labor of

embalming old ideas with ink. As for the restful summer on Vancouver Island, it had all but banished the thought of thesis writing from his mind. Now, with five different courses to prepare and teach over two semesters, there would be few hours left for other work, even if he could harness his energy to a single purpose.

Fortunately, the heavy teaching load was coupled with challenging variety, making it sheer pleasure to contemplate after a year of routine drilling in the principles of composition at Madison. True, he was scheduled for a section of freshman English again, but also the English Renaissance, Shakespeare's Comedies, Reading and Discrimination, and Studies in Milton. He would be able to put not only his Cambridge training but over a decade of independent reading to full use, spread his intellectual wings in a way that had, for the most part, been possible only *outside* classes in Wisconsin. He was moving to a larger city, a larger university, a larger perspective. McLuhan thrived on intense mental stimulation, needed to soak it up and pump it out all at once. St. Louis held the promise of satisfying that need and soon delivered on it. It also brought him "up against America" even more than Madison had. In St. Louis, he discovered what to do about it.

The first thing he noticed was the dust and the noise. As soon as the air cleared a little, he took note that "the girls are better looking than the northerners."[46] Within a week of his arrival, he was prepared to declare St. Louis "quite a livable place,"[47] and soon after he called it "a pleasant place, offering a variety of attractions."[48]

McLuhan took a room with the Gerardot family at 4343 McPherson Avenue and plunged into his work at the university. One meeting with his Shakespeare seminar was enough to satisfy him that he could manage to keep ahead of the students. He was suddenly grateful for his experience in Madison; he could now take the shocks in stride. His first paycheck arrived. At more than triple the amount he had received in Madison, it seemed "quite unreal."[49] He added that "the transition from student to teacher is imperceptible, whereas it is distinctly marked in monetary terms."[50]

The English department chairman was Father William McCabe, a Cambridge Ph.D., with whom McLuhan felt the bonds of shared faith and common scholarly interests. McCabe was a man in whom the new convert and young professor found a compelling model of the spiritual and the intellectual inseparably twined. Writing to Watson Kirkconnell in Winnipeg,[51] McLuhan described McCabe as "a most alert and aware sort of person, possessing the solid humanism which has its roots in Theology and Aristotelian philosophy. Such an atmosphere is free from fog at every point and does not prevent the clarification of sensibility, which is the proper function of the arts."[52]

Other clerics from the ranks of both faculty and students began forming part of McLuhan's new circle — among them Father Clement McNaspy and Father Walter Ong, who would later cite as members of this group the young Jesuits George Klubertanz, William A. Van Roo, and Charles Leo Sweeney.[53] In his first year at St. Louis, McLuhan also met Bernard Muller-Thym, a dynamic Philosophy department instructor who was completing his Ph.D. for the University of Toronto's Pontifical Institute of Medieval Studies. Muller-Thym's thesis supervisor, the founder and director of the Pontifical Institute, Etienne Gilson, regarded him as a genius. Muller-Thym and McLuhan quickly became friends for life. Later, when McLuhan would return to St. Louis, after a second sojourn in Cambridge, Felix Giovanelli had joined the faculty as an instructor of French and Spanish. Giovanelli was to play an important role in the sometimes tortured evolution of McLuhan's first book, *The Mechanical Bride*. Together, these friends gave McLuhan a sounding board for his ideas, nourished new ones, and fired his aspirations.

It was, above all, the influence of McCabe that eventually brought the ebullient McLuhan energy to bear on his Cambridge Ph.D. program. After his first two months in St. Louis, and with much appreciation for some excellent students and the freedom he was given in course organization, he noted that "the research end of it is the most interesting."[54] In this regard, he mentioned McCabe, who had already encouraged him to take a leave of absence whenever he wished to pursue the doctorate. Knowing that McLuhan was "puffing [the] *Scrutiny* approach"[55] of F. R. Leavis and I. A. Richards at the university's journal club, and that he was "keen about getting Leavis across to my classes,"[56] McCabe gave him an enormous added stimulus by inviting him to introduce a graduate course on Practical Criticism as early as the second term. McLuhan had already commented:

"Extraordinary how hard work lulls one's critical faculties. It is a drug, an escape perhaps."[57]

The new course would require an extra push, but the chance to become a voice for an approach he believed in so passionately was too good to miss. He introduced it under the title "Rhetoric and Interpretation," delivering it for the first time to an overflow class who had heard good things about this new professor. The course served to consolidate and promote what he had learned from the Cambridge English School and to move him toward the research on rhetoric that would become central to his Ph.D. thesis. McLuhan considered himself most fortunate that the opportunity to teach at St. Louis had come his way.

The students he was to influence there over the next seven years counted themselves fortunate, too. Ong would later say that he profited greatly from the courses he took with McLuhan, and in gratitude for the bibliographical research that McLuhan had done and shared so generously with him, the research leading to the publication of Ong's *Ramus and Talon Inventory*, he dedicated the book to McLuhan with the words "To HMM, who started all this."[58] Though Ong failed to detect any direct connection between the seminar in Practical Criticism McLuhan gave in St. Louis and his later media studies (only late in his career did McLuhan himself fully appreciate that the wellspring of those studies lay in Richards's teachings), he acknowledged that McLuhan "was an outpost in mid-America for the Leavis school . . . Cambridge New Criticism," adding that "this criticism was a tremendous breath of fresh air."[59]

Whether the undergraduates at Saint Louis appreciated McLuhan as much as the master's and doctoral students is another matter. In grading freshman English, he was not reluctant to follow McCabe's instruction to faculty (set down in a special version of the syllabus not intended for student eyes) to distribute failing grades freely.[60] In the same document, McCabe directed instructors that the full technique of I. A. Richards was to be used. He could have found no one more willing than McLuhan to seize on the phrase *full technique*. The exams McLuhan set for his first-year students recall the assiduous habit he formed in Winnipeg years of regularly learning new words from the dictionary: "Use the following words in separate sentences:

vehement, sedition, ingenious, paradoxical, arbitrarily . . . "[61] Sophomore students under McLuhan had to be prepared to answer questions that seemed every bit as challenging as those of a Ph.D. examination: "In what respect do rhetoric and poetic overlap?" or "Our entire conception of the nature and origins of the Renaissance is the melting pot. Discuss with specific reference [to] the work of the period and recent scholarship."[62]

As his first year at Saint Louis University drew to a close, McLuhan had already established himself as a forceful and inspiring presence. His drive and determination had allowed him to discharge his heavy teaching load evenhandedly, with time left over for undertaking the supervision of master's students and presiding over his first Ph.D. oral examination for Father Paul Smith.[63] There had even been time to think seriously about his Ph.D. topic.

It was not too early to reflect on the turn his life had taken so quickly, and a comparison invited itself between Madison and St. Louis. For all the satisfaction that McLuhan took in the community of scholars, at age twenty-six he felt a gap between himself and his undergraduate students. It was there at both universities. It had something to do with culture, but nothing to do with a Canadian teaching in the United States. It had something to do with ways of learning, ways of understanding, in young people who were the same age he had been when he said he would never be a professor. It was palpable, it was important to explore, if McLuhan was going to make a career as a professor in spite of himself. It had flickered across his mind as he wrote his last letter to Elsie from Cambridge. He needed to pursue this elusive, invisible something that had made him say he would tear the hide off Canada some day and rub salt into it.

5

From California to Cambridge Ricorso

Bought wine at the oldest winery in California.
$$-\textsc{Marshall McLuhan's diary},$$
$$25\ \textsc{June}\ 1938$$

riverrun, past Eve and Adam's from swerve of shore to bend
of bay, brings us by a commodius vicus back . . .
$$-\textsc{James Joyce},$$
Finnegans Wake

June 1938. Elsie McLuhan had enrolled in a summer workshop at the Pasadena Playhouse School of Theater; meanwhile, her son was making his way west across six states by car from St. Louis in the company of two friends. By happy coincidence, the material he had discovered he needed to begin research on the life and work of Thomas Nashe was at the Huntington Library in San Marino, a short distance from Pasadena. Elsie rented a small house, prepared for Marshall's arrival, and settled into a busy routine of daily classes and rehearsals.

Aspiring stars had come from far and wide to the prestigious annual workshop, but Elsie could not help noticing one in particular: a tall young woman of arresting and dignified beauty, with a melodious voice made all the more compelling by her Southern accent. She introduced herself as Corinne Lewis from Fort Worth, Texas. Elsie befriended her at once, charmed and intrigued by her grace and intensity. They had not been speaking very long when Elsie ventured,

WEST DES MOINES PUBLIC LIBRARY

"I have a handsome son who is coming down next week; I want to introduce you."[1]

A photograph, taken shortly after Marshall arrived, shows him in an ill-fitting jacket, bearing a startling resemblance to the young Ludwig Wittgenstein, known for his penetrating gaze. Elsie stands beside him, straight, slim, stylish in a white suit with a bold scarf and a large hat at a rakish angle. Looking far younger than her forty-nine years, she scrutinizes the camera less intently than her son and wears a look of pride.

Within a week of his arrival, Mrs. Fairfax Proudfit-Walkup, the managing director of the Pasadena Playhouse, was opening the new library wing with a flourish. She swung the champagne bottle, but it refused to break. A second swing and the bottle still remained intact. A third swing and the glass shattered, to the cheers of the onlookers. Now it was Corinne's turn to notice someone at the edge of the crowd.

Tall, very thin, with a pencil mustache, decked out in beach pants and a Cambridge rowing jacket trimmed in heavy black piping, he was leaning against the wall with a decidedly superior air, a pipe hanging from the corner of his mouth. Elsie led Marshall over and introduced him to Corinne, who thought he was the oddest-looking fellow she had ever seen. A few minutes of conversation was enough to make her realize that he lacked the elaborate charm of the young Southern men who courted her in Fort Worth. What, she wondered, makes this man tick? It was 10 July. That night, Marshall noted in his diary: "Met Corrine [sic] Lewis — worth knowing!"[2] Was she the unknown woman whose image he had been unable to shake from his mind upon awaking four days earlier?

The next evening they sat together at a performance of Shaw's *Heartbreak House*. Three days later it was "Corrinne [sic] to dinner."[3] A week later came Marshall's twenty-seventh birthday, celebrated over a festive meal Elsie had prepared. She presented him with a handsome gladstone bag that pleased him. And he was more than pleased with their only guest that evening — the vivacious Corinne. "She is not quite irresistible," he told his diary, "or else I am quite insensible."[4] On 5 August, Corinne performed in *Love on a Leash*. As Marshall sat reading his program before the show, it may have been the first time he saw her name in print; in any case, he learned to spell it "Corinne."

Marshall had thrown himself into his research work at the

Huntington Library on 12 July. By early August, he was "not seeing much but Corinne on the page."[5] On 10 August he took her to Santa Catalina, the island of romance. The day could not have been long enough for them. They swam, spent hours over dinner, climbed a mountain, where they sat watching a full moon rise, talking till dawn broke and the soft mist lifted from the seascape below.

Apart from her aspirations to a career on the stage, Corinne was teaching high school in Fort Worth and involved in the revision of the curriculum for the public schools. A voracious reader, she accepted the norms dictated by her social circle and kept her taste for literature from suitors who invariably were not her intellectual peers. With Marshall, at last, she could discuss all her literary interests. He was the sounding board she needed, as much as she was the captive audience he needed. It was a relationship of a kind she might not have dared to hope for, and the kind he had always dreamed of. For Corinne, it made the lack of genteel ways in Marshall quite irrelevant.

More than a month had evaporated in the timeless sphere they shared: the workshop at the Playhouse was ending; Corinne would be returning to Texas. They parted at noon on 15 August. Afterwards, Marshall could find no words to describe that moment except "sheer misery."[6] But very soon he would find the words for a letter to chase Corinne home, and returning to St. Louis on 11 September, he found hers awaiting him. It set off a torrent of words, and a blizzard of letters began arriving in the Lewis home in Fort Worth.

Corinne and her only sister Carolyn were not allowed to date young men, or even to have female friends, unless their family had known the other for two generations. It was the Old South. Corinne's father, Charles Lewis, was a real Southern gentleman, with no head for business matters. He had always wanted sons, but unlike Herbert McLuhan, with whom he might have been a soul mate, he had been presented with two daughters, whom he taught to ride, shoot, and fish. During the winter, he made an elaborate ritual of shining up every piece in his tackle box. In the evening, he would make a small ceremony of taking a cigar from his humidor and settling in for a good smoke, reading a book in his favorite chair, with his boots propped on the end of his bed.[7]

Emma Corinne Lewis, curious about the thick letters from

St. Louis addressed to her younger daughter and namesake, asked to see the contents. She discovered after a few attempts at deciphering Marshall's cramped hand that he was writing about arcane literary matters and decided that the flow of correspondence could continue without inspection. Though the intellectual emphasis in Marshall's letters had saved the day, Corinne would come to wish, nevertheless, that the scales were tipped a little more toward the romantic.[8]

When Marshall was not writing to Corinne, he was thinking about her. Endlessly. In September he told himself that he was not yet in love — a clear recognition that it was inevitable — but by November he had "too much Corinne on the brain"[9] and was "practically proposing."[10] There was no "practically," as Corinne read it: Marshall assumed they *were* engaged.

When he stopped thinking about her long enough to think about himself, he discovered that he had changed, that he was more self-contained. If it was an odd discovery in a man who gave every sign of being hopelessly in love, it was nevertheless an accurate observation, and Corinne had already recognized the same quality in him. It was what kept him from the expressions of adoration she would have been pleased to hear, even occasionally.

At first, Marshall felt "settled" by their exchange of letters, even "blissful." Corinne's letters were "grand."[11] They sustained him and made the enforced separation more bearable. As the fall wore on, he began to worry at the slightest delay in her replies and felt anxious about her reaction to his endless outpourings. His fear of displeasing her was confirmed when she wrote in an angry tone at the end of November. It made him wretched and "fed up with letters."[12] Within days, Corinne had written to apologize for her outburst. But then another cloud loomed on the horizon.

A young man to whom she had been all but engaged when she met Marshall was coming home to Fort Worth for the Christmas holidays. Marshall felt that in announcing this she was rubbing it in,[13] but the announcement was intended only to discourage him from coming to Fort Worth and crowding her Christmas with suitors.[14] Marshall prepared to spend the holidays alone. By 27 December, however, he could stand it no longer and informed Corinne that he was on his way.

Not only had the Lewises not known the McLuhans for two

generations, but they were Episcopalian, and Marshall was a Catholic convert. He was a Yankee, too, and it would make little difference when he emphasized that his family were Southern sympathizers. There could be no question of his staying at the Lewis home. Corinne's grandmother conveniently suffered a nervous breakdown just before he arrived, so Marshall was obliged to go to a hotel, where Corinne met him after his arrival on the morning of the 28th.[15]

In spite of the circumstances, and what might have proved insurmountable obstacles, the Lewises hosted a small party for Marshall the same evening.[16] Mrs. Lewis placed a notice in the local papers, announcing that he and his mother were visiting Fort Worth. (Elsie's presence was a pure fiction added by Mrs. Lewis out of a sense of propriety.) Corinne's near-fiancé was present, as were two other young men intent on winning her hand.[17] Within two days, according to Marshall's count, she had received proposals from eight suitors.[18] But it was he who escorted her to the New Year's Eve ball at the Fort Worth Club, with a dash of style, perhaps intended at once to convey a message to his rivals and demonstrate to Corinne that he was not as unromantic as she thought.

Resplendent in tails, top hat, and white gloves, he led her to the dance floor. Fort Worth had never seen anything like it. The other suitors were present but paled into insignificance. When it came to the last dance of the evening, they all lined up at the edge of the dance floor, trying in vain to track Corinne and Marshall as they swirled round and round, trying to see if she would let him kiss her.[19] It was the first of forty-two New Year's Eves they would spend together.

With Marshall returning to St. Louis, their grand evening would be their last for months — months of anguish and uncertainty. Each letter from Corinne, gratifying relief when it arrived, could fuel fresh anxiety when Marshall opened it. She was in a difficult position and made it clear.[20] Her family did not understand him and were opposed to her marriage to a Catholic in any case.[21] He tortured himself with endless reassessments of their situation, imprisoned himself in a maze of introspection, till he scarcely understood his own feelings.[22] Having seen the lifestyle of the Lewis family only added to the great worry and doubt he had already about providing for Corinne.[23]

To Elsie, Marshall revealed none of his confusion and apprehension, writing instead in an altogether different tone: "I have fully made up my mind that so far as Corinne and I are concerned we either get married in August or never. While leaving it entirely to her to decide, it is obvious that there are a 1000 ways in which I could break it off without even appearing to wish to do so. But the thought of becoming engaged while remote is unthinkable. I will not return to Fort Worth ever, until Corinne makes up her mind to get married."[24]

Before January had ended, Marshall, together with his friends Harold Gerardot and Addie Coleman, was planning a weekend in the country for the Easter visit he hoped Corinne would make.[25] He regretted that she did not know him better. In St. Louis, he believed, she would get her chance. But the trip did not materialize.

As spring approached, Corinne wrote to say pointedly that nothing would be possible for them that summer.[26] Marshall was already thinking ahead to the fall, when he intended to return to Cambridge and fulfill the residence requirement for his doctorate. He did not want to go without her. She, hoping that time would provide a solution for the obstacle of family opposition, suggested that he go alone. They would correspond. No, he replied, she must marry him or their engagement — still entirely unofficial — was off. More out of disbelief at such an ultimatum than out of fear of losing him, Corinne asked if he would not surely come back? No.[27] The situation was beyond handling in an exchange of letters.

With the year's teaching ended, Corinne was on her way to Austin, Texas, to continue course work at the State University.[28] Marshall joined her on 10 June. Tensions that had built slowly but surely in their correspondence were not eased as they dined together that evening.[29] It took a week to recapture the feelings they had discovered for each other on the Catalina mountain, the thrill of the Fort Worth ballroom floor. During that week, Marshall met one of the local priests, Father Riach, and introduced Corinne to him.[30] The priest was anxious to begin giving her instruction in the faith. She hesitated. I'm *not* going to marry Marshall, she thought, but why not listen, if it will enlarge my experience?[31] The next evening, near Barton Springs, outside Austin, they were engaged.[32] Feeling secure in the knowledge that they would be sailing for England together, Marshall returned to St. Louis the next afternoon.[33]

When Corinne's course at Austin ended, she decided to return home by a circuitous route — via St. Louis.[34] Alighting from the long bus ride on the evening of 17 July, she was met by Marshall, who proudly rushed her straight to the home of Bernie and Mary Muller-Thym.[35] At this time, Corinne's St. Louis cousin, Mabel Strupper, was in Fort Worth, visiting the Lewises, who by now knew of the engagement. Quite forgetting that Mabel was from the obscure Catholic branch of the family, Corinne's grandmother despatched Mabel on a speedy return to St. Louis to free Corinne from the clutches of the wicked Marshall. Ironically, with only enough money for two nights at a St. Louis hotel, Corinne would have returned to Fort Worth if cousin Mabel had not arrived home just in time to put her up for a longer stay.[36]

Corinne bought Marshall a birthday pipe, and they celebrated the day over dinner in the nearby town of St. Alban's.[37] Though there was much socializing with Marshall's friends and colleagues, the tranquil interlude they needed seemed to be taking shape. They took long walks, enjoyed lazy hours by themselves, shopped for rings.[38] Marshall was very pleased that Corinne came to mass with him.[39] Corinne worried about what her grandmother would have to say.[40] Marshall sensed that she was backing up on the idea of a quick wedding.[41] By the morning of 3 August, she was alarmed to note that she had lost ten pounds since her arrival, and she began packing to return home.[42] But the next morning, she was still there.[43] By mid-morning, they had rings, a license, dispensation, and steamship reservations. Then she wired home with the message "Am getting married in a few minutes."

Marshall and Corinne exchanged their vows at St. Louis Cathedral, on the Saint Louis University campus. Father Helmsing conducted the ceremony at the rectory, between two funerals. Bernie Muller-Thym was the best man and cousin Mabel the bridesmaid. No one else was present but Mary Muller-Thym. Afterward, a reply to Corinne's telegram awaited them, reading, "Wait at least until you come home, baby."[44]

Marshall's landlady, Madame Gerardot, feted the newlyweds with cake and wine, then they dashed away to put Corinne's passport application in order and stop at cousin Mabel's before driving off to St. Alban's and a wedding dinner for two. They spent their wedding night at the New Hotel Jefferson in St. Louis. They had had little more than forty-eight hours together when Corinne left for Fort Worth to pack for their honeymoon abroad and the sojourn in Cambridge. Marshall, remaining behind to make all final arrangements for their travel and their year away, would join her four days later.[45]

An instant trousseau was produced for Corinne by a legion of friends and acquaintances of the Lewis family, amid a flurry of activity to make the *post facto* wedding the social event of the season. Photographs for the local newspaper went ahead, despite the absence of the groom. When Marshall arrived, a day before they were scheduled to leave for New York, the air in the Lewis household was electric, though Corinne was too busy to be more than dimly aware of it. Her friends Mary Cecilia and Frank Crumley collected her and took her to the train station to meet Marshall, then earned the disapproval of the Lewises by taking the newlyweds for a drink before delivering them to the Lewis home. Corinne's trunk had not been brought up from the basement, for Mrs. Lewis still hoped that her daughter and unfathomable new son-in-law would drop their madcap plan. Firmly believing that Corinne would soon be returning, she asked her not to pack her best clothes.[46]

But leave they did. Corinne, in a three-piece suit of blue wool, and carrying a coat with red fox-fur trim, was dripping in the August heat and laden with orchids and gardenias as they arrived at the train station. One of her high school students had gathered most of the others and paraded them to the station with great fanfare. They presented the happy couple with a huge, gaily decorated box full of gifts and gave them a rousing send-off.[47] Among their traveling companions, bound for Pittsburgh, was Corinne's godmother. She seemed to be everywhere they went on the train, wearing an expression to remind Corinne that she was leaving Texas, leaving America, leaving her Episcopalian heritage.[48]

They were bound for New York via St. Louis, where Marshall and Corinne hoped Elsie could meet them. Corinne had formed a very close bond with her new mother-in-law during the summer in Pasadena. But the time was too short for a rendezvous. Elsie, ever resourceful, sprang into action. Obtaining timetables for their whole route and making telephone inquiries, she determined that they were sailing on the 60,000-ton Italian luxury liner *The Rex*. Armed with every detail down to the pier, the street, and the time of departure, Elsie arrived to see them off, accompanied by cousins from New Jersey. She shared their happiness, relieved that Marshall was not returning to Cambridge alone. Now he would have to take care of himself for Corinne's sake.[49]

The Rex slipped its lines at noon on 12 August, bound for Naples.[50] Marshall and Corinne, making their way below to third class, were greeted by "No! No! No!" from stewards who, seeing Corinne's armful of gardenias, assumed they were traveling first class and tried to redirect them. When they finally reached their tiny cabin, they found it awash with more flowers from well-wishers. The magnificent public rooms of the ship would have to make up for the challenging logistics of lateral movement in their cramped quarters. But before the first day at sea was over, Marshall had arranged for a move to tourist class. Then the next day, they were summoned to the purser's office and told that their side of the ship was too heavily loaded. Would they mind moving to a cabin on the opposite side? It proved to be a first-class suite with tapestried walls, ample room for their floral train, and enough left over to allow their trunk to be brought up from the hold.[51]

They enjoyed sumptuous meals, grand weather, and the luxury of leisurely hours to themselves. Their dining-room steward, seeing that the newlyweds wanted to hold hands throughout their meals, served Marshall from the left and Corinne from the right. Marshall recorded a magnificent view of the Azores, first sight of Portugal and Gibraltar, less with the delighted eyes of a tourist than out of a sense of a diarist's duty. Read in succession, his entries have the cadence of throbbing engines. Believing that studying and honeymooning were compatible, he noted on their fifth day out, "Life on the Rex [is] very pleasant, but we get nothing done."[52] But by the time they disembarked on 20 August, he was able to put all pretense of scholarly pursuit aside.

Early morning arrival in Naples, mass at the cathedral, a day on the hill, on to Rome, grand rooms on the Via Liguria, the Colosseum by moonlight.[53] It was Corinne's first trip abroad and a thrill at every turn.

Still in Rome on their fifth day as sightseers, Marshall and Corinne emerged from the Vatican museum[54] and soon after paused at a sidewalk café, in spite of the light drizzle. An idler in resplendent naval uniform nearby prompted a comment from Corinne about handsome Italian males, and then they were off to visit the graves of Keats and Shelley at the Protestant Cemetery.

With few other tourists about in the rain, it was inevitable that they would spot the man from the café following them. They rose to the occasion and moved nonchalantly toward the cemetery gates, planning to give him the slip in dramatic style. As a tram approached, they bolted for it. The conductor, apparently aware that they were quarry, refused to take any fare. They made their way to the train station, where they congratulated themselves on having eluded the mysterious agent, only to see him arrive breathless, minutes before the departure of their train for Florence, and take a seat behind them. Though there was no sight of the man after they arrived at their destination, the newlyweds decided to report their adventure to the American Embassy. Conspicuous by their height, Marshall and Corinne had attracted extra attention to themselves on arriving in Italy by the unfortunate choice of gray clothing with brown shirts.[55]

They toured Florence before moving on to Venice, where they took a room in a hotel beside St. Mark's Cathedral. The trip from the train station to the hotel was a holiday in itself: "En route we came out onto the Grand Canal, where all the buildings were floodlit with pinks and blues and where there were simply thousands of gondolas festooned with Japanese lanterns. We had hit on a fiesta night when the whole town stays up till dawn. There was a moon too."[56] It was only with Venice behind them, as they set off for France, that Marshall could confidently write in his diary: "Goodbye to our bothersome waiter."[57]

Taking more care this time to avoid any unintended expression of political sympathies by their dress, Marshall and Corinne spent the closing days of August absorbing the sights of Paris. They had been advised to leave Italy because of German troop movements, but the situation seemed no less ominous in France.[58] The Louvre, libraries, and art galleries were all closed in anticipation of the worst. Stained glass had been removed from churches and art treasures sent to the provinces. Marshall confidently predicted that there would be no war.[59] But descending from their room on their third day, he heard that Gdansk had been taken by the Germans.[60] Stepping out of the pension, he found the streets streaming with women carrying gas masks and weeping at the news of the army's mobilization.[61] It was 1 September 1939.

Marshall returned to the hotel with a basket of pastry and a bottle of Benedictine and broke the news to Corinne. They packed and dashed for the train to Boulogne, where they caught the last packet boat that would cross the Channel for weeks.[62] Arriving in London at midnight, they moved on to Cambridge in a jammed train the next day. The British ultimatum to Hitler was delivered on 3 September. Returning from mass that morning, their first full day in Cambridge, Marshall and Corinne learned that England was at war.[63]

THE DECLARATION OF WAR brought instant transformations to Cambridge. In temporary quarters on Rose Crescent scarcely two days, Marshall and Corinne heard their host answer a knock at the door and learned later that a government representative had called. The house was to be put at the disposal of the Lord Chancellor, and a dozen men were to be billeted for the duration of the war. A steady stream of civil servants and clerical workers would be arriving and would have to be accommodated in the colleges. Already 26,000 children had been evacuated from London, "all taken and freely supported by voluntary hosts."[64] Soon after, Corinne was to write a feature article on these children for the Fort Worth newspaper. Observing that it was "difficult to realize that the inhabitants of this tranquil countryside are officially at war," she compiled personal stories of evacuees and adoptive families for American readers, concluding that the evacuation movement was "nourishing many ills" but that balanced against these were "benefits accruing from this rude transplanting of the population." The upheaval had also exposed the appalling living conditions of countless city children.[65]

The McLuhans found a flat on the top floor of a house in Grange Road occupied by the vicar of Great St. Mary's. It was a large and elegant house, with imposing front steps, where soon a steady stream of priests and barefoot friars arrived to visit the vicar. (Thereafter, the McLuhans were asked to use the side entrance.) The good man lived with his two maiden-lady sisters, and the trio were soon ready to adopt

Corinne, because of the black Catholic to whom she was married.[66]

Marshall had successfully completed the examinations for his Cambridge B.A. and the residency for his M.A. (the only formal requirement) in 1936, but he had not yet officially received the latter degree. This meant he would not be a senior member of the university, with all the rights and privileges thereof, until his master's degree was conferred, some months after he and Corinne arrived in Cambridge. He was obliged, therefore, to respect the college rules for undergraduates, wear a cap and gown if outdoors after dark, and be in by midnight. Corinne thus took on a role with official status: she was designated by the university as his landlady. She would be required to write a report on the nature of his behavior, proper or improper. Marshall wrote to his father-in-law, asking, "Do you think she would dare to tell the truth?"[67]

After a trip to London to clear their luggage through customs, the McLuhans began setting up house in earnest, outfitting their one-bedroom quarters with furniture offered by Marshall's former study tutor, Lionel Elvin.[68] With a seventeenth-century bedroom suite, modern living-room furnishings and bookcases, as well as a mahogany dining-room suite and piano, the spacious flat was transformed into what McLuhan described as "a very opulent apartment."[69] Their windows on one side overlooked the vicar's large garden; to the other side, the vast green expanse of the Trinity College playing fields stretched away.

Marshall quickly renewed his acquaintances with the Willisons, the Leavises, the Crawleys, and others; he and Corinne took up the Cambridge ritual of having friends in to tea or sherry before dinner and to coffee after dinner, or accepting invitations to do the same, almost every day.[70] Then they would finish the evening amid their books, often taking turns reading aloud to each other. By mid-September, they were beginning to feel at home with themselves, and Marshall pronounced Corinne's first grand-scale dinner, by candle-light in front of the fireplace, a resounding success. Soon her culinary achievements ranged to the production of roasts, apple pies, and gingerbread.[71]

Corinne was also learning to type and to ride the bicycle. If the typing provided little excitement, the cycling bordered on the dangerous.

After she had knocked down her first pedestrian, Marshall took personal charge of perfecting her skills.[72]

Marshall settled down to a daily routine of work for his dissertation at the university library in early October and was appalled to see the amount of work he needed to do in the nine short months ahead.[73] Father McCabe had told him that he would be eligible for tenure in his position at Saint Louis even without a doctorate,[74] but Marshall had his own standards to meet and attacked his work with a sense of urgency. Having quickly established a good relationship with his research supervisor, Frank Percy Wilson, whom he described as "stout, able, pleasant,"[75] he could say "I feel a 100 times more like working at it now."[76]

In November, Marshall addressed the Doughty Society of Downing College on the subject of American universities. Leavis and Wilson were among the large crowd that turned out to hear Marshall and ply him with endless questions until late into the evening. Then Marshall's friend Gordon Cox "let us out the back gate of the College into Fitzwilliam Street and we proceeded by starlight (the new moon had set) to Grange Road at 1:30 A.M."[77]

In the stillness of the night, the events that had overtaken Europe seemed more remote than ever. There was little evidence in Cambridge of fear or fervor over the war. Though the town was crowded, the rhythm of the days could be as tranquil as the night air Marshall and Corinne were enjoying as they made their way back to the vicar's. Plays, concerts, and social life continued in Cambridge, intensified by the presence of servicemen. Girls on bicycles rode into town for dances, stopping to change clothes at the posts of air wardens. Though the McLuhans were supposed to take shelter in the vicar's basement when air-raid warning sirens went off, after two or three alerts they dropped the precaution and remained in their flat. But by early December, planes had been overhead constantly for a week. These were English planes. Marshall and Corinne knew little more than that about the war, till they ventured to London the following month.[78]

They were the guests in London of Mr. Patton, a benevolent bachelor from Nova Scotia who stayed with the vicar on his regular visits to Cambridge. He took Marshall and Corinne to Simpson's in the Strand. Marshall described the service: "They push the joint or duck on wheels to your table, produce a vast blade with operatic flourish, flash it on a steel two or three times, and then with critical ear await your orders."[79] At this spectacle, a delighted shiver ran down Corinne's spine. She would relive it for days and thought seriously about opening such a restaurant when they would return to St. Louis. Then it was off to the theater to see Sybil Thorndike in *The Corn Is Green*. Relishing his role as host, quietly thrilled at the prospect of having a beautiful young woman on his arm, indulged and encouraged by her enthusiasm and patience, Patton whisked Corinne away to show her the sights of London and took her to all the best shops. Marshall professed to be not the least bit jealous or sorry to miss a tour he had done before. By now, he noted, London was a mess, boarded over and strewn with sandbags, though not quite ruined — yet. And everywhere was the oddly picturesque sight of thousands of helium-filled balloons, anchored to heavy cables, soaring ten thousand feet or more, forcing the enemy planes to remain at higher altitudes.[80]

MARSHALL WAS AWARDED HIS M.A. on 20 January 1940 in a ceremony marked by the same rituals as his graduation with the B.A., three and a half years earlier. Though his time at Cambridge was nearly over, it was a day for looking to the future more than for reminiscing. The return trip to America would require careful planning: a transatlantic crossing in wartime meant restrictions and complications, perhaps an earlier departure than he wished. The remaining days in Cambridge would have to be well spent.

His research for his Ph.D. thesis was proceeding very well — well enough to make him believe he could finish writing the thesis before he and Corinne would have to leave for St. Louis; well enough to convince him he could take time away from it to prepare an article for publication. Perhaps it was the approaching return to the United States that rekindled a thought he had expressed to Elsie the year before.[81] He had pondered it all the while, and now it would out. His inspiration was the competitors he had beaten, without competing, in winning Corinne's hand. A second sojourn in England had confirmed his negative impression of American men.[82]

More than a year after his grandstand performance on the Fort Worth ballroom floor, he commented to Red: "Texas men are incredibly infantile, and of course as tough outside as they are slushy inside."[83] Now it was time to expose the story of the American male in an article to be titled "Fifty Million Mama's Boys." As with his Macaulay article for the *Manitoban* and the Chesterton article for *The Dalhousie Review*, he wrote out of conviction and enthusiasm for his subject, and with an urgency to communicate his idea to readers. By the middle of April, he was satisfied that he had found just the right touches to make his portrait of effete American manhood complete. He wrote to Elsie immediately. "A few moments ago I finished the 'Mama-Boy' article, which Corinne is typing . . . You can't imagine my relief in getting the thing out of my system. Must now fly at the thesis."[84]

But the time was too short. Marshall had assembled vast amounts of research material over a remarkably short period; writing it up was a far different matter. He had seethed with ideas for the "Mama-Boy" piece till it rolled out of him. Within two weeks of putting it behind him and giving his full attention to his thesis, he admitted that "the ideally green, balmy, blossomy out-of-doors is at present a major distraction."[85] The same day, he obtained permission to submit the Ph.D. dissertation from the United States after his return. Owing to war conditions, he would not be required to defend the completed work at an oral exam.

He shared this good news with Elsie, declaring that the highly profitable year in Cambridge assured that the Ph.D. would soon be his. He responded to notes Elsie had sent him on a lecture she had recently heard dealing with education, adding: "You may have noticed that I attack the same problem from a different point of view in my 'Mama-Boys.' I have masses of material for articles on a dozen subjects including education. But I feel that I must first make my mark as a 'scholar' in English literature before seriously embarking on any other careers."[86] *Other careers.* Here was a plain and matter-of-fact statement that the professor of English in spite of himself would become McLuhan by choice and not by chance.

Their departure was set for early June. As a citizen of a country at war, Marshall was required to sail from Liverpool on the *Ascania*, bound for Montreal with a cargo of gold bullion. Corinne, as a citizen of a nonbelligerent country, would need to travel to Galway, Ireland, and board an American ship, the *President Roosevelt*, for the voyage to New York. The *Roosevelt*, built to accommodate 250 passengers, loaded over 900, assigned in fours to cabins for two. Seven sittings were needed for every meal, with the first lunch served barely half an hour after the last breakfast. Corinne was ill for the entire crossing. Arriving in New York, she traveled to Fort Worth for a much needed rest before returning to St. Louis. The *Ascania* was fifteen days at sea before docking at Montreal, and Marshall had been unable to hear one news report on the crossing of the *Roosevelt*. Anxious and exhausted, he made his way from Montreal to Toronto to St. Louis to Fort Worth, flooded with relief at last to find Corinne.

6

Breaching and Bridging

If the function of literary study is to produce emotional
thrills, then anybody would be a fool to study it today. Burke
is feeble stuff to pit against Bogart . . . If, on the other
hand, there is still some point in carrying on the study of
literature and philosophy, then the problem which every
educator must face today is that of immunizing the student
against his environment.

–*MARSHALL MCLUHAN*
PREFACE TO EARLY DRAFT OF The Mechanical Bride

McLuhan RESUMED HIS DUTIES at Saint Louis University in September
1940. "I never think of myself as a teacher,"[1] he had said earlier, but
at the same time he noted that current movies were "useful handles in
teaching."[2] This was not a matter of giving up on a carefully prepared
lecture, if students found it too difficult, and indulging them with chat
about the latest Cary Grant or Paulette Goddard. McLuhan described
the use he made of films with his students: "I always spend at least two
weeks introducing them to the writings of Pudovkin and Eisenstein
on film technique and make them adapt a novel to scenario form."[3]

Films, musical stage shows, and the backdrop of Elsie's career as a
monologist had long been with him. There was a connection with
his studies through the literary selections that Elsie included in her
repertoire. Films, on the other hand, had been pure entertainment,
nothing more than distraction, until he began teaching and realized that

"having seen them, one has much more in common with freshmen."[4] They provided an entry point for dialogue with young people whose consciousness was not being shaped predominantly by literary culture.

If films were "the opium of the people,"[5] that was all the more reason to examine their workings and alert students to their effects, to the contrasts between the forms of traditional and contemporary culture. Shunning the latter could only widen the gap. It was the same gap that Richards and his colleagues at the Cambridge English School had fought to close as educators, the gap T. S. Eliot had closed in poetry by embracing the English music hall, breaking with the conventions of nineteenth-century verse to recover the full resources of the English language. In the models of Richards and Eliot, McLuhan saw the possibility, the necessity, of simultaneously breaching and bridging; immunizing against the environment involved the symbiosis of immunity and community.

He was giving his attention to more than popular films. After returning from his first visit to Fort Worth, nearly two years earlier, McLuhan had started assembling a file of newspaper clippings that had nothing and everything to do with his trip. In the Greek myth that figures so prominently in McLuhan's later teaching on media, Narcissus, gazing into a fountain, fails to recognize as his own the reflected image that so enchants him. But McLuhan suddenly began recognizing reflections of the American men he had met in Texas every time he opened the daily paper — and here was nothing enchanting.

In advertisements, in the comics, he found confirmation of his impression that the North American male had become a shell. Was Li'l Abner not congenitally immature and vain? Had one generation not transformed "Life with Father" (a man to be endured, like Henry Selden Hall) into "Bringing up Father" (a man reduced to a problem-child, like Herbert McLuhan)? What kind of a man was that featured in the soap ad, *trapped* in the soap ad, shouting "Here Comes Herb"? McLuhan kept documenting the decline of American manhood from the flotsam and jetsam of the press.

Before long, he detected further atrocities. They all merited a publication going far beyond the scope of the "Mama-Boy" article. He would write a book whose outlines were firmly in his mind in St. Louis by late 1940. When McLuhan eventually turned his bulging

files into *The Mechanical Bride*, published in 1951, Dagwood headed
the list of the pathetic male figures emblematic of the obvious *but
invisible* ills in American society. McLuhan would give Dagwood his
full scorn in more than one airing well before the book appeared.

The McLuhans took an apartment across from St. Louis
Cathedral, where they had been married. Though the building could
boast a maid's room in every apartment and a uniformed elevator boy
named Orville, Cathedral Mansions was a touch less grand than its
name suggested, their apartment consisting of one room and a tiny
kitchenette and bath. Books and notes and the swelling press-watch
files made their way to the dinette table, necessitating a clearing operation before meals. Walter Ong was the first guest the McLuhans
entertained for dinner.[6]

Corinne, always as keen as her husband to observe a new environment, was taking in the contrasts provided by her Fort Worth–
Cambridge–St. Louis move. Cambridge had been a rich and enriching experience; coming to St. Louis no less so. It struck her as odd
that the people referred to themselves as Southerners. Back home,
anyone from Missouri was a Yankee.

Corinne's powers of observation were tested at home one Sunday
morning as they prepared to leave for church. "Notice anything
different?" a straight-faced Marshall asked, fixing her with a stare.
"No," she replied. The question was forgotten as they made their way
down the hall. A moment later the elevator doors opened for them
and young Orville exclaimed, "Oh, Mr. McLuhan, you've shaved off
your mustache!" Corinne decided she did not like her husband's clean
upper lip, so he promptly grew an even thicker mustache.[7] Over the
years, a variety of mustaches appeared and disappeared unpredictably.

St. Louis also reunited McLuhan with Bernie Muller-Thym, whose
encyclopedic knowledge had drawn McLuhan to him from his earliest
days in the city. Here was someone who shared his zest for ranging
over ideas at light speed. They talked endlessly, attended the theater
together, raced to find each other when a parcel of new books arrived.
Mary Muller-Thym had fed McLuhan during his bachelor year and
her husband had given him counsel when he announced his engagement to Corinne. It was Muller-Thym who now opened whole new
fields for McLuhan, such as the study of Provençal poetry. When they

turned their attention to Joyce, they took themselves to a tavern one evening with a copy of *Finnegans Wake*. They had the book open between them on the bar when another patron approached, with unsteady step, to inquire what they were reading. Not satisfied to wait for a reply, he leaned over and took his own introduction to Joyce. One page was enough. The reveler blanched as he looked up, exclaiming, "My God, I really am drunk."[8]

F. R. Leavis had first stimulated McLuhan's interest in Joyce's writings. Joyce's "efforts in the *Wake* to make language physical"[9] reflected the emphasis on the training of perception that McLuhan took with him from Cambridge. The collaboration that Joyce demanded from readers was also the basis of the critical method McLuhan learned from Richards. This was an intellectual challenge to full participation in a creative process, a challenge McLuhan enjoyed above all others, one he would later fling at his readers in *War and Peace in the Global Village*, where quotations from Joyce run riot in the margins. But that came after the book he was incubating in 1940, long after Joyce's inebriating prose had worked a sobering effect on one St. Louis citizen.

It was in St. Louis in 1941 that McLuhan took to the airwaves for the first time. Ezra Pound had published *How to Read* ten years earlier; Mortimer Adler had published *How to Read a Book* the year before. Showing the influence of Richards, McLuhan condemned the Adler book for its narrow focus on argument and procedure. Richards himself was about to publish *How to Read a Page*, a corrective for Adler's approach that also gibed at his hyping of "great ideas" by its subtitle, *A Course in Efficient Reading, with an Introduction to One Hundred Great Words*. McLuhan, seeing that Adler's method was faulty for prose and irrelevant for poetry, prepared a radio talk entitled "How to Read a Poem."

In ten minutes of airtime he managed to touch on Keats, Shakespeare, Matthew Arnold (condemned as conventional in the grand Miltonic-Wordsworth manner), Eliot, Tennyson, and Kipling. His parting words to the radio audience were pure Richards: "The way to read a poem is to read it many, many times. Read it with close attention to the images. Find out what the images are intended to do. Explore their significance and interrelatedness. Ask yourself whether they hang together. And listen to the rhythms, realizing that they give the clue to the meaning as much as the images."[10]

McLuhan was encouraged by the response to his talk, opened a new notebook on the subject, fully expecting it to grow into the manuscript of a book he would title "How to Read Poetry." In his enthusiasm, he mentioned the project at a departmental meeting and was reminded that, under his contract, any royalties from the book would revert to the university. It made the project slightly less appealing.[11]

Neither his small excursion into broadcasting, his endless combing of the popular press, nor his teaching duties distracted McLuhan from working on his Ph.D. thesis. Its outline was taking shape and surfacing even when he was directing his attention elsewhere: "Adler has no idea of *grammatica* or *rhetorica* as means of analyzing either social or poetic products . . . "[12] By its terminology, the comment looks forward to the trivium of grammar, rhetoric, and dialectic that would unify McLuhan's thesis.

Corinne was pregnant with their first child as they celebrated their second anniversary and then their third Christmas together. She delivered a son on 19 January 1942. Following Southern tradition, Corinne wanted to call him Herbert Marshall McLuhan II. Herbert Marshall McLuhan I would have none of it. Friends Karl and Addie Strobach were consulted in the serious business of name selection. It was Addie who suggested Eric, noting that the name means "strong," and adding: "He'd be well-named to have to put up with a lot of your guff."[13] The new father wanted to honor St. Thomas, and Corinne was not prepared to give up her idea completely. The baby was christened Thomas Eric Marshall McLuhan.

Elsie was as proud as the new parents. She sent Marshall money to buy Corinne nineteen roses as soon as he telephoned the news to her. The next day she wrote: "So! He looks like Mr. Lewis does he! Well, I'll have something to say about that — he is Capricorn — must have large brown eyes and round face . . . I'm jealous right now . . . Next time he opens his eyes tell him I've been waiting to love him and to gain a few more pounds so I can give him a very big hug . . . That this little fellow will bring the joy to you that you have to me is the most I know how to wish him. Love, Mother."[14]

BECOMING A FATHER WAS apparently a stimulus to McLuhan to work even harder. He relished the vast scope of inquiry the research on Thomas Nashe was now plainly demanding, a demand he imposed himself. He began planning to stage his debut on the academic conference circuit, using background material on Nashe as a pretext for advancing a hidden agenda with overtones of the later McLuhan: "Meantime thesis advances. I am on the M[odern] L[anguage] A[ssociation] program this December when I shall let loose some of it. 'The twenty minutes that wrecked my life' sort of thing. The problem is to convert a bomb into a spacerocket which will convey the auditors safely into a new world rather than blasting them in their present mud huts. I must manage to seem naive, oblivious of what I'm about, needing guidance and encouragement. There's just a possibility I can manage it."[15]

When McLuhan had first pondered the choice of a Ph.D. thesis topic, the sixteenth-century dramatist, satirist, and pamphleteer Thomas Nashe had not even come to his attention. He had settled first on the idea of recasting Raymond Wilson Chambers's *Continuity of English Prose* (1932), extending its scope beyond Thomas More to the end of the sixteenth century. Retaining Chambers's view that English humanism had suffered a dislocating effect at the hands of Henry VIII's headsman, McLuhan began work on a definitive survey of the prose writers from More and Hugh Latimer, through Thomas Stapleton and Cardinal William Allen, to Robert Parsons and Edmund Campion. Unable to resist the call of an emerging pun, McLuhan made the connection with Chambers's book clear by styling his dissertation proposal "The Arrest of Tudor Prose." He intended to examine the writings of theologians, preachers, pamphleteers, historians, romancers, annalists, even anonymous authors of newsletters and broadsides.

But McLuhan quickly became dissatisfied. Though the topic remained interesting, treating it from Chambers's perspective was beginning to look unsatisfactory, for it implied that the rich variety of prose in the sixteenth century was an anomaly in relation to a longer tradition among English writers. The problem was serious enough to convince McLuhan to abandon his original thesis and turn to consider Thomas Nashe as a journalist.

At this early stage, Nashe was for McLuhan like one of the objects in the Maelstrom for Poe's sailor: "Once he had emerged, he tended to submerge himself again and again in what at first appeared to be a welter of conflicting objects of interest."[16] But just as the sailor came to see a pattern amid the chaos engulfing him, McLuhan began to detect order in the multiple traditions represented in Nashe's writings: "From those strengthening perceptions the figure of Nashe began to assume some definition."[17]

In the nineteenth century, Nashe had served as a resource for Elizabethan scholars documenting and illustrating editions of plays and other historical research. By the time McLuhan undertook his study, the prevailing view of Nashe was as the journalist par excellence of his age. It seemed, therefore, that McLuhan's task would be to relate Nashe's prose techniques to those of less well known and less successful writers. But it quickly became apparent that such an approach would be fruitless, leading to a dissertation no more defensible than the amplified Chambers. The variety and virtuosity of Nashe's styles made it untenable to derive them from their impoverished journalistic cousins.

In Nashe's apparently unstudied brilliance of style, McLuhan detected a pose. And from Morris W. Croll's Preface to John Lyly's *Euphues* came a hint that this was a studied pose, calling for extensive investigation of the medieval and patristic models of euphuism.[18] So, he undertook a full-scale study of medieval and ancient rhetoric, and the connection with Nashe soon became increasingly evident.

In the standard edition of Nashe's writings by Ronald B. McKerrow,[19] McLuhan observed inappropriately dismissive comments on his engagement with rhetoric: "McKerrow's impatience with this side of Nashe, and his deliberate refusal to consider it further, perfectly express the limits which not only he but many scholars since his time have set for themselves."[20] McLuhan set himself no such limits. The thesis would aim to fill the void in McKerrow's scholarship by considering Nashe on his own terms.

McLuhan's study of Nashe's style began with an overview of the theory and practice of rhetoric in his period. He examined its myriad forms at every level of expression in England, Italy, France, Spain, and Germany and quickly realized that the sixteenth century was an age of rhetoric. In this context, Nashe seemed insignificant, dwarfed by the monuments of rhetorical exuberance that dominated the culture of his day. It was only in moving to a longer perspective that McLuhan found what freed Nashe from the marginal stature imposed on him by his contemporaries.

What began as a study of Nashe became first a survey of the entire rhetorical canon from Cicero to Nashe, and then an investigation of the modes of education through the centuries separating them. Moreover, as the rhetorical treatises involved made very little sense when isolated from the full tradition of ancient and medieval education, McLuhan took the further step of investigating grammar and dialectics. (Grammar is not to be understood here in the narrow modern sense of parts of speech and sentence structure but as the art of interpreting phenomena. It takes in all of literature and includes etymology and exegesis. Dialectics is, variously, a way of testing evidence, the study of kinds of proofs for an argument, a method of dialogue, and logic. Grammar was primarily a humanistic activity; dialectics a philosophical one.) Since education continued to be based on the cycle of the three liberal arts till Nashe's day, McLuhan's task was to demonstrate this and to explain its major literary consequences.

McLuhan noted that the so-called trivium of grammar, dialectic, and rhetoric endured with enough vitality into the eighteenth century to make Nashe more accessible to Warton than to McKerrow. McLuhan wrote in his thesis: "But the rapid displacement of the linguistic disciplines by the mathematical . . . has been carried on so much in an atmosphere of controversy that even scholars have come to the point of patronizing sixteenth century writers and sixteenth century education. This attitude has not advanced understanding."[21]

From the earliest pages of the Nashe thesis it is possible to detect the themes McLuhan would continue to develop to the end of his career: "The great alchemists . . . were grammarians. From the time of the neo-Platonists and Augustine to Bonaventure and to Francis Bacon, the world was viewed as a book, the lost language of which was analogous to that of human speech. Thus the art of grammar provided not only the sixteenth century approach to the Book of Life in scriptural exegesis but to the Book of Nature, as well."[22] This is the central idea, more than forty years later, in *Laws of Media*, where the subtitle

The New Science is also a deliberate echo of Francis Bacon's *Novum Organum*. In the dissertation, the overview of grammatical art is repeated, and emphasized, and advanced as a key element in the work's originality: "[Grammar's] claim to be viewed as an important basis of scientific method, both during antiquity and continuously throughout medieval times, and in the work of Francis Bacon, has, I think, never been indicated till the present study."[23]

McLuhan was attracted as much to Bacon's style as to his grammarian's orientation. Once he is well into his work, McLuhan quotes Bacon's statement that "knowledge, while it is in aphorisms and observations, it is in growth," commenting that "the ensuing discussion makes perfectly clear that Bacon considered his own aphoristic style in the Essays as part of a scientific technique of keeping knowledge in a state of emergent evolution."[24] McLuhan's predilection in later years for aphorisms and the tentative statements he would call "probes" may be attributable directly to his study of Bacon and to what he learned of Bacon through I. A. Richards at Cambridge. Richards's lectures were seven or eight years behind McLuhan by the time he was completing his doctoral dissertation, but their powerful influence endured.

McLuhan weaves together an account of Plato's *Cratylus* and the new significance of its doctrine at the opening of the Christian era, referring again to Francis Bacon and his claims for metaphysical knowledge, then bringing the discussion full circle to the *Cratylus* by way of Alfred Korzybski's general semantics. All this is accomplished in the first five pages of the dissertation's opening chapter, setting the pace and establishing the approach characteristic of the work as a whole.

McLuhan is quick to take issue with received opinion from the outset. Explaining how the concept of the Logos, or universal reason,[25] placed grammatical art at the center of both Stoic physics and the earliest Christian theology, he notes that the Stoic interest in etymology as a source of scientific and philosophic knowledge was perfectly natural, adding that "it is somewhat misleading to accept the suggestion of Sandys that the Stoics were interested in etymology because 'they regarded language as a product of nature and onomatopoeia as the principle on which words were first formed.'"[26]

McLuhan also detects misreadings among the standard commentaries on Plato: "Jowett's impatience with the *Timaeus* as 'most obscure and repulsive to the modern reader' is owing to his supposition that Plato's knowledge represents 'the infancy of physical science' and to Plato's 'desire to conceive the whole of nature without any adequate knowledge of the parts.'"[27] And yet, as McLuhan acknowledges, it is Jowett who makes clear the relationship the ancients held to exist between the order of speech and language and the order of nature. This relationship is anchored in the recognition of the effect of the physical senses on the development of human language. McLuhan was already keenly attuned to this view as he wrote his dissertation — long before he would develop his own perspective on media effects, the sensorium, language, and their interconnections.

The Logos, spanning universal reason and constitutive utterance, and informing the Greek view of the life and order found in all things, including the mind of man, is also the view that would inform McLuhan's later writings. In the early portion of his dissertation, he began working toward this view by focusing on the history of the trivium and the dynamics unifying grammar, dialectic, and rhetoric. In particular, he stressed that while the reception of the doctrine of the Logos into Christianity had always been duly noted, the intermediate stages of that reception through the discipline of the grammatical arts had been largely overlooked. This neglect was ensured by perspectives such as those of Sandys and Jowett, mentioned above.

McLuhan rises to the defense of the use and perpetuation of allegorical and etymological methods by the Stoics, Plato, and later thinkers such as St. Augustine, rejecting the characterization of it as a holdover from a primitive worldview or an uncritically held mythology finally eclipsed by the Renaissance and the Enlightenment. "However much this account may satisfy the emotional needs of the modern world, it certainly does not satisfy the needs of historical explanation. The Stoic interpreters of poetry and mythology knew very well what they were doing, and did not derive their doctrines from, but applied them to, these matters."[28] Here McLuhan insists again on the metaphysical character of the Logos.

In developing his own view in this matter, he clearly acknowledges that of Etienne Gilson, whose major works to that time all appear among the references for the dissertation.[29] But for all that the work owes to Gilson with respect to certain key ideas, the overall design is

McLuhan's alone. More than three hundred pages are required to set the stage for the proper treatment of Thomas Nashe. There McLuhan documents the modern failure to understand the nature of grammar in the ancient and medieval worlds, and traces the unbroken tradition linking Francis Bacon, Thomas Urquhart, the Cambridge Platonists, James Harris, Etienne de Condillac, Auguste Comte, Alfred Korzybski, and the Chicago University school of encyclopedists. The objective is to demonstrate the outgrowth of the tradition uniting science and grammar by the concept of language as the expression *and* analogy of the Logos.

McLuhan shows how the patristic school, whose objective was to combine Plato's intellectual concepts with the religious ideas from the Gospels, adopted not only the methods of grammar but the interest in mythology and in science that characterized the grammatical school. The fundamental difference between the grammatical and dialectical schools begins to emerge in McLuhan's presentation with the help of a key quotation from Gilson's work on the philosophy of St. Bonaventure.[30]

Gilson observes that the role of things as signs in the order of revelation sanctions the same role for them in the order of nature. Once this transfer is in place, it functions by a method distinguishing it radically from dialectics. McLuhan characterizes the contrast: "M. Gilson proceeds to show that these guiding principles of interpretation are managed in their application not by the logic of dialectics of Aristotle, which are adapted to the analysis of a world of natures and leave us 'without the means to explore the secrets of a symbolic world such as that of the Augustinian tradition,' but by the reasoning of analogy."[31] Here one can detect a source of both McLuhan's principle of the probe and his preference for the analogical over the logical, as well as a worldview demanding the investigative technique of closure based on relationships — a worldview shared by McLuhan and the ancients of the grammatical school. He freely acknowledges this link in noting that the history of the trivium is essentially a history of the rivalry amid practitioners of grammar, dialectic, and rhetoric, adding that it cannot be written without adopting the viewpoint of one of them.[32] The analogists viewed words and phenomena as interrelated by proportions and etymologies — a view

retained and reworked by McLuhan long after he wrote his
Cambridge dissertation.[33]

The mention of Thomas Nashe fifty pages into the dissertation is
the first since the introduction. But McLuhan has far to go before
he can focus his attention exclusively on the enigmatic satirist. The
interactions of the trivial arts need to be set out, and these prove to
be very complicated indeed. Dialectics is described in grammatical
terms from a rhetorical point of view by the Sophists; the dialecticians
subordinate grammar and rhetoric to their art; the rhetoricians subordinate dialectics to the first two divisions of their art. But there is
harmony as well as rivalry among the arts of the trivium. Stoic physics
and the art of grammar were so closely linked as to make dialectics
and grammar all but inseparable studies.

McLuhan rises to the challenge of both assembling the massive
evidence required to support his thesis *and* reducing it without giving
his conclusions the appearance of bald assertions. In this respect, his
dissertation is exempt from the charges critics would bring against the
published works of his later career.

Among the topics set out and discussed by McLuhan are the five
divisions of classical rhetoric — a subject that would preoccupy him
again at the end of his career. They are *inventio* (discovery), *dispositio*
(arrangement), *memoria* (memory), *elocutio* (style), and *pronunciatio*
(delivery).

McLuhan traces the misunderstanding of the interrelation of the
arts of the trivium through the major European historians of rhetoric,
noting how they all adopted the Renaissance habit of skipping over
the medieval period, and concluding: "But whereas Valla, Vives, and
Ramus[34] and the rest did this deliberately and belligerently, not
because they regarded the preceding ages as insignificant, but because
they were rhetoricians engaged in a very real war with the dialecticians of Paris, subsequent historians have innocently assumed that
there was simply nothing to be investigated."[35]

From these observations McLuhan proceeds to demonstrate that
the Ciceronian ideal of the Renaissance was not a matter of retrieving
the teachings of the great orator from antiquity, but the outcome of a
continuous tradition that included a vigorous adherence to his ideal
throughout the Middle Ages. Seen in this light, the quarrel between

the ancients and the moderns becomes a continuation of Cicero's conflict with the philosophers and the medieval dialecticians' clash with the grammarians.

In advancing this revisionist view of intellectual history, McLuhan moves for the first time toward the observation he will eventually place at the center of his media analysis: "A consideration of the Ciceronian ideal and tradition, therefore, has claims to being one of basic importance in the history of western culture, and its comparative neglect must be ascribed to impercipience of the ubiquitous, rather than to mere indifference on the part of scholars."[36] Nestled amid McLuhan's rhetorical flourishes here is the notion that one of the biases of Western culture is rooted in the failure to perceive environments.

Pursuing his commentary on Cicero, who denounced professors of rhetoric and described as bogus their claim to be able to fashion orators by mere schooling in a set of rules, McLuhan aligns himself with Cicero in condemning the segregation and specialization of the arts. Together with the emphasis on analogical method, the refusal to compartmentalize knowledge will form the essence of the McLuhan approach throughout his career.[37]

By a third of the way through the dissertation, McLuhan is in sufficiently full stride to pronounce on the principles of historiography: "For the historian of culture the matter of significance is not so much to determine the precise content of this teaching [of the four phases of discussion of logic in the Middle Ages] as to note how it functioned in relation to the disciplines of grammar and rhetoric."[38]

In discussing the work of scholars such as Edmond Faral and Richard McKeon, McLuhan pursues the full implications of the criticism that if the definition of rhetoric is couched in terms of a single subject such as style, literature, or discourse, it has no history during the Middle Ages. While he finds Faral too narrow in scope, there are passages from McKeon suggestive of McLuhan's own emerging method: "The many innovations which are recorded during [the Middle Ages] in the arts with which [rhetoric] is related suggest that their histories might profitably be considered without unique attachment to the field in which their advances are celebrated."[39]

As he builds steadily toward a characterization of the sixteenth-century humanism of Nashe, McLuhan launches into an account of the role of the late medieval Church in maintaining the ideals of classical learning: "Grammar and classical culture had been preserved by the Church after the fall of the Empire because grammar was then the indispensable mode of theology. The advent of dialectics was, therefore, sheer gain for theology but almost a total overthrow for grammar."[40]

Seeking to make Erasmus and sixteenth-century humanism intelligible as developments from vigorous medieval traditions, McLuhan places some of the great representatives of culture in the twelfth and thirteenth centuries in the lineage from Plato to Bacon. He sets out to dispel the confusion created where other chroniclers had failed to see figures such as Hugh of St. Victor as radical opponents of scholasticism. McLuhan reminds his readers that Hugh shared with Plato, the Stoics, the ancient grammarians, and the scholars of the patristic tradition the view of the universe as an organism. Here is the link to Francis Bacon and the argument for grammar as the most basic art of all, because "Man cannot look with understanding on the book of nature until he has been perfected in the art of grammar."[41]

McLuhan is sufficiently secure in his line of argument about the history of the trivium to dispose of lesser commentators one after another. He calls Foster Watson's *The English Grammar Schools to 1660* a fresh perception of the Renaissance with respect to school texts but a "stale controversial view based on hearsay and conjecture about the twelfth and fourteenth centuries."[42] Watson failed to see that the struggle between grammar and dialectics was to decide which would serve exclusively as the framework for theology. "Watson misses the main point about his own period. He narrows the subject of grammar almost to its nineteenth century nonentity. Thus restricted, it certainly will not function as the key to the literary modes of its great period of success and cultivation."[43] The commentary clearly shows McLuhan's own ideal of using as wide a context as possible as the key to understanding. In the dissertation, the scope of his task goes beyond contextualizing Nashe to provide the historical correctives required for rescuing him from undeserved obscurity.

Gilson remains a powerful ally to McLuhan's arguments throughout the dissertation, cited at key points such as the discussion of why the syllogism of Aristotle remained powerless against the allegories of the Trinity supplied by grammar:[44] "Adapted as it is to a universe of nature which it is able to analyse, it leaves us without the means to explore the secrets of a symbolic world such as that of the Augustinian tradition . . . "[45] Implicit in Gilson's view as described by McLuhan is that analogic method is inevitable, if the object of inquiry is relationships, as it will be for McLuhan throughout his career as both literary scholar and media analyst.

Since the grammarian is concerned with connections and the dialectician with divisions, it is hardly surprising to find McLuhan hunting out critical bias and seeking to redress historical error where these have arisen from distorted perceptions of the legacy of the two camps: "The modern view that allegory is a product of medieval scholasticism is the precise contrary of the facts. The modern distrust of allegory and parable is demonstrably rooted in the prevalence of the mathematical modes of abstraction which becomes general in the seventeenth century but is no less typical of Abelard and the dialecticians. It is the Cartesians who distrust fancy with its metaphors, allegories, and similes. Just as the grammarians distrusted abstraction, so the dialecticians contemned the concrete models of language."[46]

McLuhan's dissertation was intended to provide a tool for modern scholars. It also provided a task. By fostering an understanding of the full implications of the basic distinction between grammar and dialectics, it opened the way to recasting the whole of the histories of European literature since the fifteenth century. The entire golden age of Spanish literature, for example, could be reinterpreted as an expression of patristic rhetoric and exegesis. Such a reinterpretation would require looking beyond questions of style to more fundamental matters of method and placing the entire study in the full medieval perspective McLuhan set out.

Having taken 350 pages to build the only scholarly apparatus he believed fit for the purpose, McLuhan turned his full attention to describing the writings of Thomas Nashe. But the description would also be a test of the apparatus.

McLuhan begins with a review of specific sources for Nashe's method and style, a question opening at once onto the much larger one of his aims as a member of the patristic party within the Anglican church. Nashe's opponents prove to be the Calvinist party, armed with scholastic method in theology and manning Ramistic ramparts in dialectics and rhetoric.

McLuhan's correctives for the conventional view of the antagonism between Nashe and Gabriel Harvey emerge quickly: "It is a mistake to suppose that, in opposing Harvey, Nashe appeared reactionary to his contemporaries; for in the sixteenth century Harvey seemed to be tied to the scholastic Ramus, whereas Nashe belonged to the party of the ancients who were defending the cause of the reformed grammatical theology of Erasmus."[47]

There are also mysteries to be solved: the link between Nashe and the Parnassus plays proves to be their anti-Ramistic view of the arts; and others to be dismissed: Nashe's turn away from the pseudo-eloquence of what he himself termed "bragging blank verse" is no anomaly when the two principal themes of his writing are viewed as part of an overarching commitment to patristic union of poetry, eloquence, and theology. And this is the essence of the thesis McLuhan advances: "Nashe's writings present an almost uninterrupted texture of patristic implication."[48] He describes Nashe as a "fully enlightened protagonist in an ancient quarrel,"[49] the contest for supremacy between dialectic and grammar chronicled by McLuhan.

It was not doctrine at issue but methods of exegesis in theology and preaching. Some Catholics and some Protestants held patristic views, while others took up scholastic positions. Consequently, Nashe could align himself with Erasmus, More, and Rabelais, among others, and still escape the charge of adhering to Catholic views. As a patristic partisan he could also describe the Calvinist position of Harvey, with its ostensibly "advanced" character, as mere "drifat duncerie" borrowed from medieval scholastic philosophy.

McLuhan returns repeatedly to the framework he has erected, demonstrating how it clarifies Nashe and how Nashe consolidates the framework: "Nashe's defence of Aristotle is always with reference to Ramus. It never commits Nashe to the monopoly which Aristotle held in some of the late medieval schools . . . The responsible historian should guard himself from repeating the opinion that the 'authority of Aristotle' was absolute at any time in the history of European thought."[50]

Even at the level of specific textual commentary, McLuhan's

examination of Nashe is anchored in the trivium and its role in intellectual history: "When Nashe praises the poets for having cleansed English of barbarism[s] . . . he means the dunsticall, inkhorn terms of scholastic grammatica and dialectics . . . The words 'dunce' and 'barbarism' are not loose terms of vague application with Nashe. His observation that 'ouerflowing barbarisme' had 'withdrawne to her Scottish Northren chanell' is a reference to the inveterate scholasticism of Scotland in his own day."[51] The variety in Nashe's writing styles is similarly explained in historical terms. Thus, McLuhan views *The Unfortunate Traveller* as a satire on medieval romances, forming part of Nashe's attack on Duns Scotus and the Calvinists.

It becomes clear that Nashe both validates McLuhan's history of the trivium and personifies the argument of the ancients for its indivisibility. This emerges not from any argument on McLuhan's part but simply from the compelling quality of his close reading. McLuhan detected that Nashe's power as a writer extends beyond mastery of a variety of styles to skill in remolding his array of verbal tools.[52] In this respect, Nashe may have provided part of the initial inspiration for the later McLuhan of the probes. In any case, as the dissertation draws to a close, amid illustrations of Nashe's allegory, hyperbole, paradox, the prolonged metaphors typical of patristic sermons, and a host of dramatic devices, the echo of I. A. Richards is strong once more: "Perhaps more than enough has been said to indicate that the locus of any solution for the problem of the professional and artistic status of Nashe must be sought in the character and purpose of his rhetoric."[53]

The dialogue of art and scholarship, which McLuhan viewed as both inevitable and indispensable, is evident here and as he summarizes the prospects he has opened for transcending conventional views of Elizabethan literature: "It required, perhaps, the advent of such a successful devotee of the rhetoric of the second sophistic as James Joyce to prepare the ground for a scholarly understanding of Elizabethan literature."[54] It was at this point that McLuhan said, "And so I interrupt what I hope to be able to conclude another day" (p446). As he worked toward that day, he would return to Joyce again and again.

7

Duelogue

But what complete isolation governs the maturing of any thought in this country!
—*MARSHALL MCLUHAN TO WYNDHAM LEWIS*
17 JANUARY 1944

That Dagwood, himself, should come forward to grapple with me is a bit of luck I scarcely deserve.
—*MARSHALL MCLUHAN*
Columbia, *MARCH 1944*

OWING TO THE DIFFICULTY of wartime travel, McLuhan was not required to defend his dissertation in the standard oral examination. It was approved *in absentia* on 11 December 1943. Professor Wilson noted in his report that he had learned more from it than from any he had read in years. He later wrote to McLuhan on several occasions, urging publication. Professor Douglas Bush of Harvard and Professor Maynard Mack of Yale also read the work, made suggestions that McLuhan found helpful, and encouraged him to publish it at once.[1]

But McLuhan's mind surged with ideas, all of them demanding attention as urgently as the Nashe and the revisions it would require to be fit for any publisher's eye. The ideas needed airing; McLuhan needed money — and a distraction from the irritants of the classroom: "I have been writing 'learned' papers lately, since publication is the only way out of the morass of petty pay and inferior students."[2]

The quotation marks around *learned* are a signal of skepticism over prevailing standards in the academic community, the same standards McLuhan had found wanting in undergraduate days in Manitoba, standards that did not come up to his own or connect with his vision, his scope, his priorities.

He had published "Aesthetic Pattern in Keats' Odes" in the *University of Toronto Quarterly* in January 1943 with no difficulty. Soon after, John Crowe Ransom, editor of *The Kenyon Review*, turned down McLuhan's essay on Forster and Kipling.[3] McLuhan was not about to produce the terser version of the essay that Ransom hoped to see, and certainly not disposed to recast what he had to say in light of recent work by Lionel Trilling, as Ransom suggested. Instead, McLuhan mailed off an article on Leavis, Richards, and Empson, but Ransom declined it, too. At the same time, he encouraged McLuhan: "I don't think you should stay on the sidelines. I admire the authority and the excellent writing in your paper. I wish we might publish it, but I think we have other items more pressing."[4]

Though it was clear that McLuhan's thought was far from the perspective that informed Ransom's editorial policy,[5] McLuhan eventually broke into print in *The Kenyon Review* with an article on Gerard Manley Hopkins's "analogical mirrors" and a satirical piece on the "New York wits," condemning them for imposing "a paralyzing orthodoxy in taste and culture" and skewering them one by one: Edna St. Vincent Millay, a "purveyor of cliché sentiment"; Dorothy Parker, with her "mechanism of sensibility which is about as complicated as a village pump"; and Alexander Woollcott, "a sort of Thackeray of Broadway."[6]

A McLuhan article on metaphor was turned down by *The Quarterly Journal of Speech* in March 1944 "because of the scope of our publications rather than the inherent worth of your study."[7] Two months later, an evaluation of McLuhan's submission on Francis Bacon to the *Journal of the History of Ideas* arrived along with a rejection slip.[8] This time there was no talk of excellent writing, no encouragement. The anonymous appraiser commented on abrupt shifts into philosophical realms, an incorrect definition of *decorum*, the author's tendency to metaphorical play. "The metaphor of Nature as a book is widespread," the reader observed. "It is also used by Galileo. Does that make of Galileo a grammarian?"[9]

McLuhan had a question of his own: how could the evaluator of his manuscript have branded him "completely scholastic" when his point was to show that Bacon was anti-scholastic?[10] "This man can't read,"[11] McLuhan fumed, as baffled by the complete misunderstanding of his work as he was appalled by the ignorance of the classical trivium it revealed. He addressed a long reply to the editor, beginning: "The purpose of my paper was to show not Bacon's intrinsic importance but his tradition. The problem which remains with regard to Bacon is simply 'Why has Bacon enjoyed the reputation he has?' My answer was left implicit in my evidence and my argument."[12]

One by one, McLuhan disposed of his commentator's criticisms: all ancient grammarians regarded textual analysis as a grammatical activity, even when it involved ancillary domains as diverse as geometry, metaphysics, and biology; the definition of decorum he discussed was not his own but Bacon's. He pointed out that no specific objections had been raised against his article that a careful check of his references would not clear up. And he defended the metaphor of the book of nature.

McLuhan admitted that he had aimed for shock effect: "This Bacon paper was intended as a raid, but not as a raid to set up a scholastic regime — merely a raid to upset a mass of complacent cliché." To this he added candidly that "the main reason for presenting this paper in its present form is not to produce conviction . . . but to get the scholarly world by the ear."[13]

Having defended his method and explained his motives, McLuhan launched an appeal to have his work published, and concluded with speculation and prediction: "The only kind of research which interests me is of an unconventional kind which cannot show immediate marketable results. Moreover, when it is ready, it is bound to raise resistance and resentment in the very quarters from which help alone can come. Perhaps these difficulties will, during the next twenty years or so, force me to do a better job than a modicum of time and means would permit."[14]

Recognizing that the problem with the Bacon essay stemmed from his attempt to cram in more than four hundred pages of background from his Nashe study, McLuhan realized he should give priority to revising the Nashe. But too many other projects claimed his attention and his time.

WHEN MCLUHAN FIRST became acquainted with Wyndham Lewis's work is not clear, but Elsie, directing a play in Detroit in 1943, recalled her son's references to Lewis in his letters from Cambridge and alerted him to the artist's presence across the river in Windsor, Ontario. She had heard Lewis lecture on "Rouault, Painter of Original Sin," in the Christian Culture Series and learned from the organizer, Father Stan Murphy, of Lewis's move from Toronto to Windsor, where he had set up a studio and was teaching at Assumption College.[15]

Toronto had been a catastrophe in more than one way for Lewis. Born of a British mother, on his American father's yacht in the Bay of Fundy, Lewis had been christened in Montreal[16] and retained dual British and Canadian citizenship. World War II forced him to abandon his London art studio, and he found himself exiled in Toronto. He called it a "bush-metropolis of the Orange Lodges."[17] In the heavily autobiographical novel *Self Condemned* Lewis would publish in 1954, Toronto became "Momaco" — echoing the name of the Toronto suburb of Mimico, and more importantly, according to McLuhan, providing a link to McLuhan's own theme of the feminization of the North American male. Toronto was the very metaphor of the glacial soullessness of colonial culture for Lewis — a prison full of the self-condemned. In February 1943, fire swept the city's Tudor Hotel. Lewis and his wife Anne were among those who fled. Two prized portraits, two unfinished manuscripts, and hundreds of his books perished.[18] It was the end of Lewis's association with Toronto.

In some disbelief that the man Elsie had located could be *the* Wyndham Lewis, the man whose quarrel with Roger Fry had earned him the name "ogre of Bloomsbury," McLuhan made inquiries and confirmed that it was.[19] Arranging first for Father Murphy to tell Lewis of his wish to meet him, McLuhan then introduced himself by letter.[20] After a frustrating wait to finish his summer-school teaching commitment, he boarded a train with Felix Giovanelli and set off for Windsor.

Avant-garde painter, novelist,[21] and essayist, Lewis was the leading figure in the British art movement dubbed "Vorticism"[22] by Ezra Pound. Lewis worked, by his own account, "like the mason bee or the woodpecker from a fundamental need."[23] He collaborated with Pound to found the journal *Blast* — a short-lived publication that did not fail to deliver the effect promised by its title. Its pages filled with "Blast" and "Bless,"[24] echoing the "Merde" and "Rose" of Guillaume Apollinaire's *L'Antitradition futuriste*, Lewis's journal proclaimed the demise of British provincialism and heralded the international environment of the new art in dark symbiosis with the internationalism of technology. T. S. Eliot (whose portrait Lewis painted) and I. A. Richards considered Lewis the supreme living master of English fiction.[25] Like his paintings, Lewis's imaginative prose focused on the artist's role in an age engulfed by technological change.

A satirist, above all an inquirer, at his best form in dialogue, committed to exposing the inadequacies of Naturalism and Symbolism alike, steadfastly refusing to articulate a canon that could only have undermined Vorticism, Lewis had boundless interests that embraced sculpture, architecture, cinematography, and what he called "the visual revolution."[26] In *Time and Western Man* he analyzed the world of advertising. Little wonder that McLuhan, assembling material for *The Mechanical Bride*, would come looking for Lewis. Lewis had said in *Time and Western Man* that "we want a new learned minority as sharp as razors, as fond of discourse as a Greek, familiar enough with the abstract to be able to handle the concrete. In short we want a new race of philosophers, instead of 'hurried men,' speed-cranks, simpletons, or robots."[27] Lewis was also looking for McLuhan.

They met in Lewis's basement apartment in downtown Windsor. As impractical as he was brilliant, Lewis had arrived in town and simply stood at a street corner asking passersby where he could find a place to live.[28] After the disaster of Toronto, anything would do. He was grateful to have found the cramped quarters where he was now hosting McLuhan, Giovanelli, and Father Murphy, accepting the two newcomers with an easy informality McLuhan had not expected. It was a meeting of minds and all the incentive McLuhan needed to hatch a scheme for bringing Lewis to St. Louis.

He threw himself into finding painting commissions and lecturing engagements for Lewis, who was perpetually impoverished, and in this he was successful enough for Lewis to warm to the idea of yet another relocation. McLuhan discovered through his neighbor, Edna Gellhorn, mother-in-law of Ernest Hemingway, that Joseph Erlanger, the Nobel prize-winner in Physics at Washington University in St. Louis, was to have his portrait done. McLuhan eagerly proposed Lewis to Mrs. Gellhorn, who telephoned at once to Hemingway in Cuba for his opinion. Hemingway not only endorsed the idea but gave Lewis an enthusiastic buildup, paving the way for him to earn a handsome $1,500 fee and launch his career as a portrait painter of the St. Louis gentry.[29]

The good burghers of the city knew little of Lewis's reputation. He was asked to give a lecture, and the matron in charge of the event, knowing only that he hailed from England, suggested that he give his presentation a title along the lines of "Famous People I Have Put in my Books and on Canvas."[30] It was the sort of situation McLuhan would need to head off over and over to keep Lewis from exploding, managing on this occasion to confront it boldly and with humor, suggesting that Lewis make the lecture "a chatty, breezy sort of account of the bigwigs you know, letting them know that your wig is even bigger."[31]

Lewis's self-portrait, painted when he was fifty, is that of a younger man. Styled with high-definition lines and geometric patches of shading, it shows an apparently reluctant subject raising a patrician eyebrow, his expression captured in bold, angular forms, repeated in the outline of a wide-brimmed hat. Lewis faithfully drew the oval shape of his face but obscured it with the dark triangles etching his features. His hat further obscures a feature that prompted a remark from McLuhan, the sometime phrenologist: "I mentioned to Lewis that his cranial profile was that of a tomahawk."[32] Lewis was upset.

Lewis painted McLuhan's portrait in 1944, making him expressionless and showing him face on, full figure, sitting cross-legged. Just as television would soon shift human sensory balance by giving mankind an eye for an ear, Lewis gave McLuhan no right eye, but enlarged his left ear. Years later, in a dream, McLuhan asked Lewis why he had painted him that way, but got no reply.

When Lewis arrived in St. Louis, he entrusted himself to the guardian angels McLuhan and Giovanelli.[33] Living for a time in the Giovanelli apartment, vacated for his benefit, he enjoyed the attention and the services of the endlessly obliging McLuhans. Lewis was even the beneficiary of generosity on the part of Elsie McLuhan, who lent him money when he was in a desperate position. When he found it necessary to move from the modest Giovanelli quarters to the Park Plaza Hotel, in order to accommodate both his work and his callers, he enlisted the help of McLuhan, who appeared in a shabby old shirt and paint-splattered pants. Lewis found him inappropriately attired and ordered him home to change before the move could begin.[34] Telephoning Corinne on one occasion an hour before he was due to arrive for dinner, Lewis asked about the menu. She was delighted to be able to announce a Virginia ham, prepared from a special recipe. "Ham," Lewis growled, "I'll come another night."[35] The epithet of "ogre" that had clung to the artist in his London days took on its full meaning for a terrified two-year-old Eric McLuhan, who shrieked whenever Lewis approached him.[36]

Having benefited from so much goodwill, Lewis returned to Windsor to teach a summer course at Assumption College during July and August 1944. Before he left, McLuhan told him: "You had been, for years before I met you, a major resource in my life. These past months have been a very great experience indeed. To recruit understanding students for your work will always be part of mine."[37] But six months later, by which time McLuhan was also in Windsor, Lewis wrote him an extraordinary letter, telling him that he must stop "posing as a friend and 'admirer' of Mr. Lewis." Still reeling from this opening shot, McLuhan was overwhelmed by the inexplicable barrage of venom and insult to follow: "I neither care much for you nor for the way you behave towards those you are the 'friend' of and 'admire.' I am ashamed to say you inveigled me down to St. Louis. You came up here to avoid the draft. We chan[g]ed places.[38] But I returned two months ago to this city — not the college — for a period, and do not want or intend to be interfered with. I have not the time to write more now. I send you this as a preliminary warning off, and I hope you will take it to heart."[39] Desperate to learn how he had offended Lewis, McLuhan wrote him letter after letter, but received no reply. It would not be till eight years later that Lewis, by then comfortably reestablished in London, saw fit to reopen their correspondence with a note to McLuhan saying only "How are you?"[40]

Lewis's influence is profoundly stamped on McLuhan's work. The notion of media as extensions of the physical body, along with the Narcissus corollary, find a source in Lewis's writings.[41] In Lewis, McLuhan had a model for eschewing categorical judgments.[42] McLuhan's integrating and synthesizing approach in all phases of his work is born of the same spirit as Lewis's ideal of reintegrating the arts of sculpture, painting, and architecture.[43] In the first volume of *Blast*, Lewis explicitly stated that the Vorticist is not the slave of commotion but its master,[44] just as McLuhan, the navigator of the electronic maelstrom, taught the understanding of media as the means to keep them under control. Lewis understood the fragmenting effects of technology and spoke of them in terms closely paralleled in McLuhan's writings, beginning with *The Gutenberg Galaxy*.[45] Lewis's views on space contain the germ of the idea McLuhan would develop, with input from anthropology and psychology, as the distinction between visual and acoustic space.[46] McLuhan believed, with Lewis, in the importance of names.[47] McLuhan moved, like Lewis, beyond his original interests in the world of the arts to a profound under-standing of their relationship to technology.[48] McLuhan shared with Lewis a conception of the artist inextricably linked to the inundating effect of technological advances.[49] Both accepted to face those effects as detached observers of their causes.[50] Lewis's notion of the vortex as a mask of energy in relation to both art and technology was applied by McLuhan to language *as both art and technology*.[51]

In spite of these heavy parallels between their work, and McLuhan's clear recognition[52] and acknowledgment of them, he was critical of Lewis, in light of the analytical framework that would become familiar to students of classic McLuhan: "Another person to whom I owe a good deal in terms of structural awareness is Wyndham Lewis, the painter. He spent his life defining what he considered to be the values of the eye by which he meant the audible, tactile, boundary line of abstract and sculptural form. He, by the way, did not under-stand that cartoon and sculpture are not visual forms. Since Lewis never got this straightened out, it is not surprising that students of his have trouble too."[53]

NONE OF THESE THOUGHTS had yet crossed McLuhan's mind in 1943, when he discovered his own name on a publicity flyer prepared by

Father Stan Murphy titled "Who is Wyndham Lewis?" In the same week that he was awarded his doctorate for his Nashe dissertation, McLuhan wrote to Lewis about the flyer and announced that he had another publication forthcoming. "It is sad that your prestige should have to stoop to such a green prop or crutch as mine. Perhaps my article on 'Dagwood's America' coming out in *Columbia* may help you in this regard."[54] The circulation of *Columbia*, the publication of the Knights of Columbus, stood, at that time, at about half a million. In spite of this enviably large forum for his work, McLuhan regretted "becoming entangled in Catholic journalism before having properly won my spurs in other fields."[55]

The article appeared in January 1944, reserving its sharpest barbs not for the hapless husband of the piece or his "efficiently masculine" wife[56] but for the society that had shaped their relationship and their family.

A spirited reply followed two months later in defense of the father figure McLuhan had skewered so mercilessly. The author, Joseph A. Breig, missed McLuhan's main point as surely as the reader who had evaluated his Bacon essay. By way of conclusion, the indignant Breig wrote: "I give you the greatest of American husbands and fathers; the happiest, most humorous and most human of the lot; I give you, Mr. McLuhan, Dagwood Bumstead, that you may learn of him; for he is meek and humble of heart."[57]

Ruling out ironical intent on Breig's part, the *Columbia* editor allowed McLuhan to have the last word: "That Dagwood, himself, should come forward to grapple with me is a bit of luck I scarcely deserve . . . Of course, I was somewhat embarrassed by the opulent maternalism of the fury which has been unleashed. My detached observations have been mistaken by Mr. Breig for an attack on his personal integrity, calling for anguished self-justification. With the feminine faculty for viewing all things in the light of strictly personal emotion, he enmeshes himself in the phrases of my essay until he is in danger of self-strangulation. In short, Mr. Breig does not answer my arguments. He illustrates them. Involuntarily, he proves that a book on the feminization of the American male is urgently needed. In fact, there is not a moment to be lost. And his article will do what I could never have done. It will convince any publisher in America that my book will 'fill a longfelt want.'"[58] The book was the one McLuhan had conceived at least four years earlier, the one that would still be more than seven years coming to publication as *The Mechanical Bride*. McLuhan closed his reply with a tongue-in-cheek invitation to Breig to write the preface for the book.

Another powerful and enduring influence on McLuhan came in the person of Sigfried Giedion, whom he met in St. Louis. The Swiss historian of architecture was the author of *Space, Time and Architecture: The Growth of a New Tradition*, in which he "attempted to establish, both by argument and by objective evidence, that in spite of the seeming confusion there is nevertheless a true, if hidden, unity, a secret synthesis in our present civilization. To point out why this synthesis has not become a conscious and active reality has been one of my chief aims."[59] Giedion's focus was on the connection between new developments in architecture and other domains. He sought to identify a methodological core spanning not only architecture and the related fields of construction and urban planning but painting and the sciences. It was this breadth of vision and its connection to McLuhan's emerging emphasis on the role of environments that attracted McLuhan to Giedion's work, making it a shaping force in his own thinking: "Giedion gave us a language for tackling the structural world of architecture and artifacts of many kinds in the ordinary environment."[60]

Father William McCabe had left Saint Louis just as McLuhan returned from Cambridge, but McLuhan did not fully feel the loss till Bernie Muller-Thym went away to do service in the U.S. Navy. The sense of community on which McLuhan relied so heavily to sustain his intellectual energy was weakened. Felix Giovanelli, a stalwart and steadfast friend much cherished by McLuhan, remained, but McLuhan was brooding more and more about what he perceived as a change in his fortunes since Father Norman Dreyfus had come to replace McCabe. His dark mood came to a head when he felt, at last, there was something he could do about his situation.

Dreyfus was steeped in traditional philology. McLuhan interpreted this as antipathy to the Cambridge New Criticism, and deep shadows fell across the path of his thinking: "My new head hated his predecessor and everything he stood for. That meant me too. Since then there has been a campaign of attrition against me. Shunting me into the

K.P. duties of the department where others took on the jobs I had done and for which I was especially qualified. Sabotaging of my work among the students and general tabus invented to keep intelligent people away from my contact."[61]

McLuhan had not sought a position in another department, he told Lewis, because until he had completed his Ph.D. he "was thus like a man presenting himself in a bathing suit at an embassy ball."[62] To this he added: "Of course, with the draft hanging over me, the head was able to tighten the thumb-screws considerably."[63] This was the remark that prompted Lewis to call McLuhan a draft-dodger, but in the shorter term Lewis provided him with the recommendation he needed[64] to make the move from Saint Louis University to Assumption College.[65] It was a "little bay of silence — a little back-water in a stagnant stream,"[66] not on the Canadian prairies that McLuhan had known as a child and then as an undergraduate at the University of Manitoba, not in the Tory-blue, Baptist-Orange Toronto that so revolted Lewis, not in the rural Ontario of an earlier generation of McLuhans or the Maritimes the Halls had left behind, but in Windsor, Ontario, between Lake Erie and Lake St. Clair, a small city, peering at its huge American neighbor across the Detroit River, planted on the map in a hook of Canada pressed against the lower eastern rib of Michigan. It was a starting point for tearing the hide off Canada.

THREE

McLuhan's Canada

8

Conversations with Congenial Minds

Who am I? Whose? What should I do? Better the Yankee
assurance after all.

–*Marshall McLuhan's notebook,*
27 November 1946

McLuhan was secure enough in his own emerging identity not to
need the Yankee assurance, pugnacious enough to return to Canada
to stir things up, secure enough to remain in Canada even when he
saw he would be misunderstood.

"I'm done with Catholic schools,"[1] he had written to Wyndham
Lewis from St. Louis, while awaiting his arrival from Canada. Saint
Louis University being the best of America's Catholic institutions, he
would need to look to a large secular campus, because "the next step
must be up."[2] But the U.S. military draft meant that the next step
must also be to Canada, and the road to Windsor in 1944, paved for
McLuhan by Lewis himself, brought him to a small Catholic college.

If he was at Assumption in spite of his ambitions, still a professor in
spite of his "negative capability"[3] — a potential for action that would
allow him to "impinge in some sort of way, but whether academic or
not I am unable to see"[4] — there would, at the very least, be the benefits of a Catholic community: "I need conversation with congenial
minds — Catholic minds."[5] If he was in Canada by dint of circumstance, it was with no regret. He had not forgotten the isolation
he felt in the United States, which had prompted his remark about the

country's stifling maturity of thought. In England he had found his role models, but the United States offered an intellectual climate as inhospitable as the one he remembered in his home and native land, without the abrasive stimulation he would later come to recognize in the Toronto environment.

Commentators on McLuhan's scholarship, such as American historian Marshall Fishwick, have always been ready to find a distinct break brought on by his early years of teaching. Fishwick wrote to him much later, "The McLuhan who taught in Wisconsin, and courted Mechanical Brides, was indeed from the elitist (Richards–Lewis) womb. Then something happened, one imagines: Joyce seems to have been the catalyst, student apathy with the old 'hot' lectures, the barb. Somehow you stopped being Platonic and became Aristotelean."[6] Quite apart from the wholly fanciful Platonic/Aristotelian "conversion," such speculation disconnects the developments in McLuhan's career not only from each other but from the *preparation* that shaped them decisively during his Cambridge years, giving them coherence, acting more powerfully than later "catalysts" (the Joyce influence having begun during his Cambridge training in any case).[7] The "something happened" view of McLuhan fails to apply his notion of "resonant interval," or interaction of components, to the evolution of his own teaching and writing. The principles for understanding poetry and understanding media were one and the same for him. He added the role of media analyst to that of English professor.[8] There was no break between the two roles, no redirection of his thinking as he moved back and forth between them, no break in moving from Madison to St. Louis or from St. Louis to Windsor.

McLuhan was pleased when Father Stan Murphy offered him a summer session course as an initiation to his teaching duties at Assumption. He was equally pleased by Murphy's suggestion that he undertake extramural lectures, for he believed that presentations before a wide variety of audiences would help him to clarify the ideas he was pondering as book-writing projects.[9] The hopes he expressed to Murphy, before arriving, of finding a place to live in the country ("Would like space and safety for Eric to prowl about in")[10] were met. The McLuhans settled well beyond the city limits of Windsor on the Tecumseh Road, renting a "rather baronial" farmhouse.[11] It was all the country McLuhan could have wanted, with fringe benefits. Their landlord, a man known to them only as Barthos, was building a new house for himself on the adjacent property; he stored cream and eggs in the McLuhans' basement and invited them to help themselves to all they wanted. A Jersey cow roamed the property.

Corinne was emboldened by the wide open spaces to tackle once again the job of teaching her husband to drive. Though he had never driven before, he had rented a car when he came courting in Austin. The gears were beyond him, so they had driven around in low all evening. Corinne convinced Marshall that the other gears were useful, and he accepted a lesson from her, as their evening ended, on shifting into reverse. Now that they were settled at the Barthos property, Corinne encouraged him to take the wheel once again. He did so, and promptly backed into the resident cow.[12] Corinne suggested that he rely on the bus to get to campus, and he agreed.

"Oh the mental vacuum that is Canada,"[13] McLuhan wrote after six months in Windsor. His comment was addressed to Wyndham Lewis, the last person who needed to be told. "There is terrible social cowardice," McLuhan added, "and all action here seems so furtive that one can only conclude that some unacknowledged guilt is behind it all. Canada needs about two million Jews to bring life to it."[14] McLuhan sustained himself with his reading, drafting material for articles and papers, and correspondence lashing out at student lethargy and professorial mediocrity. A glance at the program for the Modern Language Association meeting of December 1944 depressed him. "No form of Groucho Marx-like defiance or ridicule is undeserved there," he wrote to Walter Ong and Clement McNaspy in St. Louis.[15] Though he felt out of touch with intellectual developments, his frame of mind was sour enough to bring disenchantment even with the work of Leavis. "Of course the trouble with Leavis is that his passion for important work forbids him to look for the sun in the egg-tarnished spoons of the daily table. In other words, his failure to grasp current society in its intellectual modes . . . "[16] McLuhan too was having trouble seeing the sun.

Watson Kirkconnell wrote to say he was looking forward to hearing an address McLuhan was preparing for delivery in the spring: "[I] shall be curious to know what is meant by 'An Ancient Quarrel in

Modern America.' At any rate, it will have nothing to do with Dagwood."[17] But Dagwood and the full cast of characters for *The Mechanical Bride* were marching through McLuhan's mind; he did a page of advertisement analysis every evening before supper. At home, he was also "devising barricades against the insolent ingenuity of Eric."[18] McLuhan tried to protect his study time by keeping his two-year-old son in a playpen, but he regularly escaped.

Summer brought the violent storms common to the region. Then a tornado. "What a bee-yew-teefull sight,"[19] McLuhan called it. The white funnel with its black top came gracefully, snaking across the fields toward their house. Less than two hundred yards away, it paused and changed course, moving parallel to the road. Others were still huddled in the safety of the basement, while McLuhan and his friend Carrol Hollis busied themselves taking pictures of the roaring maelstrom of air, watching as several houses were caught up. The next-door neighbor ran down the road, following the tornado, shooting into it with his rifle. It crossed Tecumseh Road, tearing the bridge loose, and seemed to die at the river's edge. "We saw it collapse," McLuhan wrote, "ever so leisurely, beautifully. Like the Indian rope-trick. Something out of the Arabian Nights."[20]

In his second year at Assumption, McLuhan served as head of the English department, an administrative post he was not to assume again at any time in his career, for lack of patience and skill. He was also looking for a new position. There were few universities offering opportunities for teaching other than freshman English. Even those who might have gladly engaged his services commented that he seemed to be worthy of a better appointment.[21]

THE DOCTOR HAD HEARD the double heartbeat but did not want to alarm his new patient with the news that she was carrying twins. It was not till the babies arrived, seven minutes apart, on 26 October 1945, that Marshall and Corinne learned they had conceived twin daughters.[22] Eric, now three years old and approaching four, not only took the news calmly but professed to have known all along that he was going to have twin sisters. What's more, he announced, the Jersey cow had just had a calf.[23] "Come as soon as convenient," a mildly panic-stricken McLuhan wrote to Elsie, "you can certainly be a big help to Corinne with the babies."[24] *To Corinne*.

Fatherhood, once again, inspired McLuhan to a renewed effort in his research and writing. His concern was to meet his financial responsibilities, and possibly to escape mundane ones. He complained at how long it took to feed the newborns, one on a three-hour schedule, the other on a four-hour schedule, during the daytime. Eric, for all his precociousness, was only a slightly less bewildering phenomenon to his father than the new babies. McLuhan reported to Elsie that Eric was threatening to shoot one of his playmates because she did not like Barthos, remarking "you will see some changes in him."[25]

The twins were christened Teresa Carolyn and Mary Corinne in a pre-Christmas ceremony that brought Elsie to Windsor.[26] Herbert McLuhan made a separate visit to his son and young family the same month and "managed to be quite helpful."[27] The greatest help with the twins, however, came in the person of Miss Amy Dunaway. A stalwart Englishwoman, she had come to stay with her sister in Windsor, but found her quarters very cramped and was only too happy to become a live-in weekend baby-sitter for the McLuhans. A grateful McLuhan described her as "a great boon. A cliff, a rock, an oak. An abyss of good nature."[28]

McLuhan was on the road in the spring of 1946 to give lectures in Montreal and Woodstock, Ontario, with a stopover in Toronto that proved to have enormous consequences. In both Montreal and Toronto, McLuhan made contacts formed through Pauline Bondy, a teacher of French at Windsor's Kennedy Collegiate who became a great friend of the McLuhans through Father Murphy. Her friends in Montreal welcomed McLuhan and hosted him during his brief stay. In Toronto, McLuhan reestablished contact with Father Phelan and Pauline's brother, Father L. J. Bondy, then president of St. Michael's College, who had met McLuhan on visits to Windsor. Bondy expressed keen interest in bringing him onto the faculty. On the same trip, McLuhan met Northrop Frye, already something of a fixture in the Victoria College English department and soon to launch his illustrious scholarly career with the publication of *Fearful Symmetry: A Study of William Blake*.

McLuhan's *The Mechanical Bride* also had a connection to Blake, who had influenced McLuhan's program for the training of perception; McLuhan would mention this, in passing, when he published *Understanding Media* in 1964.[29] In 1946, *The Mechanical Bride* was a set of slides McLuhan used for lectures; files of magazine and newspaper clippings that had been growing since 1939; a protean manuscript with any number of titles: "Guide to Chaos," "Typhon in America," "Folklore of Industrial Man."[30] Felix Giovanelli, having left St. Louis for New York, acted as agent for McLuhan, who gave him a free hand in approaching publishers: "No need to use my name or 'Typhon in America' title. Use some other title such as 'Jitterbugs of the Absolute' or '60 Million Mama's Boys.'"[31]

McLuhan felt an urgency over getting the work published that had nothing to do with enhancing his dossier. In Madison, it had been important to contrast words on the page with words in the mouths of film actors and ask students Richards's question: what difference does it make? Now it was becoming important to engage an audience beyond the classroom, beyond the walls of a Catholic institution, on topics beyond the printed word and film. In 1946, the word *technology* began to appear with noticeable frequency in McLuhan's writings.

At the beginning of the year, he had written to Father Clement McNaspy at Saint Louis University about the work he sensed he should be doing, stressing at the same time that he did not "wish to take any step in it that is not consonant with the will of God . . . My increasing awareness has been of the ease with which Catholics can penetrate and dominate secular concerns — thanks to an emotional and spiritual economy denied to the confused secular mind."[32]

This did not make the project a Catholic mission. McLuhan felt, in any case, that no group of Catholic educators was fit for the task he had in mind, consisting essentially of shocking the world into awareness of its confusion, illiteracy, and somnambulism. "There is no need to mention Christianity. It is enough that it be known that the operator is a Christian. This job must be conducted on every front — every phase of the press, book-rackets, music, cinema, education, economics. Of course, points of reference must always be made. That is, the examples of real art and prudence must be seized, when available, as paradigms of future effort. In short, the methods of F. R. Leavis and Wyndham Lewis applied with all the energy and order denied them

from faith and philosophy — These can serve to educate a huge
public, both Catholic and non-Catholic, to resist that swift oblitera-
tion of the person which is going on."[33] The hope of meeting this
daunting educator's challenge was part of McLuhan's motivation in
looking to the University of Toronto, where he could be at a Catholic
college but within a secular university. Regardless of where the future
would take him, meeting that challenge was his imperative in *The
Mechanical Bride*.

The early drafts of material for the book are angry, sarcastic, scatter-
shot pages, under the title, at this point, "Guide to Chaos." The
enemy was wearing a velvet glove over an iron fist; McLuhan fought
back wearing no gloves. A toothpaste ad, a Walter Winchell column,
Felix the Cat, Frank Sinatra — what made them all the targets of
McLuhan's jabs? He answered in his preface to this draft: "These
items have in common the fact of invisibility. They are too obvious to
be seen. They are intended to be absorbed through the pores or to be
gulped in by a kind of mental breathing."[34] This was the leitmotif
McLuhan carried through to his final page, where, in summary, he
wrote: "In that darkness we must learn to see."[35]

Much of the "Guide to Chaos" remained unpublished when it was
eventually transformed into *The Mechanical Bride*. There was simply
too much material. Some McLuhan pruned and toned down himself;
some his editor at Vanguard Press cut, when she found it too academic,
too Canadian, or too feisty — for instance: "The average parent today
should be detained in a mental-delousing institution until cleansed of
the verminous accretions of pseudophilosophy acquired while rolling
around in the Circe sty of sensate culture."[36]

In the early manuscript, McLuhan served up such items as the
following on *Time* magazine, which was promoting itself as a weekly
report of history in the making and suitable for classroom use: "Yes,
kiddies, you need trouble no more about History. You *are* history. As
for teacher! With *Time* in hand you can feel your spine corrugate with
the thrills that come only from being the cromium [sic] tip of the
radiator cap of the *Zeitgeist* as you plunge onward into time . . . How
does *Time* regard its readers? That is a simple matter. The reader is a
moron who has to be babied, tickled, prodded, propped and paddled.
He can escape this infantile treatment only if he joins the gang of

nose-thumbers."[37] A considerably tamer treatment of *Time* appeared in *The Mechanical Bride*, titled "The Ballet Luce."[38]

The logic of McLuhan's comments on passive reader acceptance of photographs of death in *Life* magazine was compelling: "But when Dali or Picasso produce a canvas loaded with the necrophilia of a sado-masochistic society they are called 'unhealthy.' The fact is that we get the jitters about everything the moment anything is made intelligible to us. So long as we can splash about in a big hygienic tub of scented sex and death we imagine we are safe and happy. But a pox on the prying intelligence which would withdraw to contemplate and evalue [sic] these closely inter-related activities."[39]

"Guide to Chaos" offered documentation for McLuhan's thesis that the male ego had begun to totter as early as 1890. And it castigated ads with "layer on layer of moral insentience," those that registered "calculated oblivion to every normal human impulse,"[40] and still others that offended his Christian sensibilities: "That the Nativity gets smeared is all in the day's work for the admen."[41] At the same time, "Guide to Chaos" hints at visual versus acoustic space and other themes to become perennial favorites in McLuhan's later work: "The modern soul laughs at space, but time sends it into a blue funk. The mental and moral continuity of past, present and future is an intolerable burden for the sensualist. Jazz is the poor man's answer. It kills time. It hints at order and continuity just enough to satisfy the harassed listener that these things are being successfully invaded by destructive chaos. Jazz provides for the the lazy and illiterate precisely what Stein and Joyce offer to more earnest folk. A carefully arranged reduction of consciousness to a moment by moment inconsequentiality. The latest name for this elaborate game of evading and abolishing reason and the rational content of experience is called *Existenz* (existentialism)."[42]

Among the advantages a move to Toronto would bring, McLuhan counted a traveling allowance generous enough to take him to New York four times a year.[43] (Yankee assurance may not have been necessary, but the Yankee stage was.) Above all, being among scholars from the Pontifical Institute such as Etienne Gilson, from whom he had drawn so deeply in preparing his thesis on Thomas Nashe, would allow him to continue learning — an objective at least as important to him as teaching.[44] He also planned to start a magazine, recognizing that it "might function well in Toronto by reason of the very hostility of the environment."[45] "The house problem will probably lick us," he told Elsie. "It's hopeless in Toronto. But while I think we might do *very* well in Toronto, we are not set on it."[46]

Any number of ideas distracted McLuhan from the wait to learn if the move was to be. He was beginning a study of Poe, and of Faulkner's awareness of the impact of technology, and continuing his study of Joyce. Though he still found Joyce difficult, he had made "so many discoveries I don't know how to keep the business under control. Like bringing in an oil gusher."[47] (McLuhan was somewhat startled to discover on the last page of *Finnegans Wake* a parody of the last part of the mass, and it was only some time later that he came to regard Joyce's comic perception as the element that freed Joyce from diabolism.)[48] Also, John Crowe Ransom had encouraged him to submit further writing for *The Kenyon Review*, an opportunity he welcomed.[49]

On 14 May 1946, McLuhan traveled to Toronto alone and learned that the position at St. Michael's College was his. Faculty housing was available. He inspected the premises offered at 91 St. Joseph Street — a three-bedroom flat with two fireplaces — and said yes at once. After two years of shuttling between downtown Windsor and Tecumseh Road, he would be living within a two-minute walk of classes, office, library, and church. Four-year-old Eric, who had "emerged into a more moderate phase of childhood, more self possessed, less urgently personal"[50] toward his parents, would be sent off to study Latin and Greek with Sister St. John around the corner. Mary and Teresa, not yet having celebrated their first birthday, were, nevertheless, "as little trouble as children can be. They are so unlike that they are really a great source of quite satisfactory small-talk with us. We have never regarded them as anything less than *blessed* events."[51] Best of all, Miss Dunaway agreed to come to Toronto with the McLuhans and continue as their live-in baby-sitter. McLuhan felt that he was at a great turning point in his life. "So, Walter," he wrote to Father Ong, "I must regard this move as a permanent one. I must pitch in and do, for the first time, an uncompromising and unremitting job."[52]

When the McLuhans had first settled in Windsor, Corinne took instruction in the Catholic faith from an intrepid priest who cycled out to Tecumseh Road once a week. Two years later, she was, in her husband's words, "teeter-tottering towards the Church."[53] When they arrived in Toronto and took up residence in the closely knit community on the St. Michael's College campus, Father Bondy told her "I'm not going to let you escape."[54] With her dramatic flair, Corinne had always appreciated Episcopalian pomp and ceremony, and she had continued worshiping at her own church, even though she attended mass regularly in Cambridge, St. Louis, and Windsor. Now Father Bondy sent Father Lawrence Shook along with Father Anglin to give her instruction. The conversion that had been coming gradually needed only a week to be complete, inspired in large part by the example of good friends and neighbors. Pauline Bondy, already a god-mother to Teresa, became godmother to Corinne. As a new convert, Corinne went to mass twice a day and developed a special love for the Latin liturgy.

Hugh Kenner, from the University of Toronto, took the position McLuhan had vacated at Assumption College.[55] From Kenner, McLuhan had learned enough about life on the Toronto campus to believe that he was taking up his new position without illusions. "I know what to expect. *But*, some very good students are there. That's all one can ask. A few good colleagues, good library, good music, and good students. Also a living wage, fine surroundings and suitable cir-cumstances for raising children."[56] McLuhan and his colleague Larry Lynch were the only two members of the St. Michael's faculty who were not priests. They became known as the "civilian Basilians."[57]

McLuhan was to find himself just as disturbed on meeting his Toronto classes in the fall of 1946 as he had been at Madison ten years earlier, though for different reasons. The students expected him to dictate notes and were bewildered when he asked them for opinions. "I am absolutely stunned by this discovery. When with the fact fresh upon me I hurried to Father Shook, he looked very embarrassed. 'Of course,' he says, 'what else can we do?' He doesn't seem to realize that this is the only university where such utter dishonesty prevails. It is hypocritical because by this means the exam questions are made to seem very mature. I was struck by this fact. But the exams are not *studied* for at all. Only class notes are memorized. A few variations are then played on these hackneyed themes."[58]

McLuhan began meeting his new colleagues. On his spring visit to Toronto, he had already met the sixty-two-year-old Etienne Gilson and found him effervescent, witty, and looking for all the world like a football coach.[59] "Gilson and Maritain do belong to a community in which a general awareness of our age at all its points is cultivated. Yet both of these men have evaded (or for lack of time and faculty they have done nothing) the application of Thomistic principles to the area of Freud, Fra[z]er, and Malinowksi[60] — psychology and anthropology."[61] The mention of these fields, the note of disappointment, hint already that McLuhan would soon be organizing an interdisciplinary seminar reaching outside St. Michael's. But first, he tried to engage Catholic minds in the exploration of disciplines that had "not found their Newman," to address questions "no Thomist has ever faced."[62]

To Walter Ong, McLuhan had waxed lyrical on his ideals for education: the training of sensibilities, fostering the interplay of thought and feeling as a basis for value judgment of artistic works, the need for the liberal arts to coalesce in order to rebuild a human community on the wasteland of modern life. These were the same objectives and concerns McLuhan had expressed to McNaspy only months before. Now they were focused even more sharply by his thoughts about his role as a teacher of literature. He saw literature as "not a subject but a function — a function inseparable from communal existence. That it should be taught — these 150 years — according to the modes of a debased scholasticism is the first fact to be exploded with a maximum amount of noise. I myself have plans to make such a noise fairly soon, but many people are needed to co-operate in such matters."[63]

The move from Windsor to Toronto authorized musings on the Canadian psyche and Canadian literature: "Looking at Canadian poets, I see some tendril-like groping for contact which appears in Southern letters. But more luxuriously and tragically in the South. Because there the defeat of man was dramatized not only in a war but in the rape of the soil by a tribe of Lovelaces."[64]

McLuhan's reflections during his first term of teaching at St. Michael's also show his increasing preoccupation with psychological and social effects of technology: "The church can never be alive enough, in a technological world, to be hated,"[65] he observed in his notebook, adding that in the family of Dagwood the masculine principle is dead, because there is "neither dignity in technological toil nor support for the male ego in demagoguery."[66]

The students who had shocked McLuhan with their complacency were shocked themselves to be hearing so much about Dagwood and technology from their new English professor. It was the era of the Friday afternoon gatherings in the student common room at the Pontifical Institute, known as the Institute Teas.[67] On one occasion, a clutch of graduate students stood not far from Gilson and Fathers Flahiff, Shook, and O'Donnell, their talk gradually becoming loud enough to reach the professors. McLuhan's name figured prominently, and the complaints were clear. The keen-eared Gilson, whose teaching style and expectations of his students were much like McLuhan's, excused himself, and moved over to join the other group. "Gentlemen," he said, "I have been listening to your discussion. I have the impression that you do not really appreciate Marshall McLuhan for what he is. But I want to tell you what I think he is. And I'd like you to think about it. I think he is a genuine genius. The time will come when you will be proud to say: 'I knew Marshall McLuhan when he was at Toronto, and I was a student there.'"[68]

McLuhan had already collected rejection slips for "Guide to Chaos" from three publishing houses in England when a prospect arose for placing it in the United States.[69] This should have been a cause for rejoicing, but McLuhan was disappointed, because it would require a financial commitment on his part, when he had hoped the book would provide at least a little extra income.[70] He wrote to Felix Giovanelli about the matter, displaying the same impatience he felt throughout his life with the publishing game: "Apropos of *Typhon*. It is not going to be easy to dig up the $250 . . . Why not try Knopf or Doubleday or some big brash outfit that might like to play up the book not as Typhon but as Sixty Million Mama's Boys? What do you think of selling it to somebody not as a sober thesis but as a spectacular item? Not something to be understood but just a smash hit? I think the book can sell on two or three levels. And the big level of buyers won't understand or want to understand a word of it. They will be quite happy or angry with its sporadic impudence . . . What about playing it as a hot number? 'Can only leave this with you for one week. Material won't keep. It's a best seller. Got to hit the Christmas trade' sort of note? . . . I think you could play that game for one or two publishers very advantageously even for the sake of merely testing their attitudes. Let's leave the serious publishers till the last."[71]

The hundred-headed Typhon had still not found a home in America, or anywhere else. In spite of his comments to Giovanelli, McLuhan himself was promoting the work as a textbook that belonged in every high-school and college classroom to help students develop immunity to their media environment.

McLuhan had constructed his book like a vortex, where readers could make their own observations and discover a means of escape from the maelstrom by making connections for themselves: "When the interrelatedness of many things is made plain, then the mind is freed from any watchful fretting over any one of them."[72] In this respect, McLuhan had predecessors, to whom he called attention, in Kenneth Burke, Sigfried Giedion, and Laszlo Moholy-Nagy, all of whom detected the interrelatedness of the most casual and disparate objects in a manner which served McLuhan as a model of perceptual acuity.[73]

The agenda of "Guide to Chaos" involved nothing less than the rescue of rationalism: "In any age which boasts of its extension of reason to everything, is it not strange that reason has so seldom been allowed to explore the assumptions and attitudes of daily life? . . . After studying the exhibits in this book, the man who is concerned about the political chaos of the world will readily see why the most reasonable plans are bound to fail. The gap between political pronouncements on one hand and the jungle of lethal appetites daily aroused and propiti- ated by current entertainment illustrates why people are not basically convinced by reasonable policies. Reason is not an accepted criterion. Reason imposes limits. And there is nothing limited about Sherlock Holmes or Superman . . . Certainly [exhibits presented] were never intended for rational consumption, since that destroys their value as anodyne, dope, or directive. Rather they are intended by their authors to be absorbed by a sort of osmotic inattention . . . "[74]

[handwritten margin note: Jefferson Missouri]

Deceptively amorphous at its edges, and full of luminous mysteries that could appear and disappear as unpredictably as electrons and pho-tons, "Guide to Chaos" nevertheless had a carefully wrought four-part structure: Book 1 — Know-How or Daedalus; Book 2 — Sex and Technology or Pasiphae and the Minotaur; Book 3 — Jitterbugs of the Absolute or Dionysus; Book 4 — Sixty million mama boys — or Typhon.[75] McLuhan explained the rationale of the four sections: "The American immersion in matter is shown at four levels of existence in the USA . . . The four levels go progressively deeper into the effects of mechanism and technology on the total human response to what in the first section appears as a whimsical vagary."[76] This sophisticated structure was not to be retained in the version of the work eventually published as *The Mechanical Bride*. The loss might have disturbed McLuhan less than the delay in publication, had he been able to foresee either one in 1946.

As for the purpose of the work, McLuhan emphasized that its attack on advertising was not to galvanize the public into sales resistance, "a frivolous expenditure of effort which would only land the reader deeper than ever in the emotional morass of irrational reactions."[77] His purpose, he said, was much more radical. "Nothing less, in fact, than fully conscious awareness of the multiple inter-relations of all these things."[78]

McLuhan confessed that writing the "Guide to Chaos" had been fun, and that he intended readers to share it. He qualified this as "fun through intelligibility,"[79] though he fully expected that reviewers would brand it a "bilious book."[80] When the reviews of *The Mechanical Bride* appeared, it would be called everything from "brilliant" to "baloney," but not "bilious."

THE MCLUHANS EXUDED hospitality. Graduate students were invited into their home one night a week for poetry readings. McLuhan concentrated on the poem as text, in the manner of Richards and Leavis. When the fall term ended, the McLuhans hosted their first Christmas party, welcoming guests from faculty to freshmen, along with good friends like Jack and Mary Wilson, neighbors and members of the St. Michael's enclave. Corinne, resplendent in an evening gown, fueled an atmosphere of warmth and cheer. Frothy chitchat among the guests did not keep McLuhan from the serious business of thinking. He went to work, launching the trial balloons of his latest thoughts.

He had a captive audience, reacting to his ideas, bringing him the same enjoyment Elsie knew when she performed her monologues and recitations.

When Elsie was present at these gatherings, she found herself astonished. The students were calling her son — a professor, a scholar with a doctorate from Cambridge — "Marshall." Jack Wilson offered an explanation. He told Elsie that her son regarded and treated every person in the intellectual community as a peer, and that he expected everyone else to do the same. There was nothing to be lost by dropping "Professor McLuhan" or "Doctor McLuhan" and everything to be gained by a meeting of minds.[81]

By the spring of 1947, McLuhan had high hopes that his "Guide to Chaos" would appear in the United States under the imprint of Dial Press.[82] Negotiations fell through. To a manuscript large enough to startle most publishers, McLuhan kept adding pages. His new material was beginning to show the focus that would eventually be reflected in the title *The Mechanical Bride*: "The *Life* [magazine] stereotype, therefore, is technology and sex. Stress on eroticism, nudism and primitivism being only too obviously the futile efforts of the mechanized slave to get the machine out of his guts."[83] McLuhan's media analysis at this early stage found its roots in I. A. Richards, who analyzed what McLuhan would later call mankind's first technology — language. In analyzing the media of popular culture — magazines and newspapers — McLuhan focused on both form and content; later he would move to analysis of the effects of form alone: typography in *The Gutenberg Galaxy*; television's cathode-ray tube in *Understanding Media*.

By the time he began his second year of teaching at St. Michael's, in the fall of 1947, McLuhan's mind had shifted from high gear to overdrive. He had been promoted to full professor. "A good thing to have been before leaving academic life," he wrote to Elsie,[84] but his output and his involvements made it plain he was not about to leave. He published "Inside Blake and Hollywood," a review of Frye's *Fearful Symmetry* and Parker Tyler's *Magic and Myth of the Movies*, a rich example of the literary McLuhan in easy union with the McLuhan of popular culture, hinting at his full program for educational reform, grandstanding ever so slightly for Frye's benefit, hinting too at the rivalry between them that McLuhan was ready to foster.[85]

He resumed writing a book on Eliot he had begun at Saint Louis University,[86] split the mountainous manuscript of "Guide to Chaos" in two to permit its further circulation at double speed,[87] wrote an introduction to Hugh Kenner's *Paradox in Chesterton*, describing it himself as containing "spectacular indiscretions"[88] because its overview of Catholic thought implicitly condemned modern Thomists for relinquishing social and ethical problems to artists. His railing at these "indiscretions" was symptomatic of his discontent at St. Michael's, where he sensed that intellectual inquiry on the scope he knew to be necessary could only come about if he turned himself into a one-man academy: "I heard [Gilson] on the puns in St. Augustine's *Confessions*. He noted that they were inseparable from the multi-levels of simultaneous presentation without seeing that this is precisely our contemporary 'cubist' sensibility. What is true of Gilson at only one level is the crippling condition of most present-day Thomists . . . What a state of affairs when one has to do everything oneself! No use to ask any colleague in any other department a single question bearing on a specifically contemporary development as it is related to the past."[89]

McLuhan's most satisfying contacts were with his correspondents. He praised Walter Ong for his publications, offered commentary on them (in case Ong had missed the full significance of his own words), and gave him specific suggestions for further writing that could spark sorely needed educational reform and sound an alert to somnolent scholars.[90] In McLuhan's correspondence with Ong at this time, it is possible to find him expressing an idea that was never to be stressed in his articles and books: "But it is plain enough to me that the abiding achievement of the past century has been in analytical psychology . . ."[91] Other observations bring out coincidences illuminating the evolution of technology traced in McLuhan's later work: "There was a widespread revival in France of the Fathers from 1800 on."[92] There is even a Catholic twist on an idea that would absorb McLuhan during the last six years of his life: "The Fathers fathered French symbolical linguistic technique."[93]

McLuhan became a father again in 1947. Stephanie (for St. Stephen) Lewis (for her maternal grandparents) McLuhan was born on 14 October. Eric, now five and approaching six, articulate beyond his years, could not muster a memorable comment for posterity, as he had on the arrival of the twins, whose second birthday was less than two weeks away. If the new parents were relieved to be spared another surprise set of twins, this too went unspoken. McLuhan amused himself in later years by making twins out of Stephanie and Teresa — referring to them as "Tepi" and "Teri." (Teresa chose her own nickname; "Tepi" was her father's invention.)[94]

At the end of his second year of teaching in Toronto, while traveling with Hugh Kenner, McLuhan detoured to Washington, D.C., to visit Ezra Pound. The poet had been indicted for treason against the United States because of his wartime radio broadcasts from Fascist Italy. But psychiatrists judged him unfit to stand trial, and he was committed to St. Elizabeth's Hospital for the Criminally Insane, where he would spend twelve years. He had already been incarcerated for over two years when McLuhan and Kenner arrived to see him on the afternoon of 4 June 1948.

Among the legends that grew up around McLuhan, after he achieved international fame, was that of his "friendship" with the poet. He commented on this when Pound died in 1972: "I once spent two hours with him at St. Elizabeth's hospital. For some reason that has been parlayed into a close relationship. My admiration for Pound's work increases constantly."[95]

McLuhan wrote to him before their meeting as "Mr. Pound," retaining this form of address in a few letters after the occasion, before switching to "Dear Pound." Their correspondence was to continue for years. Pound had clearly been impressed by McLuhan during the brief visit, asking him why he had not looked up Eliot while in England. When McLuhan replied that he would have found Eliot intimidating, Pound said, "Harumph! He's the one who would have been intimidated by you."[96] Dorothy Pound was present throughout the time that McLuhan spent with her husband and wrote to him afterward to say, "E.P. enjoyed your visit so much."[97] Pound wanted to read McLuhan's publications.[98]

Returning to Toronto, McLuhan was soon writing and deluging the poet with questions: "Are not your affinities (so far as English poetry goes) with Ben Jonson? The same plastic and sculptured world? . . . Your Cantos, I now judge to be the first and only serious use of the great technical possibilities of the cinematograph. Am I right in thinking of them as a montage of *personae* and sculptured images? Flash-backs providing perceptions of simultaneities?"[99] Pound answered: "You go right on writin' me letters, but don't xpect [sic] me to answer questions — even if answers are known."[100]

Much of the McLuhan canon from later years appears in embryonic form in his correspondence with Pound: cinema as womb-worship because of the conditions of projection in dark room, the importance of the detective story (prompted by Pound's own characterization of his early Cantos as examples of the genre), high-definition vs. low-definition media.[101] McLuhan's great admiration for Pound and the importance of Pound's work for his own becomes clear: "The vortex you created has become a kiddies' slide in the subsequent work of the Spenders, Sitwells, Audens and co. Thanks to Freud. Thanks to lack of sustained attention. Lack of energy even to contemplate what's been happening."[102]

Pound added his influence to that of Joyce in shaping the work McLuhan would eventually publish in 1970 as *From Cliché to Archetype*.[103] His verse and prose were likened by McLuhan to ideograms: "That is the sculp[t]ed item, whether historical, excerpted or invented. These he sets side by side in analogical ratios in accord with Aristotelian principle of metaphor."[104] Pound's drawing on the resources of classical antiquity for his craft in this fashion made him a powerful and attractive model for McLuhan. As for Pound's aesthetic principles, McLuhan noted that they were "pushed to metaphysical intuition of being,"[105] bringing them in line with McLuhan's own emerging thought. To Felix Giovanelli, McLuhan outlined similarities and contrasts between Pound, Lewis, and Eliot.[106]

McLuhan ascribed the neglect of Pound and Lewis and the misunderstanding of Eliot to the inattentive reading habits of the intellectual class and reliance on "four or five catch-all concepts, Freudian, socialist, etc."[107] He reverted, on this note, to his ideal for any educational program: "The appeal must be to the young . . . they have been systematically deprived of all the *linguistic tools* by which they could nourish their own *perceptions* at first hand at the usual traditional sources."[108] But the America that was not ready for *deceptively important*

Pound's ideograms, "because it had chucked out the principle of metaphor and analogy,"[109] was, for the same reason, scarcely ready for McLuhan, either.

Living at St. Michael's gave the McLuhan family the best of the city. With the broad expanse of Queen's Park separating the college from the rest of the University of Toronto campus, it was a particularly pleasant place in summer and offered easy access to attractions such as parades and concerts. Their social life in the university community, especially during term, kept them very busy. McLuhan recorded one event for Elsie's amusement: "Corinne made a big hit with Sidney Smith[110] at the dance. He's a cheerful Rotarian. But Mrs. Smith is a bluenose with a blue heart and ice-cubes in her veins. And she didn't take to it all so heartily . . . Did you hear about Sidney chasing balloons around the floor of the ballroom for Corinne? When he arrived with two for the twins she wailed 'What about Eric?' So Sid plunged back into the melee again! I thought nothing of it, but apparently it caused a sensation among the fathers and the students."[111]

By the fall of 1948, McLuhan had an agreement with Vanguard Press of New York for the publication of "Guide to Chaos," referred to in the contract with the publisher as "The Folklore of Industrial Man," the eventual subtitle of the book. He linked the book to Pound's work, telling him that its exhibits consisted of "popular icons as ideograms of complex implication."[112] Confident about bringing out his book on Eliot as well, he was already planning his next.[113] He wrote to Dorothy Pound, again linking his new project to Pound, this time via the poet's critical work *Guide to Kulchur* (1938).[114] Since McLuhan's would also be a guidebook, "an inventory of breakthroughs in all the arts and sciences,"[115] he referred to it as "a Baedeker," after the well-known series of European guides. Later he would refer to it as "the twentieth-century Baedeker." Much later. For he had no idea how accurately he spoke in saying to Dorothy Pound, "a Baedeker for the university frustrates."[116] Intended for "the kind of people who remain illiterate through the misfortunes of current educational misguidance,"[117] McLuhan's Baedeker never left his thoughts through the years that he gave to exploring media effects as the causes of that illiteracy. By the time those explorations were complete to anything like his satisfaction, more than two decades had passed, and the

Baedeker was still a pile of notes — thousands of pages of notes.

Though he was continuing to publish regularly in *Sewanee Review* and *Renascence*, McLuhan believed other journals were rejecting his work as unfashionable. This acted as a stimulus: "Has the advantage of turning one's attention to basic issues."[118] The long wait for the publication of his book ensured that these basic issues would define themselves as the study of media. For, as McLuhan would tell Wyndham Lewis once *The Mechanical Bride* was in print: "I had lost interest in its approach before it appeared. Now I see that I was try-ing to prop up the standards of book culture when we have passed out of the Gutenberg era."[119] McLuhan's frequent variations on this theme, probes of miscalculated (or uncalculated) effect in his later career, made the notion that he condemned book culture the most widespread of all the misunderstandings surrounding his thought.

As he waited for *The Mechanical Bride* to move through the press, McLuhan was both propping up book culture and bridging the gap to the post-Gutenberg era. He and Hugh Kenner were hatching ideas ranging from literary essays to a book on "Li'l Abner" creator Al Capp.[120] McLuhan felt Kenner had appropriated some pure McLuhan as though it were his own, but the high premium he put on collaboration with valued colleagues allowed him to overlook this, and he anticipated with satisfaction what they could accomplish together.[121] For his part, Kenner was not put off by a slap on the wrist from McLuhan.[122]

There was much consternation in New York, if not outright terror, as McLuhan's manuscript circulated among the staff of Vanguard Press. The work resisted the conventions of book production, defied the resourcefulness and ingenuity of the most benevolent editorial midwifery, and stunned the hapless publisher into inertia. McLuhan may have lost interest in the approach he had taken, but not in getting his book to the public. He began to boil. Giovanelli, well known to the Vanguard people, was on hand in New York, and McLuhan counted on his intervention: "This business is beginning to affect my health. Sheer rage and frustration first declared itself physically at your apartment when I arrived with that 'headache.' A kind of 'heart' condition associated with that same rage and 'headache' occurs whenever I think about [editor] Evelyn [Schrifte].

This can't go on. But they mustn't know. I really depend on you, Felix, to break up this log jam. [The Vanguard editors] would be delighted to think they were affecting my health. I mean that."[123]

AT HOME, MCLUHAN FOUND his children "getting to be more manageable and interesting."[124] They were also getting more numerous. A fourth daughter was born to the McLuhans on 2 August 1950 and christened Elizabeth (in honor of the saint) Anne. By this time, Amy Dunaway had long since returned to England. Corinne had the support and help of many good neighbors and baby-sitters from the ranks of the students. She also had a husband who was always too distracted to hone his domestic skills. Willing to perform such tasks as loading and clearing the washing machine, he minded the "waiting in between."[125] Assigned to kitchen duties, he was capable of washing one dish endlessly — a bit of stage business subordinated to his monologue — unless told to pass it along for drying. For her part, Corinne could not afford self-indulgent behavior or any other luxury. She acquired a reputation as an interesting cook with a great talent for the preparation of economical dishes of meat loaf, beef and lamb stews, and soups of all kinds.[126]

As his children were becoming more interesting, it seemed McLuhan's colleagues were growing more boring. One exception was Ted Carpenter. Meeting Carpenter, from the department of Anthropology, was just what McLuhan needed. Alert, abrasive, and iconoclastic, his energy spilled over. A match for McLuhan's quick wit, Carpenter was ready to join him and steam in the wake of Wyndham Lewis, railing against the bloodless persons and the hollow rituals that passed for life in Toronto. Together they were capable of racing to the most far-flung corners in the empires of the mind. A Carpenter anecdote finds them in their favorite Toronto restaurant over coffee.

"A stranger appeared in the entrance. Even at 50 feet it was obvious he was demented or at best, eccentric. His eyes darted about and under his arm he clutched a great scroll. Spotting us, he strode directly over, pointing a finger and said, 'Just the two I wanted to see.' Then he unrolled the scroll which showed a crudely drawn muscular

monster hurling boulders down on a factory labelled THE INDUS-
TRIAL ESTABLISHMENT. Marshall examined this briefly, blew
smoke from his cigar and said, 'Ah ha! Toronto's William Blake with
a low I.Q.' Clearly the man did not know who William Blake was, but
just as clearly he knew this was no compliment. Rolling up his scroll,
he pointed at Marshall's cigar. 'You put down that cigar. It's the product of mechanization.' 'That cigar,' said Marshall, taking a deep pull
and slowly blowing out the smoke, 'that cigar was handrolled along
the thigh of a Tahitian maiden.'"[127]

While McLuhan and Carpenter became friends for life, McLuhan
and Harold Innis enjoyed a meeting of minds only in the closing years
of the latter's life. Innis, a brilliant theorist who had joined the
University of Toronto's Department of Political Economy in 1920, was
seventeen years McLuhan's senior and a veteran of World War I.[128]
McLuhan was curious to set eyes on a thinker who had not only
endured a quarter century on the University of Toronto campus, but
had prevailed in his unique way.

Motivated, like McLuhan, by dissatisfaction, Innis had rejected the
application of conventional models to the Canadian economy in his
first book, *The Fur Trade in Canada* (1930), in which he developed the
staple theory of economic development. Here already was the link to
media for McLuhan: "The effect of a new staple or natural resource
upon an economy is much the same as the effect of a new medium.
But the sense in which a new medium is a staple depends upon recognizing that media are the technological externalization of our
senses. Such was phonetic writing, such is radio."[129]

Innis, too, had transcended Baptist roots. He had what McLuhan
called "Inniscence,"[130] a lively sense of humor that anchored "his aphoristic association of incongruities."[131] He was, McLuhan pointed out,
baptized prophetically as "Herald Innis."[132] This made him a voice in
the wilderness, and McLuhan saw why: "Harold Innis was never
understood simply because he worked with causality at all times."[133]
McLuhan's insight here was not to prevent him from working with
causality himself, to the point where he could eventually say: "My own
writing has been entirely in the world of formal causality, the study of
effects, rather than the assertion of values. This approach I owe to
Harold Innis and his *Bias of Communication* [1951]."[134]

McLuhan saw not only that Innis was misunderstood, but what he did not understand and why: "[Innis] had no training whatever in the arts, and this was his gross defect."[135] The observation prompted McLuhan to fill Innis in. He regarded Innis's 1950 study *Empire and Communication* as programmatic and told him so, in a letter showing the fundamental links between Innis's work and the framework of thought McLuhan had discovered in Cambridge, developed in his doctoral dissertation, and drawn upon for "Guide to Chaos": "Many of the ancient language theories of the Logos type which you cite for their bearings on government and society have recurred and amalgamated themselves today under the auspices of anthropology and social psychology. Working concepts of 'collective consciousness' in advertising agencies have in turn given salience and practical effectiveness to these 'magical notions of language.'"[136] McLuhan went on to enlighten Innis about the esthetic discoveries of the French symbolists and how their legacy had been nurtured by Joyce, Eliot, Pound, Lewis, and Yeats. But he recognized that, even without the benefit of this knowledge, Innis had "discovered how to arrange his insights in patterns that nearly resemble the art forms of our time."[137]

McLuhan spoke of Innis as "quite confused" and "by no means clear," going so far as to say that he "had not a clue about this kind of dynamic within the materials he was studying."[138] Innis had failed to distinguish mechanical from electronic technologies and had been misled by the consensus of the age. He had, moreover, misread Wyndham Lewis radically.

Yet McLuhan emphasized Innis's genius and his own great debt to him: "Until the work of Harold Innis, I have been unable to discover any epistemology of experience, as opposed to epistemology of knowledge."[139] McLuhan spoke of Innis's "intellectual monopoly of the study of the psychic and social consequences of technological innovation."[140] Pivotal ideas in *The Gutenberg Galaxy*, *Understanding Media*, and even later works McLuhan drew from Innis: "If you look at Harold Innis's *Empire and Communication*, you will see the evidence for the fact that phonetic writing destroyed Greek society without their having the slightest notion of how it happened."[141] When McLuhan moved to a figure-ground approach in his media analysis, he recognized that Innis had been there before him.[142] "I well remember,"

McLuhan said, "my discovery of his idea that print creates national-ism."[143] *My* discovery of *his* idea. McLuhan had not only found a gem but sensed that it was worth cutting and polishing.

He speculated on Innis's place in the development of the broad current of intellectual inquiry referred to as structuralism: "His great insight was that every situation can be studied structurally by asking the question: 'What is the primary stress or action that holds this whole structure in place?' I think he got this approach from Max Weber.[144] Weber had used it for institutions. Innis extended the approach to media. This structural approach tends to dispense with the accidents of 'content.'"[145]

McLuhan also gave Innis the credit for the basis of his own work on the economy of the human sensorium (the relationship among the five physical senses): "My own approach, following Harold Innis, is a transformation theory, thus homeostasis of the perceptual factors in a rapidly changing environment requires much redistribution of empha-sis among the senses. For example, a blind or deaf person compensates for the loss of one sense by a heightening of activity in the others. It seems to me that this also occurs in whole populations when new technologies create new sensory environments [by amputation]."[146]

McLuhan went so far as to set Innis in a pantheon, alongside the unlikely triumvirate of Abraham Lincoln, Henry Thoreau, and Albert Einstein.[147] And he traced a thread from Samuel Taylor Coleridge to Innis that is of particular interest, given the influence of Coleridge on Richards and Richards on McLuhan.[148]

Even Innis's phrase "the nemesis of creativity" ("blindness to the effects of one's most significant form of invention")[149] made its way into McLuhan's work as a chapter heading for *Understanding Media*. Qualities McLuhan identified in the work of Innis are to be found in his own: the expression of insights through aphorisms and a mosaic structure of presentation, expectations that readers will make their own discoveries, an abhorrence of the debilitating effects of the specialist approach to knowledge, a concern with the power of form to alter the action of other forms, the identification of cultural patterns in their psychic and social dimensions on the basis of a society's dominant technology, and, above all, a refusal to present ideas with any concession to the expectations of readers.

"YOU MIGHT MAKE YOUR train of thought plainer," McLuhan's editor suggested. The shock of the "Typhon" manuscript was wearing off at Vanguard Press. There were further suggestions — and complaints: the author should avoid making the reader feel like an imbecile; specialized terminology was going to restrict the audience; some points were stretched so far that the main idea was lost. "You so often attack and criticize 'industrial man,' 'science,' 'mechanical devices,' 'technology' . . . that one wonders what you would have us do?"[150] These comments were aimed at features so deeply ingrained in the manuscript, in McLuhan's style, in his way of thinking, that he was powerless to change them. For the most part, they remained in the final version of the work and, in the end, would raise few complaints among reviewers.

Changes made by his editor raised many complaints from McLuhan. To Ezra Pound, with whom he often took a swashbuckling tone, he said that Vanguard had been "castrating and textbookizing a job which originally was sprightly and not unworthy of Wyndham Lewis to whom it owes much. Publishers['] offices now are crammed with homosexuals who have a horror of any writing with balls to it."[151] To Felix Giovanelli, as weary of the whole business as McLuhan himself, he explained the crux of the difficulty: "[Vanguard Press] do not grasp the fact that this book is written on several levels and presents numerous intelligible facets of numerous items but that it is not intended that all readers possess all of it at any one time of reading. They are obsessed with the old monoplane, monolinear narrative and exposition and conceive of intelligibility as the imposition of a single concept on diverse materials."[152] And book publishing seasons came and went, with no sign of the finished product.

McLuhan rescued himself from disgust and despair over the Vanguard impasse with plans for his biggest project ever: nothing less than orchestrating a merging of the arts. This was the teaching program counterpart to his projected twentieth-century Baedeker. It meant he would have to "learn the grammar and general language of twenty major fields."[153] Sigfried Giedion, author of *Mechanization Takes Command*, was an inspiration. As was Pound, to whom McLuhan wrote: "You and Eisenstein have shown me how to make use of the Chinese ideogram to elicit the natural modes of American sensibility. But I've just begun. Feeling my way."[154] He was feeling his way toward an interdisciplinary seminar.

Alongside Giedion, Pound, and Eisenstein, transcending languages as well as disciplines, the influence of the French symbolist poets[155] and their heirs was coming to the fore: "Have discovered the meaning and value of landscape[156] in this connection. *"Paysage intérieur* à la Rimbaud Pound Joyce as means of unifying and digesting any kind of experience. Should have got it twenty years ago if I hadn't had the rotten luck to bog down in English lit at university."[157] This statement and McLuhan's impulse toward interdisciplinary initiatives do not signal his intent to move beyond literature, for he says at the same time, "I should like to set up a school of literary studies."[158] Such a school would provide training that clarified literature and all art by an understanding of the psychic and social forces of technology: "From the point of view of the artist, the business of art is no longer the communication of thoughts or feelings which are to be conceptually ordered, but a direct participation in an experience. The whole tendency of modern communication whether in the press, in advertising or in the high arts is toward participation in a process, rather than apprehension of concepts. And this major revolution, intimately linked to technology, is one whose consequences have not yet begun to be studied, although they have begun to be felt."[159]

Though a new focus on technology was inevitable, the purpose of it for McLuhan was nothing less than ensuring the survival of literature. Understanding technology was indispensable to the training of artistic sensibilities; the perceptions of artists were equally indispensable in understanding technology.[160] It was a symbiosis Wyndham Lewis had understood and evoked as both writer and painter, a symbiosis McLuhan understood and probed at such length that the public scarcely learned of the twin to his work as media analyst: a program in literary training.

MCLUHAN BEGAN HIS SIXTH year of teaching at the University of Toronto in September 1951. The family had moved from St. Joseph Street to a larger house on the St. Michael's campus, at 81 St. Mary's Street. It pleased McLuhan that the number was divisible by three. He had acquired a half-interest in a sailboat and hoped soon to own it outright.[161] He now had over thirty publications to his credit, ranging over Chesterton, Keats, Herbert, Poe, Eliot, Kipling, Forster, Hopkins, Shakespeare, Pound, Dos Passos, Joyce, and Tennyson. An impressive array of articles, but no book. He dared to allow himself a touch of optimism in the matter, announcing to Pound as imminent the release of what he was now calling "my Folklore of Industrial Man."[162]

When McLuhan's first book finally appeared that fall, it bore a title inspired by that of a painting — Marcel Duchamp's *The Bride Stripped Bare by Her Bachelors, Even*. If the painting was as little known to the average reader as the mythical figure of Typhon, it was nonetheless important for McLuhan to evoke a visual artist's sensitivity to invisible environments of the type examined in *The Mechanical Bride*. Years later, he summarized the work by saying "*The Mechanical Bride* is really concerned with the decimation of sex by simple fragmentation or mechanization."[163] To say so is to practice a simple fragmentation of the rich diversity of the book.

"Morticians and Cosmeticians," McLuhan's peppery indictment of the funeral business published in the *Manitoban* on 2 March 1934, anticipated *The Mechanical Bride* by seventeen years.[164] Though McLuhan disavowed a stance of moral indignation over manipulative advertising practices in the book's preface, some commentators have been able to detect one, by contrast to his later writings.[165] McLuhan not only continued to deny any outrage on his part but tied his method of analyzing media to the necessity of *refusing* to be outraged.[166] If such a denial was possible after the publication of *The Mechanical Bride*, it would have been impossible in 1934. Reviewers of the book would have found little indignation in it by comparison with the *Manitoban* article.

Comic strips engage a large part of McLuhan's attention in the book, less as examples of what he would later dub a *cool medium* than as a mirror of popular culture. Comics also fit McLuhan's educational program, because they have "been seen as a degenerate literary form instead of as a nascent and dramatic pictorial form which has sprung from the new stress on visual-auditory communication in the magazines, the radio and television. The young today cannot follow narrative, but they are alert to drama. They cannot bear description but they love landscape and action."[167] Whether he is condemning or praising the world of comics, McLuhan's purpose is to create awareness of its biases, the models it uses, and the values it perpetuates.

McLuhan interprets "Little Orphan Annie" as the American success story with a psychological twist: the drive to succeed by both pleasing parents *and* outdoing them; Annie as orphan by choice. The isolation and helplessness of her situation are potentially frightening, but they are offset by Annie's innocence and goodness — to say nothing of the campaign she wages so successfully against incompetence, interference, stupidity, and evil.

In the adventures of Superman, McLuhan sees a hybrid of science fiction and drama portraying the psychological defeat of technological man. Though Superman is always assured of victory through sheer force, he is nothing but the alter ego of the ineffectual and downtrodden Clark Kent, simply a wish fulfillment in a man whose personality holds the key to the real significance of the strip for McLuhan. Clark Kent embodies society's reaction to the pressures created by technological advances, the rejection of due process of law, the recourse to violence.

Tarzan, like Superman, has an alter ego in the person of Lord Greystoke. But by contrast with the vilified Clark Kent, Greystoke is what McLuhan calls "the unreconstructed survivor of the wreck of feudalism."[168] The contrast between noble savage and civilized man does not apply to him; he is an aristocrat who renounced the trappings of society for life in the jungle. Greystoke represents a fusion for McLuhan of the ideals of the YMCA, Rudyard Kipling, and Sir Robert Baden-Powell.

McLuhan remains as thoroughly irritated by "Blondie" in *The Mechanical Bride* as he had been in the pages of *Columbia*, because the strip is pure formula and cliché. Dagwood, a frustrated victim trapped in suburban life, gets little respect or sympathy from his children and none from McLuhan. Where readers might find Dagwood's snacking comical, McLuhan finds it contemptible: "promiscuous gormandizing as a basic dramatic symbol of the abused and the insecure."[169] This psychological evaluation of Dagwood is rounded out in terms that revert to *The Mechanical Bride*'s emphasis on society's values. McLuhan explains that, unlike the character of Jiggs ("Bringing Up

Father"), who belongs to the first generation to realize the American dream, Dagwood is second generation and lacking the competitiveness that assured his father's success. McLuhan's speculation that the "Blondie" strip would survive into an age alien to it, in all respects but Dagwood's somnambulism, is borne out nearly fifty years later.

To McLuhan's satisfaction, Dagwood's world of repetitive and inescapable dilemma is offset by the delightful predicaments in the Dogpatch of Al Capp's "Li'l Abner." Satirical, ironic, and free of shallow sentimentality, Capp's strip works toward the same purpose as McLuhan himself — the development of sharpened perception. Just as McLuhan approaches his objective by the use of the mosaic technique (multiple points of view), Capp fashions Li'l Abner himself from a mosaic of hero images. For McLuhan, the real hero is Capp, seeking endlessly to expose the delusions and illusions foisted on society by politicians, business, and the media. McLuhan made no prediction for the future of Al Capp's strip, and unlike "Blondie," "Li'l Abner" has not survived, confirming McLuhan's observation that society prefers somnambulism to awareness.

"Guide to Chaos" lost some of its force in the transition to *The Mechanical Bride*. Much of the earlier version was cut altogether. Despite the retention of the key phrases "know-how" and "man of distinction" as titles for exhibits in the book, the following passage appears only in the original draft: "Know-how and technology isolate man at work and play just as much as a big city and unemployment do. But this fact is also the basic condition of science. A scientific experiment has to be carefully isolated from normal conditions. And the success formula certainly sets you apart. A man of distinction. Sing Sing or a padded cell couldn't be more effective in this respect. By making each cell (home, hotel, blonde, car) in the world exactly alike, technological man manages to create the illusion of being at home everywhere and with everybody. At the same time he has created a bright and salubrious hell from which, as Sartre noted, there is 'No Exit.'"[170]

The passage repays attention with rewards beyond those of routine manuscript exhumation. The comment on the requisite of scientific experimentation is a succinct statement of why McLuhan chose the analogical and integrating techniques of classical learning over the logical and isolating techniques of modern science. As for the reference to technological man's illusion of being at home everywhere and with everybody, it anticipates much more than McLuhan's later pronouncements on the global village and the retribalization of the West. Twenty years after *The Mechanical Bride* was published, McLuhan would grow even more concerned and speak more forcefully of electronic technology turning that illusion into the reality of discarnate mankind, at home nowhere and sustained by no illusion.

McLuhan collected and carefully filed dozens of reviews of *The Mechanical Bride*.[171] According to one, he had buried a good idea under "tons of rich and purple baloney."[172] Another observed that McLuhan had used "the same razzle-dazzle technique in his presentation that the admen themselves have mastered with such advantage."[173] One reviewer called McLuhan's critiques "full-blooded thumps" and pronounced the work a "significant social document."[174] The *New York Times* found the book full of righteous anger, nearly as solemn as Nazi propaganda, and regretted its lack of humor.[175] Closer to home, the *Globe and Mail* said, "It requires merely a glance at four or five pages of *The Mechanical Bride* to cause us to nominate it for the Stephen Leacock prize for humor."[176] The *New York Herald Tribune* objected to McLuhan's excessive use of bold metaphors "because they seem smart alecky."[177] The reviewer for *The New Republic* recoiled from "the author's predilection for positively bloodcurdling puns,"[178] while *Advertising and Selling*, the organ of the vested interests whose manipulations McLuhan unveiled, greeted the whole production as "an Arabian Nights entertainment which opens the door on a new world of popular culture and mythology."[179] Walter Ong's review was the only one to offer a detailed analysis and, as far as McLuhan was concerned, the only one that made sense.[180]

With *The Mechanical Bride* selling slowly but widely read, McLuhan tried on the vantage point of the average reader and asked himself what type of book it was. He decided it was science fiction with comic strips and ads cast as characters.[181] Since his aim was, as he noted, not to prove anything but to demonstrate the community in action, this made the work a new type of novel: "But if I were writing another, it would be easy to arrange the ads according to themes and patterns of novel type."[182] This sequel took shape nearly twenty years later in

Culture Is Our Business, a work marked both by transition and continuity in relation to *The Mechanical Bride*. Though he had learned the
lesson much earlier, McLuhan noted only when the latter work
appeared that there was no ready-made audience for either book: "In
Culture Is Our Business and *The Mechanical Bride* I was not writing for
the fans of anything at all. I was looking at a world which was accepted
somnambulistically by its occupants and perpetrators."[183]

McLuhan took up the question of somnambulism with Pound.
Calling words the "cheapest and most universal drug,"[184] he asked the
poet how language could be used to combat its own diseased state, to
undo the trance induced by print. Finding McLuhan "pleasantly
coherent,"[185] Pound responded in kind, suggesting to him that he
become a one-man orthological police force, "selecting ten or a dozen
words and smacking public swine whenever any of these terms is
flagrantly distorted."[186] Even if he found the idea useful, McLuhan
was unable to follow up on it for lack of time; with *The Mechanical
Bride* behind him, he added yet another title to the list of books he
planned to write: "The End of the Gutenberg Era." His study of
media was now emerging distinctly along lines he had described to
Pound.[187] When McLuhan announced this as a priority, Pound was
unimpressed, noting simply "Nuts."[188]

Pound might have been tempted to make the same response when
McLuhan announced his year-long investigation of secret societies.[189]
It had begun with a query to Pound that seemed tongue-in-cheek.
Observing that Pound shared with Eliot and Joyce "a central guide in
all matters of letters, sounds, phrases, situations,"[190] McLuhan asked:
"Is there some secret cult knowledge in these matters? Masonic?
Something no critic should know?"[191]

The questions scarcely deserved a reply, for clearly McLuhan himself, as critic and teacher, possessed the key to the "secret cult
knowledge" shared by poets,[192] their skill in controlling the medium
of language for noble purposes. He had used that key in *The
Mechanical Bride* to expose those who exercised control over language
for baser purposes. There was no secret, other than the technique of
constantly renewing perception of language as a medium, as an environment, and refusing to allow its effects to remain invisible.

Pound might have been surprised, therefore, when McLuhan

persisted in speaking of secret societies. He seemed intent on refusing to allow them to remain invisible.[193] (The same organizations, he suspected, were conspiring to keep *him* invisible.) But Pound's situation made him receptive to McLuhan's views on unseen forces and the theatrical pronouncement that "McLuhan is banned. No mag will publish me."[194]

It was to Pound that he had first voiced a milder version of the complaint, and now he told him that "after five years of miserable health I am suddenly recovered and full of energy again. It was a gall bladder condition. Not serious. Just debilitating."[195] His renewed energy was channeled into less galling tasks than sleuthing after Masons, a phase of McLuhan's research that had apparently been serious, but not debilitating.

Expecting her sixth child, Corinne hoped for a boy to balance the family. When the doctor quietly confided to her that it would be a girl, she consoled herself with the thought that she enjoyed having daughters. A baby boy was born to the McLuhans on 19 October 1952. Neighbors told Corinne that Eric went up and down the street explaining that it was a boy and how this had happened. A nurse came into Corinne's room the next day and asked, "Why were you grinning all night?"[196] The second McLuhan son was christened Michael (in honor of the saint) Charles (after his grandfather Lewis). The McLuhan family was complete.[197]

9

A Beachhead in Toronto

I should prefer the States for personal reasons. But my
work is in Toronto. It's to be a fight all the way. But I'm made
for that.

–MARSHALL MCLUHAN TO ELSIE MCLUHAN, 1946

"LIVING UP HERE IN CANADA I have got so out of touch with people that
I have even lost the desire to communicate."[1] So said McLuhan to
Walter Ong in the spring of 1953. The comment was not very accurate. He had been traveling to conferences and taking speaking
engagements. He had many faithful correspondents and was faithful
in replying to them. At St. Michael's, contacts were less satisfying:
"I find few I can talk to among Catholics. Fewer and fewer too.
Educationally we have made a great blunder in dispersing talent
instead of concentrating it."[2] But when McLuhan made his jaded
remark to Ong, he had already received an exceptionally good piece
of news that meant excellent prospects not only for satisfying personal
communication but for seeing his vision of educational reform
become a reality.

The intellectual excitement of endless dialogue between McLuhan
and Carpenter had crystallized into a tangible project with their success
in obtaining a grant from the Ford Foundation.[3] University of Toronto
president Sidney Smith wrote to McLuhan immediately upon learning
the news, noting with satisfaction: "This grant of theirs, as far as I know,
is the first investment that they have made in Canadian scholarship."[4] It

was the Ford grant that permitted McLuhan and Carpenter to launch their interdepartmental seminar in culture and communications in 1953, and subsequently the journal *Explorations*. The Ford Foundation money made provision for offering scholarships to graduate students wishing to do a doctorate on any aspect of communication studies.

The momentum generated by the seminar and the results of its investigations eventually led, eleven years later, to the establishment of the Centre for Culture and Technology at the University of Toronto. It was to the seminar, and not to himself, that McLuhan attributed the crucial discovery that media are extensions of the human body and of the nervous system.

When he came to write a historical account of the seminar, McLuhan characterized it as the continuation of the pioneering work of Harold Innis, thanks to whom "the University of Toronto has established a unique beach-head in the study of social change."[5] It is an illuminating account, limning Innis's discovery of the shaping power of technologies in psychic sensibility and social organization and linking it to a view put forward by Samuel Butler in the nineteenth century, in which culture and technology are described as organically related self-modifying systems.

When the seminar group met for the first time in June 1953, McLuhan and Carpenter were joined by Carl Williams from Psychology, Tom Easterbrook of Economics — both old friends from Winnipeg days — and Jacqueline Tyrwhitt from the School of Architecture, about whom Sigfried Giedion had written to McLuhan.[6] Williams, though the only representative of the hard sciences among them, nevertheless had a special interest in the influence of media of communication on personality and social structure. As a psychologist, he was keen to examine the effects of new forms of perception and learning. In this respect, his interest converged with Carpenter's investigations into speech, behavioral response, and the concept of self as affected by media; his interest also resonated richly with McLuhan's Cambridge heritage. Easterbrook, as an economic historian, provided a direct link to the work of Innis, who had died the year before. Tyrwhitt, a pioneer of interdisciplinary studies in Britain, had come to the University of Toronto to foster cooperation among the departments of Economics, Political Science, Sociology, Social Work,

Anthropology, and Architecture. Her participation in the seminar was virtually mandatory, all the more so because of her interest in the city as a privileged site for special modes of communication.

The five met throughout the summer and early autumn of 1953, exploring the connections among their fields and special interests. From the survey each presented to launch discussion, parallel developments among their disciplines soon emerged, particularly in methods and points of view. This encouraged the group to hope that a unified perspective on the cultural impact of mass media would soon be within their grasp. They discussed the mechanics of the work ahead, such as selection of graduate students and techniques of investigation to be used. These quickly revealed the unique dynamics of the group. Williams had a strong preference for statistical method and was supported in this by Easterbrook and Tyrwhitt. McLuhan, preferring intuitive procedures, was backed by Carpenter, but not without support from Tyrwhitt. As an economic historian, Easterbrook's slant was not exclusively quantitative; as an expert in the visual arts, Tyrwhitt did not opt for statistical analysis alone. A healthy balance prevailed.

Word spread across campus that something interesting was in the wind. Graduate students volunteered as seminar candidates from the start. Once the project was underway, requests to participate poured in. The publication of *Explorations*, beginning in December 1953, was giving the seminar a high profile. Part of the Ford Foundation grant was used to start up the magazine. It was Carpenter's pet project. He threw himself into the editing, printing, and distribution so energetically that no support staff was required. The publication cut across the social sciences and humanities, reflecting the spirit of the seminar by treating all disciplines as a continuum. The promotional flyer noted that *Explorations* was "not designed as a permanent reference journal that embalms truth for posterity, but as a journal that explores and searches and questions."[7] The first issue included "Culture without Literacy" by McLuhan and "Nursery Rhymes" by Northrop Frye.

It soon became impossible to meet the demand for the magazine. With print runs limited to a thousand copies for all but the second number, thousands of orders remained unfilled. *Explorations* was snapped up so quickly by the curious at the University of Toronto that few copies remained for wider distribution. *Explorations* was published three times a year for the two years that the interdisciplinary seminar operated under the Ford Foundation grant. Encouraged by the interest the journal generated, McLuhan later obtained funding to produce three more issues from the Toronto *Telegram* publisher, John Bassett, between 1956 and 1959. In 1964, *Explorations* was revived as a sixteen-page insert in the University of Toronto's *Varsity Graduate* magazine for alumni and survived in that format into the 1970s.

By the fall of 1953, a report of the intellectual vitality of the seminar had already reached Claude Bissell, then vice-president of the university. He offered the use of his private office as a meeting place for the group. The term got under way with discussions on the writings of Innis. By now, a dozen graduate students from the departments of Psychology, Anthropology, Sociology, Economics, and English had joined the faculty fivesome, who set them the task of writing papers on all aspects of Innis's work. The anthropologists examined the nature of communication in preliterate societies, and the economists dealt with the communication role of money in both pre-market and market economies, while the literary specialists focused on the sensory bias of media and the social consequences. An important new dimension to the understanding of communication came from the psychologists, with their concept of acoustic or auditory space. The resulting discussions quickly showed the strengths and weaknesses of Innis's ideas. The seminar was already functioning to organize ignorance for discovery.

It was also revealing something about learning environments. McLuhan detected a typical reaction in the group on the part of both students and faculty whenever a breakthrough was achieved: "They rally to resist the unexpected light from an alien source."[8] Commenting on this tendency, he took the opportunity to decry the fragmenting specialization the members of the group were seeking to transcend.[9]

Any upheavals within the group were dwarfed by reaction from without. The success of *Explorations* enhanced interest. A trickle of copies to the Toronto establishment was enough to provoke animosity and criticism. The discussion of radio, movies, and television as culture brought the deepest suspicion of low motives on McLuhan and his group. The custodians of the humanities aligned themselves against the work that appeared in *Explorations* and everything the seminar stood for, resisting the basic premise of the need to translate and adapt centuries of civilized inheritance into modes suited to a new technological culture.[10] Only the force of argument from history made a small inroad.

Unfazed — perhaps quietly delighted and certainly stimulated — by opposition, the seminar moved headlong to new discoveries. Discussions revealed the bias of the book, its power to separate readers from both oral communication and the visual arts, to promote the notion of concept as opposed to form.[11] The informing influence of the printed page on music, painting, poetry, and drama, the contrast between European and North American culture, Gutenberg's movable type as prototype of assembly lines in the industrial age, all emerged from the seminar. *The Gutenberg Galaxy* and *Understanding Media* were in the making.

Discoveries followed from each other. When the seminar turned its attention from new media altering the culture of the day to the earlier media that had shaped it, a marked contrast emerged. The report issued at the end of two years' work in the seminar stressed the contrast: "The new media constituted an orchestra of effects, compared to the earlier cultures based on solo media. What had begun as the mechanization of writing [through print] had become the mechanization of an economy and of the human sensorium."[12]

The seminar's report twined the sweep of history and the evolution of technology with a dramatic flourish: "With television both sight and sound were out of the wire and our culture stepped free of mechanization for the first time since the invention of writing, 5,000 years ago."[13] It also sounded a warning: "The reason we are so privileged yet so confused today is, from this point of view, that there are no historical or even archaeological precedents for our state. If we are now beyond mechanization, we are also in a sense beyond history. We have stepped over all those familiar 'lines of development' which we have so long accepted as historical and cultural guides."[14]

Notions from even the latest of McLuhan's writings can be traced to the earliest days of the seminar. So, for example, the idea of technologies as words, emphasized in *Laws of Media*, was in the air by

1955: "One way of stating our condition is to say that in the electronic age our entire technology has achieved the freedom and flexibility that had formerly been available only in the verbal universe. The metaphoric parallels and discontinuities — parataxis and syntaxis — by which mankind had first learned to structure acoustic space and create a subtle world of oral and interpersonal relations is now possible visually and spatially as well."[15]

Although a certain antipathy toward the seminar came from the Canadian Broadcasting Corporation, it was with the CBC's help that a four-media experiment was conducted in the spring of 1954. More than one hundred second-year university students participated to determine the effect of receiving the same lecture material via live lecturer, television, radio, and print. The students were divided into four groups to form audiences for a lecture delivered live to one and simultaneously relayed to two others via radio and television, while the fourth group read the text delivered by the lecturer. When tested on the material, the students in the television audience scored highest, regardless of their level of previously measured academic ability. Moreover, television apparently had its greatest effect on the strongest students. Radio emerged as the second-most effective medium for conveying information and silent reading the least effective. (Mixed results on testing of the studio audience reflected the distractions and excitement of the studio itself.) Published in *Explorations*, the results caused enough stir to be reported in the *New York Times*. If there were skeptics, they might have been satisfied when follow-up testing after six months yielded similar results both in Toronto and in further tests at Princeton and elsewhere.

The seminar gave much attention to the work of Sigfried Giedion, whose work, like Innis's, was a pioneering effort at unifying separate disciplines. In Giedion's case, this synthesis was achieved by promoting techniques of attention to the language of vision inherent in painting, technology, and architecture. Tyrwhitt, a former associate of Giedion, gave the group invaluable guidance. Once again they were challenged to interact to their mutual benefit: "The Innis verbal approach to many of Giedion's interests was for her as hard to master as the Giedion language of vision was for the rest of us. Our psychologists and anthropologists soon caught the idea and enriched our insights with many new materials and procedures."[16]

In its second year of operation, the seminar carried over only one graduate student and took on eight new ones, as well as three guest members. But fresh projects were launched, involving in one instance eight hundred students from the Ryerson Polytechnic Institute enlisted to investigate visual awareness and communication. This study formed the basis of "The City Unseen" in *Explorations V*.

Encouraged by the initial grant from the Ford Foundation and subsequent discussions with its representatives, McLuhan broached the subject of funding for a permanent center to carry on the work of the seminar.[17] This initiative proved unsuccessful.[18] Nearly a decade would go by before the idea bore fruit.

JACK BIRT HAD LOST touch with McLuhan. They had known each other in undergraduate days in Winnipeg, when Birt was editor of the *Manitoban*. He came to Toronto to take up duties as editor of *The Imperial Oil Review*, not knowing he would meet McLuhan again. In the fall of 1953, Birt moved into an apartment in a converted duplex on the north side of St. Mary's Street. Across the road, the yellow brick wall of St. Michael's College playing field stretched to the western end of the street, stopping beside the only house on the south side — number 81. This situation allowed McLuhan to boast with a measure of truth that his family was installed in a large house with two acres of land in downtown Toronto.[19]

Living on the same block, it was inevitable that Birt and McLuhan would meet and pick up their acquaintance where they had left off at the University of Manitoba. They often found themselves walking in the same direction and enjoyed long talks, but otherwise had little contact until McLuhan telephoned Birt one evening.

"Jack, you have a television set, haven't you?"[20] he asked. He did indeed, though it was well before the days when most homes had TV. "Could I come over tomorrow evening and see the set? And would you mind if I bring Mother along? I'm going to be on television for the first time."[21]

Birt was very pleased to invite the McLuhans, mother and son, to the extraordinary premiere. He had met Elsie in Winnipeg and regarded her as "a definite and entertaining personality" of considerable charm.[22]

She reminded Birt of actress Rosalind Russell. He remembered her long, flowing dresses, the chiffon scarf she often carried, her elocutionist's expressive tones and waves of the scarf in wide gestures to emphasize her very positive ideas.

The McLuhans arrived on schedule. Birt turned on the TV and the threesome huddled expectantly. Within a few moments, the program, a panel discussion, began. The moderator introduced the regular panelists and then said a few words about guest panelist Marshall McLuhan. On the screen, McLuhan looked his usual self, except that he appeared to be a bit shy and nervous. The other speakers carried most of the discussion. When McLuhan's turn came, he appeared to be acquitting himself creditably, though it was difficult to hear most of what he had to say.

Elsie looked at him in close-up and burst out: "Marshall, you look dreadful! Oh Marshall, why didn't you have your hair cut?" A shot from another camera and "Oh Marshall, your hair's just terrible!"[23] Almost before they realized it, the historic debut of the man who would explain television was over. The main message about the medium that evening came from his mother.

McLuhan was enjoying his newly reopened correspondence with the ogre of Bloomsbury, reincarnated as the ogre of Notting Hill, which he had already immortalized as "Rotting Hill."[24] The end of Lewis's eight-year silence came, by chance, in 1953, the same year that McLuhan published "Wyndham Lewis: His Theory of Art and Communication" in *Shenandoah*, an essay that earned his subject's seal of approval. Lewis's latest novel, *Self Condemned*, was in press, and McLuhan wrote to tell him he had ordered his copy, noting that "Toronto has been alerted and has begun to tremble."[25] Lewis having been a source of his views on "freemasonry of the arts,"[26] McLuhan welcomed the opportunity to linger with him over a topic he had exhausted in his exchange with Pound. In concert with the appearance of Lewis's novel, McLuhan published a seventeen-page pamphlet titled *Counterblast*, which would be reissued in expanded form as a book in 1969.

McLuhan's tone as he explored the mind-numbing effects of advertising in *The Mechanical Bride* had been whimsical rather than judgmental. By way of explanation, his introduction noted that "the time for anger and protest is in the early stages of a new process. The present stage is extremely advanced. Moreover, it is full, not only of destructiveness, but also of promises of rich new developments to which moral indignation is a very poor guide."[27] The paradox of creative and destructive changes issuing from the same social forces had also been noted by Lewis, though he took a high moral tone that repelled McLuhan and served him as a model to avoid in *The Mechanical Bride*. But Lewis also gave McLuhan an attractive model in his 1914 periodical, *Blast*.

Lewis's title was a complex pun, derived from the technical term *blastoderm* in embryology, echoing the name of the then current art magazine *Germ*, and foreshadowing World War I, which broke out only a few weeks after its appearance. When Lewis published *Self Condemned* in 1954, he was still blasting — this time at the Toronto that McLuhan found so stultifying. The combined appeal of Lewis's publications, spanning forty years, inspired McLuhan to produce his *Counterblast*. He noted at the beginning of the book that "the term *Counterblast* does not imply any attempt to erode or explode *Blast*. Rather it indicates the need for a counter-environment as a means of perceiving the dominant one."[28]

THE ECHOES FROM MCLUHAN'S depth charges might not have reached as far as Lewis's "Momaco";[29] echoes from the students he was teaching at St. Michael's at this time did reach him years later: "I suppose the most familiar picture I have of you is your entrance into the English seminar room at 46 Queen's Park Crescent, a huge pile of books in your arms, to begin a class in the Pound/Joyce/Yeats/Eliot course. There were no notes to guide the hour, yet by its end you had 'dipped into' (a favourite expression that always brings you to mind) most of the pile on the table, and the talk rounded itself off apparently without effort . . . We all partook of your homelife on evenings of records and discussion when you were living on campus . . . We browsed among your bookshelves and drank beer from your fridge on those nights when we babysat for you and Mrs. McLuhan."[30]

Elsie was working on a theater production in New Jersey, in spite of declining health. Corinne and Marshall went to see her and found her seriously ill. She realized her career would have to come to an end and returned to Toronto. The McLuhans arranged for her to live nearby on St. Mary's Street in a private home. She took her meals with her son and his family. When the McLuhans moved house, they found quarters for Elsie next door to their new location, where she lived until she suffered a stroke, moving then to Our Lady of Mercy Hospital for the last five years of her life.

After more than nine years of living on the St. Michael's campus, the McLuhans moved to a comfortable Tudor-style house on quiet, tree-lined Wells Hill Avenue in central Toronto, about a mile and a half from the university campus. The neighborhood, largely unchanged for years before the McLuhans took up residence, or since, is dominated by the castle known as Casa Loma. Built between 1911 and 1914 by industrialist Sir Henry Pellatt as a private residence, Casa Loma dominates the brow of a steep hill, with its soaring towers visible for miles to the south, beggaring the phrase "eccentric stone mansion," saluting the ghost of Britain's glory with a flourish that might have left even Wyndham Lewis speechless. But the McLuhans were not living in baronial splendor at 29 Wells Hill. With six children between the ages of thirteen and three, on a salary that had driven some of his friends out of university teaching, McLuhan was concerned constantly about providing for his family. It was at this time that he got the idea for Idea Consultants — a company for the development, processing, and promotion of schemes and dreams.

A partnership contract for Idea Consultants was signed on 31 March 1956 by the McLuhans and their friends Corinne and William Hagon and Murray Paulin.[31] It was a natural for the mill of McLuhan's mind and, though intended as a business venture, often clearly related to his thoughts on media. A brief on Idea Consultants stationery from McLuhan's own hand went to the Royal Commission on Patents, Copyrights, Trade Marks and Industrial Design, outlining a new solution to the problem of patents in relation to the community of consumers. His approach was developed in terms of recent communications study and research and quickly turned into a lecture on the McLuhan theme of effects, replete with analytical tangents: "The artist himself is now habituated to regarding himself as part of the audience in his own art."[32]

Very soon the little firm with big ideas, originating in house or developed on behalf of clients, was trying them out on financial backers, entrepreneurs, ad agencies, and corporations. There were ideas for products, for services, for promotion, for methods and techniques in a bewildering variety of fields: a colony for hay fever sufferers, illuminated panels for use on public transit flashing up the name of the next stop together with a sponsor's name, television platters (videocassettes twenty years ahead of their time), a column of children's sayings for newspaper publication, vocational guidance.[33]

Sounding already like the McLuhan who would baffle television interviewers a decade later, he lectured the vice-president of Colgate Palmolive by letter: "We are today very close to a new era in relating the consumer to production and distribution . . . The more teamwork cuts out the individual the more the individual is going to demand and find expression and satisfaction. This is one reason for the public interest in individualist efforts such as those put on by the contestants in the $64,000-question type of show."[34] Idea Consultants were in business to make money, but here was the firm's head giving away vintage McLuhan as fine as a '28 Bordeaux: "I am citing here a basic *principle of reversal* which is effective in every type of operation. As human skill perfects and develops the possibilities in any given process or organization it guarantees the emergence of a new situation with opposite characteristics. Thus the age of automation is going to be the age of Do-It-Yourself."[35]

The ideas kept coming: a project for a television program featuring collective problem-solving by mass audience participation, bandages on an adhesive-tape style dispenser ("Peel-Aid"), soap, shampoo, and lotions in single-use, disposable foil capsules, talking letters (via an electronic unit to record and play back personal messages on a plastic record), a promotional device for displaying *Life* magazine material. (Was this publication not excoriated in *The Mechanical Bride*? Yes, but the public needed to be encouraged and educated in recognizing the high-quality art to be found in so much advertising.) McLuhan's infectious enthusiasm touched Bernie Muller-Thym, now a management consultant in New York: "I also have the feeling Idea Consultants is going to make a real breakthrough."[36]

When *Life* turned down the promotional display device, McLuhan sent it immediately to *Holiday* magazine, only to be told that it had been suggested many times over the years. An inconsequential rejection. No setback at all. If the world did not like McLuhan's ideas, he had plenty more. He fired off a suggestion for a small lunchtime carton for brewery products to the J. Walter Thompson Agency, who rejected it as "impractical."[37] McLuhan was not ready to let go of this idea, but switched over from campaigning for cartons to boosting the brew: "It is the view of Idea Consultants that the breweries have stressed unduly the importance of the working man as the main consumer of beer."[38] He conceived promotions featuring professionals: "'What is the dentist's view of beer?' 'Clean bill,' he will say. None of the objections to soft drinks obtain with beer."[39]

Brainstorming continued. McLuhan and Hagon were joined by artist and designer Harley Parker. They met to discuss writing a series of articles about marketing. For openers, they agreed that the phonoscope (a device for displaying properties of sound visually) restores the bazaar, and someone quickly noted that there were filing cabinets on the beaches on D-Day. Media are staples, Hagon pointed out, and McLuhan interjected that media need to be explained to the reader. Anything that alters the time factor in information flow, as well as the space factor, alters conditions of economic growth. This could be illustrated casually from the telephone to the telegraph: 1,200 words; six double-spaced pages. There was the question of touch-smell deficiencies. Parker explained to Hagon why TV is tactile. It was basic to show confusion, and they had the answers. McLuhan tossed off the notion of military products for enemy consumption for export. Spying for enemy consumption, Parker added. Staples create homogeneity. It had happened in the Canadian wheat belt. McLuhan made a note to bone up on staples but had a take on the subject already. New media, common terror, we will all be "stapled." If you push the instruments of war far enough you prevent war. Three or four articles would be required. On press, print, pricing, the tactility of tapestry, manuscript, and television. They identified four types of invention — physical, social, method, and artistic.[40]

The first three types, at least, kept flowing from Idea Consultants: overhead garage doors activated by the weight of a vehicle passing over a release bar, aluminum soft drink containers, semi-liquid soap in toothpaste-style containers for travelers, frozen diet dinners, temporary inner walls for soundproofing, tape recordings for tourists, a transparent training potty to eliminate the lift-and-check problem, a motor-powered pencil-sharpener, a muffler attachment (hose) allowing exhaust fumes to be used for killing rodents in their burrows, lawn-mower headlights, airborne gift packages (promotional samples released by balloon), modular monsters (toys) in cereal and soap boxes, and "3D fireplaces" — videocassettes of hearths, campfires, etc.[41] As for artistic inventions, pure creations of the mind and for the mind, they were McLuhan's strength. He generated them unstoppably, long after Idea Consultants had taken up a lot of time without meeting the group's early hopes for extra income, without producing much more than a letterhead.

"Is there any common basis for conversation between you (totally unknown to me) and McL/who seems headed toward aridity and discussion of safe topics?"[42] It was Ezra Pound putting the question to Ted Carpenter in the year of Sputnik. The poet had become a difficult correspondent, threatening not to answer McLuhan's letters unless he took out a subscription to Pound's favorite new publication, *Edge*. Exactly what he was referring to as "aridity and discussion of safe topics" he did not say, but McLuhan's cresting enthusiasm over media studies in 1957 and Pound's lack of it from the start make for an easy guess. McLuhan reserved his enthusiasm for other correspondents, such as Walter Ong: "The media issue concerns every minute of every teacher's day. Every problem of every catechist and liturgist . . . But how does one talk about these things in a society which hasn't got a clue about print after 500 years? The Church has more at stake than anybody. Should set up an institute of Perennial Contemporaryness!"[43] These topics were not as safe as Pound thought.

McLuhan had an idea for easing the tensions of the Cold War with "cool media" (though the latter phrase had still to appear in his work). Writing to no one in particular, he and Lou Forsdale put their ideas on paper for a Broadway show on the theme of American-Russian relations: "The idea is to develop a comic presentation of a situation in which the United States would simply throw open its doors to the Russian governing powers, inviting them to come to the USA, revise and improve our whole mode of existence with a view to making the whole world a more livable place for Russians and anybody else. This gesture would emerge from a brainstorming session in which the chiefs of the American state would be subjected to the full Madison Avenue treatment to develop 'creative solutions' to current world tension. A Broadway musical would seem to be the natural form, but it is perfectly obvious that Hollywood or straight theater or other literary treatment could be used."[44]

The key to developing the plot would be McLuhan's cherished "discovery procedure": as the Russians and Americans met, they would learn and assimilate each other's habits, customs, and art forms. The process of cultural exchange would take place through bartering activities, with the Russians offering to trade Sputnik for Marilyn Monroe or Lily St. Cyr (with a play on "sincere"). In Las Vegas the Russians would learn the value of undraped figures and dropping curtains, including the Iron Curtain. By the end of the show, both peoples would understand that they had much to learn from each other, but that they could not run each other's lives. McLuhan saw the whole production as both deeply playful and a serious attempt to help resolve the extreme tensions between the United States and Russia.

Two years after drafting his first thoughts on the matter with Forsdale, he was still keen to see it come to the stage. The play would be a lesson in media as much as a contribution to international diplomacy: "Basic, however, is the fact that the East is going West, and the West is going East. All the thrills and surprises of the musical will arise from this dynamic."[45] The idea was rejected by the Madison Avenue firm of MCA Artists in January 1961 as unmarketable. Fourteen years later, when Stephanie McLuhan brought the big Broadway hit *A Chorus Line* to her father's attention, it rekindled his old dream of writing a media play.[46] By then, McLuhan had too many unfinished projects in hand to think seriously about one that had scarcely been started. The world was not to know Marshall McLuhan as the librettist of an East-side/West-side story. But when he first pondered his musical therapy for international tensions he was already saying that "the globe becomes a very small village-like affair"[47] — a phrase that soon accompanied him to the world stage.

FROM MCLUHAN'S WRITINGS, *Bartlett's Familiar Quotations* records "The new electronic interdependence recreates the world in the image of a global village" and "The medium is the message." According to the CBC, McLuhan used the latter phrase for the first time on 30 July 1959, at a cocktail party hosted by Dr. Alan Thomas in Vancouver, after a symposium at the University of British Columbia dealing with music and the mass media.[48] But according to McLuhan himself: "I said [the medium is the message] in July 1957, at a radio conference, where people were in a panic about the coming of television. I tried to reassure this bunch by saying 'You've nothing to fear at all. Your medium is unique, and the medium is the message, and will ["stand up against" deleted by McLuhan and replaced by] relate to any new medium.'"[49]

Like all of the aphorisms McLuhan favored, "the medium is the message," a Chestertonian paradox, invites reflection and challenges us to plumb its depths, to interpret it, to put it on, to understand it by becoming its content — the very principle the saying articulates. Perceptive commentators have risen to that challenge, reworking the idea while remaining faithful to McLuhan's percept. Samuel Becker's interpretation[50] outdoes McLuhan by integrating two senses of the notion of "closure," both crucial for McLuhan but not explicitly related in his own writings.[51]

The benefit of McLuhan's personal explanation was not always enough to get across the message of "the medium is the message." Immediately after he had finished delivering an address at Montreal's Windsor Hotel, a perplexed and skeptical Alphonse Ouimet, then chairman of the board of Telesat Canada, accosted him in the men's room, engaging him in discussion and moving quickly to what he imagined would be his key point: "Surely if you remove the content, the medium remains."[52] McLuhan delivered himself of as full a reply as the circumstances permitted, noting that the user of a medium is the content, but Ouimet missed the all-important distinction between content and message, and the principle that the user is content *because* any medium is an extension of the human body.

The influence of Harold Innis, always readily acknowledged by McLuhan, is apparent in the idea that the medium is the message: "A medium of communication has an important influence upon the

WEST DES MOINES PUBLIC LIBRARY

dissemination of knowledge over space and time and it becomes necessary to study its characteristics in order to appraise its influence in its cultural setting."[53] McLuhan took the germ of the idea, confined here by Innis to media of communication, and extended it to all media.

Misunderstanding of the principle expressed by "the medium is the message" has often arisen where readers and audiences failed to make the leap with McLuhan from media of communication to *any* technological extension of the human body. This is surprising, in view of how infrequently he used mass communication as his starting point for discussion. When he did, he typically went on to cite the wider domain where the same effects obtain: "The overwhelming message of 'French' or 'English' or 'Russian' is the language itself and nothing in particular that is said in that language. Each language is a kind of corporate mask or vortex of energy to which countless millions of lives have contributed, *and so it is with each of our media* . . ."[54] Here McLuhan is giving an additional sense to "the medium is the message": the medium of language is *its own* message.

McLuhan put himself in the company of B. F. Skinner, Freud, and St. Thomas Aquinas.[55] The last, he observed, was teaching that the medium is the message with his principle of instrumentality as the "unmoved mover." McLuhan saw in this notion a forerunner of his own that all media remake mankind's perceptions and environment without undergoing any change themselves. He found further support in Aquinas for his own view that the user of a medium is the content.[56]

Discussing the principle in his correspondence, McLuhan repeatedly links it to the concepts of cause and effect. He refers to behavioral psychologist B. F. Skinner, recognizing that the study of the environment as a conditioner is the study of effects without causes. Even Freud, in his later work, McLuhan notes, became aware of the environment and conceived of it as a study of effects without causes. Freud on the environment anticipates McLuhan; McLuhan completes Freud: "When I talk about 'the medium is the message,' I, too, am saying that it is the medium as an environment of services that produces the effects. The 'message' is the total happening, as it were, and not a special bit of data or a special point of view."[57] The latter point could confound many an aspiring learner and prevent an understanding of the principle.

It was a lesson McLuhan did not tire of repeating and recasting. In addition to drawing comparisons with Aquinas, Skinner, and Freud, he assimilated his teaching to that of a technique developed by poets such as Ezra Pound: "Do you remember Pound's couplet: 'The apparition of these faces in a crowd / Petals on a wet, black bough'? The first line presents a situation. The second line presents the effect of the situation on his sensibilities. The discovery that one could present effects directly, and that one could by-pass the causes of the effect, led to many developments in art in this century. In a sense, it is embodied in my phrase 'the medium is the message' [where] I point out that the effect of the medium on the sensibilities in a way by-passes the causes, at least those causes which most people locate in the content."[58]

Less well known than "the medium is the message" is "the medium is the massage," even though the latter became the title of one of McLuhan's books (with Quentin Fiore). By the time it appeared in 1967, McLuhan no doubt recognized that his original saying had become a cliché and welcomed the opportunity to throw it back on the compost heap of language to recycle and revitalize it. But the new title is more than McLuhan indulging his insatiable taste for puns, more than a clever fusion of self-mockery and self-rescue; the subtitle is "An Inventory of Effects," underscoring the lesson compressed into the original saying. Each medium, McLuhan stressed, is unique in its properties and its effects upon our sensorium.[59]

Another McLuhan probe for exploring media effects is the figure/ground relationship: "Apropos 'the medium is the message,' I now point out that the medium is not the figure but the ground."[60] Later McLuhan added: "It is this ground that changes people and is therefore the 'message' or 'massage.'"[61] But as early as 1964, the same year that *Understanding Media* appeared, he had an alternative for his best-known phrase: "I have discovered a better way of saying the medium is the message. It is this: each technology creates a new environment. The old environment becomes the content of the new environment."[62]

The appearance of *Understanding Media* obliged McLuhan to set the record straight on what he meant by the phrase he was already well known for. Responding to *Time* magazine's reviewer, who had managed to garble much of McLuhan's thought, he switched from probe to professorial pronouncement: "To say that the medium is the message is to say that visual modalities have nothing in common with the audible, even when extended technologically."[63] *Especially* when extended technologically, but this was not the lesson *Time* readers needed or wanted, and McLuhan was ambivalent about feeding the hand he had bitten.

In private correspondence on the matter, he was candid, clear, critical of himself in a productive and poetic way: "All that I had to say about 'the medium is the message' . . . can now be put more simply, or at least more acceptably. If one says instead that each new technology creates a new human environment, it is easy to see why this new environment modifies all previous ones. It is like the 'last ring on the tree.'"[64] When McLuhan spoke of language as technology, he used the same comparison to prolong a Joycean echo: "utterings-outerings-outer rings."[65]

Joe Keogh, who had worked as an assistant to McLuhan on the preparation of *Understanding Media* and shared his insatiable appetite for wordplay, invented a corollary to "the medium is the message": "the idiom is the idea."[66] But few, even among McLuhan's closest associates, had the dexterity of mind to manipulate his media probe with any measure of control, much less extend it, a task he undertook with both relish and reluctance. "When I say 'the medium is the message' I suppress the fact that the user or audience or cognitive agent is both the 'content' and maker of the experience in order to highlight the *effects* of the medium, or the hidden environment or *ground* of the experience."[67] *I suppress*. Seldom did McLuhan acknowledge so plainly (if at all) that his style required readers to unpack his phrases. Never did he hint that his mentor I. A. Richards had invented a device to help with the unpacking — a simple rule for filling in missing words justified by context, to make the meaning of a phrase or sentence clear[68] — perhaps because it carried the terrifying name of "the third canon of symbolism."[69] Teaching others what the phrase meant was less interesting and absorbed less of his energies than learning for himself how many more meanings he could add to it.

Misunderstandings of McLuhan's thought, published in the work of high-profile authors, provided the healthy irritant he needed to develop a key idea. Charles Reich's *The Greening of America*, dismissed by McLuhan as a left-wing, lightweight survey of intellectual changes, contained what he called a "prize misinterpretation"[70] of the percept that the medium is the message. Reich was one of few critics who actually said what he thought McLuhan meant. McLuhan was grateful for this, and doubly grateful for the unintended stimulant it provided. "He assumes that I simply mean that the medium has no content, as with the electric light. It will serve as a useful quote in the revision, which I am gradually working at."[71]

Reich's mistake became McLuhan's insight: "[Reich's] statement is actually one of the few useful remarks that has ever come to my attention about anything I have written. It enables me to see that the user of the electric light, *or* a hammer, or a language, or a book, is the content."[72] McLuhan wrote to Reich to explain (and thank him for) his valuable blunder, and Reich replied: "I think actually that what you say in your letter is very relevant to the point I was attempting to make in my book — the point that people 'ignore' but are shaped by the media they use in the form of the daily life routines."[73]

McLuhan shared the insight he had gained with Peter Newman, then editor of the *Toronto Star*: "The user is always the content of any medium. He creates the *meaning* by gradually discovering the potential of the medium of which he is the content. This is just as true of language as a house or a car. The *meaning* is the interplay. We make sense by gradually focussing and exploring the various media that surround us. But in making sense, we also make new service/disservice environments which in turn become new media. If the meaning is the process of interplay between us and a technology, the effect or message results from the projection of this interplay between us and the media. To say, therefore, that 'the medium is the message' is to coalesce these stages a bit."[74]

In the month since he had written to Reich, McLuhan had already moved from thinking about one medium as the *content* of another to that of a medium as *meaning*, because it is the content of another. Or, better still, to emphasize the dynamics involved, because *of its relation* to another medium. (A year later, in his book *Take Today*, this idea appeared on the first page of the text as "the meaning of meaning is relationship.")

McLuhan was also moving toward the idea of all human artifacts as linguistic in structure. This move came gradually and under several influences, but might have been prompted at first by an observation offered to McLuhan regarding his original media probe. One of his correspondents, Max Nanny, wrote him: "By the way, I have found out that the difficulties concerning your insight 'The Medium is the Message' can elegantly be solved by a recourse to [Ferdinand] de Saussure's distinction between 'langue' [language system] and 'parole' [speech]: the medium as 'langue' is the message; the medium as 'parole' is rather content oriented, or as you said, the user!"[75]

Linking service/disservice environments, the process of interplay between user and technology, and *meaning* to "the medium is the message" brings the phrase a very long way from what McLuhan had first meant by it in the late 1950s. But these links also bring the idea and the phrase back close to its roots in the work of Harold Innis and I. A. Richards. McLuhan continued to use his famous probe, because it was still yielding new discoveries.

In a letter to *Atlantic Monthly* editor in chief Robert Manning, McLuhan was continuing to change tack while heading for new ports: "When anything unconventional or radically perceptive is uttered, the *unhappy listener* automatically translates it into the old familiar patterns. The *eye* of the beholder is quite capable of blotting out the *resonant* and the existential, and the average reader *makes* whatever he wishes to find: the user is the *content* of every medium, condemning the writer to move at that level."[76]

Here the notion of user as content has a clearly distinct sense from the earlier passages where the medium may be a hammer, a house, or a hydrofoil. And different consequences. McLuhan is now edging toward audience study and reader response theory. This is a step forward *and* only a short step back to the educational aims anchored in the training of perception that had always been McLuhan's concern.[77]

McLuhan wrote to *The Listener*, the magazine of the BBC, in response to a letter from Jonathan Miller that the magazine had printed in their issue of 9 September 1971, fully integrating the notion of user as content with his other probes. The letter bombarded Miller from a dozen directions at once and in a tone light enough to rescue their protracted exchange from any danger of dreariness. McLuhan's focus on user as content was sharpened here and once again, some five years later, as he turned his attention to formal causality and a concentrated effort to integrate the probes he had by then been developing for over a quarter of a century: "Formal causality is that which structures whole situations, e.g., environments are formal causes. The user of any technology is always an efficient, never a formal, cause. The formal cause of poetry or painting or drama is the public. Do you remember the wonderful essay by Arthur Miller on this subject entitled '1949: The Year It Came Apart'? He had discovered that 1949, the first year of network TV, was the end of his public. However, he did not relate it to TV — I did."[78]

In the closing years of his career, McLuhan was absorbed with synthesizing his work on media[79] and anticipating further discoveries. His earliest probe remained foundational: "All media tend to be subliminal in their structures, and this I have been trying to say in the phrase 'the medium is the message.'"[80] "Message" retained for McLuhan the special sense he had given it nearly twenty years earlier: "The programs and the content of media are always less significant than the resonating and pervasive ground that is the 'message' or effect of the medium."[81] Understood and misunderstood throughout those years, McLuhan's saying remained a probe and became something more. As Norman Mailer put it: "McLuhan would torment the vitals of a generation of American intellectuals with the irremovable harpoon that 'the medium is the message.'"[82]

CLAUDE BISSELL ASSUMED the presidency of the University of Toronto in 1958 and became aware of McLuhan's growing reputation the following year. After speaking at convocation at Wayne State University in Detroit, Bissell invited any questions the assembly might have about Canada. There was a brief pause, then a member of the audience rose and asked gravely, "Could you give a brief summary of the ideas of Marshall McLuhan?"[83] When asked the same question in years to come, McLuhan himself regularly emphasized that he had neither a theory nor a point of view — only percepts and probes.

As Bissell was speaking on his behalf in Detroit, McLuhan was in Toronto preparing for a year of sabbatical leave during 1959-60. He had compiled a list of projects, and was finding in himself little inclination to confine himself to one, when a piece of good news settled his priorities for him. The U.S.-based National Association of Educational Broadcasters (NAEB) approved McLuhan's proposal for a study of media in June 1959. One of their advisers had written, "He's an authentic genius, I'm sure. He is also a poet in temperament."[84] NAEB project #69 was launched; McLuhan, as always, was pleased that the number was divisible by three. He referred to the project as "Vat 69," where he tossed every idea in his purview, in the hope of someday giving the subject the fuller treatment it deserved. Later, his enthusiastic but anxious editors for *Understanding Media* would naively believe that this meant he intended to give it a more orderly treatment.

The NAEB commission to McLuhan gave him a completely free hand to design a teaching method and syllabus for use in introducing the nature and effects of media to the curriculum of secondary schools. Sponsored jointly by the NAEB and the United States Office of Education, McLuhan would carry out research, conduct interviews, and launch a program of media-testing with the assistance of the Ryerson Polytechnic Institute, Toronto. He got started on his work the same month that the project was approved, traveling to Philadelphia to confer on the design of his project with Harry Skornia, then professor of radio and television broadcasting at the University of Illinois at Urbana and president of the NAEB, and with author Gilbert Seldes.

The study would clearly take up all of McLuhan's time, with a final report date scheduled to coincide with the end of his sabbatical year. But he completed a thirty-five-page sample syllabus before 1959 was out. It began: "Teachers today face a quite different environment from the one they themselves grew up in."[85] As objectives for courses in media he listed effects of media interacting, the nature of print, and new electronic technology as top priorities. He pointed out that "increased awareness of the forms of media, as they operate upon our modes of perception and judgement, is not merely a means of understanding but of prediction and control,"[86] a notion he was to develop later in chapter eight of *Understanding Media*.

McLuhan spoke of the mental discipline required to transpose the realities of life into new spheres and the dislocating effect of media. He referred to James Joyce and cited Peter Drucker's *Landmarks of*

Tomorrow for its prescient views on the merging of purpose in education and business. McLuhan permitted himself the occasional aphorism ("Inspiration has replaced perspiration")[87] and stressed the power of the print medium, evoking sources from Rabelais to Innis as he homed in on his own vision of educational reform: "This role of the artist as herald and model-maker affords a major resource in understanding media. In fact, it indicates a natural means of integration of the curriculum, whether in history, mathematics or language and [i.e., with] media study. This syllabus will attempt, in some degree, to provide a means of overall integration, while also coming to grips with particular media."[88]

Writing as an achievement of sedentary societies, writing preceded by sculpture, sculpture as modeling of auditory space, writing as translation of auditory space, the division of labor and partial dissociation of sensory life in sedentary society, the work of Innis, manuscript culture, printing, the message of repeatability, print and perspective, print and industry — all of these were crammed into McLuhan's syllabus outline. Reader Arthur Wells Foshay commented that "media" was not in the average teacher's vocabulary and needed introduction and explanation, adding: "You understand it, and I do, but will they believe it in Dubuque?"[89]

Where McLuhan wrote that "print learnt in childhood may prove to have been a major block to learning in many subjects besides music,"[90] Foshay cautioned: "Don't underestimate the shock this comment will have, especially for teachers. You could lose a majority of your audience right here . . . Can't you ease up on this point?"[91] McLuhan was not about to ease up on anything, much less the insight that had been his starting point for the investigation of contrasting media effects. Fifteen pages into his text, he was in full flight, discoursing on the connection between ideograms and nuclear phenomena and predicting that the "Chinese will eventually be more at home with non-Euclidean mathematics and physics than anybody else."[92] Foshay predicted skepticism on the part of readers unless McLuhan gave his statements support and development, but as his final comment he offered: "This remains the most exciting stuff around."[93]

McLuhan's correspondence during the year that he worked on the NAEB project reflects his intense preoccupation with the ideas it was producing. To David Riesman at Harvard he wrote about repeatability as the subliminal message of print permeating Western thought since Gutenberg,[94] noting: "When the globe becomes a single electronic computer, with all its languages and cultures recorded on a single tribal drum, the fixed point of view of print culture becomes irrelevant and impossible, no matter how precious."[95] With Peter Drucker he discussed the contrast of emphasis between efficient causality under print technology and formal causality under electronic circuitry.[96]

Many of McLuhan's correspondents during this period were persons he interviewed in connection with his project, including Bernie Muller-Thym, to whom McLuhan wrote about his new ideas as soon as they emerged. Among these was the high-definition/low-definition contrast as a basic defining feature of media, presented to Muller-Thym through an illuminating illustration, moving from country pedestrian to petrified metropolis as an example of the evolution of a single medium.[97] McLuhan's *principle of reversal*, as a feature of both a medium's behavior and its effects, a cornerstone of his thought through to his final writings, is linked here, for the first time, to the high-definition/low-definition contrast. He was gratified to learn of independent evidence from the field of fluid mechanics to support the principle.[98] It was with Muller-Thym and Harry Skornia that McLuhan shared and explored what he regarded as the major breakthroughs propeling him to an overview of media.[99]

In correspondence with poet and English professor Wilfred Watson, his future collaborator in writing *From Cliché to Archetype*, he stressed the engagement of artists with technology and opened questions relating to the scholarship of Northrop Frye, questions he and Watson would pick up again in their book.

Though work on the NAEB project was taking him away often, his thoughts on the consequences of the reforms he would be proposing in his final report brought him home again, as he mused on the federated college system at the University of Toronto, its roots in sectarianism, and how its nineteenth-century vision worked against his own idealism, concluding: "It would of course be a triumphal irony if Irish Catholic St. Mike's should become the insistent voice for Oxford Cambridge ideals of gentlemanly liberal education."[100]

McLuhan described television to Bernie Muller-Thym as an introvert medium ("because people are the screen they are driven inward"[101]). McLuhan also reported to Muller-Thym discoveries about himself: "It is very odd, I find, Bernie, that as one moves into a faster and richer dialogue all desire for publication ceases."[102] But with his final report to the NAEB due in less than two months as he made this remark, it was no time to let rich dialogue interfere with publication.

For the benefit of impatient readers, McLuhan said plainly in the final version of *Report on Project in Understanding the New Media* that all his recommendations could be reduced to one: "Study the modes of the media, in order to hoick all assumptions out of the subliminal, non-verbal realm for scrutiny and for prediction and control of human purposes."[103] The scrutiny in question is not far from that of F. R. Leavis, and McLuhan's words also recall I. A. Richards's lessons on context and purpose.

The report's introduction identified human speech as a "master technology," a fundamental observation that inevitably made its way into *Understanding Media*, though featuring less prominently because of the size of the book.[104] McLuhan lauded the tradition of American linguistics, but upbraided social scientists who "have been unduly shy of a plenary approach to technology."[105] The remark emphasizes the inseparability of art and technology in the McLuhan view. Just as semiology was the context in which Saussure set linguistics, implicitly deferring the larger study till linguistics had been more fully developed, media provided the context for Richards's approach to language. Unlike Saussure, both Richards and McLuhan moved beyond the scope of their first inquiries to the broader domains that beckoned. McLuhan evoked this parallel in only the subtlest of ways in a section of his NAEB report titled "The New Criticism and the New Media."

He also linked work in American linguistics to his original media probe: "[Robert A.] Hall's concept of the 'organizing pattern' concerns the fact that 'there is no such thing as *experience* in the abstract, as a mode separate and distinct from culture.' Hall is saying here, in effect, what I formulate as 'the medium is the message.'"[106] This is a long way from what "the medium is the message" meant when McLuhan said it to reassure worried radio broadcasters that their medium was not threatened with extinction by television. The new interpretation is also distinct from the protean formulations the same probe was to undergo throughout the 1960s and '70s. It is much closer to the thesis of chapter four in Richards's *The Meaning of Meaning*, "Signs in Perception" — the notion that all perception demands interpretation — an idea related to McLuhan's SI/SC formula, meaning the transformations of sensory input into sensory closure.

Report on Project in Understanding the New Media paid scrupulous attention to television, allowing McLuhan to showcase what he considered to be among the most important discoveries of his year's work: "Television, I show, is a low definition medium and radio is a high definition medium. That is to say the quality of sense image offered by television is visually of poor quality, and in the case of radio the quality of auditory image is very high. When a low definition medium like television is augmented by studio gimmicks, its teaching impact is strikingly reduced. But when a high definition image like radio is similarly augmented, its teaching impact is increased."[107] This observation presumably applies to the entertainment / incantatory value of radio as well, offering an explanation of the powerful effect achieved by the 1938 Orson Welles broadcast of H. G. Wells's *War of the Worlds*.

McLuhan confessed that throughout his year-long project he had found it easier to talk to business people than to educators. Not content to make this an incidental remark, he took the occasion to unsettle his audience: "The educator feels protected by bureaucratic structures which ensure him a comfortable decade or so of culture-lag."[108]

Completing his year's work with meetings in Cincinnati, Columbus, Galveston, and Detroit in June 1960, McLuhan put the finishing touches on his report, sounding a note of evident satisfaction and giving a clear indication of where the future would take him: "Had Project 69 done nothing more than to isolate the fact the 'content' of any medium is another medium, it would have justified the expense involved many times over. Because, until this principle of 'content' as an illusion of media-mix is grasped, there is and will continue to be a futile effort to measure the transfer of content as if it were some pellet moving from point to point like Zeno's arrow. The 'illusion' of content likewise syphons off all attention from the forms and effects of media."[109] McLuhan was the first to benefit from his research, as he made plain in a section of his report entitled "What I Learned."

Foshay remained one of McLuhan's biggest supporters, encouraging him to continue the work he had started with the NAEB project.[110] McLuhan needed little encouragement. His findings were too absorbing to be left in a report gathering dust on a shelf. "I am myself staggered by the implications of discovering the high definition tactual component in the television image. This not only means that the TV image is directly tactual and sculptural but that as image it tends toward the auditory."[111] McLuhan saw that big stakes were involved, writing to Harry Skornia: "When all our senses are globally enveloping all our senses, you have an archetyped game or play situation which ensures for the whole of mankind the utmost possibilities of creativity . . . I hope you will feel that I am not letting the NAEB down nor above all your confidence in me in tackling this staggering concept."[112] Tackling the concept meant he was now committed to pursue goals beyond addressing hidebound educators.

Report on Project in Understanding the New Media would eventually become *Understanding Media*, but McLuhan had something else in the works at the same time. His energy level was higher than ever, and the momentum he had gathered on his sabbatical project was still carrying him. It had also tipped the balance of his interests far enough toward media to give him a focus and keep him writing instead of planning to write.

AFTER THANKING HIS in-laws for their gift of an elegant glass tray in a Christmas Day letter of 1960, McLuhan mentioned that he had written a book in less than a month. Of all his publications, *The Gutenberg Galaxy*, so explosive on the page, had the tidiest beginnings. The manuscript, in unusually controlled longhand, flowed from McLuhan's pen. When he had written 399 pages, he stopped, so that the number would be divisible by three.[113] Of course, the book's true beginnings go back to St. Louis, more than twenty years earlier, when he began discussing ideas concerning the print medium and its effects with colleagues and students, friends and neighbors.[114]

The cover of *The Gutenberg Galaxy*, promising by its title to be a science-fiction thriller, bore two huge "G"s. Locked in a silent mirror-image echo, the white letters gleam against a cool red ground. They hint at a vortex, mock its surge and tug in a paralyzed, stylized parody of print technology impoverishing human perception with the gift of a bias in the guise of new power. But the interlocking design is also a labyrinth with easy access to its center, a medium within a medium, the lost but recoverable world of acoustic space.

The contract for the book McLuhan signed with the University of Toronto Press referred to it as "The Gutenberg Era," a phrase found in its pages. McLuhan settled on "Gutenberg Galaxy" for the title, not only for its alliterative value but to emphasize that a configuration of events had been spawned by the invention of the printing press. "Galaxy" allowed McLuhan to focus on those events as effects and to evoke his theme of effects as a cluster of environmental changes.

McLuhan cites dozens of writers and thinkers in his opening pages, mentioning Innis briefly, at first, but soon after paying him full homage with the remark that the entire book can be taken as a footnote of explanation to the economic historian's work.[115] It is also very much a footnote to *Report on Project in Understanding the New Media* and a prelude to *Understanding Media*.

Though the mosaic format of *The Gutenberg Galaxy* with its multiple points of view creates an intellectual energy that surges into a hundred different channels, the book focuses on one question: What sort of changes did the media of the printing press and movable type bring about? It meant the end of manuscript culture, to be sure, but the consequences were much more far-reaching than the loss of jobs for scribes and monks. Printing was the mechanization of writing. It promoted nationalism and national languages, because international Latin did not have enough scope to provide markets for the printers. Print also fostered a sense of private identity (by making copies available to individual readers in such large numbers) and imposed a level of standardization in language that had not prevailed until then, thus making "correct" spelling and grammar a measure of literacy.

Print culture intensified the effects of the older technology of writing. Before writing, mankind lived in acoustic space, the space of the spoken word, which is boundless, directionless, horizonless, and charged with emotion. Writing transformed space into something bounded, linear, ordered, structured, and rational. The written page, with its edges, margins, and sharply defined letters in row after row, brought in a new way of thinking about space.

Media effects did not end when Gutenberg's invention transformed writing into print. Whereas print had mechanized writing, four centuries later the telegraph electrified it. But McLuhan teaches that new media do not so much replace each other as complicate each other. It is this interaction that obscures their effects. The technology of mankind in the age of acoustic space, the technology from which writing, print, and telegraph developed, was speech. Transformed into writing, speech lost the quality that made it part of the culture of acoustic space. It acquired a powerful visual bias, producing carryover effects in social and cultural organization that endure to the present. But there was also a loss, in that writing separated speech from the other physical senses. The powerful extension of speech permitted by the development of radio produced a similar loss, for this medium reduced speech to one sense — the auditory-aural. Radio is not speech (because we only listen), but it creates the illusion, like writing, of containing speech.

The all-at-onceness of the stories on a newspaper page contrasts with the one-at-a-timeness of ideas developed in a book. The significance of this contrast for McLuhan is the effect it produced: artists like Joyce and Picasso saw beyond the superficial chaos of the newspaper page to a higher order of harmony. The apparent dislocations that mark the work of these artists are paralleled by the discontinuities that form the basis of quantum physics and relativity theory. In the social sciences, McLuhan detects further parallels in the approaches to history and culture to be found in the writings of Arnold Toynbee and Margaret Mead, where again all-at-onceness replaces one-at-a-timeness.

Such reorganization of perception bewilders those who cling to the comfort of the older, linear order of things and a (single) "practical" point of view. In *The Mechanical Bride* McLuhan had issued a challenge to readers to become as aware of new environments as they are of getting into a bath: "The inside point of view would coincide with the practical point of view of the man who would rather eat the turtle than admire the design on its back. The same man would rather dunk himself in the newspaper than have any esthetic or intellectual grasp of its character and meaning."[116] Stepping into a newspaper is inevitable;

perceiving it as an environment is indispensable to understanding its power and its effect.

The phonetic alphabet is medium par excellence — medium as extension *and* in the basic sense of in-between or go-between. As a result, it has subtle but powerful consequences. What does the alphabet mediate? Meaning and sound. Compare Chinese characters, where there is no representation of sound in the visual symbols, no component parts used in different combinations to show how those combinations are pronounced. Here the symbol is a whole, a unit. It carries its meaning as a whole, not as a sequence of elements. In alphabetic writing, there *is* a sequence, but its parts (letters) *and* the sounds they stand for are meaningless in themselves. Meaning only attaches to complete sequences.

Before the invention of the alphabet, communication among humans involved all the senses simultaneously, speaking being accompanied by gestures and requiring both listening and looking. The immediacy and rich complexity of this type of communication was reduced by the alphabet to an abstract visual code. This is part of McLuhan's teaching on the transition from the culture of acoustic space to that of rational space brought about by the invention of the alphabet. To this he adds two points: (1) the transition involves a shift away from tribal society to a society composed of individuals with private identities and capable of pursuing private goals; (2) the transition is a one-way process. This last point means that, since alphabetization is a reductive process, a non-alphabetic culture cannot assimilate it; it can only be assimilated by it.[117]

Completed less than six months after McLuhan's 1960 NAEB report on media, and promising *Understanding Media* on its final page, *The Gutenberg Galaxy* was, in Harry Skornia's words, "not really a book in the usual organizational or formal sense. It only looks like a book. And since Marshall has to try to use the print medium, the book, to try to convey and illustrate non-print revelations, he is bound to be trapped into several approximations, exaggerations, and over-simplifications and apparent contradictions. The flashing lights, which GALAXY is, cannot be expected to have the characteristics of a steadily glowing headlight that can be traced back to its source, crossed and recrossed, sampled and analysed."[118]

Skornia understood that McLuhan's objective was to transform the hot medium of print into the cool medium of dialogue. Recalling his encounters with McLuhan as they consulted on the NAEB project, Skornia said: "When I used to preside at meetings at which he spoke, I used to say, there should be a switch on him so I could turn him off, translate and discuss, and then turn him back on after we slow pokes had gotten the point."[119] He was prepared to take *The Gutenberg Galaxy* and its author on their own terms: "In any criticism or analysis of Marshall, we miss the point if we quibble over whether he means 'the mosaic is THE ONLY way to reveal . . . etc . . . ' or whether, on reflection, he may not mean that the mosaic analogy is a convenient and useful one. He can't be bothered with details like that."[120]

Other critics were not so magnanimous. Conceding the validity of McLuhan's view of media as shapers of mankind, Arthur Efron charged that his mosaic approach had not achieved its objective of abolishing point of view: "He instead introduces it in his spoken and unspoken assumptions . . . "[121] Efron buttressed *his* point of view by invoking misconceptions about the Renaissance that McLuhan had outlined twenty years earlier in his dissertation on Thomas Nashe. Efron concluded: "In my mind *The Mechanical Bride* is a great work of cultural illumination, but *The Gutenberg Galaxy* is finally a reversion to a neoclassical or neoscholastic daydream."[122]

Such views did not disturb McLuhan, who wrote to Walter Ong: "My theory is only acceptable to Thomists, for whom consciousness as analogical proportion among the senses from moment to moment, is quite easy to grasp. But print technology actually smashes that analogical awareness in society and the individual . . . A *sensus communis* for external senses is what I'm trying to build."[123]

The years since the McLuhans had moved to Wells Hill had been crowded ones. McLuhan's saying that adults are obsolete children developed out of watching his offspring with the amazement from which no parent is exempt. Eric departed for a stint in the U.S. Air Force at age eighteen, providing his five siblings with a model for early obsolescence. Elsie, hospitalized after her stroke, declined seriously. Two weeks before McLuhan's fiftieth birthday, she died at Our Lady of Mercy Hospital in Toronto. McLuhan was disconsolate, but shared his grief with no one.[124]

"I'm not concerned to get any kudos out of this book," McLuhan said of *The Gutenberg Galaxy*, adding: "It seems to me a book that somebody should have written a century ago. I wish somebody else *had* written it. It will be a useful prelude to the rewrite of *Understanding Media* [the 1960 NAEB report] that I'm doing now."[125]

But the kudos came — and in the form of the 1963 Governor-General's Award for critical prose. McLuhan had not expected it. Nor did he know who, as chairman of the selection committee, had locked himself up with colleagues in an Ottawa hotel room, persuading them the award should go to Canada's emerging authority on media. None other than Northrop Frye.[126]

FOUR

Canada's McLuhan

10

From the Centre Out

My motive in returning to Canada was then, as now, my fear
of acceptance. I knew there was no danger of this in Canada.
It is very salutary to have a daily charade of human malice and
stupidity mingled with warmth and insight. In the U.S.,
surrounded with an atmosphere of success and acceptance, I
could have lost my bearings very quickly.

–MARSHALL MCLUHAN TO CLAUDE BISSELL,
23 MARCH 1971

THE UNIVERSITY OF TORONTO's Centre for Culture and Technology was
formed in 1963, with the aim of bringing together scholars and
researchers from all branches of science, technology, the humanities,
and the arts, for the purpose of determining the effects of any
technology — any extension of the body — on culture, society, and
institutions.

There was hostile reaction from the outset. Robert Angus Gordon,
going into the final year of his term as dean of the Faculty of Graduate
Studies, was firmly opposed to the Centre being part of his faculty.[1]
But the establishment of the Centre was approved by the University
of Toronto's board of governors at its meeting of 24 October 1963,
with the appointment of McLuhan as director, and the allocation of a
modest budget of $7,800 for its first nine months of operation.[2]
Earlier in the year, McLuhan had asked for the cross-appointment to
the Centre of painter and art historian Harley Parker, who headed up

the Department of Design at the Royal Ontario Museum. The request was acceptable to the ROM, but University of Toronto president Claude Bissell had deferred the matter, pending official status for the Centre.[3] Now the appointment went ahead. Ambitious projects were under way even as the University of Toronto board of governors brought the Centre into the world. McLuhan's account of the design for an experimental method of determining the sensory typologies of entire populations, describing a project carried out under the auspices of the Centre, anticipates passages later to become familiar to readers of *Understanding Media*.[4]

Among early initiatives to compel interest in the Centre was the plan to launch a cultural awards program. The objective was, in McLuhan's own words, "to sting" corporations into realizing the relevance of what he and his group were doing.[5] The awards would be made amid much fanfare and publicity, and business leaders, realizing how outmoded their basis for decision-making was — by comparison with the innovative ways of the award-winners — would come to the Centre to get their perceptions scrubbed. The operation would, in this way, fulfill its mission in the wider community and generate revenue to expand its activities.

There were also the Centre's Intuition Awards. When made for the first time in 1964, these went to the Canadian beaver, as an apt symbol of the country's dammed-up creativity, and to the wavers of the new Canadian flag, for their effort in promoting a salutary new cliché. It would still be several years before McLuhan spoke of flags in terms of cliché and archetype, but the unveiling of Canada's new flag in 1965 had already provided an opportunity for him to repeat an important lesson on media effects.[6] The iconic power of television creates a high degree of involvement, and this in turn makes for separatism, whether it occurs among teenagers or in Quebec. Electric technology, unlike that of steam and machinery, makes for decentralism in work, play, and politics. Against this overwhelming force, McLuhan explained, the flag-wavers were making their valiant stand.

Noting that the profound need for in-depth empathy and participation fostered in the young by television is frustrated by the sharp outlines of conventional typography, McLuhan also applauded the Pitman phonetic alphabet of forty-three letters and their shaggy design, likening it to a Beatle wig. The high sensory involvement and reading aloud required by the Pitman system made it the perfect medium for rousing typographic man from his trance.

Within a year of the Centre's inception, blueprints had been drawn up for the building to house it. The plans were featured prominently in the *Toronto Star* and described as "downright intriguing."[7] Architects Allen Bernholtz and Wilfred Schulman designed the spindly looking concrete and glass facility to reflect "the extensions of man, including his consciousness and five basic senses."[8] Bernholtz was quoted as saying: "The building is a physical embodiment of the work at the centre."[9] The projected cost was five million dollars, but no funding was in place at that time.

A year and a half after its formation, the Centre was still looking for a home. Plans under development for the construction of Innis College, as part of the expansion program at the University of Toronto, offered an ideal prospect from the standpoint of historical association, but accommodating the Centre in the new facility proved to be impractical.[10] McLuhan was undaunted: "We shall concentrate upon achieving an intellectual identity rather than a physical one."[11]

The members of the Centre as of August 1964 were Allen Bernholtz (School of Architecture), Dr. Daniel Cappon (Medicine), Prof. B. M. Carpendale (Mechanical Engineering), Prof. W. T. Easterbrook (Political Science), Dr. E. Llewellyn-Thomas (Medicine), Arthur Porter (Industrial Engineering), Prof. Carl Williams (Psychology), Harley Parker (Design, Royal Ontario Museum), Prof. Ed Rogers (Anthropology), and McLuhan.

If McLuhan knew the bureaucrat's adage "organize-delegate-supervise," he was, as director of the Centre, incapable of acting on it. To organize could never mean the tedium of imposing rational, linear, visual order; could never mean anything other than to discover the organic whole of whatever had his attention. To delegate this as a task would be to miss the thrill of the voyage of discovery. To supervise would be to make an iconic captain out of Poe's sailor.

New statutes were approved by the University of Toronto senate, making the Centre for Culture and Technology part of the Faculty of Social Sciences.[12] This change in status did not move it closer to anything like satisfactory quarters. From 1964 to 1968 it would remain crammed into the St. Michael's College English department office McLuhan shared with his secretary, Margaret Stewart.[13] The Centre offered no regular classes, but seminars, workshops, and public lectures were organized under its auspices. These took place wherever room could be found.

With his Governor-General's Award in hand and projects at the Centre taking shape to his satisfaction, McLuhan was ready to stir "Vat 69." He had been ready since the day he finished *The Gutenberg Galaxy*. "By all means call [the new] book 'EXTENSIONS OF MAN,'" Ted Carpenter advised him, "UNDERSTANDING MEDIA title classifies it with all the old and current crap."[14] The phrase "extensions of man," from Emerson's *Works and Days*, fit McLuhan's definition of technology perfectly, but he settled on *Understanding Media* to echo Cleanth Brooks and Robert Penn Warren's *Understanding Poetry*, retaining Emerson's expression as a subtitle.

McLuhan's collaborator on *Understanding Media* was to have been Harry Skornia, who read the draft and the proofs of *The Gutenberg Galaxy* and wrote the publicity, but their collaboration never progressed beyond a fond wish on the part of both men. To Skornia, McLuhan had spoken of his terror at the disaster civilization faced if mankind could not learn to use new media wisely, adding that this required understanding them in order to control their consequences.[15]

McLuhan transformed his NAEB *Report on Project in Understanding the New Media* into the manuscript of *Understanding Media* by raiding his library. References to scores of authors sprang up throughout the new text, though some of these were eventually obscured by editorial cutting. McLuhan had sent a proposal and a sketchy first draft to McGraw-Hill in New York in June 1961.[16] By the time associate editor Leon Wilson responded with an evaluation, McLuhan had sent him an expanded second draft. With it came a second proposal, for a project titled "Child of the Mechanical Bride," a study of advertising intended to update *The Mechanical Bride*.

Wilson found the *Understanding New Media* manuscript "brilliant stuff," but called it "slipshod writing," giving McLuhan criticisms by the standard editorial guidebook.[17] Changes would be needed "if your message is to be intelligible between covers,"[18] Wilson wrote to McLuhan in October 1962, without understanding or admitting

McLuhan's definition of "message" as effect on the reader. The manuscript seemed "at heart a plug for *Finnegans Wake*" to the wary editor.[19] He acknowledged some pleasure in reading McLuhan's "racy, gaudy, slashing style — when it works."[20] But apparently that was not often enough, and though McGraw-Hill committed themselves to publishing the work, Wilson was determined not to have any of it. Wrote the editor: "One of your friends and well-wishers . . . warned us . . . that we were probably in for a very difficult editorial task, citing your 'often incomprehensible tidal wave of ideas.' It was his feeling that you could not, even if you want to, make your material 'accessible and persuasive.' Marshall, get to work and prove him wrong!"[21]

McLuhan was incensed. Wilson told him he was overreacting.[22] McLuhan feared prompting the "moral point of view" criticism received by *The Mechanical Bride* if Wilson forced *Understanding Media* into a conventional mold.[23] After publicity for the book had begun, Wilson wrote again to say "[We] would be anxious to avoid what you so casually announce as 'rewriting' it."[24] McLuhan had already rewritten parts of his manuscript many times in anything but casual fashion, keeping at it with a concern for provoking his readers, satisfied only when he could find fresh twists bold enough to make himself exclaim "Ha! this will really get them!"[25] And not "*they*'ll get *this*." Here is Eliot's notion of dislocating language into its meanings, together with the lessons from the symbolist poets, Poe, Joyce, and Pound — the collective credo of early modernism — distilled into essential McLuhan. Apparently it never occurred to him to relent in this approach, even when it became clear that the world was not getting his message. But then how could he, without sacrificing part of the truth he had revealed in saying the medium is the message?

With the departure of Leon Wilson from McGraw-Hill in the summer of 1963, the *Understanding Media* file fell to David Segal. Having read all the correspondence about the work, he told McLuhan his curiosity was "wildly aroused."[26] McLuhan seemed by now — midsummer — to have formed the misconception that *Understanding Media* was scheduled as a release for the fall of 1963. Segal quickly straightened him out on this matter (indicating that the likely publication date would be the spring of 1964), but despaired of straightening out the manuscript: "I have rarely read anything that required so many unprepared mental leaps on the part of the reader."[27]

After a month in a state of shock, Segal felt an odd combination of elation and despair; he recognized that McLuhan's prose was crammed with insights, but had taken an accurate measure of the author, grasping at once that it was pointless to rehearse the standard editorial litany of clarity, brevity, unity for McLuhan's benefit. "All of which leads me to think that this is as coherent a book as you are going to write, that any massive effort at editorial assistance would be wasted. Also, I have a funny feeling that this manuscript, as you have written it, is, in a funny way, true to your intentions."[28] This was the only indication Segal gave of coming close to understanding the purpose of *Understanding Media*, but he had no more of an advantage than future readers for grappling with a book whose theme was not announced till page 329: "It is the theme of this book that not even the most lucid understanding of the peculiar force of a medium can head off the ordinary 'closure' of the senses that causes us to conform to the pattern of experience presented."[29]

McLuhan exhausted Segal, who finally said: "If you are absolutely set on your mosaic style, I will back down entirely."[30] By comparison with both earlier work, such as *The Gutenberg Galaxy*, and later work, such as *From Cliché to Archetype*, *Understanding Media* would give the appearance of a conventional book, and it was McLuhan who believed he had been obliged to back down on using mosaic style. When questioned on the reason for the stylistic transition between *The Gutenberg Galaxy* and *Understanding Media*, McLuhan replied: "I abandoned the mosaic approach in *Understanding Media* for a very simple reason. The McGraw-Hill editors wouldn't have it. One of their house rules is 'don't quote anybody at all unless you disagree with him.'"[31] As for "Child of the Mechanical Bride," the project was stillborn, apparently dropped in a mutual conspiracy of silence between McLuhan and McGraw-Hill.

In the third and final draft of *Understanding Media*, submitted in the late fall of 1963, "The Medium is the Message," previously chapter two, became chapter one. However, it no longer opened with "The 'content' of any medium is always another medium," though this idea remained the focus of the chapter. The metaphor of a cloak of invisibility cast over any medium *from within*, i.e., by its content, was dropped from the second draft, along with the original statement of media effects: "Yet the effect of any medium is overwhelmingly from the unnoticed medium itself, and the effect is always the greater when its source is ignored."[32]

Where the editors found the manuscript intolerably repetitive, they directed McLuhan to cut the limper versions of the offending passages, such as "The electric light is, perhaps, the only medium that does not 'contain' a message, or what is the same thing, another medium. The medium is the message and the only message of the electric light. Nevertheless, it is a medium that changes time and place and architecture."[33]

McLuhan made revisions principally in the early part of the book, with fewer in part two, tinkering there with chapter headings. "Clocks: Time with an American Accent" became "Clocks: The Scent of Time." "The Credit Card: The Tinkling Symbol" became "Money: The Poor Man's Credit Card" (with the tinkling symbol moving to the telephone chapter). And the long section on advertising, planned originally with illustrations in the style of The Mechanical Bride, went ahead in a drastically shortened final form without a single visual (this would form the basis of one reviewer's complaint), becoming "Ads: Keeping Upset with the Joneses."[34]

Where McLuhan discussed the wheel as an obsolete form in the twentieth century, his weary editor, unable or unwilling to follow him in one of his less daring leaps, even though a safety net of logic was clearly visible, wailed in the margin, "Why talk about clocks here?"[35] Elsewhere, in his second draft, McLuhan had written: "All manner of utensils are a yielding to this bodily pressure [to extend storage, mobility functions, and portability] . . . as in vases, jars, and 'slow matches' (stored fire). The cave or the hole in the ground precedes the house as storage place, because it is not enclosed space but an extension of the body."[36] The editor protested that "because it is not enclosed space" was a baffling statement. McLuhan scratched it out. The final typescript of Understanding Media, much revised and expanded, was shortened when the book went into production. But the chapters on "Hybrid Energy" and "Media as Translators," added by McLuhan to his final draft, were retained.

The book was released in the spring of 1964; by January of 1965

McLuhan had decided to begin work on a second edition. By late summer, perhaps recalling his offer to rewrite *Understanding Media* in Basic English, he was proposing a children's edition to McGraw-Hill.[37] This fresh burst of enthusiasm was inspired by the breakthrough McLuhan had achieved and announced to David Segal less than four months after *Understanding Media* first appeared: "Major insight on 'medium is the message' is this: each new technology, be it house, or wheel, or radio, creates a new human environment."[38] Even without this insight, *Understanding Media* was on its way to sales of over 100,000 copies.

The richness of the book defies summary. That was the whole idea. Faced with information overload, the mind must resort to pattern recognition to achieve understanding. The ideas in *Understanding Media* are for seizing each time they whirl past. Here is the notion of electric light escaping attention as a medium of communication in the chapter on the medium as message. Here is the explanation for that inattention in the chapter on hybrid energy. Here is a discussion of the work of Hans Selye and Adolphe Jonas introducing McLuhan's notion of closure as equilibrium-seeking, as displacement of perception, as completion of image . . . Here is Narcissus, a regular Halley's comet in *Understanding Media* and McLuhan's dual-purpose metaphor for the failure to understand media as extensions of the human body and the failure to perceive the message (new environments) created by media (technology). Here is McLuhan explaining that the response to the increased power and speed of bodily extensions creates new extensions. So *that's* what he meant by mankind becoming the sex organs of the machine world. Here are Chaplin, Joyce, Chopin, Pavlova, Eliot, and Charles Boyer in the same paragraph. When the maelstrom subsides, a serviceable raft for passage to other waters may be constructed by the reader prepared to lash together the ideas that have surfaced. They are ten.

1) We think of media mainly as those that bring us the news: press, radio, and television. McLuhan thought of a medium as an extension of our bodies or minds: clothing is an extension of skin, housing is an extension of the body's heat-control mechanism. The stirrup, the bicycle, and the car extend the human foot. The computer extends our central nervous system. A medium, or a technology, can be *any* extension of the human being.

2) Media work in pairs; one medium proves to "contain" another one. The telegraph, for example, contains the printed word, which contains writing, which contains speech. In this sense, the contained medium is the message of the containing one. Because this interaction of media is always obscured, and because its effects are so powerful, any message, in the ordinary sense of "content" or "information," is far less important than the medium itself. This is the fundamental sense of "the medium is the message."

3) There are exceptions to media working in pairs. McLuhan finds two. In the example given above, speech is the content of writing, but one may ask what the content of speech is. His answer is that speech contains thought. Here the chain of media ends. Thought is nonverbal and pure process. A second pure process, or message-free medium, is the electric light. It permits activities that could not be conducted in the dark, and McLuhan concedes that in this sense the activities might be thought of as the "content" of the light. But this simply reinforces his point that a medium changes the form of human relations and activities.

4) Media are powerful agents of change in how we experience the world, how we interact with each other, how we use our physical senses — the same senses that media extend. They must be studied for their *effects*, because their interaction obscures those effects and deprives us of the control required to use media effectively.

5) McLuhan teaches that new media do not so much replace each other as complicate each other. It is this interaction that obscures their effects. The technology of mankind in the age of acoustic space — the technology from which writing, print, and telegraph developed — was speech. Transformed into writing, speech lost the quality that made it part of the culture of acoustic space. It acquired a powerful visual bias, producing carryover effects in social and cultural organization that endure to the present. But there was also a loss, in that writing separated speech from the other physical senses. The powerful extension of speech permitted by the development of radio produced a similar loss, for this medium reduced speech to one sense — the auditory-aural. Radio is not speech (because we only listen), but it creates the illusion, like writing, of containing speech.

6) Many commentators thought McLuhan was penetrating in his

observations when he published *The Mechanical Bride*; just as many thought he was wrong. When he published *Understanding Media*, some disagreed even with his basic classification of media as hot or cool. It is a classification that hinges on special senses of the words "definition" and "information" — and on our physical senses more than word-senses. McLuhan borrowed the phrase "high definition" from the technical language of television. It means well-defined, sharp, solid, detailed, etc., in reference to anything visual. Letters of the alphabet, numbers, photographs, and maps, for example, are comparatively high definition. Forms and shapes and images that are not so distinct as these are low definition. For these, our eyes scan what is visible and fill in what is missing to "get the full picture," as in the case of sketches, cartoons, etc. Here is a contrast with the examples of high-definition visuals such as maps of the world, where no guesswork is involved in determining where South America ends, no doubt as to whether Spain is connected to Africa.

When McLuhan speaks of the information that a medium transmits he does not refer to facts or knowledge but to how our physical senses respond to the medium. Our examples so far have been only of the visual, but the principle applies to sounds as well. A high-definition medium gives a lot of information and gives the user little to do; a low-definition medium gives little information and makes the user work to fill in what is missing. This is the basis of the contrast between hot and cool media: high definition is hot; low definition is cool.[39] Here is how McLuhan compares various media:

HOT	COOL
radio	telephone
print	speech
photographs	cartoons
movies	television
lecture	seminar

The lecture/seminar contrast shows that hot media are low in participation, whereas cool media are high in participation. Looking at the other examples, we have a reminder that participation does not refer primarily to intellectual involvement but, like "definition" and "information," to how a medium engages our physical senses.

7) In discussing the myth of Narcissus, McLuhan begins by pointing out the common misrepresentation in which Narcissus is said to have fallen in love with *himself*. In fact, it was his inability to recognize his image that brought him to grief. He succumbed to the same numbing effect that all technologies produce, if the user does not scrutinize their operation. Technologies create new environments, the new environments create pain, and the body's nervous system shuts down to block the pain. The name Narcissus comes from the Greek word *narcosis*, meaning numbness.

The story of Narcissus illustrates mankind's obsessive fascination with new extensions of the body, but it also shows how these extensions are inseparable from what McLuhan calls "amputations." Take the wheel. As a new technology, it took the pressure of carrying loads off the human foot, which it extends. But it also created new pressure by separating or isolating the function of the foot from other body movements. Whether you are pedaling a bicycle or speeding down the freeway in your car, your foot is performing such a specialized task that you cannot, at that moment, allow it to perform its basic function of walking. So, although the medium has given you the power to move much more quickly, you are immobilized, paralyzed. In this way, our technologies both extend and amputate. Amplification becomes amputation. The central nervous system reacts to the pressure and disorientation of the amputation by blocking perception. Narcissus, *narcosis*.

McLuhan finds a lesson on the power of media once again in Greek mythology. It was the king Cadmus who sowed dragon teeth from which an army sprang up. It was also Cadmus who introduced the phonetic alphabet (from Phoenicia) to Greece. The dragon's teeth may, therefore, represent an older form of hieroglyphic writing from which the much more powerful alphabet grew.

8) In the case of Narcissus, a new medium both extends and amputates the human body; McLuhan finds another dimension of opposing effects accompanying the transition from mechanical to electronic technologies. This transition has involved a relentless acceleration of

all human activity, so extensive that the expansionist pattern associated with the older technology now conflicts with the contracting energies of the new one. Explosion (whether of population or knowledge) has reversed into implosion, because electronic technology has created a global village where knowledge must be synthesized instead of being splintered into isolated specialties.

In *Understanding Media*, McLuhan offers examples of overheated technologies and overextended cultures, and the reversals that they cause. The overextended road turns cities into highways and highways into cities; in the industrial society of the nineteenth century, with its extreme emphasis on fragmented procedures in the workplace, both the commercial and social world began to put new emphasis on unified and unifying forms of organization (corporations, monopolies, clubs, societies). McLuhan characterizes Samuel Beckett's play *Waiting for Godot* as dealing with the destructive aspects of the vast creative potential unleashed by the electronic age. This type of reversal is crucial in the integrated laws of media formulated late in McLuhan's career.

9) McLuhan's analysis identifies the effects of media in all areas of society and culture, but the starting point is always the individual, since media are defined as technological extensions of the body. As a result, McLuhan often puts his questions and conclusions in terms of the ratio between our physical senses (the extent to which we depend on them relative to each other) and what happens when that ratio is modified. Any such modifications inevitably involve a psychological dimension. In this respect, they point to the inadvisability of a rigid separation of the physical from the psychological, perhaps in all analysis, but especially for an understanding of McLuhan's teachings. When the alphabet was invented and brought about the intensification of the visual sense in the communication process, sight swamped hearing so forcefully that the effect spilled over from language and communication to reshape literate society's conception of space.

McLuhan stresses sense ratios and the effects of altering them: in Africa, the introduction of radio, a hot medium distorting the sensory balance of oral culture, produced the inevitable disorienting effect and rekindled tribal warfare; in dentistry, a device called an *audiac* consists of headphones bombarding the patient with enough noise to block pain from the dentist's drill; in Hollywood, the addition of sound to silent pictures impoverished and gradually eliminated the role of mime, with its tactility and kinesthesis.

The examples involve the relationships among the five physical senses. These senses may be ranked in order of how fragmented the perceptions are that we get through them. Sight comes first, because the eye is such a specialized organ. Then come hearing, touch, smell, and taste. Reading down the list, we move to less specialized senses. By contrast with the enormous power of the eye and the distances from which it can receive a stimulus, the tongue is thought capable of distinguishing only sweet, sour, bitter, and salt, and only in direct contact with the substance providing the stimulus.

10) Western culture, with its phonetic literacy, when transplanted to oral, nonliterate cultures, fragments their tribal organization and produces the prime example of media hybridization and its potent transforming effects. At the same time, electricity has transformed Western culture, dislocating its visual, specialist, fragmented orientation in favor of oral and tribal patterns. McLuhan retains the metaphors of violent energy in speculating on the final outcome of these changes — the fission of the atomic bomb and the fusion of the hydrogen bomb.

The hybridization of cultures occupies McLuhan most fully, but he offers other examples, such as electric light restructuring existing patterns of social and cultural organization by liberating the activities of that organization from dependence on daylight.

McLuhan emphasizes that media as extensions of the body not only alter the ratios among our physical senses, but that when the media combine they establish new ratios among themselves. This happened when radio came along to change the way news stories were presented and the way film images were presented in the talkies. Then television came along and brought big changes to radio.

When media combine, both their form and use change. So do the scale, speed, and intensity of the human endeavors affected. And so do the environments surrounding the media and their users. The hovercraft is a hybrid of the boat and the airplane. As such it eliminates not only the need for the stabilizing devices of wings and keels but the interfacing environments of landing strips and docks.

NEIL HARRIS, A HARVARD history professor, wrote to McLuhan to say what a great impression *Understanding Media* was making. As reviews began to appear, *The New Statesman* proclaimed that "Marshall McLuhan is now a power in more than one land."[40] It was not intended as a compliment. Reviewer Christopher Ricks alluded to "Mr. McLuhan's clutch of crystal balls" and found that the book's themes of electric speed, media as extensions, and media effects "cohabit not very fruitfully." Acknowledging the importance of these themes, he remarked that "they are altogether drowned by the style." (One can hear Leon Wilson and David Segal saying "I told you so.") The probes of *Understanding Media*, intended to irritate readers into thinking, proved so abrasive as to prevent Ricks from seeing that McLuhan *redefines* content in terms of media. Reviewers had identified a moral stance in *The Mechanical Bride*, though McLuhan had anticipated readers would think his detached amusement was indifference; *The New Statesman* review likewise ignored the deferral of moral judgment in the opening paragraph of *Understanding Media*, to cast McLuhan somewhere between preacher and showman.[41]

Commonweal Review called it an infuriating book full of brilliant insights and turgid incoherences, dismissing as "grotesquely inadequate" McLuhan's discovery of the rise of nationalism in typography.[42] At home, *The Tamarack Review* detected "an air of almost smug knowingness."[43] The *Toronto Star* reviewer found it a rich, sprawling book, but saw McLuhan as guilty of the same sort of exaggeration that marked Pasteur, Freud, Darwin, and Marx.[44] Reviewers began taking aim at each other: the CBC's Lister Sinclair fumed in *The Globe Magazine* that *Understanding Media* was full of words about pictures but contained not a single illustration, dismissing the book outright.[45] Alan Thomas then chastised Sinclair for his "fit of pique," noting that he had chosen "to deal with McLuhan's work by the easiest method ever known. If you don't understand something, but can't afford to ignore it, condemn it . . . "[46] Thomas offered the public advice on how to read McLuhan: "If you have any skill at reading poetry, use it."[47]

A reader responding to *Time*'s review pointed out that it had said not one word about the theme *Understanding Media* announced by its title.[48] And a popular misreading of McLuhan's thought was not long in taking hold. In a review obscurely titled "Reverse Canadian," the

Riverside Press-Enterprise of Riverside, California, branded *Understanding Media* "a book against books."[49]

THE REACTION IN RIVERSIDE must have made McLuhan wonder if the same "daily charade of human malice and stupidity" he had come to count on in Canada would await him in sunny California, where he would soon be arriving. A converted fire hall in San Francisco was the headquarters of Generalists Incorporated, a consulting firm run by adman Howard Luck Gossage and proctologist/ventriloquist Gerald (Gerry) Feigen.[50] (It was Gossage who would later produce fifty thousand bumper stickers reading "WATCHA DOIN MARSHALL McLUHAN?"[51] The firm catered to clients in the business world whose requirements could not be met by the fragmented knowledge offered by traditional, academic specialists. Gossage and Feigen needed a resource like McLuhan. A friend had sent Feigen *Understanding Media* in the belief that it was about advertising. Feigen spent long hours trying to figure out what it was about, all the while reciting "the medium is the message" like a mantra. He soon realized that "What is it about?" is the wrong question for McLuhan (though it contains the answer to the right question, where "about" means *around* or *surround*, putting the focus on medium as environment and message as effect). All the pieces of the medium-message-senses-television-effects mosaic fell into place for Feigen. He shared this with Gossage, who glanced at a few of McLuhan's pages and said, "I know more about that than he does."[52] But by the time they had gone through the whole book together, both men suspected McLuhan was a genius. They telephoned him in Toronto and invited themselves for a visit.

McLuhan was waiting for them when they arrived at the Royal York Hotel on a balmy spring evening. Feigen later described the intense look McLuhan reserved for first encounters as "a marvelous moment of inquiry."[53] It was the start of a long evening over dinner, with McLuhan's scrutiny reciprocated by the visitors. They learned that "one talks only about McLuhan's subject, and during an ordinary conversation one remark would spark multiple responses from him."[54] But there was also "a satisfying lack of conceit or egotism in his approach to discussion."[55] And it was fun for McLuhan and Feigen, who quickly discovered their mutual love of jokes and puns. Feigen had indexed over two thousand of them, and McLuhan was prepared to hear them all before he left. McLuhan also delivered many of his favorites; though his sense of timing, in Feigen's opinion, was sorely lacking, they were all lead-ins to rich observations on literature and technology. Gossage had little taste for humor, at least in the huge dollops his tablemates were serving each other, and sat through it all with a long face. When McLuhan left, after midnight, Gossage and Feigen then turned to the serious business of reviewing their impressions.

McLuhan had been in top form, answering their questions, setting out the projects underway at the Centre for Culture and Technology, soaring from topic to topic. Both Gossage and Feigen felt as if he had given them heavy reading assignments for their next meeting, less than twelve hours away. If they had any doubts at all that night, it was very clear to them before they left Toronto two days later that they wanted to make a commodity of McLuhan in the United States. It is a moot point whether Gossage, who said of *The Mechanical Bride* only that it was "bizarre,"[56] ever penetrated McLuhan's teachings well enough to understand why the man could not be packaged.

First it was to be New York. McLuhan was hesitant, because he had final exams to mark. But after Gossage and Feigen pointed out that they were opening a door leading away from such drudgery, McLuhan finished his marking and met them in Manhattan, regaling his first select audience of business types with the message that they knew nothing about media. The executives were dumbfounded; Gossage and Feigen were delighted and began making plans to bring their find to the San Francisco fire hall for the first McLuhan Festival.

Feigen recalls the event as a string of lunches and dinners.[57] At San Francisco's Off Broadway restaurant, McLuhan recognized the environment as a virtual tactorium and needed to explain to his tablemates their hopelessly visual reaction to the topless waitresses.[58] McLuhan paid the food as little attention as the girls, but displayed his usual healthy appetite for endless talk. In six days of nine-to-five sessions he explained many wonders, and then the event closed with a party, where Gossage had a twelve-piece mariachi band to herald in his Canadian discovery/discoverer. There was some question as to whether McLuhan, with his hypersensitive hearing, found the blaring trumpet stunt all that amusing. When Feigen spoke of what the future could hold, McLuhan asked: "Do you mean it can be all fun?"[59] That question too remained open.

McLUHAN TOOK NOTICE that Jonathan Miller had taken notice of him in early 1965: "Jonathan Miller is a medical man whose interest in my stuff derives from his concern with the sensory modalities. His interest in sensory modalities stems directly from his interest in neurology."[60] At their first meeting, in England, where McLuhan did a radio broadcast for the BBC, he earned high praise from Miller, who said that McLuhan was "doing for the fact of visual space what Freud did for sex, namely to reveal its pervasiveness in the structuring of human affairs."[61] Within a few weeks of returning to Canada, McLuhan heard from Miller, who declared himself a McLuhanite but had some suggestions to make, along with his own observations on the television medium: "I am one of your more vehement disciples and keep wishing that you would cool down the jargon a little bit . . . The other thing which has always worried me is the slightly promiscuous way in which you use 'cool' and 'hot.'"[62] Miller listed four distinct meanings he had discovered for these terms in McLuhan's writings, without documenting where they occurred. If Miller was a disciple, he was quickly becoming a doubting Thomas about points McLuhan had set out in *Understanding Media*; he was particularly keen to challenge him on his description of television as the cool medium par excellence.

In retrospect, Miller's reservations about this claim are not well-founded. Since *Understanding Media* first appeared in 1964, technical advances have given the world HDTV — high-definition television — without transforming TV into a hot medium. Improved sharpness and clarity of the image on the screen have been offset by the decreased visual intensity of color transmission. For McLuhan, color was tactile, not visual, a matter discussed in his later book with Harley Parker, *Through the Vanishing Point*, published in 1968. From this point of view, color is cooler than black and white, and the television medium retains the cool and tactile qualities McLuhan detected.

Furthermore, camera shots for television are most often closeups, framed for viewing on a small screen. By way of comparison, postcards and snapshots are also small, but without being restricted to close-ups, because they are high definition. The low-definition medium of television *requires* close-up shots, and it *keeps* the projected images low definition, even when viewed on a large-screen television set.

Finally, the image on a television screen is not photographic, like that of film. It is iconic and sculptural rather than pictorial. There is never any fixed image on the television screen, only a configuration in a constant state of flux. This is produced by light *through*, not light *on* — by electrons bombarding the picture tube. HDTV has brought no changes to this process. As a piece of technology, the television set of today remains as cool a medium as the box on which audiences watched the American debut of the Beatles in the year McLuhan published *Understanding Media*. Jonathan Miller was ready to challenge McLuhan on this understanding of the television medium in 1965.

McLuhan likened the image on a television screen to a two-dimensional mosaic. This TV mosaic does not have a visual structure, like the hot medium of print, where the eye races in a straight line over sharply defined forms. Nor does TV extend sight, to the exclusion of the other senses, because it has a tactile quality. It does not have uniform, continuous, or repetitive features. On the contrary, it is discontinuous and nonlineal; this is what gives the TV image the features of a mosaic. The television medium forces the use of what McLuhan later referred to as the "ear-view mirror,"[63] because the eye never receives a complete picture from the screen, just as the ear never receives a word in isolation from a stream of speech.[64]

The properties of the TV image make up what McLuhan called "mosaic space." He believed that the shift from the attitude of detachment fostered by print to the involvement stimulated by television can be explained only by the differences between visual and mosaic spaces.

Television shifted the balance among our senses and altered our mental processes. The shift was radical for two reasons. First, the abstract visual sense had dominated Western culture for centuries, through the alphabet and the printing press, but was abruptly dislocated by the new medium. Second, TV is primarily an extension of the sense of touch. Though received by the eye, the image on the screen has the type of texture associated with touch, which creates an interplay of all the senses.

Non-phonetic forms of writing that preceded the alphabet, as well as those that coexist with it in non-alphabetic cultures, are, like television, media that *integrate* the physical senses. Phonetic writing, by contrast, *separates* and *fragments* the senses. The low-definition TV image reverses this effect of phonetic writing and replaces the process of analytic fragmentation with a reintegration of sensory life.

The impact of such a shift was particularly strong in North America and England, where the cultures had been intensely literate for so long. In these countries, television moved people toward the tactile model of continental European cultures. As for social trends and values influenced by television, McLuhan noted that Europe began Americanizing as quickly as America began Europeanizing.

The effects of television began to make themselves felt as soon as television was introduced in the 1950s. North Americans acquired new passions for tactile involvement, in everything from skin-diving to the enveloping space of small cars. The TV western took on new importance, because the television image is highly compatible with the mix and tactility of textures of saddles, clothes, hides, and rough-hewn wood of the western's sets. A taste arose for all experience *in depth*. This affected language teaching (where reading knowledge alone was no longer favored) as well as clothes (with a new emphasis on textured materials), food, wine, and car styles.

A television screen is a mesh of dots. Light shines through them with varying intensity to allow an image to form. But the spaces in the mesh need to be closed before the image can form. McLuhan refers to this process of closure as "a convulsive sensuous participation that is profoundly kinetic and tactile."[65] Because touch is central among the senses, McLuhan defined tactility as the interaction of the senses, following St. Thomas's definition of touch as the meeting place of all the senses. There is, of course, no contact between the skin of the viewer and the television, but the eye is so much more intensely engaged by the television screen than by print that the *effect* is the same as that of touching. And it was the study of effects that interested McLuhan most. On these points, too, Jonathan Miller was to argue against him.

McLuhan cautioned that not even the type of insight he was trying to provide into the operation and power of media could offset "the ordinary 'closure' of the senses."[66] Here "closure" refers not to the closing up of the spaces in the mesh of dots on the television screen, but to a shift toward a new balance among our senses, such as that performed while the eye views television images. Television simultaneously reawakened the tactile sense and diminished the visual sense, as it is used in a purely print culture.

Sensory closure causes conformity to the pattern of experience presented by a medium. In making this observation, McLuhan sounded another caution, introducing medical metaphors and the principle of the numbing effect of media. The warning also shows us most clearly that to take McLuhan as a promoter of television is to miss an important part of his teaching: "The utmost purity of mind is no defense against bacteria . . . To resist TV, therefore, one must acquire the antidote of related media like print."[67] In his privately expressed views, McLuhan eventually went further when he became a grandfather, cautioning Eric: "Try not to have Emily exposed to hours and hours of TV. It is a vile drug which permeates the nervous system, especially in the young."[68]

The cool TV medium is unsuited to persons who represent a type or group with easily recognized features, because types deprive the viewer of the task of closure or completion of the image. Because of the medium itself, the sensory involvement it demands, and the habits of perception it imposes, the viewer comes to expect not a fixed image but one which must be fixed. Anyone whose physical appearance is a statement of role and status in life overheats the cool medium of TV, with disastrous consequences for themselves.

Successful TV personalities require texture and sculptural quality. These can be provided by highly stylized hair, mustache, beard, small nose, large teeth, craggy brow, high cheekbones, etc. McLuhan offered such observations and related advice to Canadian politicians, beginning with federal cabinet minister Mitchell Sharp: "For months I have been expounding to American and Canadian audiences that as soon as [U.S. presidential candidate Barry] Goldwater appeared on TV he was a 'dead duck.' He is fine on all media except TV. As far as TV is concerned he is a conventionally classifiable item and his verbal line is altogether too hot for the medium. You are not only unclassifiable, but you have a quiet and easy verbal manner that is as effective as Jack Paar's."[69]

Persons who are neither shaggy, craggy, nor sculptural may nevertheless project an acceptable television persona through cool and casual verbal skill, and it was *Tonight Show* host Jack Paar, in the earliest days of television, who demonstrated such skill, *and* the fundamental need of the medium for free-flowing chat and dialogue, which still informs it to this day.

McLuhan drew no sharp distinction between entertainment and education. The implications of the TV medium for education are the same as for entertainment or any other aspect of social and cultural organization. And they are equally far-reaching, because the medium has imposed closure of the senses. Pedagogical techniques that developed with the visual bias of print became less effective with the advent of television. But the solution to this problem is not to let students learn from teachers teaching on TV, a useless overheating of a cool medium. Noting that TV makes for myopia, McLuhan called again for an understanding of the dynamics of the medium, its action on our senses, and its interaction with other media, stressing at the same time the futility of confining attention to the TV "curriculum."

And so the conclusion that McLuhan draws as to what TV can do that the classroom cannot, regardless of subject matter, is inherent in the medium itself: "TV can illustrate the interplay of process and the growth of forms of all kinds as nothing else can."[70] He adds that it is the teacher's job not only to understand the television medium but to "exploit it for its pedagogical richness."[71]

Such are the points McLuhan makes in explaining television to the world in *Understanding Media* — illuminating points for some; debating points for Jonathan Miller. Miller differed with McLuhan above all on the nature of the image on the television screen, and noted: "The filling in which occurs in watching TV . . . really comes down to the simple matter of completing perspectives and not giving some spatial meaning to the different patches of grey tones. In this respect, therefore, I do not think that you can really put too much weight on the participation which an audience brings to TV. *It is important certainly in the neuro-psychological argument.*"[72]

Here Miller was conceding a point that would eventually be demonstrated by psychologist Herbert Krugman in support of McLuhan's view,[73] but Miller continued, insisting on a notion radically different from McLuhan's: "In fact TV does work by a series of frame by frame presentations and although within each frame the picture has a grain which is due to the scanning line on the camera, the picture which the audience gets is a compilation of *frames* and the scanning process which makes up this picture does *not* impose scanning on the *observer*. In a sense, both movies and TV are particulate presentations . . . The difference between the two is purely quantitative and not, in fact, qualitative."[74]

Miller would not retain this argument in his later writing on McLuhan's ideas, but in 1965 he maintained that the iconic quality of television was purely metaphorical, ascribing it to "the smallness of the screen which makes it like a tiny devotional object in the drawing-room."[75] McLuhan ignored the absurdity of this observation and confined his response to an explanation of his approach in *any* area of investigation: "Don't allow my terminology to 'put you off.' I use language as probe, not as package. Even when I seem to be making very dogmatic statements, I am exploring contours."[76] Miller did not respond to this implicit invitation to challenge McLuhan on his metaphors, and events were to suggest that the lesson on the McLuhan method had meant little to him.

Four years later, however, McLuhan was delighted to learn that he was to be the subject of a book by Miller in Frank Kermode's Modern Masters series.[77] He described himself as "enormously flattered that Jonathan Miller should take the trouble to even look at my stuff."[78] The trouble would prove to be McLuhan's. Miller's book was a virulent attack that McLuhan did not bother to read until he realized how much attention it was attracting. With equanimity, he wrote at first to Frank Kermode: "[Miller] is not inquiring nor discussing along the lines I have opened up. He assumes that our sensory order is not violatable by new technologies. This is a universal assumption of our entire establishments, humanist and scientific alike. Merely to challenge it creates panic, for it means that we have polluted not just the physical but the psychic and perceptual order of our societies without questioning our procedures. To argue whether there is any quantitative proof of this is part of the panic. Nobody *wants* any proof. Most people desperately don't want it."[79]

Later, McLuhan took counsel with the BBC's Martin Esslin: "May

I ask you whether you think it reasonable that I should write a letter to *Encounter* concerning Jonathan Miller? In his book he refers to my work as a pack of lies, without referring to any of my percepts whatever. In what sense do you think he means 'lies'? Does he imagine that I have consciously and deliberately falsified evidence? Surely Miller is a clown with the habits of a sixth form debator?"[80]

The little book stayed in the public eye. McLuhan was irritated, and began referring to Miller's "anti-McLuhan crusade."[81] Eventually he eased his irritation by deciding to treat Miller's work as a spoof: "Apropos your review of Miller's *McLuhan*. Dr. Miller, remember, is the cabaret artist and satirist who did 'Beyond the Fringe,' in part at least. His book is a spoof, of course. Quite deliberately, he ignored my Cambridge work on Thomas Nashe and the history of rhetoric, of the trivium and quadrivium from the fifth century to the present. He ignored all my symbolist poetry studies in order to create the nostalgic image of a prairie boy yearning for the fleshpots of culture."[82]

McLuhan's new interpretation allowed him to deal with the matter in good humor when Miller's book began to appear in translation and follow McLuhan around the world on his lecture tours: "Last night Corinne and I returned from Caracas where we had spent a most interesting week, and where we were surrounded by two to five security guards, night and day. Corinne found this very exciting, and I found it very suffocating. One of our guards proudly presented me with a Spanish copy of Jonathan Miller's book, in which I wrote 'he is an *enamigo.*'"[83]

AT THE 1965 MEETING of the American Association for Public Opinion Research, Dr. Herbert E. Krugman, then manager of corporate public opinion research at General Electric, advanced the idea of television as a medium of low involvement by comparison with print. The researcher defined involvement by the number of spontaneous thoughts that subjects made while viewing television — thoughts linking the content of their viewing to something in their own lives. Such a definition contrasts with what McLuhan meant by a "cool medium" in *Understanding Media*. Krugman was examining subjects registering mental reaction; McLuhan was describing a physical process where a medium provides little information and requires highly active involvement of the eye or the ear to fill in what is missing.

Once they became aware of each other's work, McLuhan picked up Krugman's description of the contrast between the active responses to print and passive responses to television in terms of fast versus slow brain waves. For some observers, this might have signaled that McLuhan was moving from physical to mental criteria for describing the contrast between cool and hot media, or a tacit recognition that the contrast was blurred by the neurophysiological realities underpinning it. Krugman believed the world should be moving toward McLuhan. He did not regard the differences he had uncovered as controversial, but he thought that few people had fully appreciated them, and he added: "We need now to spell out, if we can, the meanings of these differences, and to catch up, if we can, with Marshall McLuhan . . . In a sense he could not really be understood by a world raised on print and print theory about communication."[84]

McLuhan eschewed *transportation* in favor of *transformation* as a model for describing the process of communication, and Krugman grasped the contrast well: "It seems to me that McLuhan might characterize our field of communication theory as horse-and-buggy, or at best a 'Pony Express' type of theory. That is, we are wedded to a view of someone preparing a message, the message carried across a distance . . . and a receiver reading or decoding the message at the other end."[85]

Krugman also understood that it was the technology of television broadcasting that had led McLuhan to scrap the old model. In fact, television could not even be called mass communication in the old sense. The transportation model was no longer valid, because viewers were not decoding anything on their screens. Even when a printed message is shown on the screen, the letters must first be processed by the eye in a manner which is not required of letters in ink on paper. Krugman captured the essence of McLuhan's lesson on television's effect on the human sensorium, and the paradox of television, when he said of viewers that "their eyes and ears have been 'extended' into the situation portrayed on the screen. *They are participating in an experience* — even if it is passive participation."[86]

The EEG data emerging from Krugman's experiments confirmed

McLuhan's observations on the television medium, including the paradox that it is and is not a medium of communication.[87] The only way to salvage the old transportation model for the communication process was to think of the television viewer as transported. But that would reduce the model to a metaphor, and McLuhan's sensitivity to the power of metaphor would not allow him to debase it.

In their correspondence, McLuhan reminded Krugman of a principle articulated in *Understanding Media*: "There is a sense in which the 'content' of any medium is another medium. This is a natural fact of figure-ground relationships."[88] Striking a rare historical note, McLuhan alluded to a source for the work of his own mentors and peers: "The work of I. A. Richards and Empson and F. R. Leavis in part stems from the psychological explorations of F. C. Bartlett in his *Remembering*. His discovery that all perception is in effect the re-structuring of any situation whatever led Richards and others to test this on the printed page. They discovered at once that people rearrange whatever is presented to them in patterns that do not remain unchanged. From week to week and year to year the same experiences are, according to Bartlett's recorded observations, undergoing perpetual change. The objects on a table seen twenty years earlier are given new patterns, etc. Hence his title *Re-membering*."[89] As for television, he pointed out that "TV is not merely rear projection. There is also the entire electric mesh — what Joyce calls 'the charge of the light barricade.'"[90]

MCLUHAN BEGAN DEVELOPING his own proposal for a television series intended to reproduce the 1960s in themes. With himself as primary host and a prominent television commentator as cohost, the series would recreate actual events through stock footage and enjoy the benefit of McLuhan's commentary. This was not produced.[91] Another proposal followed: "Up Against the Wall" was to feature not McLuhan but the audience as actor. "The drama inherent in genuine human need was the motivating force which led to the creation of this program format . . . the problems dealt with in this program will be genuine and will arise from the real or imagined needs of people . . ."[92] The program was not produced.

But McLuhan made his point "with brilliant style," according to the *Christian Science Monitor*, in NBC's *Experiment on TV* series: "The viewer was tugged, eyes blinking and ears tingling, through a demonstration of TV's profound effects on our civilization. Flash cuts, double dissolves, 'stills' superimposed on action shots, elliptical editing, split screen, op art, pop art, bop art, all pummeled the viewer as Mr. McLuhan translated the message in his cool Canadian voice."[93] McLuhan dismissed the program, produced entirely from edited clips, as "grotesque trash."[94]

McLuhan's unsuccessful attempts to explain television on television demonstrate what he sought to explain: "Recently, on the David Frost show, I had the opportunity to explain why the TV viewer tends to be 'stoned' [or stunned, bombarded]. TV as a kind of inner trip disposes people to many changes of outlook, including loss of outer goals. I had other opportunities to explain this matter, but from this vast audience there was not one phone-call — not one question by way of follow-up."[95] But when a magazine ad for ABC News, featuring extracts from McLuhan's evaluation of the network, offered readers the full text of his comments, it drew response day in and day out for over four months.[96] The two episodes could hardly have been a more telling comment on the contrasting effects of television and print.

McLuhan did not neglect the positive interaction of these media: "In North America . . . TV has not been the friend of literacy *except* to encourage depth involvement in language as a complex structure. In other words, TV fosters the *Finnegans Wake* approach to language."[97] Though such comments from McLuhan were rare, it was widely believed that he embraced television, when in fact, he made dire predictions about the new medium: "When TV is older it will use the cognitive dance of our brain cortex directly via the cathode x-ray tube. This may be utterly disastrous, like nuclear weapons . . . "[98] Such an opinion, privately expressed by McLuhan, carries less force than a public one calling television "that Christ-killer of the ages." The phrase originated with Norman Mailer and was never used by McLuhan.[99]

11

The Good Ground

Electric man is discarnate man, sharing a consciousness, or at least a *sciousness*, as fully as any native tribe.
—*MARSHALL MCLUHAN TO FATHER LAURENCE SHOOK*
20 JUNE 1972

Discarnate man is not compatible with an incarnate Church.
—*MARSHALL MCLUHAN TO CLARE BOOTHE LUCE*
5 APRIL 1979

AFTER THE PUBLICATION OF *Understanding Media*, McLuhan became increasingly concerned with the spiritual implications of the human subconscious externalized by electronic technology. He saw a new responsibility for mankind to develop consciousness of both pure process (as the governing dynamic of the world, from atoms to the arts) and of the effects of specific processes. At the same time, in the suspended value judgment fostered by sensitivity to process (to which he had adhered himself since writing *The Mechanical Bride*), he recognized a metamorphosis of a Christian imperative: "Awareness of process tends to push value judgments into abeyance. In fact it has a sort of secular mode of Christian charity about it."[1]

The saying "God is dead" was much in vogue in the same counter-culture of the 1960s that was adopting McLuhan (and missing the double irony of giving a man of faith the status of an icon). He dismissed his apparent popularity as mere tolerance of his thought, to

be explained by the movement of the Western world into tribal organization,[2] but he pondered the popular slogan and came to a
somewhat improbable interpretation of it through his own contrast
between visual and acoustic space: "Suddenly really got the 'God is
Dead' message. They mean that the incarnation was his death because
he became visible. Now in the non-visual time, the visual alienates
them."[3]

McLuhan repeatedly saw the principles of his media analysis as
applicable to the Church: "The church is so entirely a matter of communication that like fish that know nothing of water, Christians have
no adequate awareness of communication. Perhaps the World has
been given to us as an anti-environment to make us aware of the
word."[4] (And perhaps of the Word.) McLuhan explored another
dimension of this theme with graduate student Allen Maruyama:
"There seems to be a deeply willed ignorance in man. 'Sin' might also
be defined as lack of 'awareness.'"[5] McLuhan was referring not to
awareness of self, for that came to Adam and Eve after the Fall, but
to a lack of awareness of environments and their effects. Elsewhere,
he quoted Joyce expressing the same thought: "As for the viability of
vicinals, when invisible they are invincible."[6]

The theme of environments proved to be a rich vein in McLuhan's
dialogue with Maruyama, who led him to an explanation for North
Americans going outside to be alone, while the people of other
cultures go outside to be together. (Conversely, North Americans stay
at home to entertain, while others reserve their homes as private
space.) McLuhan had been thinking about this for a long time when
he mentioned it to Maruyama. As their conversation took various
turns, McLuhan wondered aloud why the Western world typically
shunned investigation of the effects of technology. Maruyama spontaneously answered that the Western mind fears invasion of privacy.
The observation brought McLuhan back at once to the "inside/
outside" question. Here was the key he had been searching for:
Western habits could be explained as a safeguarding of privacy by
moving communal activity to the controlled environment of the home
and eliminating the threatening environment of public space by
reserving its use for private individuals.

McLuhan wrote at once to Ted Carpenter, sharing the insight into a cultural contrast that had puzzled them both since the earliest days of their seminar. "There it is, Ted, after all these years. The Western psyche is a fragile, specialized product of the phonetic alphabet which stands in terror of any snooping around for its credentials, whereas tribal men welcome such study."[7] Before long, McLuhan was applying his fresh hypothesis: "Since North Americans go outside for privacy and inside for community, whereas Europeans go outside for community and inside for privacy, Henry James was able to use these antithetic modes in many different patterns."[8] He took the matter up with Margaret Atwood, writing: "'Why do North Americans, unlike all other people on this planet, go outside to be alone and inside to be with people?' I knew that the answer would be massive, since if it were anything else, it would be easy to spot. You provide the answer in *Survival* when you indicate the North American crash program for conquering nature."[9]

A verse of Scripture served McLuhan as a means of integrating two of his much-favored analytical tools — figure/ground analysis (the emergence of form against a background) and the concept/percept distinction (ideas as opposed to the physical sensations in which they originate): "[It] is the same as the difference indicated in Luke 8:18: 'Heed *how* you hear.' The entire text depends on understanding that. Those who get the word of God as a wonderful idea or concept soon lose it. Those who get it as a percept, a direct thing, interfacing and resonating, are those who represent the 'good ground.' The sower and the seed image is a direct anticipation of the gestalt figure-ground relationship. All those who are having difficulty with their Catholic faith today tend to be the victims of a post-Renaissance conceptualized theology and catechism."[10] McLuhan also linked his notion of user as content to chapters 16 and 17 of the New Testament's Acts of the Apostles.[11]

Such reflections were in the nature of the McLuhan probes; others were rooted squarely in his Christian convictions and brought him back repeatedly to his perception of the tension between Christianity and electronic media: "It is not brains or intelligence that [are] needed to cope with the problems which Plato and Aristotle and all of their successors to the present have failed to confront. What is needed is a readiness to undervalue the world altogether. This is only possible for a Christian . . . All technologies and all cultures, ancient and modern, are part of our immediate expanse. There is hope in this diversity since it creates vast new possibilities of detachment and amusement at human gullibility and self-deception. There is no harm in reminding ourselves from time to time that the 'Prince of this World' is a great P.R. man, a great salesman of new hardware and software, a great electric engineer, and a great master of the media. It is his master stroke to be not only environmental but invisible, for the environmental is invincibly persuasive when ignored."[12]

With his former student Father Walter Ong, McLuhan shared his concern that the clergy were as ignorant as their parishioners about the impact of technology. He identified the problem as the Gutenberg legacy of visual space, the source of literate mankind's demand for connectedness as a condition for the world making sense. That demand fostered neglect of the dynamic and creative disconnections McLuhan called *resonant intervals*. The problem reached into the bureaucracies of the Catholic Church, which were marching into the late-twentieth century with no understanding of the rationale of electronic technology. "There was no one at the Council of Trent who understood the psychic and social effects of Gutenberg," McLuhan wrote to Ong, adding that "the church is no better off now, humanly speaking."[13]

Nor were humans, in contact with the whole world under electronic conditions, any better off, McLuhan told Allen Maruyama, for that contact eliminated individual freedoms. The only hope McLuhan saw for restoring them was through the transformation of mankind by the sacraments of the Church, and the development of the awareness of self through the community.[14]

McLuhan pursued this idea and widened its scope. It preoccupied him, and he wrote to many friends and colleagues about it. He explored the consequences for contemporary Christianity of Eric Havelock's assertion that the private individual is a development from the technology of the phonetic alphabet, confessing that he was "completely baffled by the relation of the Graeco-Roman tradition to the church at the present time."[15] The dissolution of that tradition and the threat to Western literacy resulting from the pressure of electronic technology brought McLuhan back to Havelock's claim and an apparently inescapable conclusion: "If the private person is an artefact, then it becomes criminal to perpetuate him technologically in the electric age."[16] McLuhan's correspondent, Alexis de Beauregard, subtly suggested that, historically, the Mediterranean is the message, but to this McLuhan made no reply.

The urgency of the question for McLuhan made him impatient and irritated that the Church could provide nothing more than ineffectual cosmetic changes to the liturgy: "Cat-gut and cat-calls cum Gregorian. The mass gets longer, limper, lumpier."[17] This complaint did not keep him from attending mass daily, reading Scripture every morning, and praying confidently.

McLuhan so distressed Etienne Gilson with his urgent questing over the matter of faith and Western culture that the venerable philosopher was unable to sleep. Gilson did not share McLuhan's view that Western culture was sloughing off the Gutenberg legacy, and he admitted that he did not understand what McLuhan meant by saying that the electronic revolution was terminating the Church's marriage with the West. But Gilson continued to wrestle with the ideas. He wrote to his St. Michael's colleague Father Lawrence Shook: "I am wondering if McLuhan's problem has been answered; I even wonder if his question is answerable at all?"[18]

McLuhan too wrote to Father Shook, summoning all his key percepts to describe the conundrum of the Church in the electronic age, citing Scripture again in linking Christianity to media analysis: "There has been a tremendous 'rip-off' of the human flesh and bones, as it were, a fantastic 'hi-jack' job performed by electric engineering . . . Although the church began, and continues, with a communication theory or doctrine, Western philosophy has had none since the Greeks. That is, in Western philosophy I have been able to find no doctrine of the changes which man inflicts upon his entire psyche by his own artifacts. The Old Testament is full of awareness of these changes, which St. Paul, 1 Romans i, calls 'vain imaginings' etc. Christianity is itself a theory of communication, an announcement of change in the structure of the human being, body and soul, since Christ."[19]

With this last observation, McLuhan was emphasizing not so much the tension between the Church and electronic hegemony as a second one intersecting it — the tension between the Church as institution and the dynamics at the core of Christianity: "There is one vast paradox related to the fact of the Christian involvement in the Graeco-Roman intellectual matrix because this matrix resists all possibility of change, while the Christian thing is concerned with change at every level and in every facet."[20]

McLuhan did not believe that he had made any progress either in understanding the matter himself or communicating his thoughts to others, in spite of two years of energetic discussion and much correspondence. He viewed electronic man's discarnate state as sinister and predicted it would soon create chaos in the ranks of the theologians.[21]

But he continued to ask his questions. Considering the Church and literacy, he wrote: "Let me make a little note here about the church and literacy. Alphabetic man is the only one who ever tried to transform other cultures into his form. Oral societies never try to convert anybody. The early church began with a liaison with the Graeco-Roman and the alphabetic. Ever since, the church has made inseparable the propagation of the faith and of Graeco-Roman culture, thus ensuring that only a tiny segment of mankind would ever be Christian. Would it appear to you, now that literacy is technologically expendable, that the church can also dispense with Graeco-Roman forms of literacy and hierarchy? I have been able to find no ecclesiastic or theologian for whom this is a meaningful question."[22]

When McLuhan became fully immersed in his new linguistic discoveries, he found a link even there to questions of faith and belief: "All of man's artifacts are *structurally* linguistic and metaphoric. This discovery, unknown to anybody in any culture, would justify a book without any other factors whatever.[23] Remember the [James] Watson autobiography of his discovery of the double helix in the DNA particle? Literally speaking, this breakthrough about the linguistic structure of all human artifacts is incomparably larger and deeper-going. I am, myself, unable to grasp the implications. Certainly it means that the unity of the family of man can be seen, not as biological, but as intellectual and spiritual."[24]

It was neither the question of faith and Graeco-Roman culture nor the conundrum of the incarnate Church in the age of discarnate mankind that McLuhan put to God when he dreamt in later years of a conversation with Him. The setting was "rather like the White House lawn — large, elegant and expansive, a sort of American Olympus. God was altogether charming and urbane and one had the impression of His being a man of complete (i.e. unostentatious) knowledge."[25] (Was McLuhan casting President Jimmy Carter, a man of God, a Southerner in the oral tradition that keeps the Logos whole, in the role of God Himself?) McLuhan wanted to know what God thought of *Finnegans Wake* and was about to favor Him with a reading when he woke up.

ON 8 MARCH 1966, McLuhan agreed to let his name be used in a circulation letter promoting subscriptions to *Time* magazine. In exchange, he received one dollar. In the draft copy he is styled "Marshall McWhoan" and "Marshall McGoohan," in the sardonic style of *Time* he described in *The Mechanical Bride*. *Time* executive Bernard M. Auer wrote to him two months later. Whether inspired to metaspoof by the publicity copy or in an honest mistake, Auer addressed his letter to "Mr. McLahan."[26]

Amid these slightly surrealistic events, McLuhan was Poe's sailor, not in the Maelstrom but on the fishing ground, and about to land a big one. If *Time* publisher Henry Luce III knew of *The Mechanical Bride* and its scathing comments on his publication and his person ("Mr. Luce and his advisors are content to enjoy the irresponsible manipulation of these arts and techniques as entertainment without directing them to the achievement of direct political power"),[27] it did not keep him from trekking to Toronto just to meet the feisty father of *The Bride*. Luce certainly did not know McLuhan had also said: "Like all simple men of single mind (and success is certainly not to be had or desired in a technological world by complex men with varied outlooks) Mr. Luce understands what he is doing only in a small degree."[28] McLuhan welcomed the opportunity to illuminate Luce. The publisher arrived with a delegation of six other Time Incorporated executives and "got a crash course in Canadian politics and sociology . . . and some candid comments."[29] So said *Time*.

"It seems you are taking over from [actress] Tuesday Weld and Batman as the pop hero of the mass media," Bob Ellis of *Time* told

McLuhan.[30] *Life* and *Newsweek* featured him in the same week. (Only Barbra Streisand had ever been so fortunate.) "It must be your cold personality that intrigues them," Ellis joked.[31] Though McLuhan managed to baffle the *Newsweek* reporter, he was clearly attaining celebrity status. Some of his associates thought he was becoming overexposed and underappreciated.[32]

OTHERS WERE MORE CONCERNED for his health than his cachet. Ted Carpenter, Lou Forsdale (McLuhan's friend at Columbia University's Teachers College), and colleagues at St. Michael's knew he was ignoring spells of dizziness and blackouts. He had already been denying these signs of serious illness, even to himself, for nearly eight years.[33] Now they were growing worse. Though he tried to conceal his episodes from Corinne, she was quickly becoming aware of them. She also knew he regarded any sickness as a sign of a weak constitution, that it made him angry, and that his dislike of doctors would prevent him from seeking a medical opinion about his condition.

There was no time to be ill. The spectacular sales of *Understanding Media* and the San Francisco symposium had brought a steady stream of invitations to speak; unofficially, 1967 was the Year of McLuhan. He addressed the American Marketing Association, the Pharmaceutical Advertising Club, the Texas-Stanford TV Seminar, the PEN Congress, the National Housewares Manufacturers Association, the 28th Annual National Packaging Forum, AT&T, IBM, the American Association of Advertising Agencies, the National Bureau of Standards, the International Symposium on Technology and World Trade, and the Container Corporation of America — among others. In less than a year.

In March 1967, NBC aired "This is Marshall McLuhan" in their *Experiment in TV* series.[34] *The Medium Is the Massage* appeared, even as McLuhan was signing contracts for *Culture Is Our Business* and *From Cliché to Archetype* with publishers in New York. He collected honorary doctorates from the University of Manitoba, Simon Fraser University in British Columbia, and Iowa's Grinnell University, along with a citation from Niagara University and West Germany's Carl Einstein Preis. He had already received his first two honorary doctorates from the University of Windsor and Assumption College. That spring, Herbert McLuhan died peacefully in his eighty-eighth year. His son's blackouts became more frequent, but even in the privacy of his diary, he said nothing about his own deteriorating health. Though he could go for days without the sudden bouts that paralyzed him for a minute or two, they came often enough for most of his acquaintances to know that something was seriously wrong.

During the summer months he was asked to appear on TV with Groucho Marx but declined because of other commitments. He completed a third and final draft of *Culture Is Our Business*, working at an old ping-pong table in the basement at Wells Hill, and did an interview on Rudolf Nureyev with *Esquire* when the magazine was directed to McLuhan by George Balanchine of the Ballet Russe, who had said "McLuhan talks our kind of language."[35] Later in the year he would travel to Vancouver for a presentation ceremony, when chosen along with author Anne Hébert and architect Arthur Erickson to receive a Molson Prize. At home, he gave the University of Toronto's Marfleet Lectures and spoke to the Systems and Procedures Association and the National Conference of Christian Broadcasters. The release of a Japanese book on McLuhan in August opened the way to the publication of all of his writings in Japanese translation when sales reached a quarter-million copies within two months.[36]

As soon as Fordham University officials heard of their success in the bid to secure one of New York State's newly created Schweitzer Chairs in the Humanities, Father John Culkin, recently appointed as director of Fordham's Center for Communication, approached McLuhan. They had first met when McLuhan spoke at a conference at Brandeis University in 1963, opening his address with the remark: "Of course, it's very difficult for a naked person to learn how to read."[37] They became friends at once. To the astonishment of Culkin, who had been studying McLuhan's writings for five years and corresponding with him for two, McLuhan asked him to write a letter to University of Toronto president Claude Bissell, attesting to the importance of his work. McLuhan began making annual trips to New York during summer sessions to lecture for Culkin at Fordham and for Lou Forsdale at Columbia University's Teachers College.

Culkin feared that McLuhan would refuse to uproot his family and come to New York for a full year, but the prestige of the new Schweitzer Chair at a major American Catholic university was a powerful attraction. Upheavals could be minimal. Eric, who had returned to Toronto after a four-year stint in the U.S. Air Force and was already proving to be an invaluable assistant to his father, would join him to teach at Fordham. Ted Carpenter and Harley Parker also received official positions as assistants and formed the Schweitzer team along with the McLuhans, father and son. Teri would complete her degree at Fordham, Liz would join the first class of Fordham's newly opened Thomas More College, and Michael would continue studies at Roosevelt High. Stephanie knew she wanted to remain behind and complete her degree at the University of Toronto, while Mary, married in December 1966, was living in California. A fine house, elegantly furnished and with spacious grounds, on Bronxville's leafy Kimbal Avenue, was available for the year and could be ready and waiting for the family to move in. McLuhan accepted.

Culkin and his colleagues set out an academic program for twenty senior students to work full time with the Schweitzer team. A course of lectures to be conducted by McLuhan, Carpenter, and Parker would meet three times a week. Interest and enthusiasm ran high, as everyone at Fordham awaited McLuhan. But trouble arrived first.

New York State attorney general Louis Lefkowitz, a Fordham graduate, announced that the university would not be eligible to receive a Schweitzer Chair after all, because it was a Catholic institution. The press and TV corps descended on the campus. Much indignant comment was generated over such shabby treatment of a university that had shown the initiative to bring Canada's guru of the electronic age to the Bronx. Fordham did lose the Schweitzer Chair but honored its commitment for the year to McLuhan, Carpenter, and Parker.

"Splendid quarters," McLuhan said, as the family took up residence on 31 August 1967, adding: "The tactile world of the interval has preoccupied me more and more."[38] The family found themselves neighbors to Jack Paar. McLuhan illuminated Paar on the subject of television, and Paar put McLuhan on to a good toupee-maker. As a result, he began making TV appearances wearing his new hairpiece, and Paar would be promoted in the second edition of *Understanding Media* from pages 29 and 309 to page 1.

Ruth Anderberg, who was appointed secretary to the Albert Schweitzer chair, recalls McLuhan as "rather stoic" and not given to much laughter. She was soon to understand why.

The reaction to the Lefkowitz decision was strong enough to bring unsolicited donations to Fordham in support of its program. It also brought more requests for interviews and speaking engagements than McLuhan could have managed even in good health. He was far from it. In October, he suffered a paralyzing blackout in front of his class.

Mild epilepsy had been the diagnosis from a Toronto doctor years earlier. Now Culkin and Carpenter were alarmed and took medical counsel. They were told McLuhan should be checked for a brain tumor.[39] Knowing his aversion to doctors, Culkin chose to confront him with the latest medical opinion in the presence of Corinne. McLuhan agreed to enter New York's Columbia-Presbyterian Hospital for tests. Three would be required. He discharged himself from the hospital after two. That had been enough to determine that he had a brain tumor — benign, operable, and discovered in just enough time to prevent irreversible damage. McLuhan went back to his teaching, but the high energy level that was his trademark had disappeared, and the spells kept coming on.

The media were still on a partial state of alert to events at Fordham after the Schweitzer matter, and now students, faculty, and the family were being deluged with questions about McLuhan's health. He agreed to return to hospital to complete his testing but kept opposing the idea of an operation, finally giving consent only in late November. Surgery was set for the Saturday after Thanksgiving Day, to be performed by renowned neurologist Lester Mount. In the days leading up to the operation, Culkin spent long hours at the hospital with McLuhan, who asked him on Thanksgiving: "Do you think that Dr. Mount drinks?"[40]

Mount anticipated a five-hour procedure to remove the meningioma under McLuhan's brain. As McLuhan was wheeled to the operating theater at 8:00 on Saturday morning, Culkin and Eric began their vigil, assuring Corinne that they would relay hourly reports to the rest of the family in Bronxville. At the end of five hours, the medical team did not emerge; instead a second team joined them. Ten hours. A third team. Only at 5:00 on Sunday morning did the

news come that the operation had been a success. McLuhan, awaking
in the recovery room, looked at the clock and supposed it was 5:30 on
Saturday evening. Corinne, Teri, and Liz arrived at the hospital by
8:00 a.m. and found McLuhan engaged in lively conversation. Over
two hundred representatives from the media had been in contact with
the hospital. The reports they filed were not the ones they had already
prepared. It was the same day that Father Gulkin's beloved assistant,
Vivian Kaplan, died of cancer.

When the anesthetic wore off, McLuhan was in blinding, searing
pain. Filling in the blank pages of his diary later, for the day of his
operation he wrote only "ruddy gore."[41] Soon he would discover
other blanks that could not be filled in — five years of reading were
lost, and Corinne had to be at his elbow to remind him of names. But
he appeared to hold her responsible for having subjected him to the
operation.[42] McLuhan's hypersensitive senses, his impatience, and his
high-strung nature all became intensified by his ordeal.[43] One of
his doctors wondered if he should be committed to an asylum. Dr.
Mount spoke of three months as the normal period for full recovery
from brain surgery; McLuhan's would take three years.

Before he left the hospital, McLuhan's spirits were boosted enormously when Eric arrived with a publishing contract for his father to
witness. Father-and-son dialogues had inspired a work cracking the
code of the thunders in *Finnegans Wake*.[44] The youngest McLuhan
had been slated to break on the publishing scene at the same time as
his brother. Michael had been commissioned by *Esquire* editor Tom
Hedley to write an article on the "flower children." This he did, the
article was accepted, and Michael received payment, but for reasons
that were never explained the work was not published.[45] As Christmas
drew near, McLuhan was cheered at the prospect of Stephanie's
arrival from Toronto and Mary's from California. But he refused to be
discharged from the hospital on 13 December . "To start a new life on
the 13th seemed a bit much," he wrote.[46]

The return to his comfortable surroundings in Bronxville flooded
McLuhan with relief, and he resumed his correspondence and work at
once. To Harry Skornia he described the removal of his tumor,
noting that it "was not connected to the brain at all — a work of pure
symbolic juxtaposition."[47] To Wilfred Watson, whose trip to New

York for work on *From Cliché to Archetype* had been canceled because of McLuhan's surgery, he wrote with the same confidence that caused him earlier to predict "we can complete that book in ten days."[48] By Christmas Eve the entire family was gathered. "All in together,"[49] McLuhan wrote on Christmas Day. He was hard at work on *War and Peace in the Global Village*.

Despite his decreased vitality, the second half of McLuhan's year at Fordham was both productive and pleasant. Perhaps the most creative collaboration McLuhan developed during this time was with Tony Schwartz, the award-winning sound artist and maker of commercials. Schwartz's innovations provided concrete examples of McLuhan's teachings on media, and McLuhan provided the framework for Schwartz's art.[50] McLuhan resumed his Fordham teaching commitments in January 1968 and even undertook outside speaking engagements by February.

The McLuhans were invited to a personal, private screening of Stanley Kubrick's *2001* before the film was released, but ten minutes proved to be enough to bore McLuhan. It was only at Teri's urging that he remained for the full showing, sleeping through much of it. It was a typical McLuhan reaction, summarized in his aphorism "It's nice to have the avant-garde behind you."[51] Any multimedia artist who claimed to have drawn inspiration from McLuhan for existential commentary via strobe-lit exhibits of ball bearings cascading to the beat of heavy rock drove the inspirer away, asking, "What has this got to do with my work?"[52]

The question points to the same conclusion that journalist Michael Horowitz drew in reporting on McLuhan's year in New York, saying, "What's happening with Marshall McLuhan at Fordham? Only a few are getting the message."[53] The slant of the piece was typical; the media seldom knew what to make of McLuhan and relied on the tired Hollywood cliché of the nutty professor.[54] This was never more apparent than on McLuhan's return to Toronto.

A YEAR IN THE United States, after twenty-three in Canada, had not caused him to lose sight of his objectives, and the irritants against which he had pitted himself for so long offered themselves afresh. He was ready to renew his battle. But first came a triple move. From New York back to Wells Hill Avenue; from there to a new home in Toronto's Wychwood Park; and, after more than twenty years in the same office at 91 St. Joseph Street, McLuhan relocated in the new quarters of the Centre for Culture and Technology, on the edge of the St. Michael's campus at 39A Queen's Park Crescent East. Amid the inevitable chaos, two new McLuhan books appeared in print (*Through the Vanishing Point*, coauthored with Harley Parker, and *War and Peace in the Global Village*, with Quentin Fiore and Jerome Agel), along with the first issue of his *DEWLINE* newsletter. This multimedia forum alerted subscribers to the cultural impact of the electronic age. McLuhan returned to full-time teaching and a heavy schedule of speaking engagements. By the end of 1968, he had been honored at the Lord Mayor's dinner in London and interviewed in *Playboy*.

Their Bronxville house had inspired the McLuhans to make a move to a neighborhood they knew well and had walked through many times during their twelve years on Wells Hill Avenue. In the heart of Toronto, Wychwood Avenue, a wide street running south from St. Clair Avenue West, is free of heavy traffic, even at rush hour. Designed to accommodate vehicles turning in and out of the Toronto Transit Commission barns, the roadway appears, at a quick glance from St. Clair, to come to a dead end. On its west side, an acre of overgrown tracks and a skyscape of trolley wires are separated by a steel fence from the now disused streetcar barns. At the end of the street is a small brown gate that provides the entrance to Wychwood Park. On Davenport Road, the south entrance to the Park is opened only during snowstorms to allow residents to negotiate the steep hill. There are no other entrances, and tangled brush has overgrown a disused footpath where a road had once been planned to connect Wychwood to neighboring Burnside Drive.

Conceived at the turn of the century as an artists' colony by landscape painter Marmaduke Matthews, who had been commissioned by Canadian Pacific Railway builder William van Horne to paint the Canadian Rockies, Wychwood Park took its name from Matthews's birthplace in England, Shipton-under-Wychwood. When Matthews died in 1913, his sylvan retreat had attracted few of his fellow painters, but a community had grown up around his own rambling house, until it comprised the fifty-four residences that stand there today. It is the only place in Toronto where Taddle Creek, running southeast through the middle of the city to Lake Ontario, surfaces as a pond. The Park acquired its own lore. A young lieutenant who lived at the Matthews house was said to have stocked the pond with goldfish, which still populate it, on the night before he left for France in 1914.[55]

Dominated by the centuries-old oaks lining its meandering streets, Wychwood Park casts a spell. It cast a spell over McLuhan from the time the family took up residence in the fall of 1968, aiding his convalescence, soothing and invigorating him through the busiest years of his life, and then imparting its tranquillity to him through the days of his final illness more than a decade later.

McLuhan was proud of his new home and neighborhood, describing it at length to friends far and near, as he invited them to share its charms: "We are the only house on a beautiful pond filled with large goldfish. It is fed by an artesian spring and is the headwaters of a little river that runs across the Toronto campus . . . Have decided to dub the pond 'Walden III' and use it as a basis for P.R. and meditation. It is a campus version, as it were, of my Dew-Line, since it runs all across the campus. Joyce quips: 'Sink deep or touch not the Cartesian spring' as variant on Pope's 'Drink deep or taste not the Pierian spring.'"[56]

To Frank Kermode, who had asked McLuhan for a book on Joyce or Eisenstein for the Modern Masters series, McLuhan proposed instead to write about Wychwood Park: "The pond ripples outward into a heavily treed neighbourhood of twenty-two acres and fifty-four houses. The Park has no 'roads' or sidewalks, but simply these 'Viconean' circles of homes and people in a most unusual, dramatic relationship. Naturally I could tie these patterns into many features of cities past and present."[57]

McLuhan would have gladly lived without the adventures he logged in his travels away from home. Returning from a conference in Acapulco where he had been the keynote speaker, he told one correspondent, "Personally, I prefer Wychwood Park."[58] And though he had long since lost the manual skills of his youth (or lost interest in maintaining them), McLuhan readily agreed to painting a portion of the Wychwood fence every summer, as was expected of each householder.[59]

Years after moving to the Park, McLuhan was still thrilled by it and called it his first experience of living in a community: "Previously, I have lived only on streets, which sometimes have the quality of neighbourhood, but lineality is not compatible with community. The community character of Wychwood Park is a direct result of the circular compositioning of the houses, resulting from Wychwood pond. When houses interface by their circular or oval compositioning, a kind of social resonance develops that does not depend upon a high degree of social life or visiting among the occupants. Rather, there occurs a sense of theatre, as if all the occupants were, in varying degrees, on a stage. Something of the sort happens in any small village, and builders and planners could easily achieve rich community effects (even without a pond) simply by locating dwellings in non-lineal patterns."[60]

The move to Wychwood coincided with the time when McLuhan began enjoying his adult children in a way he had never been able to enjoy them as youngsters. It had something to do with the sort of whirlwind he thrived on and a sense of homelife as theater. Recounting his children's travels to Red, he commented: "You see what I mean by 'the global village'?"[61] His only concern was for Michael, who had "disappeared into the hippie jungle."[62] The youngest of McLuhan's children was on a voyage of self-discovery that took him to Toronto's Yorkville district and New York.

McLUHAN'S THIRD MOVE was already well under way before his return from New York. In McLuhan's absence[63] Arthur Porter, acting director of the Centre, had inspected the new facilities offered by the university at 39A Queen's Park Crescent East, a former coach house, and opined that they would be quite suitable. "The 'coach house' is ideally located from the Centre's point of view, and in most other respects it is ideal."[64] What "other respects" might have made the seedy little building on the fringe of the St. Michael's College campus ideal is not clear, but it soon came to be furnished in a manner so whimsical as to make the visitor overlook its dinginess. Years later, journalist, author, and editor Peter Newman would observe that the most prominent decoration on the premises was McLuhan's rowing oar from Cambridge.[65] The official opening of the Centre was held over till the spring following the move, when festivities went ahead at a modest cost of $382.58.[66] The *Toronto Star* captured the event in a report entitled "'Guru' McLuhan boy at heart."[67]

"FOR GOD'S SAKE, how do you explain Trudeau?" *Esquire* editor Tom Hedley needed a take on Canada's second-best-known personality from its first.[68] "Trudeaumania" was gripping Canada in the run-up to the 1968 federal election. McLuhan was preparing to address a Liberal Party of Canada seminar, and he knew just what Trudeau was all about: "The story of Pierre Trudeau is the story of the Man in the Mask. That is why he came into his own with TV. His image has been shaped by the Canadian cultural gap. Canada has never had an identity. Instead it has had a cultural interface of 17th-century France and 19th-century America. After World War II, French Canada leapt into the 20th century without ever having had a 19th century. Like all backward and tribal societies, it is very much 'turned on' or at home in the new electric world of the 20th century."[69]

That fall, McLuhan wrote a review of Trudeau's *Federalism and the French Canadians* for the *New York Times Book Review*.[70] The *Toronto Daily Star*'s Kildare Dobbs commented that if a book is written by a cocker spaniel, the *New York Times* will find a dog to review it, adding that McLuhan had not said much about the book, but a good deal about Trudeau. Dobbs said nothing about the book, but saw the review as revealing a good deal about McLuhan: "McLuhan displays with rare candor his long-standing admiration for the type Trudeau represents, the Catholic aristocrat who is at once cooly mundane and other-worldly. It is a contemporary apology for the purest tradition of conservatism."[71] By now, the correspondence McLuhan had initiated with the newly elected Canadian prime minister was flourishing.

McLuhan had made a study of U.S. politics over the recent election year, focusing on the conflict between policies and images. These reflections he had been sending to Trudeau since the eve of his own election. "After seeing the Kennedy-McCarthy 'debate,'" McLuhan told him, "I wish that you were not going to be on TV at all. It is not a debating medium."[72] But the fear behind McLuhan's wish was soon confirmed when Trudeau debated Conservative leader Robert Stanfield on national television. McLuhan offered Trudeau a pithy postmortem: "The witness box cum lectern cum pulpit spaces for the candidates was totally non-TV."[73]

In the same letter to Trudeau, McLuhan plucked a lesson on the TV medium from a magazine cover: "The cover of the June 8-14 *TV Guide* is a Dali masterpiece. It manifests in detail the tactile quality of the TV image. The extension of the central nervous system via electricity is environmentally indicated in the upper right hand corner by a segment of brain tissue. The two thumbs with the TV images on the nails are carefully separated to indicate the 'gap' or interval constituted by touch. The age of tactility via television and radio is one of innumerable interfaces or 'gaps' that replace the old connections, legal, literate, and visual."[74]

Trudeau found McLuhan's observations stimulating and helpful, and their correspondence soon led to meetings. They shared a playful nature, and a relationship that both were proud to call friendship developed between them. Before 1968 was out, McLuhan had written to Trudeau with suggestions for dialoguing on television and "government of the air"[75] to bypass bureaucracy, signing himself "Medium-mystically yours, Marshall McLuhan."[76]

AMONG THE SATISFACTIONS McLuhan registered as 1968 drew to a close was the praise he won from American critic and editor Cleanth Brooks, who told him that the freshly released *Through the Vanishing Point* — a joint effort by McLuhan and Harley Parker — was McLuhan at his best.[77] The book brings poems and paintings together to illuminate the world of space created by language. We see *how* an artist depicts space in a painting, even if we are unaware of painting techniques; with language it is just the opposite, because knowing how to talk and write is no assurance that we will notice how the world of space is expressed in words. It becomes easier to start noticing space in the world of words by coming at it through paintings.

The "vanishing point" is a technique that was invented by artists in the sixteenth century. It is fundamentally an optical illusion — an illusion that the space "inside" a painting and the viewer's space are the same — as if you could step into or out of the painting. Looking at a painting done in the vanishing point technique, one becomes part of the lines of force that focus *in* the vanishing point, *in* the painting.

Before the sixteenth century, no such technique existed. Up to the Middle Ages, the focus of a painting, and where it came together with the space of a viewer, was *in the viewer*. It wasn't until the vanishing point technique was developed that the observer of a painting and the artist shared a point of view. It is a matter of perspective. McLuhan and Parker point out that perspective itself is a mode of perception involving a single point of view, or fragmentation, in space and in time, in painting and in poetry.

McLuhan and Parker call poetry and painting "sister arts" and use them side by side to do the same job all McLuhan's books are intended to do — train our physical senses and raise them to a new level of sensitivity. This is why Brooks was so enthusiastic about *Through the Vanishing Point*. It bombards readers with paired-off poems and paintings, stimulating thought about how they connect with each other by adding short quotations from other writers and observations by the authors.

Through the Vanishing Point is a brief book, but the introduction alone deals with: how deodorants have created the bland, undifferentiated spaces typical of American culture; what those same deodorants have done to our memories (McLuhan is always interested in how our perceptions relate to each other and it turns out that perception itself is an act of remembering); why the Balinese say "we have no art"; what René Descartes and Shakespeare's Hamlet have in common (as victims of visual culture, they both experienced alienation); why the newspaper is a Romantic art form.

All this was to help readers through the maze (and the haze) of technologies — new *and* old — and to explain why primitive times and the world of the Middle Ages share much with our electronic age. The guided tour of the centuries in *Through the Vanishing Point* teaches about the effect that Isaac Newton's great work *Optical Lectures* had on eighteenth- and nineteenth-century painting and poetry. It encouraged great emphasis on visual and uniform space, and that uniformity "neutralized" the way artists showed nature.

But then came a reaction by the Romantic artists, who began taking an interest in such things as the effect of light on natural colors. These artists also started turning away from showing things in themselves and put a new emphasis on process (another McLuhan favorite), the English artist Joseph Turner with his paintings featuring storms, steam, mist, water, and light being a good example.

With French artist Georges Seurat, a whole new technique came into painting: divisionism, where every dot of paint on a canvas became a light source. All of a sudden, traditional perspective was reversed — the viewer became the vanishing point. All this provides a clue for McLuhan and Parker to the link between the sensory life of Paleolithic Man and Electronic Man. We are back to McLuhan's idea of the retribalization of the Western world.

McLuhan viewed *Through the Vanishing Point* as another stage of the literary criticism he had learned in Cambridge: "Whereas the new criticism had discovered multi-semantic levels, Parker and I deal with the multi-levels of sensory space in poetry and painting. In fact, it is concerned with the training of the whole sensorium, i.e. with the different kinds of space created by each of our senses."[78]

In 1969, the second year of recovery after his brain surgery, the demands on McLuhan's time were heavier than ever, though still not as crushing as they would become during the 1970s. He taught full time, lectured in Canada, the United States, and England, attended the first Bilderberg Conference in Elsinore, Denmark, sponsored by Prince Bernhard of the Netherlands, and collected an honorary doctorate of Humane Letters from the University of Rochester. There were more invitations than McLuhan could accept. He and Corinne were selected to join the Equestrian Order of Knights of the Holy Sepulchre but declined the honor because of a backlog of commitments.[79] McLuhan's schedule caused him to reflect that "when one comes into the public domain, one becomes a thing and everybody does that thing except oneself. All I do is on the back burner."[80]

His list of regular correspondents grew steadily, and throughout 1969 his letters show a marked emphasis on spiritual matters. He told James Taylor of the *United Church Observer* that he did "not think of God as a concept, but as an immediate and ever-present fact — an

THE GOOD GROUND   239

occasion for continuous dialogue."[81] He declared himself "a Thomist
for whom the sensory order [the sensible world] resonates with the
Divine Logos. I don't think concepts have any relevance in religion.
Analogy is not a concept. It is community. It is resonance. It is
inclusive. It is the cognitive process itself. That is the analogy of the
Divine Logos. I think of Jaspers, Bergson, and Buber as very inferior
conceptualist types, quite out of touch with the immediate analogical
awareness that begins in the senses and is derailed by concepts or
ideas."[82] McLuhan was demonstrating how his religious views were
compatible with the philosophical views of a range of thinkers
including Coleridge, Charles S. Peirce, and I. A. Richards.

To anthropologist Edward T. Hall, whose work McLuhan admired,
he explained that "I deliberately keep Christianity out of all these
discussions lest perception be diverted from structural processes by
doctrinal sectarian passions. My own attitude to Christianity is, itself,
awareness of process."[83] There was no breach between McLuhan's
intellectual and spiritual views, just as there was no need to reconcile
his faith with the view of the dynamics of communication he shared
with Richards and others, since God is not accessible through the
senses, even though He is expressible through analogical percepts.

At the Centre, McLuhan's days — and nights — were rarely less
theatrical than at home. Monday night seminars at the Centre were
dramatic happenings where ideas were animated and truths distilled
from dialogue that gave those present a sense of community."[84]

The coach house was crammed with filing cabinets, books on
shelves, in piles, and in cartons, a photocopier, and tiny work areas for
McLuhan's secretary, Margaret Stewart, and administrative assistant,
George Thompson. The jumble came to a visual focus, only to dissolve
again, in the seminar room with the stunning René Cera mural titled
Pied Pipers All.[85] The absorbing and eloquent commentary on media
effects, dominated by rich hues of gold and turquoise, shows monoc-
ular figures responding to the clarion call of pipers on a television
screen. In ambiguous postures of joyful dance or impotent flailing in
a struggle to escape, they manage only to ring the screen in a ghostly
and entropic parody of itself.

An inflated plastic model of an Air Canada jet hung from the ceiling,
and a collage of Wyndham Lewis drawings occupied a privileged and

prominent spot. Posters with photos and artwork, charts and sayings, festooned the walls, drawing the visitor's eye to the iconic Chaplin, to a model of the communication process, to a sign stating the need to acquire perception and understanding.

In the small rooms of the Centre's upper floor, the decor gave way from late-whimsy to timeless-eclectic and featured a venerable green couch, plastic chairs, folding table, and a rusty air-conditioner. In the bathroom, lined with books, the top shelf was reserved for St. Thomas's *Summa Theologica*. Gutenberg's was the dominant technology in the Centre.

McLuhan's brother Maurice left the United Church ministry during the days of communes and "flower children," because he felt his message was losing relevance. He dropped out to get back in touch. After working at a series of jobs in Vancouver, he felt he had come to a dead end, so he called his brother. Was there any place for him in Toronto? Yes, came the answer. The Centre had just lost an assistant at the very moment when there was too much work to handle. Maurice felt more than a little trepidation at having to work alongside a brother who had achieved international notoriety. Moreover, he had not read any of his books and had no clear idea of what the work of the Centre involved. But McLuhan understood that Maurice's talent for communication would be his chief asset and felt confident that everything else would fall into place as a result.

For his first assignment, Maurice joined McLuhan and Barry Nevitt as they dialogued their way toward the manuscript of *Take Today*. This on-the-job training was combined with a bewildering series of unpredictable and unrepetitive tasks to teach Maurice the meaning of the McLuhan percepts. Maurice said that at that time he "walked about the Centre with head high and mouth wide open."[86] A year had gone by when McLuhan asked Maurice to begin accepting speaking invitations on behalf of the Centre. There was a particularly heavy demand from the organizers of educational conferences, and it was here that McLuhan knew Maurice would excel. The highlight came with the invitation to the White House conference on education and the glowing report on Maurice's participation that followed him back to Toronto. He continued to represent the Centre at many conferences across Canada and the United States.[87] Coming to the realization, after three years at the Centre, that nothing grows under an oak, he struck out on an independent teaching career, without forgetting either his brother's gesture toward him or the McLuhan percepts themselves.[88]

When McLuhan was not going to the world, the world was coming to the Centre — business executives, teachers, media moguls, entertainers, and royalty. Sometimes they would pull up to the coach house; sometimes they stopped in the long narrow driveway of 39 Queen's Park Crescent. The building housed the University of Toronto's Experimental Phonetics Laboratory. Year after year the traffic increased, and the laboratory's director, Pierre Léon, had his own message about media as environments for those who left their motors running. Was that John Lennon and Yoko Ono getting out of a white limousine? No matter. Léon had a small flag ready to thrust out the window reading "Stop Polluting."[89]

McLuhan's message on pollution was out of this world. *Apollo 11* was on the launchpad and McLuhan was ignoring his camera cue at ABC Studios in New York. He was explaining to the world how the whole space program had scrapped the earth and "turned it into planet Polluto." "Nature ended with Sputnik." Here the lesson on technology as new environment was clear. Everyone could understand that the old environment was now surrounded by earth-orbiting satellites. All this seemed more important than the unfolding epic of three men traveling a quarter of a million miles from earth. In private, McLuhan spoke of the necessity for humans to learn to laugh at the pomposity of moonshots.[90] The *Apollo 11* astronauts set foot on the lunar surface on McLuhan's fifty-eighth birthday. It was the same year that he began to expand his own global journeys.

FIVE

Closure

12

To the Four Corners of the Global Village

The west shall shake the east awake . . . while ye have the
night for morn . . .

–JAMES JOYCE, Finnegans Wake

"I HAVE COME TO have a deep dislike of travel and dislocation of all
sorts," McLuhan wrote to Dalhousie University English professor
Malcolm Ross on 6 July 1970. It was the very time he began traveling
endlessly: the Bahamas, Washington, New York, Montreal, Greece,
St. Louis, Ottawa, San Francisco before 1970 was out. These were
speaking engagements in between teaching commitments, his investi-
ture to the Order of Canada, and receiving the Institute for Public
Relations (U.K.) Award. He was diagnosed with a blockage of the
carotid artery and hospitalized. Blood-thinners were prescribed. The
doctors decided to wait and see if an operation would be necessary.
McLuhan could wait for nothing. Corinne knew it was useless to try
to dissuade him from accepting speaking engagements. Cautions from
his doctors about his condition were in vain, and he regularly forgot
to take his medication.

It was no longer necessary for McLuhan to write his own books, or
even to dictate them. In 1969, *The Interior Landscape: The Literary
Criticism of Marshall McLuhan 1943-1962* had been presented to him
as a fait accompli. Unbeknownst to McLuhan, it had been compiled,
edited, and introduced by Eugene McNamara, from the English
department at the University of Windsor.[1] But 1970 also saw two

genuine "McLuhans" appear in print: *Culture Is Our Business* and *From Cliché to Archetype*, published by McGraw-Hill and Viking Press respectively.

Compared with *The Mechanical Bride*, *Culture Is Our Business* reveals much more ambivalence on McLuhan's part toward the world of advertising, the perpetrator of somnambulism, and its arsenal of techniques, as amazing as they are insidious. If McLuhan appears to have more admiration than condemnation for these techniques, it is only because he deliberately holds the latter in check. When McLuhan's disapproval of advertising becomes clear, it is disapproval of the end, not the method, which is after all his own: "[Making someone ill, then selling the cure is] the way advertising is done. They start off with the effects then look for the causes. That's how I prophesy. I look around at the effects and say, well, the causes will soon be here."[2]

In *Culture Is Our Business* McLuhan identifies advertising as the cave art of the twentieth century; neither is intended to be examined in detail but to create an effect. There is a further similarity in that cave art and advertising both express corporate aims rather than private thoughts. McLuhan comments on the social and emotional upheavals brought about by twentieth-century technology but continues to withhold judgment: "It would have been self-defeating for me to have said years ago 'the medium is the mess-age': such judgments distract attention from the events and processes that need to be understood."[3]

Culture Is Our Business does for the advertising of the 1960s what *The Mechanical Bride* did for the advertising of the 1940s. The effect of television made this update necessary. The title was a deliberate put-on of the nineteenth-century idea in North America that "business is our culture." With the advent of radio, movies, and television, culture had turned into the biggest business in the world. Only rarely does McLuhan comment on the hundreds of ads reproduced in the book. His preferred method, as in *The Mechanical Bride*, is to put the ads side by side with statements probing their significance, questions to the reader, or quotations and observations from writers as diverse as James Joyce, T. S. Eliot, William Congreve, Alfred North Whitehead, Ashley Montagu, and Karl Polanyi. A bumper crop of McLuhanisms sprouts like figures over the ground of Joyce's puns:

"costume is custom," "the end of the muddle crass," "Jung and easily Freudened," "freedom from the press."

Culture Is Our Business pushes the mosaic approach found in virtually all of McLuhan's works to its most playful and thought-provoking extremes. A section entitled "Rear-View Mirror" begins by juxtaposing James Joyce's observation that "pastimes are past times" with a travel ad showing a British beefeater under the caption "On a clear day you can see a long, long time ago." Then the mosaic quickly takes on the quality of intellectual sandpaper: a banana ad headed "this page is dedicated to the proposition that all bananas are not created equal" sits across from a quotation from Pierre Trudeau's *Federalism and the French Canadians* to teach us that the concept of nationhood has been made obsolete by the electronic retribalization of Western culture. At the same time, the cliché "banana republic" is tossed back on the compost heap of language. McLuhan also slips in a word about gaps and interfaces — as much a part of his method as of the new environment he evokes.

McLuhan was less than enchanted with the book when it appeared. "Did I tell you about the McGraw-Hill blooper with *Culture Is Our Business*? It may be a collector's item, since the book appeared before it had been proofread by anybody at McGraw-Hill and before I had seen any galleys or proofs. It is packed with errors and omissions. The jacket was botched,[4] like everything else. It was intended to be a cyclops, i.e. the image of the hunter in the new world of the information environment."[5] Instead, the book designer had parodied a well-known advertisement for Hathaway shirts showing a man with an eye-patch.

Joe Keogh, McLuhan's former student and assistant, friend, and sometime collaborator, drafted a review and sent it to him.[6] Keogh viewed the book as "a sort of *Bride* stripped bare by the x-rays of color tv,"[7] noting that it "reads as if, by a commodius and vicarious recirculation, the excreta of *Finnegans Wake* were finally making a splash in the dry waste land of Madison Avenue."[8] Jacques Ellul had written to Keogh to say that because of McLuhan all was not lost. Though this was the thrust of the review, and Keogh pointed out that McLuhan refrained from moralism, McLuhan was not entirely pleased with the passage that put him at the end of the tradition begun by Eliot and

Joyce, or with finding himself compared to George Orwell.[9] When McLuhan indicated this to Keogh, he replied: "What *you* assume is that the conventional poses in my review represent *me*; I am sure you've never reacted that way to Mr. Eliot. Of course your approach is not 'moral' — but in my little metaphysics, there are two other categories, and 'truth' is only one of them. 'Good(s)' count for a lot, and you've obviously got the goods on twentieth century culture. If you weren't a Catholic and didn't respect the sacramental system, you couldn't do it. (But you didn't expect me to say that in a review for a secular magazine.)"[10]

In sharp contrast to the mosaic form of organization of this book is the encyclopedia format of *From Cliché to Archetype*, published in the same year. The book was the product of more than ten years of sporadic cooperation between McLuhan and Wilfred Watson and was more sporadic than cooperative. Watson had wanted to do a play based on *The Mechanical Bride*, because he found the book "not so much a study as a superb piece of idiosyncratic satire, with the best prose I've seen yet by a Canadian."[11] The play did not materialize, but Watson accepted McLuhan's offer to collaborate.

The husband-and-wife team of the Watsons, Wilfred and Sheila, held appointments as visiting professors at the Centre for Culture and Technology during 1968-69, when McLuhan and Watson were to make the final push on their joint effort. Watson, who had begun to feel overwhelmed in his solo runs at the work, looked forward to the year in Toronto as the solution for bringing the project to completion.[12] It brought only conflict. Seeing that he and McLuhan were at a serious impasse, Watson said, "All right, Marshall, I'll write my portion on the left-hand pages, and you do yours on the right."[13] Of course, it was a jest — and perhaps a reminder to McLuhan of his own observation that jests are based on grievances. Looking back long after *From Cliché to Archetype* was finished, Watson put their troubles down to McLuhan's preferred method of writing by dialoguing with his collaborator and getting Margaret Stewart to record the outcome.[14]

The terms *cliché* and *archetype* appear as separate entries in the book, but the reader soon learns that they are inseparable in their operation. McLuhan and Watson explore the various meanings of *archetype*, including the basic one linking it to *type*, referring to a pattern or model. In literary analysis, an archetype is a symbol or image, recognizable because it is met repeatedly. But clichés are also repeated. It is repetition that makes them clichés. For this reason, McLuhan and Watson emphasize the connection between the two terms.

An archetype is an expandable category; a cliché is neither a category nor expandable. But it can be modified, and McLuhan and Watson have much to say about how this is done in the hands of artists. Just as McLuhan stretched the sense of "medium," he and Watson stretch the sense of "cliché," defining it at different times as an extension, a probe, and a means of retrieving the past. The resonance among these notions demonstrates how fundamental the study of cliché is in the McLuhan canon.

McLuhan and Watson call perceptions clichés, since the physical senses form a closed system. They regard all communications media as clichés, insofar as they extend our physical senses. And even art is cliché, because it retrieves older clichés.

The simplest definition of cliché for McLuhan and Watson is that of a probe. Here is an apparent paradox, as the authors freely acknowledge.[15] But art is the sharpening of clichés into probes, into new forms that stimulate new awareness. What is familiar, even worn out, becomes new. McLuhan's favorite example to illustrate this process comes from James Joyce, whose writing wakes up language (creates new clichés) by putting it to sleep (destroying old clichés). Or, as McLuhan put it in commenting on the treatment of this theme: "All cliché is always being put back on the compost heap, as it were, whence it emerges as a shining new form."[16]

Between archetypes and clichés there is both contrast and interaction. A cliché is incompatible with another, even when they are of similar meaning. One may choose between the expressions "getting down to the nitty-gritty" and "getting down to brass tacks" but not combine them into "getting down to brass nitty-gritty" or "getting down to nitty-gritty tacks." But an archetype is an open set or group to which members (clichés) can be added.

McLuhan and Watson define the archetype as a retrieved awareness or new consciousness. Such awareness is created when the artist probes an archetype with an old cliché. Eventually, the probe itself turns into a cliché. *From Cliché to Archetype* views all form — whether in language, visual arts, music, or other domains — as reversal of archetype into cliché. But cliché also reverses into archetype.

Beyond language, cliché occurs in past times, fixed and unalterable, because they are irretrievable. These become the archetype of pastimes — an open category the hobbyist may modify endlessly. While McLuhan and Watson emphasize that clichés are not confined to the verbal, they also note parallels between the verbal and the nonverbal type. They find strong similarity between phrases like "green as grass" or "white as snow" and the internal combustion engine. These similarities relate to both the form of the clichés involved and the key McLuhanean teaching on new environments created by technology. The banal phrases in question and the engine operate without any control over their *form* by the user. This is ultimately less important than their environmental impact. Both the clichés and the engine create new environments in three distinct ways: (1) meaningless communication and endless commuting, respectively; (2) invisible/visible junkyards of speech/writing — the vehicles of thought — and visible junkyards of the road vehicles of yesterday, respectively; (3) disfigured mindscape and landscape, respectively.

McLuhan and Watson probe the connection between verbal and nonverbal clichés and archetypes. They observe that language provides extensions of all the physical senses at once, reminding us that these are integrated when language is spoken, whereas the visual sense becomes highly specialized with written language. Because McLuhan and Watson take clichés as extensions or media or technologies, they can discover not only similarities but direct links between the effect of past technologies and the accumulation of clichés in language. So, hunting with dogs gave English the phrases *to turn tail, top dog, underdog, bone of contention, to give the slip to, to run to earth, to throw off the scent, to be on the track of*, etc.

Inspired by W. B. Yeats's poem "The Circus Animals' Desertion," McLuhan and Watson develop the idea that the interaction of clichés and archetypes in language has counterparts beyond language. Examples include that of a flagpole flying a flag. The flag by itself is a cliché — a fixed and unalterable symbol of the country it represents. Citizens don't have the option to modify it at will. But a flag on a flagpole is an archetype, since any flag can be hoisted in place of another.

Any cliché can interchange with another in the archetype.

McLuhan and Watson challenge readers to discover the full meaning of their thought throughout *From Cliché to Archetype*. The book's table of contents appears neither at the beginning nor at the end but alphabetically under "T." Since all the material in the book is arranged in alphabetical order, the table of contents is useless, except as a reminder that archetypes can reverse into clichés. This careful order was botched by the publisher, who insisted on printing the footnotes ("Notes on Sources") at the end of the book instead of alphabetically under "N."

The interplay of cliché and archetype, and the close connection of both to McLuhan's most fundamental preoccupations, are perhaps best seen in the following passage: "The archetype is a retrieved awareness or consciousness. It is consequently a retrieved cliché — an old cliché retrieved by a new cliché. Since a cliché is a unit extension of man, an archetype is a quoted extension, medium, technology, or environment."[17]

McLuhan had looked forward with optimism to the appearance of *From Cliché to Archetype*, telling Frank Kermode that it "may be a bit of a blockbuster."[18] But if he was in any measure satisfied with the book at first, he became ambivalent afterward.[19] And he found the French translation superior to the original, ascribing the credit for this to his personal collaboration with the translator.[20] Even so, the work could irritate him when he returned to it. "A stupid book," he fumed, on one occasion, because he could find nothing to learn from it on rereading.[21] Yet it led him to the discovery that the interplay of cliché and archetype is the interplay of figure and ground.[22]

The concept of archetypes also gave McLuhan a take on structuralism, in which he identified the paradigms of European structuralists as a set of archetypes.[23] His decision to develop a complete book around the term *archetype* might have been motivated in the first place by a desire to appropriate it from his rival, Northrop Frye. There are five references to Frye in the book[24] including a "Frigean Anatomy of a Metamorphosis" for Eugene Ionesco's *The Bald Soprano*[25] and an extensive quotation from a commentary by William Wimsatt criticizing Frye for failing to maintain his own distinction between *value* and *criticism* in *Anatomy of Criticism*.[26] McLuhan wrote to Cleanth Brooks with some satisfaction of his discovery in Jean Piaget's writings that archetypes, as defined in Frye's approach, were unnecessary.[27]

The archetype was nevertheless a useful enough tool to have appeared eight years earlier in the closing pages of *The Gutenberg Galaxy*. As for cliché, McLuhan linked it even to his personal experience in the aftermath of brain surgery: "*Cliché* appears in many modes. All media whatever are environmental clichés. The effect of such surrounds is narcosis or numbing. This is a kind of *arrest* which, mysteriously, results in metamorphosis. Even anaesthesia has this effect. I was told after my long operation that many recent memories would disappear and many older ones would re-appear. This indeed happened. It also happens with the environmental clichés that are media."[28]

McLuhan's preference for percepts over concepts[29] was a strategy for avoiding clichés and capta[30] by recourse to pure process. In his correspondence with Herbert Krugman, he linked this process to his original probe, pointing out that any medium surrounds both its users and earlier media. The result is resonance and metamorphosis between media and their users. This nonstop process was the subject of *From Cliché to Archetype*.[31]

Within the body of McLuhan's work, *From Cliché to Archetype* marks the emergence of the notion of *retrieval* — the fourth of the media laws he would integrate with those of *extension, obsolescence,* and *reversal*. "Retrieval" is the only entry in the book under "R." McLuhan's correspondence following the appearance of the book indicates the central place *retrieval* occupied there and in his evolving thought: "I had asked the publisher to put on the flap of the jacket this formulation of the process that is cliché to archetype: Print scrapped scribe and Schoolmen and retrieved pagan antiquity. Revival of the ancient world created the modern world. Electricity scrapped hardware and industrialism and retrieved the occult."[32]

When the reviews of *From Cliché to Archetype* appeared, Hugh Kenner, then teaching at Harvard University, wrote: "No art can step up the voltage of boiled spinach."[33] This was a phantom blow for McLuhan, an echo from one of his own favorite sayings, attributed to the Balinese: "We have no art; we do everything as well as possible."[34] Now his old student and friend was telling him that he had neither done everything as well as possible nor been artful enough to cover it up. Other reviewers also spoke of a rehash and raised the usual charge of obscurity, reactions prompting a *Toronto Daily Star* editorial by Peter Newman entitled "McLuhan, hurrah!" calling him "the most influential prophet of our age."[35]

THE LABEL "PROPHET" WAS not one that McLuhan could live up to without conceding to the demand for personal appearances — or without accepting pressures that exacted a toll. To the cautions of Dr. Hans Selye, the pioneer of research on biological stress, he replied: "As for the 'stress' that besets my ordinary existence, there is probably little to be done about that short of withdrawal from the world."[36] He was no more capable of such withdrawal than Poe's sailor was of extracting himself from the Maelstrom. McLuhan kept on the move. As did the entire family. Eric, who had stayed behind in New York to edit the *DEWLINE Newsletter*, was also preparing to take up teaching in Wisconsin, and his father was much pleased that it should be at the same university where he had begun his career. Elizabeth was continuing art studies at Fordham University and spent five weeks in the summer of 1970 in London, where Teri, working for BBC News, found her a job with a magazine editor, while Stephanie was working with CBS in New York. McLuhan left for the eighth annual Delos Symposium, organized by the Athens Technological Institute and its president, C. A. Doxiadis, accompanied by Corinne.

At home, the "daily charade of malice" McLuhan had come to count on continued. His former student Donald Theall, teaching at McGill University, had drafted a book on McLuhan and wrote, sending the manuscript, to ask permission to quote from his work. Disappointed that one of his students had understood him so poorly, McLuhan wrote: "My approach to the media is never from a point of view but is in fact a 'swarming.' Since this is an inexhaustible process, it has to be arbitrary . . . As for the book in general, Don, I think you take me too 'seriously.' It is really more fun to join the quest for discoveries than to try to classify and evaluate the processes in which I am involved. You are, in a sense, trying to translate me into an academic fixture. Perhaps that is what I mean by 'serious.' On page 222 you refer to my retaining Joyce as my major authority. Please

consider that there can be no 'authority' where the game is discovery
. . . What I *have* found is an enormous enjoyment and thrill in
experiencing the events that are on every hand. It seems to me that
this steady enjoyment of these events is a sufficient value system, as it
asserts the joy of mere existence. Naturally it does not rule out the
possibility of moral judgments, in particular, existential situations, and
you know that I am not averse to these in private."[37]

Writing separately to Theall's publisher, McLuhan pointed out that
the quantity of Theall's quoted material exceeded his original estimate
by ten times, adding that "any reader would sense from the outset of
the book that the author is 'snarky' and 'snide.' McLuhan has been
classified and be-clowned as well as be-nighted. Even where
Don doesn't [*sic*] mean well, he doesn't understand me anyway."[38]
McLuhan denied permission to quote, but Theall's publisher decided
that the quotations were within the bounds of fair use for a scholarly
work and proceeded. Theall agreed to some revisions when his editor
echoed McLuhan's sentiments about a snide tone in the work, but the
impression of a "be-clowned" McLuhan remained in the final version,
titled *The Medium Is the Rear View Mirror*. Responding when the publisher sent him a complimentary copy, McLuhan said: "I found the
book very dull and confused."[39]

At the height of his fame, McLuhan was lionized and lambasted. In
between came the rare, balanced evaluations of his work — and much
misunderstanding. Joe Keogh regarded McLuhan as a Christian
prophet, "perhaps much more than Père Chardin."[40] Lille bookseller
René Giard, a fan since he had read *La Galaxie Gutenberg*, told
McLuhan his ideas were too important for television debates against
the lesser minds of Sorbonne professors.[41] Toronto businessman Sam
Sorbara worried about McLuhan wasting his substance: "I want
McLuhan to be held high. He must not speak to groups such as the
one he addressed yesterday. I wonder just how much those present
derived from the talk . . . You have made my life richer."[42] Journalist
Cy Jameson noted that "critics have scraped away at McLuhan's body
of work . . . rubbing away at brash sentences — but rarely getting the
message,"[43] adding that his media analysis was rarely acknowledged as
a relevant contribution to the debate on literacy.

Only a few commentators were prepared to give McLuhan the

freedom he required to be effective: "To systematize McLuhan is to misunderstand him. Even to confine him to print is to distort him."[44] Broadcaster and communications lecturer Samuel L. Becker said that half of his students had been frustrated in their attempts to verify McLuhan's pronouncements in *Understanding Media*, as if they were "descriptions of the real world, including human behaviour."[45] If absence of true originality was a fair criticism of McLuhan, Becker saw that it was also irrelevant: "The critical criterion is not whether he has made startlingly new discoveries or whether his statements are accurate; it is whether he has caused others to think and to make such discoveries."[46]

Becker's counsel on how to approach McLuhan remains among the best: "Instead of responding to McLuhan's work as though it is scientific research, historical or anthropological observation, or even serious criticism, we ought to respond to it as the object it most closely approximates — a projective test. We ought not to read it for what it or McLuhan means, but rather for its help on loosening our imaginations, for stimulating us to think about communication in fresh and imaginative ways, for causing us to dredge up out of the very recesses of our own minds the ideas about communication which are lurking there. This is what a good projective test, such as Rorschach, can do for us; this is what McLuhan can do for us."[47] Becker took his own advice even as he offered it, producing an excellent analysis of McLuhan that yielded a new interpretation of "the medium is the message" by integrating McLuhan's two senses of "closure,"[48] and thereby outperforming him in the use of his own technique.

Commentaries such as Becker's were all too scarce. Instead, notorious misreads were the norm. The *Saturday Evening Post*'s self-advertisement in its own pages proclaimed that "McLuhan's argument has little application to our own sophisticated media-saturated society."[49] The magazine first misrepresented McLuhan as saying that television is a hot medium, print a cool one, and then took exception to such a statement and hit its punch line: "The *Post* invites the active involvement of reading."[50] But this refers to reading as a *mental* activity and in no way denies any statement about the human eye processing print, from the man who loved few things more than sitting by a fire with a book. The irony of a text begun as an argument against

McLuhan and ending with an inadvertent twist on his own lesson about the obscuring of content was lost on the copy-writers.[51]

An interviewer asked McLuhan whether he had been given an accurate reading in the universities. "Oh no, no, no," he replied, "they thought that everything I had to say was an absolute attack on their values."[52] Despite the fact that McLuhan likened television to bacteria and poison and prescribed the antidote of reading,[53] journalists could confidently report that "he excoriates print."[54] Some commentators were confident enough in their misreadings of McLuhan to publish them amid absurd flourishes: "You tolled the knell a bit early sir. The book isn't dead. You see it as a pile of dry leaves on an otherwise tidy lawn, an organic embarrassment in this transistorized age. Put down your rake, Marshall."[55]

When McLuhan appeared on national television in France, interviewer Pierre Schaeffer brought out his big question with the alacrity of a fox and all the insight of a mollusk. How could the book be a technology? It is too small.[56] And this after the microchip had made its way to the shores of France.

McLuhan concluded on good evidence that he was not faring any better across the Channel. Journalist D. A. N. Jones could find no significant lesson in McLuhan beyond the idea of mankind manipulated by media. He proposed to illuminate McLuhan by introducing him to the working-men's clubs of Sunderland that "represent workers' control in leisure."[57] Clearly McLuhan's "generalisations"[58] did not apply here, because: "he forgets that people can, collectively, control their environment, deliberately maintain 'old-fashioned' cultural habits."[59]

McLuhan did not always help his own cause in the U.K. When a *Manchester Guardian* reporter asked him what "the medium is the message" meant, he replied that he was not sitting, he was moving.[60] Suspecting that the interview had not gone well, McLuhan called after the man as he left, saying "We are fellow literates." "I hope not," came the reply.[61]

One of the most trite arguments raised against McLuhan was that he wrote about communication but could not communicate effectively. It was a popular saying over coffee among students, even if they had not read much McLuhan, but it also graced the features pages of major dailies: A *Toronto Daily Star* article reported a front-page review of

Understanding Media from the *New York Herald Tribune*: "The review stated that McLuhan, having discussed communications in his book, displayed a lack of that quality in his work."[62]

Letters to editors, even when they addressed McLuhan's ideas, often missed the mark: "[McLuhan's] pronouncement that knowledge rather than ignorance is the greatest obstacle to problem-solving is little served by his example. The point he is presumably making is either the axiomatic one that it is necessary to be ignorant of the solution to a particular problem in order to solve it or the hardly less shopworn notice that necessity and not knowledge is the mother of invention."[63] The writer seized on McLuhan's key word "obstacle," but missed the related notions of knowledge as cliché, problem-solving as process, and the role of archetype.

Some commentators were content to be dismissive without entering the analytical fray: "[*Understanding Media*] struck me as the largest collection of unsupported assertions since Burton's *Anatomy of Melancholy*."[64] But Pittsburgh attorney Henry Venable larded his criticism with rhetorical trappings, though confining himself to a valiant effort at vivisecting McLuhan's emerging laws of media.[65] Others said all they had to say by way of style: "Space is the ultimate loudspeaker capable of refracting effluvial syllogisms in a perfectly inverse measure to the voltage applied — a holdover from the Industrial Revolution . . . Turning a radio 'off' is an outmoded concept. So is turning a radio 'on.' It matters little to the sender who will go about his business regardless of individuated decisions in the megastructure."[66] Despite her father's voracious reading habits, Stephanie McLuhan did not trust his taste to extend (or descend) to *National Lampoon*. Not wanting him to miss this delicious satire, she took out a subscription for him.

McLUHAN HAD BEEN CLEAR of vertigo and blackouts since the removal of his brain tumor, but on 16 May 1971, after a year on anticoagulants for the blockage of his right internal carotid artery, he was admitted to St. Michael's Hospital in Toronto. The medication had relieved his numbness and weakness, but throughout the year he had felt a constant humming in the left side of his body. Fresh test results came back revealing serious narrowing of the arteries supplying blood to both sides of McLuhan's brain. On the right side — the dominant hemi-sphere of the left-handed McLuhan — scarcely any blood flowed through the major vessel. Beyond the major obstruction only an insignificant amount of blood — nothing approaching the brain's demand — could pass. Even on the left side, the vessel was irregular and narrowed to nearly 50 percent, but on the right side, the blockage was nearly 95 percent. Surgery would be far too dangerous. But along with the alarming report came astonishing findings.[67]

McLuhan's *external* carotid circulation (the external carotid artery supplies blood to the face, scalp, and jaw muscles) had formed huge connecting channels through the base of his skull and through the orbit with the internal carotid artery inside his head. While common in some mammals, particularly in the cat family, such connections in a human are rare and had never been seen in such size and complexity by McLuhan's doctors. The pictures resembled those produced in experiments at Oxford University, using dye injections, of the cerebral circulation of tigers. McLuhan's channels had opened "magnifi-cently," the doctors said.[68] The patient called it a miracle and accepted it as the work of God.

Though he had experienced some mild sensory loss, McLuhan was discharged from the hospital after a two-day stay. A discharge diagnosis cited transient ischemic attack and right internal carotid artery stenosis.[69] For the doctors, there was nothing to do but to continue treatment by anticoagulants. For McLuhan there was much to do. His address to the American Society of Medical Technologists in Las Vegas was already scheduled and less than a month away. Then it would be Toronto, Ottawa, Edmonton, Italy[70] . . . And there were books to write.

McLuhan had told his former student Richard Berg that he thought he had too many books on the market,[71] but even as he made the remark he was faced with further publishing commitments to honor. *Take Today: The Executive as Dropout* had begun as a project in collaboration with Ralph Baldwin, a McLuhan acquaintance from St. Louis days. A contract for the publication of the work had been signed with Harcourt Brace Jovanovich in 1968. McLuhan saw it as a two-month job to write a ninety-page essay on the subject of the business executive in the electronic age.[72] Three years later, it was a behemoth and still in the works.

Baldwin defected at a very early stage in the project, and McLuhan took on Barrington (Barry) Nevitt as his new collaborator. Nevitt was an electrical engineer and an international consultant in his field. He also had experience in marketing and management and was working for the Ontario government at the time he gravitated toward the Centre for Culture and Technology to join forces with McLuhan. They began dialoguing the book over the inexpensive lunches McLuhan favored at the cafeteria of the Ontario Legislature Building in Queen's Park — a five-minute walk from the coach house. With Nevitt this near by, arranging their work sessions was easy. Nevitt was a regular at the Monday night seminars and never far away at any time. The McLuhans awoke one morning and came down to breakfast, only to find Nevitt sitting in their living room, chafing to begin the day's jam session. For all his energy, exuberance to match McLuhan's, and eagerness to work side by side with him, Nevitt also conducted substantial research for their project on his own and puzzled McLuhan at times by his reluctance to share his findings.[73] But that proved to be no obstacle to generating over a thousand pages of text; alongside it, McLuhan's original plan looked like a small spit in a torrent.[74]

McLuhan would still describe *Take Today* as "a fun book with a serious message"[75] shortly after it appeared in print, but soon planned to revise it for translation without "the funny verbalism,"[76] an extraordinary reversal for the author who had rewritten the manuscript of *Understanding Media* endlessly, rubbing his hands in glee whenever he found the best spots to plant verbal landmines and exclaiming, "This will really get them!"[77] By the spring of 1971, *Take Today* had taken shape as something McLuhan had never imagined: "I am now finishing a book but it is by no means the book that I contracted to write for HBJ. It has a different title, it is more than twice as long . . . and it deals with a different subject matter."[78]

As far as the beleaguered editor, Ethel Cunningham, was concerned, whatever it was that had taken shape could not be called a book. She spent hundreds of hours cutting, editing, retyping, and copy-editing. McLuhan and Nevitt had reduced their 1,000 pages to 600, but they were also planning to divide this into two books.[79] Revisions were carried out by Nevitt alone, who readily agreed to Cunningham's every suggestion for a cut, proceeding then to make two additions elsewhere.[80] Yet within a couple of months, the book was in "more-or-less-final form" and looked acceptable to Eric McLuhan.[81] Nevitt was exhausted and left for a holiday to recover from what he called three years of seven days a week without a break.[82]

McLuhan was disgusted and remained behind to fret. He did not resent the time he had spent on the project but felt that Nevitt had forced his own pattern onto the manuscript. "The result is an opaque tapestry with some very weird features."[83] Worst of all, for McLuhan, at the proofreading stage, also in the sole charge of his collaborator,[84] Nevitt had inserted the phrase "Print Oriented Bastards," against McLuhan's express wishes. "The phrase was invented by John Culkin and has never been used by me in conversation. The feeling of animus in it is not characteristic of me."[85]

In his review of *Take Today*, Canadian actor Mavor Moore evoked the roots of the McLuhan method in performance: "McLuhan the entertainer is in fine form — changing viewpoints as often as a quick-change artist changes hats. ('Change itself has become the main staple.') McLuhan is an actor — at least that's my working hypothesis. This is not to devalue philosophy but to raise the currency of acting. In a day when understanding other roles is essential and when one must fill several roles oneself, the art of the actor becomes the art of living."[86]

McLuhan noted that Moore's review failed to mention the theme of the book.[87] In an exchange of letters with another reviewer, Sam D. Neill, McLuhan soon realized why — the theme had been obscured: "The overall theme of the book is the shift from hardware to software, and centralism to decentralism, and specialism to full understanding. The fact that you did not get this kind of pattern out of the book tells me what Nevitt had done to the book. I think he is instinctively afraid to appear in the open and likes to plaster on McLuhan like ornaments as a means of disguising himself. When the book is translated into French, I am going to cut it down by at least 50%, and re-arrange the patterns in it loud and clear."[88] These had been anything but clear to Neill.[89]

At least one of McLuhan's most devoted students rose to the challenge of *discovering*, in the McLuhan sense, what the book offered: "Although to your students you always disclaim any philosophy or 'point of view' in your work, I find through reading *Take Today* that this is a volume of philosophy which may well be sub-titled THE UPANISHADS OF THE ELECTRONIC AGE. It sets forth in modern terms the Upanishadic Aryan Hindu philosophy."[90] Though McLuhan felt that "the great mistake about *Take Today* was (a) the ridiculous headings and (b) the excessive length,"[91] and recognized that "[i]t is not for reading straight through, but for sampling and me ditating,"[92] he continued to promote the book among his correspondents for years after its publication. To publisher William Jovanovich he announced, more than a year and a half after the book had been released, that a new promotional opportunity had arisen: "Surely it would be very appropriate to exploit the electronic confusion in the White House [re Watergate] for promoting *Take Today*, since it is no exaggeration to say that it is the only book that exists that tackles the entire problem of the results of decision-making under electronic conditions."[93]

Jovanovich discounted the opportunity: "Any attempt to give *Take Today* a pertinence and importance in this avalanche of imagination-boggling information and practical interpretation seems utterly hopeless in any feasible way. It would amount to little more than a whisper in a hurricane."[94] To this McLuhan replied: "Your remark about *Take Today* as 'a whisper in a hurricane' echoes the complaint of the practical man about the poet: 'The poet's head is in the clouds,' to which Victor Hugo replied 'And so is the thunder.'"[95]

Three years later, feeling triumphant over the world's tardy recognition of his work on brain hemispheres, McLuhan wrote to Jovanovich once again: "I enclose a note from J. J. Dronkers explaining how the new medical work in brain surgery completely validates all the work of McLuhan . . . We are now in a position to launch a proper promotional campaign for *Take Today* . . . "[96] Two years later he was ready to begin over: "Very few people read *Take Today*, so I am in favour of the idea of doing a small book on that subject [of predicting the future]."[97] By then a thousand remaindered copies of *Take Today*, strapped to a pallet in one bundle, had been dropped at the door of the Centre for Culture and Technology.

McLUHAN THE FIRST-TIME author had claimed to abjure a moral point of view on advertising in *The Mechanical Bride*, without convincing reviewers; McLuhan the international celebrity now claimed to abjure a moral point of view on abortion, without drawing criticism. The opportunity, real or imagined, that he gave hostile critics to find a contradiction between his pronouncements on abortion and his faith was not seized. This may have been a measure of how little the world knew about McLuhan's Catholicism — or of how lightly his disclaimers were taken.

"Moral" was simply the wrong take on abortion for him. The right take, as usual, came from his analysis of media: "What are called moral matters in the twentieth century often turn out to be merely private points of view left over from the [print culture of the] nineteenth century."[98] Shortly after writing these words, McLuhan was invited to participate in a conference on abortion at St. Michael's College. He found the issue of abortion "confused and confusing,"[99] but like any question that engaged his attention, it stayed with him for weeks and months. He was impelled to start writing a "wee essay" on the topic, but this never progressed beyond notes that remain unpublished.[100]

Two years later, McLuhan was to take the matter up again, approaching it with his tried and trusted method: "Without rehearsing the arguments in the abortion matter, I would like to draw attention to some of the hidden *ground* of this matter."[101] Abortion could be viewed as figure against the ground of a larger issue that now had great urgency for McLuhan: the discarnate state of mankind under electronic technology. Even if he took no moral stance on the matter, the intellectual apparatus he was committed to made it impossible to treat abortion as a question unto itself and difficult to discuss in a dispassionate manner.

The dominance of electronic technology was producing a rip-off of flesh, McLuhan taught. It had fostered a new attitude toward abortion, moving a world of mechanical brides toward a world of mechanical wombs. "Electric speeds of information *literally* create the mass man."[102] This is the human, born or unborn, whose mass is reduced to zero as an electrically configured world approaches the speed of light. "If this can be called a trend, it is a trend to the loss of all life values whatever."[103]

McLuhan called attention, as ever, to an environment too obvious to be noticed: "It is important to realize that all our 'thinking' about abortion is taking place in the smogged-over world of tv."[104] As a result, "it is becoming monstrous even to mention the *individual* rights of the born, or the unborn . . . Is it too late to point to our universal victimization by media in which private identity has been abolished?"[105] In so saying, he could hardly continue to claim that he was detaching himself totally from the values that had prevailed under print. But he did continue to place his emphasis on the consequences of electronic technology: "Only huge categories will serve, such as the 'rights of pregnant teenagers' or the 'rights of all pregnant mothers.' Only very large quantities of organic material (crowds) can now command attention."[106] And more than twenty years before Pope John-Paul II coined the phrase "culture of death," McLuhan said: "Abortion 'thinking' is entirely in accordance with the trend toward the mechanization of death and of birth alike."[107]

McLuhan's views were reported with a faithful reflection of the emphasis he laid on technology: the surfeit of information in the global village as a threat to human values; the elimination of the experience of private identity under electronic technology; the paradox of the involvement of everybody in everybody (and every body) creating the illusion that new life is cheap and even superfluous; the hysteria created by the inner trips of the TV image as an intensifier of panic over abortion."[108]

Technology, probes, and predictions proved to be not quite the right emphasis in at least one forum on abortion where McLuhan was the featured speaker. The *Toronto Daily Star* captured the punch of his pronouncements in an address to the Media Club of Canada: "The Apocalypse is at hand. To discuss the dignity of an unborn life is ludicrous. There are worse things happening than abortion . . . Buchenwald and Dachau were just a taste. We're on the verge — the very verge — of another binge of human slaughter. The reason, according to McLuhan, is that twentieth century man has sucked in too much electricity into the right hemisphere of the brain."[109] McLuhan congratulated himself that he had used his emerging interest in brain hemispheres to good effect, but the newspaper recorded a slightly different reaction: "'I'm going to kill him,' one debate organizer whispered."[110]

EVEN BEFORE *Take Today* had appeared in print, McLuhan was once again circling around his cultural guidebook, the twentieth-century Baedeker project. He could call it "a book I have been writing all my life."[111] He developed a new approach in the hope of seeing it done, and wrote to Ted Carpenter: "It now occurs to me that it might be far more effective to do quite brief sketches of each [figure], merely spotting the structural genealogies shared by poets, mathematicians, biologists, psychologists, etc. Instead of 1000 word essays why not 100 word groupings of aphoristic observations. Why not aim at a small 100 page book with lots of type variation and one page per author?"[112]

If this was an appeal (of uncharacteristic subtlety for McLuhan) for Carpenter to come aboard as a collaborator, it failed. Within a month, McLuhan broached the subject openly with Ruth Nanda Anshen: "I never stop thinking about that intellectual Baedeker that I would like to collaborate on with you!"[113] Proposing the same revised scheme for organizing the work he had outlined to Carpenter,[114] McLuhan also tossed off a phrase revealing of his views on the conventions of prose writing: "At present I am inclined to think of much shorter essays in which the patterns and structures would stand out very starkly without the *chiaroscuro of paragraphing*."[115]

Chronology was not enough to carry the Baedeker. It needed to be a structural study, in McLuhan's sense of focusing on patterns — the patterns he was always ready to trust readers to discover with a minimum of prompting from his text. McLuhan outlined the scope of the structural emphasis of the Baedeker for T. C. Clark: the link between Max Planck's quantum mechanics and Sigmund Freud's *Interpretation of Dreams* through the doctrine of discontinuity; the overlapping of both Planck and Freud with the development of "multi-locational" painting and sculpture, later to be called "cubism"; the analysis developed by Ferdinand de Saussure in linguistics, by Sigfried Giedion in art, and by Claude Lévi-Strauss in anthropology. The latter made it possible to "read" whole cultures as "texts," and it was to the reading of the texts of arts and sciences since 1900 that the Baedeker was directed.[116]

It seemed that McLuhan finally had a framework that could turn his unruly and bulging resource files for the Baedeker into a book. He found this framework satisfactory enough to leave it in place for a year's work on the project,[117] and soon he was able to say "it is well on its way."[118] Not only would the Baedeker make sense, a unified sense, of the twentieth century for its readers, it would reveal what McLuhan had known since Cambridge days and what had served ever since as his own guide, "that the arts are always a generation or two ahead of the sciences in developing new forms of perception."[119] He had taught this lesson many times throughout the years that the Baedeker remained unwritten. Recalling skeptical reactions, he wondered: "Do you think that this 'revelation' will be useful or beneficial to anybody?"[120]

The answer was not to come from readers' reactions to the Baedeker. It remained a jumble of notes as McLuhan shifted his attention once more — this time to the roots of structuralism in the work of Ferdinand de Saussure, to audience study, phenomenology, and brain hemispheres — in the closing years of his career.

IN 1972 MCLUHAN MADE more than thirty appearances in person and on television, addressing audiences with his blend of entertainment and education. He spoke to teachers and writers, clubs and power brokers, medical doctors and business managers. But he aimed few remarks at their particular interests, and made no concessions to those unwilling to be jolted into awareness of media effects by his inseparable weave of style and message: *Sputnik* put an end to nature, turning the earth into an art form and the planet Polluto . . . Roles have replaced goals . . . we put on our technology as evolutionary clothing . . . childhood was unknown to the Middle Ages — it began in the Renaissance with painting and ends now in the TV age.

"When we'd go on a trip," Corinne McLuhan recalls, "Marshall just wanted to get there, talk, and get right back . . . He just didn't want to be away from his work."[121] It was a condition of any trip that Corinne would accompany him. An agent to book the speaking engagement, a secretary to make the travel arrangements, and Corinne to pack — so it had to be, for McLuhan was incapable of organizing anything but ideas. And they did not really need to be organized, only rubbed together: when media put on the public, the figure of criminal becomes ground, the public is on trial, and the criminal becomes hero . . . the U.S. space program is a surrogate for war . . . the small leak that had been the political trial balloon is succeeded by the big leak as participatory democracy, i.e., from vertex to vortex.

The itinerary for McLuhan's visit to the University of Hawaii, 13 April 1972, was crowded — dominated by informal group discussions before his afternoon lecture to a large, general audience. Despite his taste for seminar-style meetings, his diary entry for the day says "ghastly day at U of Hawaii." The problem was not so much the pace but the audience reaction, as McLuhan read it. At the Chaminade College of Honolulu, where he had spoken the day before, some in the audience had said, "McLuhan is too rich for our blood."[122] Also discouraging was his reception at the University of Hawaii's East-West Center, where "there were very few friendly voices."[123] McLuhan concluded that "there's not a single person at the University of Hawaii who has a clue as to what I'm talking about."[124] Then came the aggravation of a long trip home.[125]

Some three months later, with the letdown of the Hawaiian tour forgotten, McLuhan gazed out the window of his Holiday Inn room in Kingston at the sailboats sifting through the light chop on Lake Ontario. A brilliant summer day, perfect down to the stiff breeze drawing the boats across the lake. It would have been impossible not to think of the best of his sailing days on the Red River, forty years earlier. McLuhan was in Kingston to address the Students' International Meditation Society. Eric, who was now teaching and had become McLuhan's favorite collaborator, was along, and the two of them completed preparations for the 2:30 lecture. The curious, the casually interested, and those with a total commitment in their quest for spiritual truth began to arrive. The Maharishi Mahesh Yogi and geneticist David Suzuki had spoken to an attentive and receptive audience the day before. Now it was McLuhan's turn. He had had a long chat with the Maharishi about religion and politics and had enjoyed speaking with people individually. It augured well. This time a meeting of minds seemed to be in the offing.

Neither the audience nor the speaker was disappointed. When McLuhan finished, the Maharishi rose to thank him and intoned, "He is a seer."[126] McLuhan got a standing ovation. A few hours later he was home again, and the next day hard at work on revisions of his thesis on Thomas Nashe, with an eye to its publication, at last.

When McLuhan had first started revising the Nashe in the early 1950s, he projected that two summers of work were required. The two summers went by, then ten, and more. By 1968, the copy of the dissertation in the Cambridge University Library had been "read to pieces."[127] It was also widely used without acknowledgment, McLuhan complained. Amid his commitments to numberless projects, McLuhan continued to give the revision of the thesis high priority — in his thoughts, if not in his work schedule. In the wake of the success of *Understanding Media*, he had broached the subject with McGraw-Hill: "The tradition I present extends unbroken through Swift, Sterne, Burke, Newman, Joyce, Eliot. It has far more relevance now than ever. I don't think Nashe need be on the title. In revamping the dissertation I would play up Ovid and the Orphic tradition much more. The book will be a very large commercial success but I don't want it to get in the way of the more immediate work of making the current environment available as a teaching machine. All my 'non-books' are ways of teaching how to perceive the total environment in the way in which a hunter perceives his."[128]

Though discussions with McGraw-Hill proved unfruitful, and the manuscript was still far from meeting McLuhan's own standards for revision, McLuhan remained so confident about finding a publisher that he announced the book as forthcoming in 1970.[129] But by 1974, the dissertation sat on the desk of an unenthusiastic R. I. K. Davidson at the University of Toronto Press. Of the first three chapters, Davidson opined, "an outsider would be labyrinthed, without sense of progress or enough design."[130] He ventured that much revision would be required to update the work. For fear that McLuhan might think himself falling victim to Canadian indifference toward home-grown talent, Davidson concluded: "I doubt if we'd get hyped up over Eliot's or Marcuse's thesis either."[131] Davidson's communication contained not a shred of encouragement, but McLuhan told his diary that Davidson had "accepted my Nashe for U of T Press."[132]

Eric, who had already spent countless hours dialoguing revisions with his father, remained enthusiastic and churned out insights for the next two years: "Have been mulling over lately the distinct possibility that the trivium came directly from the split-up of the Logos under the pressure of Greek writing."[133] Preoccupied with his own Ph.D. dissertation on Joyce for the University of Dallas, he nevertheless kept up a barrage of letters to encourage his father to pursue the revisions of the Nashe, even taking charge of the material organization required.[134]

McLuhan was short of time, but not of ideas: "Nashe-Ramus: Scholastic drive to reduce C-M grammatica (Ramus) to C/M logic and private interp[retation] flips via Gut[enberg] into C/A of pagan antiquity and disappearance of scholasticism and rise of extreme C/M classif[ication] of Nature Linnaeus."[135] The text was not quite ready for a reading public. But two years later, it finally seemed that McLuhan's hope for transforming his dissertation into a book would be realized, when Ian Montagnes, general editor at the University of Toronto Press, wrote to say: "The Manuscript review committee has given us the green light to negotiate an agreement with you for publication of your manuscript on the trivium."[136] It would be another year before Eric delivered the outline of chapters for the work, now conceived as a two-volume set, to the editor. By then McLuhan was far too committed to take it on. The Nashe project was interrupted again, once and for all.

By 1973, MCLUHAN HAD collected eight honorary doctorates (and turned down at least as many others for lack of time), been made a fellow of the Royal Society of Canada, received the Christian Culture Award from Assumption College, the Gold Medal Award from the president of the Italian Republic in recognition of his work as a philosopher of the mass media, the President's Cabinet Award from the University of Detroit, and been appointed by the Vatican to the Pontifical Commission for Social Communications.

And it almost looked as if Idea Consultants was back in business after nearly twenty years. McLuhan was promoting "Prohtex." Intended for the mass market as a replacement for deodorants and perfumes, McLuhan thought of it as a process rather than a product, a positive approach to personal hygiene, a way of retaining valuable body chemistry with potential for communication, while eliminating sour odors. The invention was the brainchild of McLuhan's cousin Ross Hall, a biochemist at McMaster University; the name was

McLuhan's invention, with the "h" intended to add the suggestion of restraint (by association with *prohibit*) to that of protection. The principals in the process called Prohtex were McLuhan, Hall, and Bill Bret.[137] McLuhan patented the "Prohtex" name in Canada and the United States, but as a business venture it went the way of the 3-D fireplaces and airborne gift packages.

In Ireland McLuhan spoke on radio and television and addressed a meeting of the Royal Dublin Society. Then it was off to Paris, where Teri had acquired an apartment on the rue Mazarine. It was to become a special place for McLuhan in the years ahead. He preferred to give his interviews in the cramped but airy five-flight walkup, sometimes cajoling Teri into the daunting and thankless task of translating for him. Mazarine was pure enjoyment for him and a rendezvous for discussions with a host of European intellectuals. It was here that Teri introduced him to Jean Duvignaud from the University of Tours, "a keen media man teaching this under the guise of the sociology of art."[138] Duvignaud, his colleague Paul Virilio, McLuhan, Teri, and Corinne were to dine with Eugene Ionesco, and the evening began on an appropriately absurd note. When they boarded the elevator for the assent to his atelier, it promptly sank to the bottom of the building, leaving the fivesome stranded in the bowels of Montmartre for nearly an hour. They did eventually have dinner, followed by a visit to a theater near the Odeon, where one of Ionesco's plays was being performed. From Paris it was on to Athens to join yet another Delos Seminar on shipboard. McLuhan found the gathering larger and more hidebound than ever: "earnest men, rather all 19th-century types, still preoccupied with bricks and mortar."[139]

Asphalt and concrete preoccupied McLuhan at home. He summoned his finest rhetorical skills in writing to Ontario premier William Davis on the subject of the Spadina Expressway projected to run into Toronto's downtown core, addressing him as a man with awareness and vision and ability and . . . He delivered his punch line with a metaphor: "Your vision of the seventies cannot survive a cement kimono for Toronto."[140] Davis, when he was minister of education, had been bombarded by letters from McLuhan and found them intriguing. He valued McLuhan's views enough to write serious replies to even the oddest of his suggestions. This time the matter warranted the most serious of answers. Though McLuhan played only a small part, the expressway was stopped.

In the wake of the "Stop Spadina" movement, he became a champion of public transportation. He was also a member of fifteen boards, from Planetary Citizens to the Annex Village Campus, a private school offering instruction from grades nine to thirteen, and he lent his name and support to other local causes.[141] A rally was to be held just across Queen's Park from the Centre. McLuhan was prepared to make the short jaunt and join in. But rain threatened the event just minutes before it was to start, and McLuhan called for a car and driver to take him over.[142]

Visitors passed through the Centre as though it had revolving doors. Three scholars from Bombay. Thirty Japanese exchange students. Fifty Tarheels from Chapel Hill, North Carolina. McLuhan was not the only one to see past the chaos. McLuhan's former student, Kathy Hutchon, a Toronto teacher, brought "a bunch of hippies" to a Monday night seminar.[143] At the end of the session, a young girl with needle tracks on her arms did cartwheels in the parking lot, shouting "I know why I did it! I don't have to do it anymore."[144]

The crush of visitors put McLuhan further and further behind in his research and interrupted his full schedule of teaching. He was reluctant to take advantage of the obvious solution: "Currently there is some move being made to extend the activities of the Centre, but this would involve reducing my commitments to English literature. There are some rather dubious aspects to this, and I am going to have to think about it a good deal."[145]

McLuhan was off to Ottawa, Hartford, Montreal, Los Angeles. His talks brought every listener reaction, from head-scratching to "aha!" and "a moist-eyed female fan who rushed up to confess passionately 'Professor McLuhan I just think you're God.'"[146] He traveled to the University of Western Ontario, where he received an L.L.D. Inevitably, McLuhan turned his lateral thinking on the airports where he was spending so much of his time: "Have you ever thought of the possibility of an airport university? My idea is to set up a seminar to involve people who are simply waiting for planes. They represent a wide range of interests and might be induced to sit around and chat while enjoying some refreshment."[147]

Home once more, he lectured to an overflow crowd at Toronto's Empire Club and an audience of more than 1,500 assembled for the annual meeting of the Life Office Management Association. The talk had preyed on him for weeks "because of the impossibility of focussing them."[148] The next day he was poring over Frederick Jackson Turner's *The Frontier in American History*, preparing another talk, when he "realized the frontier was the medium. The vortex the figure as ground."[149] The medium is the edges.

In his twenty-eighth year of teaching at St. Michael's, McLuhan had a fresh question for college president Father John Kelly: "I teach undergraduates here, and the teaching of poetry requires a very wide range of theological reference. Up until now I have refrained from exercising my 'right' of private interpretation. I would like to know from you whether you think I should withhold my reflections on the kinds of teaching which these undergraduates seem to have imbibed hereabouts."[150] Kelly replied: "Your restraint in commenting on the value of theological opinions of your colleagues here is entirely your own . . . I cannot see where your silence is better for St Michael's."[151]

It was not the only local matter that troubled McLuhan. He suspected that animosity and resentment of his celebrity status were giving way to outright acts of sabotage on the part of the university administration.[152] This was confirmed for him when a new graduate student reported that others trying to register had been told "you can't take McLuhan's course just because it is McLuhan. You must have a very special reason."[153] The student was also told that the course was oversubscribed, when in fact enrolment stood at just five or six.

McLuhan kept silent and kept traveling. New York, Venezuela, Denver, Paris, Rome, Ohio, Alberta, North Carolina, Texas . . . He received a citation from the Religious Educational Association of the United States and Canada and accolades from Duke Ellington. In New York he lunched with Betty Friedan and Alvin Toffler, dined with Kurt Vonnegut ("a sober American academic") and Andy Warhol ("yokel type").[154] Fan mail arrived from Bob Newhart, Ann Landers, and from Peter, Paul, and Mary.

If any of McLuhan's days had a pattern, it was those he spent on the St. Michael's campus, when he would attend noon mass. Visitors to the Centre were invited to accompany him or asked to wait until he returned. Like community and communication, communion was a focus of McLuhan's life.

He blasted the telephone as the chief villain of the electronic vortex and blessed it as a personal boon.[155] "Tom?" The phone line crackled with the excited energy of the discarnate McLuhan early on Easter Sunday morning. Tom and Jeannine Langan, getting their children ready for church, had been favored with a call announcing a breakthrough. "Tom, I have the answer to the Greeks." Langan was not sure of the question, but persuaded McLuhan to defer his revelation till lunch on Tuesday. But two days was long enough for him to have gone on to a more important question. Neither Langan nor the Greeks got their answer.[156]

McLuhan was up regularly between 4:00 and 5:00 a.m. reading Scripture in French, Spanish, Italian . . . He said it was like having different cameras on the same action. Before the day and classes and appointments were over, he would find time for a walk, the indispensable dialoguing sessions, and more reading. Though he was fond of saying that he always opened books at random to page 69 or 96 (numbers divisible by three), it was not a hard and fast rule.[157] But no reading held his attention unless it was a stimulant to fresh discoveries.

THROUGHOUT 1974, MCLUHAN was on the road again — Montreal, New Jersey, Windsor, Stockholm, Connecticut, Athens, San Francisco, Charlottetown, Acapulco, Kansas, Philadelphia. He returned home from a speaking engagement at the University of Southern Florida with his left eye swollen and hemorrhaging. In a rare admission the following day, he conceded that he was not well enough to work.[158] But he did.

By now he had an outline for a revised version of *Understanding Media* with thirty new chapters,[159] but another project was commanding his attention. It had been with him since he wrote his dissertation on Thomas Nashe. After more than thirty years, it seemed to have a new urgency. McLuhan plunged afresh into the study of the five divisions of classical rhetoric: *inventio* (discovery), *dispositio* (arrangement), *memoria* (memory), *elocutio* (embellishment), and *pronunciatio* (delivery).

"[The study of the five parts of rhetoric] all began when I noticed that Dr. Slop, the midwife, was playing the role of delivery in *Tristram Shandy*, just as surely as Uncle Toby was dispositio, or whimsical arrangement. Walter Shandy is inventio, or learning and perception, as Corporal Trim is ornament or style, and Yorick (Sterne himself) is memoria."[160] McLuhan's easy linking here of learning and perception anticipates the inevitable find he would make in Joyce, whose work is consistently a hybrid of *dispositio* and *inventio*. It was not long in coming. Working on the thunders in *Finnegans Wake* with Eric, McLuhan found the five characters of Joyce's book corresponding, like those of Sterne's *Tristram Shandy*, to the divisions of rhetoric.[161]

The floodgates were open. The five-part division was everywhere: the Lord's Prayer, the Decades of the Rosary (three times five), Swift's *Tale of a Tub*, Voltaire, Cervantes, Rabelais, St. Augustine's *Confessions*, Eliot, Dante, Shakespeare. Ovid had the strongest connection to Joyce and no connection: "I have read a good deal of Ovid . . . and the vibes with [Joyce's] *Dubliners* are getting stronger. However, as you know, in the very nature of things there can be no connections between Ovid and *Dubliners*, but only parallels and interfaces."[162]

Approached in this way, the parts of rhetoric constituted a hidden ground. They were rhetorical logos, not seen because analyzed as content instead of as relation. This was the link for McLuhan with the huge analytic framework he had set out in his Nashe dissertation: "For centuries these parts were considered as inherent in the *Logos*, or the *Verbum*, as resonating simultaneously. Hence Horace's remark that 'every play must have five acts' has been misconstrued since the Renaissance [i.e., Gutenberg] as if it were referring to something sequential or seriatim [like type]."[163] Here was not only the appeal of the study for McLuhan but its link with his media analysis: "[*elocutio*] is mimesis mode — that of put-on, i.e. its concern is with ground (not matter), hence audience study. But as mode of ground, it is properly medium, i.e. media study 'figures' etc. are all techniques for configuring a ground, for constructing a medium. It is mode of ground for speaker and hearer equally; for rapport . . . interval between them."[164]

Here too was a tie-in with McLuhan's apparently sudden new interest (in fact it dated from Cambridge days) in the epyllion, or little epic, stimulated recently by Marjorie Crump's study *The Epyllion from Theocritus to Ovid*,[165] a McLuhanean preoccupation-of-the-moment that baffled even the erudite Northrop Frye. The link with the five divisions of rhetoric and in a more general way with media solves the mystery: "I think that the reason why awareness of the five divisions [of rhetoric] tended to get submerged in the later 18th century was owing to the steady pressure of Gutenberg lineality. The parts of the rhetoric are sequential, but the divisions are simultaneous; and whatever is simultaneous tends to be contrary to the Gutenberg pressure . . . Marjorie Crump is not aware of the epyllion outside the narrow field she uses. Even the sonnet tends to be an epyllion form, as does the heroic couplet. Again the key to epyllion is the interval and not the connection; so when visual man took over, the interval tended to disappear in favour of the connection."[166]

The infectious McLuhan enthusiasm brought aspiring neo-rhetoricians into the fold: "Kathy Hutchon called long distance to report her find of the 5 parts of rhetoric in the pedagogical program of the Jesuit *Ratio Studiorum*."[167] There were also skeptics. In the belief, perhaps, that McLuhan was edging over the line between the genius of seeing all things in one and the madness of seeing one thing in all, Gene Bier offered him a lesson to call his discovery into question. Returning from a visit to Disneyland, Bier announced that it was "structured in accordance with the five divisions of rhetoric: Mainstreet — pronunciatio, Tomorrowland — memoria, Fantasyland — elocutio, Frontierland — dispositio, Adventureland — inventio."[168]

McLuhan spoke to four hundred disc jockeys and record producers, received the City of Toronto's Civic Award of Merit (along with Northrop Frye), explained to the Sandoz Chemical Management seminar that the streaker who appeared in a doorway during his talk was merely a dramatization of the disappearance of goals in American life, attended the weddings of three of his children, and on a rare winter evening experienced the "joy of dinner alone with Corinne."[169] He rose at 4:00 a.m. to prepare his Stockholm lecture to Swedish publishers and at 3:00 a.m. to organize his talk to the Society for Management Information Systems in San Francisco. In Paris, he found himself "utterly exhausted," suffering from an endless cold, and his left leg wobbling.[170] He was disgusted with the endless string of interviews foisted on him and refused to speak at a luncheon in his honor.[171] When he returned to Toronto, his body took its revenge.

At the Centre, on 21 June, he was just starting to explain the five parts of rhetoric to Joe Keogh when a blood vessel burst, resulting in a spectacular nosebleed. A startled Keogh, along with Eric, sprang to his aid. They gave him wads of tissue, cold compresses, helped him to stretch out on his back, but nothing could staunch the flow of blood from McLuhan's nose. He wanted to wait it out and sat at the bathroom sink with water and blood running while Eric tried to call his father's doctor, with no success. Harley Parker arrived, and they decided to drive McLuhan to the Toronto General Hospital, where he was admitted for observation with no protest on his part. Eric returned to the hospital a few hours later with the fresh clothes, glasses, and books his father was asking for. "Between nurses, we went through Nashe and found most of his works use the trivium, 4 levels of exegesis, 5 parts of rhetoric, etc."[172] McLuhan was writing letters before his short hospital stay was over, casually mentioning the episode and putting it down to "too much travel and too much festivity over the past few weeks."[173]

Driving home after a Monday night seminar some months later, McLuhan asked Eric: "Is it worth it? All this effort to alert people, when they just attack the bearer of news and do nothing. Do I have the right to, am I supposed to, should I continue to keep investigating and making discoveries? Why bother, if the West is being discarded and no one will do anything about it or even listen?" Eric judged rightly that the comment was a simple inquiry and not born of despair, for his father continued his investigations and discoveries and bearing the news for another five years.[174]

It was only in the closing weeks of 1974 that a measure of something like tranquillity settled on McLuhan's life. December was a rare month, completely free of speaking engagements. He and Corinne delivered Christmas cards by hand to their Wychwood Park neighbors and spent their sixteenth New Year's Eve in a row with friends Jack and Marion Johnson. McLuhan closed his diary for the year saying: "Blessing God for Corinne above all in these years. What a woman!"[175]

HIGH BLOOD PRESSURE, recurring hemorrhaging in his left eye, and massive nosebleeds did not keep him from using his sabbatical leave to undertake his busiest year ever in 1975. In Toronto he gave the Gerstein lecture series at York University, taped a special for BBC Television, spoke to IBM and the Great Lakes Megalopolis Symposium, the Conference of Chartered Accountants, the University of Toronto Dentistry Faculty, and the Chesterton Society at St. Michael's.

The year's globe-trotting began in Barcelona, where he was honored with a reception by the mayor and received a solid silver sculpture of the Barcelona fountain. He spoke to a massive audience and was beset by a crowd of radio and television reporters, describing the experience later as "a nightmare."[176] From Barcelona he went on to St. Louis, where he and Corinne visited St. Louis Cathedral again, more than thirty-five years after their wedding, and found it "superbly completed in mosaic cloisonné."[177] Then it was Atlanta, the Bahamas, Montreal, Philadelphia, New York, Mexico . . .

In between there was time to collect his "Man of Achievement" Diploma from the National Biographical Centre in Cambridge, England, attend the christening of his second granddaughter,[178] and spend a month in the Eugene McDermott Chair at the University of Dallas. McLuhan judged the month at the University of Dallas to be most satisfactory. "Quite apart from the fact that the people were extremely friendly and wide awake, I found the students very intelligent and very well prepared. The result was we got a lot done. The university is small by choice, limiting itself to 1800 students. The result is that there is a very great deal of community and dialogue in every part of the school."[179]

But even the month in Dallas was interrupted by travel — this time to lecture at a conference in Switzerland. The McLuhans returned from this trip via New York, visiting briefly with Teri, missed a connecting flight to Toronto, arrived at Wychwood Park near midnight, and dropped in on a neighbor's party. McLuhan was up and making phone calls by 7:00 the next morning. By mid-morning he and Corinne were on their way to the airport and heading back to Dallas.[180]

A neighbor growing gloomy about the onset of old age prompted McLuhan to remark that he had always been very happy. "She said I was restless and that happiness should inspire calm and serenity in all around me. She seems to have in mind dullness."[181] It was true that McLuhan could not tolerate dullness, but his itinerary and his family disposed of that danger, at least, and gave him much to be happy about. Michael arranged a sailing party for his father's sixty-fourth birthday; friends gathered and showered him with gifts. He took pride in the artistic, academic, and literary achievements of his talented children, and his work was every bit as absorbing and interesting as ever. McLuhan was profoundly grateful for all this. As another year of staggering commitments drew to a close, he simply looked forward to more of the same in 1976, though he broke his usual silence about the state of his health and complained of "much misery with swollen leg and sore midriff."[182]

The year 1976 began with a mixture of disappointments and encouragements for McLuhan. He received a letter from journalist-playwright Clare Boothe Luce showing him clearly that she understood nothing of his work. He called this "a real blow,"[183] for his correspondents were a lifeline rescuing him from irritations that had continued unabated for thirty years. He told Sheila Watson: "My own position here at the University of Toronto is no better than yours at the University of Alberta. Total isolation and futility! . . . I can have serious and satisfactory relations with people off campus and abroad, leaving the local yokels to gnash their molars!"[184]

The comment ignores the many satisfying contacts that McLuhan had made and was continuing to make regularly at the University of Toronto: psychologist D. E. Berlyne, philosopher Tom Langan, English department colleagues at other colleges such as Kay Coburn, Millar MacLure, and John Robson, French department colleagues such as Laura Rièse and Pierre Léon. Many of his former students were still on campus or regular visitors to the Centre, Derrick de Kerckhove having translated *From Cliché to Archetype* into French and Kathy Hutchon collaborating with McLuhan as joint author along with Eric on *City as Classroom*.

Physicist Bob Logan had a particular appreciation for McLuhan's turn of mind and his intuitive understanding of quantum physics.[185] They first met when McLuhan agreed to speak at a symposium organized by Logan to launch the Future Studies program at New College. For his Poetry of Physics course, Logan was trying to understand why science had started in the West. He was working with the hypothesis that monotheism and codified law had interacted, giving rise to universal law. McLuhan provided the key Logan needed to go further: the interaction of alphabet and analytic process, logic, and science as its consequences. They began meeting two or three times a week for work sessions that Logan recalls fondly. In the endless hunt for references and cross-references, their worktable often grew so cluttered that McLuhan found himself obliged to go to the library and sign out copies of books he knew he owned but could not locate. Logan became a regular at the Monday night seminars and soon had his own chair in the politburo alongside McLuhan, Barry Nevitt, and Harley Parker. McLuhan and Logan began signing publications jointly.[186]

Retirement was looming for McLuhan, but he gave it little thought.[187] He spoke in Toronto to the Royal Commission on Violence, the Provincial Judges Association, the Women's Press Club, and the World Organization of National Colleges. And he was off to Louisiana, Florida, Harvard, Venezuela, New York . . . The University of Toronto awarded him an honorary doctorate, the Maharishi Institute conferred their "Citizen of the Age of Enlightenment" award, and the contestants in the Miss Universe pageant, somewhat improbably, chose McLuhan as their favorite author.[188] In the course of a full day at the Centre, he admitted he had a "bit of a stroke,"[189] adding "worked right through as if usual."[190]

In 1976, McLuhan also made his film debut. Woody Allen called and asked if he would agree to play himself in a cameo in *Annie Hall*.[191] After years of teaching and lecturing and explaining the principle of the put-on, McLuhan now had a chance to offer his subtlest lesson ever in how the medium could be the message. He accepted with professional aplomb and boyish glee.

The scene was set for an early-morning shoot in Manhattan. Corinne was astonished, as they drove up, to see so many New Yorkers queuing in front of a movie theater before breakfast.[192] These were in fact the extras assembled for Allen's whimsical "deus ex machina" scene featuring McLuhan berating a Columbia University professor of communications who is spouting rubbish about McLuhan's teachings. When Allen handed the script to McLuhan, he promptly scribbled a few changes to his lines. Allen agreed to what seemed like minor revisions, but they brought unexpected results, cracking up the extras and ruining the first take.

Whether it was Allen's perfectionism or, as McLuhan later suspected, his resentment that McLuhan had stolen the show, he made him redo the brief scene fifteen times. It exhausted McLuhan and brought him that much closer to another serious illness. He and Corinne left the filming location and went to Stephanie's apartment, where they watched the destructive force of a hurricane making its way up the East River.

The film commitment was not over. A telephone call came, announcing that the rushes had been screened and all were without sound. McLuhan would have to stay over, go to a studio, and record fresh dialogue. In shooting the scene he had ad-libbed one of his long-standing favorite comebacks to hecklers: "You mean my whole fallacy is wrong?" But even with the rerecording of the sound track, the final print of the film portrays him delivering this as a statement. Without the force of a question, the authority McLuhan is supposed to represent is undermined. But he was too tired to argue the point, perhaps too tired to remember what the point was.

When he had had enough time to recuperate, McLuhan wrote appreciatively to Allen about the experience; Allen responded praising McLuhan for his performance and saying "it was a real treat working with you." McLuhan received a glowing comment about his performance when a rough cut of the film was screened, fan mail and requests for autographs when it was released. He knew nothing about the movie apart from his scene, not even the title, until he and Corinne tramped off to the theater to see it with a group of nine Wychwood Park neighbors. He described the event as "a fun evening but a poor show."[193]

Monday night seminars at the Centre were always a good show. Many people came to see who else would be there. The attendance list was stolen regularly.[194] An atmosphere of warmth and community prevailed. McLuhan was always good-humored and having fun, but he had an agenda that made him intolerant of time-wasters. He used the word "dope" on more than one occasion, and quickly cut graduate students down to size if their questions and comments were calculated for personal glory, but he welcomed the presence of high school students and was always willing to lead them through ideas.[195]

Pierre Trudeau called, asking to have dinner with the McLuhans on a forthcoming visit to Toronto.[196] It was arranged — a sparkling occasion on a Monday evening at the Provençal restaurant. McLuhan asked the guest if he would agree to come along to the seminar at the Centre. Delighted. The scheduled speaker did not arrive at all. Barry Nevitt and Bob Logan jumped into the breach and had a discussion in full swing, but McLuhan was still not there, forty-five minutes after it had begun.

Eric suspected why his father was late. Then he heard the cars coming up the driveway. When a quick glance outside confirmed his suspicion, Eric strode to the door of the seminar room and intoned, "Ladies and gents, the Prime Minister."[197] No one appeared to take him seriously, and the buzz of discussion continued. Then Trudeau appeared. Applause and then silence, a flurry of activity to arrange chairs for Trudeau, McLuhan, Corinne, and Teri. McLuhan, inordinately proud to be playing a trump card, was somewhat taken aback when Trudeau spotted Logan, saying "Hello, Bob . . . what are you doing here?"[198] The director of the Centre for Culture and Technology had been slightly upstaged by a sometime policy adviser to the Prime Minister of Canada.

Somebody commented that Parliament on television was a terrible show; Trudeau replied that the actors have a terrible script. He spoke of federalism and Quebec for an hour and a half, wearing the cool mask that McLuhan so admired, projecting a calm, urbane, and powerful persona, addressing the intimate group as though in the presence of a large crowd. After nearly a decade of advice from McLuhan, Trudeau knew how to wear an audience.[199]

McLuhan was to rejoice in the election victory of his second-favorite politician, Jimmy Carter. McLuhan saw Carter, like Trudeau, as "a *figure* in search of a *ground*."[200] He kept saying of Carter: "I know this guy, he's me."[201] And he understood why Carter's time had come: "I do not think that it is accidental that Carter is the first man from the deep South to be in the White House since the Civil War. The TV generation has swung unconsciously into an ancient orbit, and it was the resonance of the old oral tradition in Carter's voice that appealed to this new generation and defeated the battalion[s] of the North which have no such oral tradition."[202]

McLuhan was now on to brain hemisphere research: "The hemisphere thing has become an obsession with me, simply because it is so refreshing to switch strategies. There are no concepts involved in the hemispheres, only medical empirical data."[203] McLuhan spoke of Julian Jaynes's *The Origin of Consciousness in the Breakdown of the Bicameral Mind* as a source of his new interest and its link to his long-standing one in the psychic and social consequences of technology: "The bicameral mind is the tribal man before he has developed private consciousness."[204] His own experience of brain surgery and its enduring effects was another influence, but the original stimulus had come from neurology researcher Stevan R. Harnad, who had written to "draw your attention to the possibility that there may be a cerebral hemispheric basis to some of the dichotomous distinctions you are making in your work (eg. linear-sequential vs. simultaneous-spatial)."[205]

Harnad sent McLuhan offprints of publications on brain hemispheres dating back to the mid-1960s, along with extracts from his own correspondence with researchers in the field. It was more than five years before McLuhan acknowledged the full impact of the study to which Harnad had first alerted him: "'Way back in 1973 you sent me a group of papers relating to the hemispheres of the brain. It was only two or three years ago that I got around to noticing the work done on these two hemispheres. Since then they have been a major resource in my life."[206]

Left hemisphere/right hemisphere opposition became the new McLuhan probe: "In the last year I have switched from explaining the different effects of the visual and acoustic modes à la James Joyce into study of the twin hemispheres of the brain."[207] Naturally there was a link to the earlier probes: "Since my *figure/ground* approach is entirely right hemisphere, it cannot be tested quantitatively . . . In order to translate my work into left hemisphere terms, one has only to pull the *ground* out from under the figure. That is, to write in narrative style about the consequences of figures in historical development, one must leave out the *ground of effects* created by the technology in question. I can give it to you in one phrase: 'Keeping up with the Jones's' is figure without ground [because effect invisible/unexpressed], whereas 'keeping upset with the Jones's' is figure *and* ground [transformation of cliché recovers ground]."[208] Working with Eric, McLuhan discovered that all fragmenting and civilizing technologies and tools, all those that elevate the left hemisphere, have the hidden right-hemisphere dimension of being words with a four-part form as an aspect of their hidden ground.[209] This finding was crucial in determining the final form the McLuhans would give to the integrated laws of media.

McLuhan investigated the character of the logical bond,[210] revised the description of his myth and media course,[211] continued trying to stimulate dialogue within the Pontifical Commission for Social Communications on the effect of television on the liturgy but to no avail.[212] He was plagued by nonstop colds, but it was time to travel again. Fiji, Sydney, Auckland, Honolulu, Los Angeles, Pasadena, Sacramento, New York . . . He felt "like a convalescent again with poor circulation in left leg."[213] Italy, Baltimore, and a sleepless night before his lecture, New York, Chicago, Detroit, Windsor . . . His doctor diagnosed pleurisy and angina . . . the University of Idaho and a highly successful lecture on Ezra Pound to an audience of over one thousand: "Poe's 'Descent into the Maelstrom' has structurally much in common with the vortices of the Cantos. Similarly, the 'Saragossa Sea' is a vortex that attracts multitudinous objects but which also tosses things up again in recognizable patterns which save for survival."[214]

Now it was summer, time for respite. McLuhan was not looking or sounding well. Eric put this down to the strain created by Margaret Stewart's extended absence from the Centre and the pressure of preparing a Canada Council grant application for another project. McLuhan was also preparing for more speaking trips: Virginia, Puerto Rico, Windsor . . . [215]

The North Carolina Tarheels arrived at the Centre for their annual visit — a contingent of eighty[216] — a viral infection and "infernal misery,"[217] a speech outline solved in the middle of the night, very high blood pressure, orders from his doctor to stay in bed, planned a book on Pound and Eliot, discovered the epyllion structure in Plato's theory of knowledge . . . patterns which save for survival . . . angry at the phenomenologists . . . talk to five hundred at Hartwick College in the Catskills[218] . . . New York . . . "my talk a flop"[219] . . . Paris flight . . . wanted a seat number divisible by three . . . reading . . . "grateful and angry for the huge delay in finding this mountain of crucial crap . . . my media studies have kept me away from this left hemisphere resurgence"[220] . . . all France was blacked out by a power shortage . . . "Traumatic heeding of my advice to pull out plug in order to get back the physical body"[221] . . . patterns which save for survival. And he had a heart attack.

13

The Final Vortex

Conversation is, for me, something like Jonathan Livingstone Seagull, a game in which you play all sorts of nose-dives and air-tumbles.

–*Marshall McLuhan to Pete Buckner,*
28 October 1971

He had the title "Maelstrom" on his mind, but no further words would come to him. It was like a conversation he couldn't begin, never mind finish . . .

–*Jane Urquhart,*
The Whirlpool

The heart attack was a mild one. On 30 October 1976, after a two-week stay in hospital, McLuhan was discharged and went home to convalesce. His rapid recovery gave him the confidence to begin accepting speaking engagements for 1977, and he resumed full-time teaching in January.

Before the year was half over, he had addressed audiences ranging from the International Institute of Integral Human Science to the American Association of Collegiate Schools of Business. McLuhan tailored his lessons to their interests, developing as themes the role of media in parapsychology and the hidden information environment. He also spoke to the Christian Culture series at the University of Windsor on the subject of a people's guide to the media. At the Alliance for Life Festival in Ottawa, his talk was titled "Electronic

Man and the Loss of Private Identity." By the end of the year, he had addressed architects in Minneapolis and booksellers in Tampa. McLuhan explained to his university audience in Ann Arbor, Michigan, that computer hardware was becoming soft, and he enlightened the public at the opening of the Karl Appel Art Exhibition in Hamilton, Ontario, on the subject of art in relation to play and sanity.

In 1978 McLuhan took on speaking engagements in California, Illinois, Texas, New Jersey, North Carolina, and Wisconsin. In Toronto his schedule remained crowded with his regular teaching, lectures to the American Psychological Association and the Centre for Industrial Relations, and a stream of visitors to the Centre that continued unabated. But McLuhan put a premium on private time for study. Throughout 1978 he gave particular attention to structuralism and managed to find enough hours to investigate the writings of Jacques Derrida, Michel Foucault, Jean-Marie Benoist, and Paul Ricoeur. McLuhan was not about to convert to structuralism; he was more interested in converting structuralism to his purposes, in setting the structuralist approach to language and literature alongside all the other large ideas he had been trying to tie together — cause and effect, formal and final causality, figure/ground, left hemisphere/right hemisphere.

In early 1979, McLuhan finally had some sense of satisfaction arising from the synthesis he was striving to achieve. Along with his massive commitments on the international lecture circuit, this project had occupied him so fully that — apart from his contribution to *City as Classroom* — he had not published a book in seven years. His final push had been a foray into linguistics, and though it had yielded important results, just bringing to publication a six-page review of a book on the subject exhausted him: "I personally have been through an ordeal by linguistics in the last few weeks."[1] *Understanding Media* was fifteen years behind him, and its sequel, *Laws of Media* would fall to Eric to complete and publish nearly ten years later. The true ordeal for McLuhan lay a few months ahead.

The year had not started well. McLuhan was having serious trouble with his eyesight. He could barely see from his left eye. He consulted a specialist and learned that a globule of cholesterol in his eyeball was interfering with his vision. For the first time in his life, he was worried about his health.[2]

By February he had rallied and traveled to Boston to give lectures. In March it was Texas and Monte Carlo. May took him to Las Vegas as the keynote speaker at a cable television convention, and later in the month he collected an honorary doctorate from the University of Wisconsin. When summer arrived, McLuhan was staying closer to home.

Though most of McLuhan's activities began to dwindle as a debilitating illness grew nearer, his correspondence remained vigorous; it shows reflections and opinions on important intellectual themes. Roger Poole wrote, reminiscing about his recent stay with the McLuhans and describing an interview he had conducted with Jacques Derrida in the meantime (they spoke for an hour but the interview lasted only five minutes): "On the question of whether or not a text refers to the world 'out there' he was not, really, prepared to commit himself."[3]

McLuhan replied that Derrida's playfulness was a deliberate put-on of his public and a strategy for retaining sanity. McLuhan's University of Toronto colleague Mario Valdes had offered him an explanation for Derrida's approach, suggesting "that the supremacy of the sciences over the humanities had exasperated the Derrida type decades ago, and that they had responded in the first place by structuralism. When it had become 'old hat' in France it swept over the USA. I asked about Derrida at Yale and Valdes pointed to Hillis Miller as the agent in bringing him to Yale. He said that Miller is very much on the inside of this game of high comedy at the expense of the academic establishment. It is Menippean all the way, in the sense of being ridicule of the academic rackets."[4] This seemed to McLuhan a plausible way of accounting for Derrida's intellectual comedy and ambiguous nihilism. The hypothesis also appealed to McLuhan because it ascribed to Derrida a motive McLuhan could easily identify with: "This would make the hidden ground of his game the grievance against the blight of academic mediocrity."[5]

Though it is tempting to find in McLuhan's description of Derrida something of McLuhan himself (the McLuhan who readily acknowledged he was a satirist), James Maroosis, who had studied under McLuhan and was writing a thesis on semiotician Charles S. Peirce, noticed that Derrida fitted McLuhan's description of alphabetical man. "As I understand the issue, because of this, there can be no greater difference between two thinkers than there is between your own thinking and the thinking of Derrida . . . It is through an examination of the nature of this difference that the full import of your Laws of Media becomes truly apparent."[6]

In spite of a much lighter schedule of speaking engagements, the balm of pleasant summer weather, and long hours in the garden at Wychwood Park, McLuhan was weakening. After years of ignoring his health, he was suddenly obsessed with avoiding germs. Eric arrived at Wychwood Park for a work session, but when his father heard him sniffling with a cold, he refused to come within ten feet of him. They dialogued from adjoining rooms, lunched separately, accomplished nothing.[7]

The next day, while attending Sunday mass, McLuhan turned ashen and grew unsteady on his feet. By the time a frightened Corinne had managed to get him home, he was unable to walk. McLuhan refused to report the incident to his doctor. Twenty-four hours later, he was still suffering pain in his right shoulder, neck, and back, could barely turn his head or stand up . . . and he was still putting his trouble down to "a cold."[8]

News came that Marion Johnson had died. The McLuhans had spent every New Year's Eve with the Johnsons since 1959. McLuhan, still racked with pain three days after his episode in church, went straight from the funeral, under extreme protest, to see his doctor, who did a blood test, diagnosed the shoulder pain as a pinched nerve, and recommended a visit to a chiropractor. The latter, working with "alternative medicine," told McLuhan not to bother coming in; he could treat him from a distance.[9]

As the fall 1979 term got under way at the university and activities resumed at the Centre, McLuhan was preparing for speaking trips to Virginia and Brazil. Because he had for a long time wanted to extend the notion of "the medium is the message" to Christ,[10] he was excited about the renewed Christianity and Culture forum at St. Michael's and had promised to deliver a talk in the series to be titled "The Eucharist and Contemporary Media."[11] Neither Virginia, nor Brazil, nor the St. Michael's talk was to be.

By the end of September, the routine of seminars, visiting delega-
tions, and meetings over projects was in full swing at the Centre.
McLuhan was on his way to lunch at the University of Toronto
Faculty Club to draw out a German department colleague on the
subject of Hegel when he turned to Eric, speaking gratefully of his
help in seeing projects through, carefully choosing the words "You are
indispensable."[12] It was the first time in their years of collaboration he
had ever made such a remark. Did he know what awaited him the next
day? That he would be unable to articulate thanks and appreciation to
the son he called his "mainstay"?[13]

Late in the afternoon of 26 September, McLuhan collapsed at the
Centre and was rushed to St. Michael's Hospital with a massive stroke.
His friend and neighbor, artist York Wilson, was taken to hospital the
same afternoon; his mentor I. A. Richards had died three weeks earlier.

He grew a little worse overnight, declined even further in the
morning. When he regained consciousness, he said "Eric, Brazil" and
then did not speak again.[14] He was able to move, but the doctors took
the precaution of keeping him flat on his back. The family gathered.
McLuhan was glad to see them, but could manage to say nothing
except "ah, ah." His blood pressure was still high. The doctors said his
speech could return within a couple of days — or weeks — or months
— or never. It was too early to know the extent of the brain damage he
had sustained; there was a distinct danger it could spread and result in
partial paralysis. Father Sheridan, with much experience among stroke
victims, was quick to point out that he could also recover rapidly.[15]

Within forty-eight hours of being admitted to hospital, McLuhan
seemed improved — better color, less tension, lower blood pressure.
Scores of people wanted to visit him. The doctors allowed only immediate family, and only two at a time, to avoid stress. On the third day,
Corinne pronounced him much better. He wanted to start drinking
water by himself and without the help of a straw, then a cup of coffee,
laughed once or twice. His color continued to improve and his blood
pressure lowered further.

Another day seemed to bring more improvement. McLuhan, sitting
in a chair when Eric and his wife Sabina arrived for a visit, was able to
get to his feet. He was looking more composed and rested. Eric asked

him if he wanted a blackboard and chalk, but he refused the offer. Corinne was telling him jokes, and he laughed heartily at all of them. Stephanie read to him. Teri took him back and forth to the bathroom. Nurses made themselves scarce. McLuhan's volatility quickly became legendary. He could not wait to leave the hospital.

By now the media had learned of McLuhan's illness and the phone calls began. The family played down the seriousness of his condition.[16] And it was serious. At the end of his first week in hospital, the doctors were not satisfied with McLuhan's progress. He seemed to be losing sensitivity and mobility in his right arm. He kept the arm by his side, and Corinne noticed he was barely able to move his fingers. His treatment with blood-thinners was being reduced so that tests could be performed to determine the location and extent of the arterial blockage he had suffered.

The test results were not good: a 95 percent restriction of the artery supplying the left hemisphere of his brain, and a major reduction in the blood supply to the right hemisphere. It was too early for the doctors to determine if surgery could clear the blockage. And while they waited, it left McLuhan in danger of having another stroke.

Ten days after he had entered hospital, McLuhan underwent successful surgery. The doctors were now speaking of "damaged" rather than "dead" areas of the brain.[17] He had all his bodily functions, but he was aphasic. In spite of his ordeal, he was in remarkably good spirits and eager for news. Eric had filled in for his father at the speaking engagement in Brazil, and Sabina brought him a souvenir, a little statue of goggle-eyed St. Francis, with a dove on his head, on each shoulder, in each hand. The patient cracked up with laughter.

Within two weeks of his operation, McLuhan was discharged from the hospital. Though he had atheroma (arterial thickening and hardening accompanied by pronounced degenerative changes) and was at risk of a heart attack or stroke at any time, the doctors said they were unable to do anything more for him and that his home environment would bring more benefits than a longer hospital stay. They told the family to prepare for a recovery period of two years. Whatever functions the patient failed to recover by that time, he would not recover. The chief neurosurgeon, Dr. Alan Hudson, refused to hold out any false optimism.

At the university, things were moving quickly. Before McLuhan had even been released from the hospital, the administration had appointed Professor E. A. McCulloch, assistant dean of the Faculty of Graduate Studies, as acting director for the Centre and made the decision to shut down McLuhan's course on media.

At Wychwood, McLuhan was in the care of a full-time nurse and beginning a program of exercise, physiotheraphy, and speech therapy. He was relieved and happy to be home. Within a week he started to show signs of recovering his speech, managing a few monosyllables. But when he tried to put words together, his thoughts crowded each other, collapsed in a senseless swirl of sound; every word became a vortex from which there was no escape. He did, however, begin to recover the use of his right hand. Reached out. Touched the edge of a table. Said "table." For the most part, all he could manage was "baba, baba, baba . . ." Sometimes there would be an "oh boy, oh boy, oh boy." Now and again, with a mischievious grin and intense concentration, he pointed at a kitchen cabinet and uttered "scotch." From time to time, he could say "yes" and "no." During the many times that he walked the paths of Wychwood with Teri, he relearned the names of his favorite trees. They would stop before each one and study them. After prompting him, she would hear "oak," "birch," Japanese maple," and the one that always made him laugh uproariously: "devil's wart." McLuhan began developing a gesture language that gave life at Wychwood the air of a game of charades, but one tinged with sorrow. He created a special sign for Eric — a circle in midair with a dot at the center — and would lead people to the telephone as he made the sign. It was a silent but heart-rending cry for a son and partner whose absence McLuhan could scarcely bear.[18]

His speech therapist coordinated the efforts of family members. Teri provided relaxation therapy consisting of early silent films of Chaplin, Keaton, W. C. Fields, and the Marx brothers, which she brought in regularly from New York. McLuhan roared with laughter for hours. Several nurses warned Teri that such uncontrolled laughter was unhealthy and would most certainly lead to another stroke. She thought otherwise. Coupling Norman Cousins's account in *Anatomy of an Illness* of the role humor played in his successful fight against crippling disease with her own reflections and insights as a filmmaker, she chose all silent films for her father to view. William Sloan, the librarian of the Circulating Film and Video Library at the Museum of Modern Art, notes: "The irony and insight of Teri's choice to use like to encourage like, the splendid world of silent film to elicit communication from another silent universe, is not lost on me." The films were the highlight of McLuhan's day, brought a sense of frivolity to the household, and rekindled his gift for mime. Stephanie served as voice coach, and they launched a full-scale program to teach him English word by word, sound by sound. At times he could get only one word in ten with any accuracy. McLuhan's impetuous and high-strung nature had been intensified by his earlier illnesses; now he showed patience for the first time in his life, in spite of endless frustration.[19] Slowly, very slowly, it became easier for him to mime and repeat a cue, but he could not initiate any speech.

Teri took charge of one aspect of his speech therapy. Day after day, she and her father worked from a large print version of the King James version of the New Testament and the Book of Psalms. She would place her index finger under a word and urge him to say it aloud. He made an immense effort, but it was slow going and produced minimal results. It seemed he knew it was futile to engage in a promethean effort. Blood would rush to his face from sheer frustration, and he would explode in anger. Teri sensed his humiliation deeply.

For the convalescing York Wilson, McLuhan "painted" a birthday card — a few brilliant slashes of red and yellow. Corinne typed her husband's name in the corner and he drew an X through the signature. A fine and delightful spoof for the artist Wilson, and Herbert Marshall McLuhan's only daub. As 1979 drew to a close, he felt well enough to turn to serious work with Eric and carefully reviewed the pages Eric was preparing for *Laws of Media*.

A COMMITTEE OF SEVEN from the University of Toronto's School of Graduate Studies was struck to review the Centre for Culture and Technology in early 1980. Without exception, those who appeared before the committee agreed that the Centre could not continue as it was in the absence of McLuhan.[20] The committee decided to recommend the closing of the Centre as of June 1980, and though this decision was kept in house at the beginning, letters of support to keep the Centre open began to come in at once.

Before long, it was a deluge — carefully engineered by Teri McLuhan. Her long-time friend Rubin Gorewitz reveals that "she had drafted a letter to mobilize support to save the Centre. We discussed the import of the letter and mailing list, and I encouraged her to include people from all quarters of the globe . . . I asked Teri if she had mentioned her intentions to her father. She said before doing anything she had taken him aside at Wychwood and told him they should stand up to the university. She said his eyes filled with tears. That was enough for her . . . I learned she typed the letters herself with her father silently beaming over her shoulder at this inspired daughter's desire to give it her all. It was a fight for hope on all levels. She allocated the stamping task to Marshall and over a two-week period together they would walk in the late evening accompanied by Corinne to the Alcina Avenue mailbox to deposit the day's work. It was their one and only collaboration. I was touched beyond words by Teri's expansive spirit, her nuts-and-bolts idealism, and her simple desire to relieve her father as best she could from what she called an 'unimaginable darkness.'"[21]

Gerald M. Goldhaber, chairman of the department of Communications at the State University of New York, Buffalo, pointed out that some of the most exciting work of McLuhan's career was under way, particularly investigating the dual hemispheres of the brain and their relationship to understanding of the media, adding that no other researcher in communication was studying this extremely important phenomenon. Gerald Feigen wrote that time would prove McLuhan to have been a titan of learning, and a prophet with honor.[22] Author and media critic Neil Postman of New York University invoked a special reason for asking that the decision be reconsidered. Noting that more than one hundred students had received Master's degrees and more than forty had received Ph.D.s in his department, he concluded that none of this would have happened if not for the inspiration and intellectual guidance received from McLuhan and the spirit of the Centre.[23] D'Arcy Hayman, head of the arts section of UNESCO, added that McLuhan's ideas and concepts were serving as the basis for many projects in all branches of the organization's programs worldwide.[24]

Offering another global perspective, Florida book dealer Frank Taylor spoke of his recent trip to China, where he had found McLuhan's work topping the list of questions with which intellectuals bombarded him.[25] An indignant Tony Schwartz wondered if the committee really understood the importance of McLuhan, and called him a comet whose trail others in the communications world necessarily followed.[26] Letters by the hundred continued to arrive: Walter Ong, Woody Allen, Edward Hall, Buckminster Fuller, Tom Wolfe . . . Composer John Cage wrote: "His views corroborate and extend the far-reaching perceptions of the most advanced artists of this century. He exemplifies the usefulness of criticism opening minds to possibilities of action, creative action, that had escaped attention."[27] Ivar Blackberg raged against the University of Toronto's "clanking, chomping termites of ignorance."[28] Supporters combined their outrage with words of encouragement to McLuhan: "May your recovery shock these pygmies!"[29] Others prophesied: "Closing down that rickety shed of an office won't stop the McLuhan legend. The embarrassing point will happen years from now when foreign intellectuals come . . . like Chinese patriots looking for Bethune artefacts . . . and we will have to scurry around and put up a fake memorial to Marshall McLuhan."[30]

Peter Newman came to the defense of the Centre in a *Maclean's* editorial, noting that its research projects and seminars were going ahead even as McLuhan convalesced. He added: "His dozen books, his Schweitzer Fellowship at New York's Fordham University, his countless lectures and what he likes to describe as his 'probes' have turned McLuhan into a contemporary Aristotle. Ironically the province of Ontario declared him a 'natural resource.' The term 'McLuhanism' was recently listed in The Oxford English Dictionary and he is almost certainly the only Canadian whose name has been transmuted into that ultimate of accolades by appearing in graffiti — such as 'McLuhan reads books'!"[31] This outpouring exploded the myth that the Centre was simply McLuhan, and McLuhan the Centre.

But in the School of Graduate Studies, it was a foregone conclusion that the Centre would close. Even before the committee charged with reviewing it had met, prospective students for the fall of 1980 were turned away with regret, but also with the words "we must be quite firm on this issue."[32]

"You should see some of the letters we've received," Dean John Leyerle acknowledged, as the deluge continued, admitting that "it's a pretty unpleasant situation."[33] In the time-honored tradition of bureaucracy, Leyerle stated that many who were protesting the closing of the Centre had not taken the trouble to check the facts. He separated the issue of closing the Centre from McLuhan's retirement, stating that the latter had already been scheduled when the Centre came up for review. On the subject of the efforts to keep the Centre alive, Leyerle was considerably more testy.[34]

Assistant dean E. A. McCulloch, himself a member of the review committee, acknowledged that it was conducting its work in unusual circumstances. In his report of 19 February 1980, he characterized the Centre as having been "built upon the unique scholarship of Prof. Marshall McLuhan."[35] Because of McLuhan's illness, his inability to prepare a report for the committee or to appear before it, the decision had been made not to strike a widely representative committee, on the grounds that it would have "little documentary evidence to consider."[36] And while the committee proposed to canvass members of the graduate faculty of the Centre for their opinions, a notice of motion nevertheless went ahead immediately calling for the Centre to be discontinued. The committee had required only one closed meeting to decide to proceed in this fashion. Whereas Leyerle responded to protests against the closure by separating it as an issue from McLuhan's retirement, McCulloch pointedly brought them together as the rationale for proceeding with the closure: "Since the Centre exists to further his scholarship, there seems little reason to continue it."[37]

Amid all the opinions expressed as the fate of the Centre hung in the balance, a long, detailed, and balanced account came from former University of Toronto president Claude Bissell. Though he was writing about a close friend, Bissell maintained an objective tone and dissimulated nothing: "The simple fact is that the Centre was formed as the result of presidential initiative with the co-operation of the Dean-designate of the Graduate School. The Graduate School as such was either indifferent or opposed. Since [the Centre's] inception, there has been an uneasy relationship between the Graduate School and McLuhan. I don't say this by way of criticism of the Graduate School, since McLuhan was no respecter of departmental boundaries and was more interested in his international dialogue than in meeting graduate school requirements. At the same time, his influence was never strong within this University, and there was considerable scepticism about the work he was doing. His natural associates were in New York, Los Angeles, Paris, etc."[38]

On 19 June 1980, well after its pro forma review had been completed, the review committee for the Centre presented its report to Graduate Council, where it was adopted by a large majority vote. McCulloch forwarded the report and the official news of the Centre's closure to McLuhan, along with an announcement: "It is my personal hope, and, I am sure, the hope of council that you will be pleased by the honour proferred to you by the action of council in the naming of the McLuhan Program in Culture & Technology. The honour is unusual and is richly deserved."[39]

Nine projects were ongoing at the Centre when it closed officially on 30 June 1980. These were concerned with laws of media, a library project, visual and acoustic space, the hemisphere of the human cortex, left-hemisphere television, the impact of communication on environmental studies and futures, visual ambiguity, "blind sight,"[40] and teaching in relation to media and society.[41] The Centre had influenced the development of similar units in New York, Paris, Vienna, Dublin, and Delhi. Some activity continued unofficially at the coach house through the summer of 1980. In the once crowded appointment book, the page for 24 September was marked simply "moving."[42] It was the last entry made, except for a staffer noting the telephone number of the Unemployment Insurance Commission.

THE MCLUHAN CHILDREN WERE stepping into the breach for their father. Eric fulfilled many of his father's commitments to speaking engagements; Mary, long active in educational circles in California and across the United States, continued to address groups on McLuhan themes.[43] At home, Corinne kept up a steady stream of visitors to cheer him, and he loved every minute of it. He would pace around the living room, his attention riveted on whoever was speaking.[44] The ebullient Bob Logan told him he would have quite a story to tell when his speech came back. McLuhan gave only a small grunt by way of reply. He knew he was not going to recover. Teri, walking around Wychwood Park with her father, asked him if he was ever going to speak again. He shook his head and tears ran down his cheeks. TV journalist Patrick Watson came by for a visit. McLuhan looked out the window at the light spring snow falling and managed to start reciting "April is the cruelest month . . . " And like his grandfather Hall, in spite of his aphasia he was able to sing all the hymns at Sunday mass.[45]

Although McLuhan was unable to speak, he was perfectly able to think. Eric redrafted paragraphs and pages of the material they had already written together on the laws of media and read them aloud to his father. Much of the chapter on brain hemispheres was rewritten at this time using the present experience for verification.

Perhaps under the influence of Stephanie, who had been making her own plans to whisk McLuhan off to the United States for treatment, the McLuhans left for New York to confer with doctors who had said they could "easily" have him "speaking in sentences in 2-3 months."[46] This was not to be, though the dyspraxia (decreased ability to coordinate muscular actions) that had affected McLuhan's right arm cleared almost entirely.

Corinne put on a big garden party for her husband's sixty-ninth birthday on 21 July 1980. Two weeks later they celebrated their forty-first anniversary before leaving for a visit with McLuhan's old friend Ted Carpenter in New York.

McLuhan traveled to Cape Breton, Nova Scotia, in late September 1980 for the opening of Teri's feature film *The Third Walker*. (Starring William Shatner and Colleen Dewhurst, the film also featured McLuhan in a cameo performance filmed before his stroke.) In his aphasic state, it was a monumental act of courage, love, and solidarity with his daughter. The McLuhan party was piped into Glace Bay's Savoy Theatre with Nova Scotia premier John Buchanan. In the newly refurbished art deco auditorium, McLuhan heard himself speaking in the role of the judge who delivers judgment on the meaning of identical twinship. The five autumnal days in Cape Breton were McLuhan's last distant travels from the hearth of Wychwood.

The enchantment of summer days in Wychwood Park had given way to the glory of blazing red and brilliant gold. Then the Park began to turn soft and damp underfoot. An early winter brought temperatures plummeting into a deep freeze, high winds, and icy snow. McLuhan was in much discomfort. His pains were diagnosed as a ruptured hernia, and he underwent surgery in a private clinic in Toronto on 8 December. Eric visited him immediately afterward and found his father's complexion ashen, his movements slow and wobbly. McLuhan's lingering pain was obvious. But by Christmas he had gained strength and was determined not to miss any festivities.

Father Frank Stroud from Fordham University, who met Teri through John Culkin in early December, had met her father in the early 1970s. He had become a great fan at once, and, distressed now to hear of McLuhan's condition, he offered to help out in any way he could. Quite spontaneously, Teri suggested that Stroud make a trip to Toronto, believing that he might be able to bring some solace to her father. The priest was overwhelmed by the suggestion, so obviously motivated by a daughter's urgent desire to bring her father comfort and love at a time of unspeakable sadness and incomprehensible suffering. Teri checked the family's Christmas schedule and cautioned Stroud that Corinne was not enthusiastic about the prospect of a visit by a stranger — priest or no priest. But he had already decided to go.

He arrived at Wychwood on 29 December. Corinne greeted him cordially, but he read the strain in her face. McLuhan welcomed him with great enthusiasm, ushering him into the living room and showing him to the sofa, where he took a seat beside him. Teri had suggested that Father Stroud could quickly create a meaningful communication with her father by celebrating mass on each day of the short visit he intended. This event became the focal point of McLuhan's day.

Teri had also stressed that her father's speech was limited, but Stroud was unprepared for the shock of hearing McLuhan's animated silence punctuated by nothing more than "baba, baba, baba, baba" or "oh boy, oh boy, oh boy" in complex cadences. It seemed to Stroud that McLuhan believed he was communicating quite sensibly through his forcefully articulated babble. Inhibited at first, the Jesuit father found a way, with the help of Teri, Liz, and Corinne, to navigate the maelstrom of gibberish to McLuhan's satisfaction.[47] This consisted principally of reading to him and taking him for walks. Stroud read the entire life of St. Ignatius of Loyola to him on the first day of his visit, which ended with dinner at Fenton's restaurant. McLuhan was delighted when another diner recognized him and came over to say hello. But midway through the dinner, he was in sudden pain and turned to Teri, motioning toward his arm and neck. She asked if he had taken his medication; he mumbled and shook his head without giving an answer one way or the other. No one realized it would be his last night out in public.

McLuhan was reluctant to let Father Stroud leave at the end of the evening. When they parted, Corinne invited Father Stroud to return the following day. He was only too glad to accept and arrived in the afternoon to conduct mass at the house before a festive dinner complete with champagne and cigars that he had provided to mark the end of a hard year and to instill a little hope for the new one. Stroud planned to leave Toronto the next day.

The dinner at Wychwood on the evening of 30 December was a very happy and memorable occasion. McLuhan and Stroud retreated to the basement after a wonderful meal to smoke their cigars and watch television. McLuhan was in great spirits all evening and unwilling to see it end. Shortly before 1 a.m., Teri suggested that it was time for her to drive the visitor back to the parish house where he was staying in downtown Toronto. They all embraced as they said their farewells. In spite of the mercury at fifteen below zero, Teri suggested to Stroud that they go somewhere to talk. Much to his astonishment, she insisted that they talk about the meaning of a direct experience of God. Had he ever had one, she asked. It was only later, when he learned that McLuhan had died near the time of that startling conversation in the early hours of 31 December, that he could answer yes.

They found him in his bed the next morning, turned on his side, the left side of his face purplish, eyes partly open, a crumpled figure . . . The family gathered, paid their respects at the bedside. The doctor arrived and made out the death certificate. Herbert Marshall McLuhan. He had died of a stroke, some time between 3:00 and 5:00 a.m., peacefully, as he slept. Father Stroud anointed the body.

The telephone was ringing by mid-morning, rang all day. At Corinne's request, Eric and Michael went to make funeral arrangements. As they returned to Wychwood later, a neighbor stopped them to offer sympathy and note that he and his wife had just that day brought their fourth baby boy home from the hospital. It was the seventy-first anniversary of the wedding of Elsie and Herbert McLuhan; it was the last day of the last month of the first year of a decade for which McLuhan had made optimistic predictions. And it was a leap year. That made the date divisible by three.

SIX

McLuhan's Legacy

14

Understanding McLuhan

He had a mind that could only think in metaphors.
—*NORMAN MAILER*
"MARSHALL MCLUHAN: THE MAN AND HIS MESSAGE"

Do you really want to know what I think of that thing? If you
want to save one shred of Hebrao-Greco-Roman-Medieval-
Renaissance-Enlightenment-Modern-Western civilization,
you'd better get an ax and smash all the sets.
—*MARSHALL MCLUHAN TO TOM LANGAN,*
WHILE WATCHING TV

GOLDIE HAWN GIGGLED OUT the words of the McLuhan bumper sticker
— "WATCHA DOIN MARSHALL McLUHAN?" — on Rowan
and Martin's television program *Laugh-In*; a cartoon showed a waiter
looking at a crowded table of revelers and saying to his barman, "This
is the round that gets them going on Marshall McLuhan" — such was
the McLuhan of 1960s pop kultch. A few years later, a *New Yorker* cartoon showed a couple leaving a party, she with a worried look, asking,
"Are you sure it isn't too early to ask, 'What ever happened to Marshall
McLuhan?'" Much has happened to him since.

In his time, McLuhan inspired[1] and exasperated, pleased and
provoked.[2] Pleasing his listeners and readers was far less important to
him than provoking them, and explaining his own meteoric rise
into popular consciousness was less important than measuring the
success of his provocations. He taught that the reader is content;

discontented readers must look for a way out. Above all, McLuhan the media analyst sought to make his audiences ask: "How can we escape the inevitable changes that new technologies bring?"

This McLuhan did with his probes. Like the speculative instruments of I. A. Richards — the words Richards used to expand his own understanding and that of his students — McLuhan's probes were drills. He used them to pierce the crust of mankind's dulled perceptions, but his main interest was rarely, if ever, in getting a hole finished, for that would be a goal-oriented and linear activity. The drill, after all, is a spiral, and what it churns up was the important matter for McLuhan. The drill is the hardware counterpart to the spiral and the vortex, symbols of becoming, of pure process. Drill is to spiral is to vortex as hardware is to myth is to nature.

The McLuhan probes raised charges against his ideas that came to be repeated frequently:

McLuhan makes mankind a prisoner of media. Not all of McLuhan's critics are easily pinned down. Take John Fekete: "McLuhan's critical theory . . . is effectively cut off from its genuine ontological basis in a similar fashion to any other objectivistic rationalism."[3] Translation: McLuhan's observations make mankind powerless to escape media effects. If this were so, why would he write a book called *Understanding Media*? In fact, McLuhan says that media effects come about inevitably, as a result of altered sense ratios, but not that we are powerless to deal with them. Fekete knows, and eventually (mis)quotes, McLuhan's reference to bringing media into orderly service, but persists, even then, in painting McLuhan as a technological determinist who "renounces questions of human needs, interests, values, or goals" and is guilty of "anti-humanist dismissal of the whole of humanist history."[4]

Other commentators, such as George Steiner, speak of McLuhan's "very powerful humanistic position."[5] And McLuhan himself describes his position by saying: "In the sense that these media are extensions of ourselves — of mankind — then my interest in them is utterly humanistic."[6] A more balanced view of McLuhan than Fekete's is available in Arthur Kroker's *Technology and the Canadian Mind*. Here McLuhan is situated in relation to two other thinkers, George Grant and Harold Innis, who represent for Kroker technological determinism and technological realism respectively, while McLuhan emerges as the champion of technological optimism.

McLuhan misrepresents the role of the visual sense. Fekete seems to be disappointed, even exasperated, that McLuhan ever left the strict confines of literary criticism to explore media analysis. When Fekete grudgingly meets McLuhan on his new turf, he misinterprets him: "Not only is [McLuhan's] vision-tactility opposition phony, but the hand and sight, combined in the work process and tool formation, were both crucial variables of human evolution from the pre-human. By minimizing the role of vision before the alphabet, McLuhan makes his own claim that man is a tool-making animal (*Gutenberg Galaxy*, p.4) unintelligible."[7]

McLuhan does *not* minimize the role of the visual sense before the development of the alphabet; he simply observes that it became powerfully privileged by the alphabet. As a new technology, the alphabet required a new set of habits that carried over from reading to virtually every area of human thought and endeavour. Media effects. How could this state of affairs make the claim for the toolmaking animal unintelligible? Vision and tactility are integrated for the toolmaker, but they are separated for the book-reader, to the point where the visual sense dominates the world and experience of it.

Electricity has not unified the world into a global village. Where McLuhan speaks of the global village, his key word is *interdependence* — a far different matter from *unity*.[8] Here is McLuhan himself on this question: "There is more diversity, less conformity under a single roof in any family than there is with the thousands of families in the same city. The more you create village conditions, the more discontinuity and division and diversity. The global village absolutely insures maximal disagreement on all points. It never occurred to me that uniformity and tranquillity were the properties of the global village . . . The tribal-global village is far more divisive — full of fighting — than any nationalism ever was. Village is fission, not fusion, in depth . . . The village is not the place to find ideal peace and harmony. Exact opposite. Nationalism came out of print and provided an extraordinary relief from global village conditions. I don't *approve* of the global village. I say we live in it."[9]

McLuhan's death brought tributes and retrospective appreciations.[10] And though interest in his thought never waned entirely in the 1980s, it was a period marked principally by works following directly from his own,[11] while it is particularly since 1990 that critical reassessments have begun to appear (see Appendix 2).

THOUGH THE STORY OF McLuhan's life is an intellectual odyssey, the hero is no wandering Ulysses. In retrospect, the coherence of his work becomes apparent; it stems from his genius for returning constantly, not to a single point, but to a single strategy: probing and testing the forms and limits of an idea, forging links among ideas, developing a method for escape into understanding. This he did by using the prison walls of language as ramparts.

McLuhan's thoughts on language are linked to his reflections on spiritual questions as early as his undergraduate days at the University of Manitoba. His meditations on Pentecost at that time, written more than thirty years before *Understanding Media* put the name of Marshall McLuhan in the public eye, are closely tied to one of the least-quoted passages in the book, closing chapter eight, "The Spoken Word." It is a speculation on the potential of electronic technology for recreating the Pentecostal experience in the global village. Tongues of fire empowering believers on the day of Pentecost is not simply part of the imagery that McLuhan carried with him both before and after his conversion to Roman Catholicism. Fire is the ancient symbol of becoming, of the process of transformation, of transcendence, and so of the power of the Holy Spirit and the power of a medium, combined at Pentecost in language.

Understanding Media refers to language as mankind's first technology for extending consciousness.[12] It is the technology that has both translated (thought into speech) and been translated by a succession of other technologies throughout the course of civilization (hieroglyphics, phonetic alphabet, printing press, telegraph, phonograph, radio, telephone, and television). Language is central to McLuhan's teaching on media, their transformations and interactions. It was central in the work of those artists who first understood the upheavals that accompanied the transition from literate to retribalized culture in the Western world. Among these artists were the French symbolist poets who perceived language as decayed past the point of allowing a new Pentecost. But McLuhan, realizing that electronic technology does not depend on words, sees further. The computer is the extension of the central nervous system. It offers the possibility of extending consciousness without verbalization, of getting past the fragmentation and the numbing effect that makes the Tower of Babel the counterpart to Pentecost, of providing a way to universal understanding and unity.

The intellectual ferment of the Cambridge years, with their emphasis on the training of perception, prepared the way for the innovations that marked McLuhan's thought till the end of his career, but also produced early results in his thesis on Thomas Nashe. The McLuhan who detected coherence in the multiple traditions represented in Nashe's writings is the McLuhan who challenges readers to detect coherence in his own writings. The McLuhan who admonished earlier commentators for refusing to take Nashe on his own terms is the McLuhan whom few commentators took on his own terms. Above all, the McLuhan who discovered that the illumination of Nashe's work demanded nothing less than a study of the classical trivium was the McLuhan who took from that study the analogical method of the ancient grammarians as the unifying element of his own life's work. Though the study of Nashe might have become the focus of a lifetime of scholarship for McLuhan, Nashe remained in the background once McLuhan gave priority in his published work to the training of perception.

This was the focus of McLuhan's teaching, writing, public lecturing, and the intellectual investigations that informed them. A summary account of these investigations is given below, with McLuhan's probes serving as headings. As such, the probes should remind us that McLuhan sought not to isolate the concepts behind the words but to integrate them as percepts. Viewing the McLuhan probes in this way is a first step toward recognizing unity in the rich variety of thought he left as his legacy.

Acoustic Space

Acoustic space was a key topic for McLuhan. The idea was developed at the University of Toronto by Professor E. A. Bott of the department of Psychology, and news of it came to the interdisciplinary seminar through Carl Williams. Though McLuhan never met Bott, he acknowledged his work as a stimulus for his own "study of olfactory space, tactile space, and the rest."[13] Writing to Jacques Maritain, McLuhan brought faith, physics, philosophy, and language through the vanishing point[14] by way of acoustic space: "The ear creates acoustic space whose centre is everywhere and whose margins are nowhere.[15] This has often been mistaken for God by tribal societies as well as by neo-Platonists and the Oriental world."[16]

As for modern physicists, those "visual naifs"[17] incapable of recognizing acoustic space or its features, McLuhan saw their idea of quantum mechanics as bedeviled by the misguided effort to reduce Linus Pauling's rich metaphor of *resonance* for the chemical bond to visual terms. With or without the snare of metaphors, philosophers and psychologists had fallen into equally serious error, in McLuhan's view, by treating the human sensorium as "passive receptors of experience," by preferring "to study the mechanisms of the senses" (an insidious metaphor) "rather than the worlds created by them."[18] A promising alternative came from the approach of anthropologist Edward T. Hall, who "directed attention to the amazing variety of social spaces created by different cultures of the world."[19] Hall's study appealed to McLuhan because it left room for the dynamics of cognition and avoided any hint of technological determinism.

Less than a month before his devastating stroke of September 1979, McLuhan was wedding his latest interest, as intellectual historian, to one of his teachings on media effects from the earliest days of the interdisciplinary seminar: "I have begun to work on the relation between Kant and Hegel and their followers to the coming of the electric age and the return of acoustic space."[20]

A rare challenge to McLuhan to change one of his key probes came from his former student Richard Berg: "[Buckminster Fuller] gets his ideas of discontinuity and decentralization from atomic structure and from modern transport and communications. It is not necessary to think always in terms of acoustic space to understand discontinuous structures and properties. The drift now in communication theory, as you are aware, is toward the study of how the whole range of the electromagnetic spectrum affects human beings."[21] This appeal by

Marshall (standing) and Maurice McLuhan, c. 1914.

McLuhan when he received his M.A. in English from the University of Manitoba, 1934.

A promotional flyer with this photo of Marshall McLuhan's mother read "Elsie McLuhan, Impersonator, in her Original Character Sketches, One Act Plays, Monologues, Etc."

A relaxed McLuhan in Pasadena, California, where he met his future wife, Corinne Lewis, in 1938.

Punting on the River Cam, Cambridge, England, c. 1939.

Corinne and Marshall McLuhan immediately after their wedding, St. Louis, Missouri, 4 August 1939.

McLuhan with Father Stan Murphy at Assumption College, Windsor, Ontario, where McLuhan taught from 1944 to 1946.

McLuhan as Wyndham Lewis sketched him in 1944.

Herbert McLuhan delighting his grandson Eric during a visit to Windsor, Ontario, in 1945.

The McLuhans' twin daughters were christened at St. Theresa's Church, Windsor, Ontario, in November 1945. Seated (left to right) are Pauline Bondy holding Teresa Carolyn and Amy Dunaway holding Mary Corinne. Standing are Elsie McLuhan, friends Mr. and Mrs. McLean, Corinne, Marshall holding Eric, and Father M. F. Dwyer.

Marshall and Corinne try out the
tandem bicycle given to them by their
children as a thirtieth wedding
anniversary present. Teri (Teresa) is
ready to lend support.

Marshall and Corinne with their
children Eric, Teresa, Mary, Stephanie,
and Elizabeth in 1951. Michael was
born the following year.

McLuhan at work with artist Harley Parker during McLuhan's year at Fordham University
(1967–68). *Conrad Waldinger*

McLuhan with
Buckminster Fuller
in the Bahamas, 1970.
*Robert J. Fleming
& Associates*

McLuhan
emphasizes
a point with
John Barnes
at the Salzburg
Music Festival,
Salzburg,
Austria,
August 1971.

George Baldwin congratulates McLuhan as he receives his LL.D. from the University of Alberta, 1971.

McLuhan beams for the photographer and adjusts the antenna on a radio at Wychwood Park in the early 1970s. *Robert J. Fleming & Associates*

A guide escorts Marshall and Corinne at the tenth and last Delos Conference, Delos, Greece, July 1972.

McLuhan speaking at the Centre for Culture and Technology, August 1972. Behind him is the René Cera mural *Pied Pipers All*.

McLuhan with Canadian
Prime Minister Pierre
Trudeau in Toronto,
1977. *Toronto Star
Syndicate*

Marshall and Corinne in their
garden, Wychwood Park, c. 1975.
Barbara Wilde

McLuhan listens as Eric Havelock speaks,
October 1978.

McLuhan
with his
grandchildren,
Emily, Anna,
and Andrew,
in 1978.

McLuhan and Ted Carpenter enjoying the sun and surf in East Hampton, New York, August 1980. *Adelaide de Menil*

way of the transformation theory of communication came well after McLuhan had championed it himself, and the reference to Fuller provided little incentive to scrap the idea of acoustic space. Though he had enjoyed many meetings with Fuller, McLuhan found him incurably linear in his thinking. Besides, there was enough evidence for acoustic space to give it more status than that of an expendable probe.

Figure and Ground

In the early pages of *Understanding Media*, McLuhan refers to "the unified 'field' character of our new electromagnetism."[22] Only his quotation marks around *field* hint that the familiar word has a special meaning. Much later in the book, McLuhan discusses the automobile and how it "has quite refashioned all of the spaces that unite and separate men."[23] The first passage invites a reference to the "field theory" shared by linguistics, physics, and gestalt psychology,[24] while the second fairly cries for a McLuhanean twist on the figure/ground analysis provided by the gestalt approach.[25] But only in the year following the publication of *Understanding Media* did McLuhan add figure/ground to his intellectual toolbox. It eventually became his favored probe. The automobile could now be described as a figure against the ground of highways, service stations, motels, billboards, drive-in theaters, and suburbs.[26]

In April 1965, McLuhan circulated a draft of a paper emerging from the research and discussions conducted at the Centre for Culture and Technology during its first year of operation.[27] By then he had fully realized that the great potential of figure/ground analysis lay in its application to media ("radio service is ground, whereas radio program is figure"),[28] to the unnoticed environments they create (the restructuring of cityscape and landscape alike under the effect of the automobile), and to the equilibrium of the human senses altered by technology (mankind given an eye for an ear with the advent of television).

McLuhan applied figure/ground analysis at first to advertising and journalism: "Any connection medium is useful to the ad or, 'good news industry,' only so long as [the ad] has the character of a 'figure' in relation to some larger 'ground.' As circulation expands, the figure tends to become a ground and its relation to both the reader and ad client is finished. (This is complementary to the basic fact that advertising as 'good news' is a threat to everybody's way of life, whereas 'hard news' or 'bad news' has the opposite effect of releasing survivor emotion and general euphoria.)"[29]

Returning to his literary studies, McLuhan saw the part figure/ground had played in the perceptions of his favorite authors: "Perhaps it was Flaubert who first hit upon the procedure of taking the social *ground* itself as *figure* for structural study. It is to this that Pound alludes in *Mauberley* when he says: 'his true Penelope was Flaubert.' A mob of aesthetes had been trying to make the art figure an object for their quest while ignoring the hidden social *ground* which was the true *figure* for their pursuit."[30] McLuhan applied the same principle to his analysis of the work of Wyndham Lewis: "In figure ground terms I think it is easy to see that Lewis saw the artist *figure* as enemy of the social ground. The artists, apropos, instead of attacking the enemy, merely befriend one another, as it were. Put that way, I think Lewis's work becomes a great deal clearer."[31]

McLuhan recast Harold Innis in the gestalt mold: "More and more I see the Innis approach as a gestalt *figure-ground* approach. Innis was one of the very few people to recognize the *ground* or environment created by technologies as the area of change."[32]

Aquinas could be seen in the same way: "By the way, the word *medium* in Aquinas refers to the gap or interval, the emptiness between matter and form as such, i.e., the *hidden* ground of Being, and in every sense, it is the message. The work I am doing with Bob Logan on the alphabet and ancient science will provide a beach-head for exploring the effects of the alphabet in giving priority to efficient cause over others. Formal causality or total surround returns with the acoustic and simultaneous electric environment, i.e., we move into the pre-Socratic position once more."[33]

Figure and ground offered an explanation for the mechanism of dreams: "In dreams the symbol is minus the *ground* of effects and ergo more bearable as abstract, but the *figure* is the area of causation and direct responsibility."[34] And communication theory could be profitably reworked through the figure/ground approach: "Communication is not transportation. Communication is change. It is change in both the maker and the user — the user being the public.

Communication is the study of ground rather than of figure. In the case of Plato, it is not a study of his thought but of the people he worked for, and the people he tried to help."[35]

The discovery of figure/ground was one of breakthrough proportions for McLuhan, a key to liberation from the shackles of visual bias: "Visual man is unaware that visual space is figure minus ground. The symbolists were precisely the ones who broke through this visual structure into the acoustic structures of figure/ground. Ezra Pound is always figure/ground, always concerned with the public and the effects and changes to be introduced into that public."[36] McLuhan sensed that an approach through figure/ground could hold the answer to very large questions: "For reasons I have not yet grasped adequately, alphabetic or visual man has constantly blanketed or suppressed *ground* in all his studies of the arts and technologies."[37]

Figure/ground also provided a means of describing the contrast between film and television, confirming and giving cogency to McLuhan's earlier pronouncements on these media: "Movie is a figure-ground pictorial form, TV is iconic in the full sense that iconic merges figure and ground . . . The Platonist, with his specialized and merely visual archetypes (figures without ground rather than merged with ground), gets a sense of divinity from his abstraction of figure from ground. The Aristotelian, with his hylo-morphic figure and ground interplay, seems more earthy and rooted. In the same way, the movie would seem to many to be Platonic and visual compared to TV with its mingling of the senses in an iconic merger."[38]

By the time he made these observations, McLuhan considered the figure/ground probe indispensable: "The inability to play with *figure* and *ground* is like trying to get along with a wheel without an axle or vice versa."[39] Figure/ground analysis became a cornerstone of McLuhan's media analysis because it dealt with perceptions, whether of the whole panoply of electronic extensions of the body and nervous system or of mankind's first technology — language. The ground for poetry, on this view, is the entire language. The poet's experimental figures both stand out against this ground and interact with it.[40]

With figure/ground analysis came an insight for McLuhan into learning strategies and media effects: "A child can see the ground or environment as easily as figure. Is not this a clue to the ability of kids

C-M [center without margin] learning of language? Having no bias for figure such as comes with literacy, they can accept the ground itself as figure . . . An example of 'rip-off' would be the effect of phonetic literacy in substituting eye for ear, thereby switching figure and ground."[41]

Figure/ground was irresistible for McLuhan, but his audiences resisted it. He met with much skeptical reaction and was even accused of having either invented figure/ground analysis or being an agent for spreading such a nefarious notion.[42]

McLuhan had greatly enjoyed meeting Yousuf Karsh, who had done his portrait. Karsh professed trouble in understanding McLuhan, who sought to enlighten him with the teaching tool of figure/ground: "I want to 'pick a bone' with you about your supposed difficulties in understanding McLuhan. Let us simply use your own medium, the camera. What I study is not the content but the *effects* of the instrument itself on whole situations. The camera obviously turns the user into a hunter . . . In your case, the camera turns you into a 'lion' hunter, a big game hunter. What does it do to the game or the people involved? Obviously, it turns them into extremely self conscious and sensitive beings. The camera represents an enormous increase in self-consciousness. Do you find anything difficult about what I've said so far? Notice that what I say requires that the reader pay precise attention to the *figure/ground*, or the total situation . . . The pretense that McLuhan is incomprehensible is surely a way of protecting people's laziness and impercipience."[43]

Undeterred by audience reaction, McLuhan was well on his way to integrating figure/ground with his other probes:

1) It coalesced for him with the study of causes, in that causes could be viewed as ground while effects corresponded to figure: "The peculiarity of ground, however, is invisibility . . . The satellite as ground transforms planet Earth into figure."[44]

2) The figure/ground distinction aligned, in turn, with efficient and formal cause. McLuhan wrote to Eric: "Ignorance is hidden *ground*, i.e., formal cause! A man's knowledge would be *figure*, i.e., efficient cause, while his ignorance is *ground*. It is worth thinking about the ways in which the ignorance is the predominant shaping factor . . . The enclosed sheet from *The Listener* ["Does TV keep us in the

dark?" – 11 November 1976] states the amazing proposition that we should not talk about the effects of the media lest it put weapons in the hands of the *hoi polloi*. Explains a lot about their attitude to me."[45]

3) With Eric he had already discovered hot media as figure and cool media as ground.[46]

4) When searching for equivalent terms for figure/ground in French, McLuhan realized that his distinction between cliché and archetype constituted a parallel to figure/ground.[47]

5) There was even a link to the original McLuhan probe: "Apropos 'the medium is the message,' I now point out that the medium is not the *figure* but the *ground* . . . Also I point out that in all media the user is the content, and the effects come before the invention."[48]

McLuhan also made a connection between figure/ground and . . .

1) linguistics:
"Saussure explains that a sign is an *effect* of a hidden process, whether it be a word or a finger-post. From this point of view . . . it is possible, I think, to say that any technology whatever is a *figure* in a hidden ground or vortex of complex processes."[49]

2) his emerging tetrad of media laws:
Figure/ground yielded an explanation for the law of obsolescence: "It is, of course, the change in the *ground* that obsolesces the *figure* and draws attention to the interplay between *figure* and *ground* as the means by which relevance is achieved."[50]

But McLuhan could also see uses for figure/ground outside media analysis in relation to . . .

1) pornography:
"Pornography and obscenity, in the same way, work by specialism and fragmentation. They deal with figure without ground — situations in which the human factor is suppressed in favour of sensations and kicks."[51]

2) politics:
"Have just been doing a piece on inflation as a new form of crowd

behaviour . . . Our present inflation has nothing to do with supply
and demand . . . What has happened is that the old economics and the
old commodity markets are now old figures embedded in a new subliminal ground of instant and worldwide information. The new
ground of electronic information is a 'software' information world of
instant promises and instant delivery in which the old markets are
used as mere *pastimes*."[52]

Among McLuhan's devoted and thorough students, Kamala Bhatia
declared that his use of *figure* and *ground* was "a cornerstone of Hindu
logic. What appears to be true of a thing in one of its aspects may at
the same time be false in another."[53]

Roger Poole, a visiting Commonwealth Fellow at Toronto's York
University during 1976-77, questioned McLuhan carefully on the
matter of figure/ground:[54] "I find myself blocked and frustrated [in
trying to answer McLuhan's questions] by never being quite sure
whether you are operating your figure/ground distinction as (1) a
media-technological affair only or as (2) a philosophical affair as well
or whether in fact you aren't really hinting at (3) a theological level,
which you never state but only assume . . . Whereas linguistics and
logic generally are sophisticated toys (intellectual substitutes for
children's red and blue bricks, books) there is no reality, no certainty
whatever, except in the theologically conceived Logos. In the opposition linguistics-logic/logos you surely have the major fundamental
opposition figure/ground do you not? Am I entirely wrong in intuiting
that the basic model in your mind, the unstated ground of all your
own figures, is the Bible? [Commenting on McLuhan's own comment
in his letter of 24 November 1977 that when he says medium is
message medium is always ground and not figure:] What you really
seem to me to be indicating is the lack of a Logos in which the
Hegelian Logic can be 'grounded' . . . It does not seem to me that you
open the possibility anywhere in your thinking (or rather in your
published work) to what one might call 'theological space.'"[55]

McLuhan replied: "It was while reading Newton's *Optics* . . . that I
came across his observation about the occult qualities which underlay
[*sic*] any phenomenon. Somehow this enabled me to recognize
phenomenology as that which I have been presenting for many years
in non-technical terms. It does not seem to matter whether it is

Hegel, or Husserl, or Heidegger, phenomenology is the light coming through a *figure* from a hidden *ground* and this leads to all the techniques and doubts and 'bracketing.' I think that the obfuscation via jargon which has been going on under the name of philosophy during these centuries is a professional racket."[56]

To this McLuhan added: "*Finally* discovered what happened to the Greeks via the alphabet — it developed the acoustic world of Homer into the visual world of Plato and Parmenides."[57] Did he really not know this before? Of course he did. It is in *The Gutenberg Galaxy* sixteen years earlier, but here it is a new discovery because it can be described in terms of figure/ground, allowing the fact to be integrated with every other one that is covered by figure/ground. What is discovered is thus a new relation, and the validity of the figure/ground analysis is confirmed by the discovery.

After twelve years of working with figure/ground McLuhan could say: "It is only recently that I realized that 'understanding media' means study of their subliminal *ground*."[58] The final transformation and integration of the figure/ground probe was still ahead.

Effects

The study of effects is the thread running through all of McLuhan's media analysis — if not its entire rationale. It takes its roots in his training in Practical Criticism, where McLuhan learned to heed I. A. Richards's call to "give a fuller and more entire response to the words" of poetry and to develop "the fullest realization of their varied powers upon us."[59] Examining and revealing effects remains a constant objective, even as the McLuhan probes change. Unarticulated, left to the reader to discover, and obscured by the sheer good fun of *The Mechanical Bride*, McLuhan's focus on "effect" surfaces amid the chapter glosses of *The Gutenberg Galaxy*, then becomes a key word from the opening paragraphs of *Understanding Media*.

As he wrote his report for the NAEB project in 1960, McLuhan realized how closely the discovery of effects was linked to his other interests, particularly the classification of media in relation to how the physical senses process input: "The break-through in media study has come at last, and it can be stated as the principle of complementarity: that the structural impact of any situation is subjectively completed as to the cycle of the senses. That the effect of a medium is in what it omits and what we supply, but the factors of high or low definition image may qualify this radically. That in telephoning, for example, we are dealing with such a low definition auditory image that we are engaged in completing that rather than filling in the visual, etc. Low definition, on the other hand is the basic principle of organized ignorance, and of the technique of invention."[60]

McLuhan found even more compelling reasons to study the effects of media. In an unfinished manuscript he was preparing on the work of American author and critic Lewis Mumford, he explains: "Personally, having found the utmost ambiguity in all human technologies, and having never discovered a fixed position from which to view or measure them, I have settled for studying their on-going effects on the users."[61] Writing to Frank Kermode, McLuhan went further, speaking of the *impossibility* of studying media from a fixed point of view.[62] Like Poe's sailor, McLuhan found himself obliged to observe the maelstrom of the media from multiple points of view — and to observe effects.

Shortly after *Understanding Media* appeared, Harry Skornia published *TV in the Court Room*. It gave McLuhan fresh insights into the scope needed to fully treat the question of media effects as the sum total of their impact on the human psyche and on society. Such a treatment required history to serve as the laboratory in which to observe change, and Skornia's article offered McLuhan a model of this approach. McLuhan wrote to Skornia, noting that "it is contemporary history, of course, but history for all that. By showing the effect of a medium upon a diversity of institutions, you gain the historical dimension in the present."[63] Here McLuhan is already working his way toward the notion of transcending the synchronic/diachronic distinction — a topic to which he attached considerable importance when he discovered the work of Swiss linguist Ferdinand de Saussure (see following chapter).

McLuhan's notion of electronic technology as an externalization of the human subconscious on a global scale (made possible because such extension requires no connections of a linear nature) brought an even greater prominence to the question of effects: "The new responsibility is to develop awareness of *process* and the effects of specific processes."[64] To this McLuhan added a comment relating to the moral viewpoint he so often claimed to abjure, and which his critics just as often persisted in attributing to him: "Awareness of process tends to push value judgments into abeyance."[65] Those who could not, like McLuhan, work *backward* from effects to causes doggedly advanced a moral point of view they assumed or expected him to share. McLuhan later attributed this tendency to left-hemisphere dominance.

McLuhan found himself in distinguished intellectual company as a student of effects:[66] Ovid, Darwin, Joyce, and Harold Innis.[67] Like Innis, McLuhan became absorbed with causality. "I have been forced to observe that most of the effects of any innovation occur before the actual innovation itself. In a word, a vortex of effects tends, in time, to become the innovation. It is because human affairs have been pushed into pure process by electronic technology that effects can precede causes."[68]

To James W. Carey, director of the Institute of Communications Research at the University of Illinois, McLuhan wrote: "In a simultaneous world which structures information at the speed of light, effects are simultaneous with their causes, or in a sense 'precede' their causes."[69] *In a sense.* Quotation marks. Rare qualifiers to find in McLuhan's writing.

The effect of electronic technology that most troubled McLuhan personally, because of its implications for Christianity, was the loss of the physical body: "One of the effects of instant speed is that the *sender is sent* . . . That is, man has become essentially discarnate in the electric age. Much of his own sense of unreality may stem from this. Certainly it robs people of any sense of goals or direction."[70]

McLuhan was puzzled by the willful somnambulism that made audiences react with hostility to his teachings on media effects: "It is almost like the anger of a householder whose dinner is interrupted by a neighbour telling him his house is on fire. This irritation about dealing with the effects of anything whatever, seems to be a specialty of Western man."[71] But he came to an understanding of this reaction: "Bob Logan mentioned that many people resent me because I have made so many discoveries and from the point of view of subliminal life this may well be a clue. People feel angry when something they had 'known' all along surfaces. It happened with Freud. The point is, we

create our subconscious ourselves and resent anybody fooling around
with it. When I study media *effects*, I am really studying the subliminal
life of a whole population, since they go to great pains to hide these
effects from themselves!"[72]

Eventually, McLuhan merged his observations on media effects not
only with the question of causality but with his preoccupation with the
notion of the figure/ground relationship. In one of his last extensive letters on media effects, McLuhan sets the topic in a much larger context,
providing incidentally one his most illuminating examples of the merging of effect and cause. He tells Sister St. John O'Malley of his push
with Eric to revise his Ph.D. thesis (referring to it not as "the Nashe"
but identifying it for what it really is — "my history of the trivium"),
noting that the effort paid off by unexpectedly revealing odd and arresting features in the history of logic and dialectic: "We have discovered
the reasons for the streamlining tradition which leads to the omission
of grammatica in dialectics."[73] Here "discovered" means extending one
of his observations from *Understanding Media* to a wider field of application. "[The streamlining tradition] began with the phonetic alphabet
itself, which was business man's (Phoenician's) invention for expediting
his transactions. The Alphabet is the supreme streamlining which gets
rid of the spoken word, and all manner of corporate paraphernalia.
Once launched on this pattern of getting to goals with expedition, the
appetite has grown to include the computer and the moon-landing.
Logic itself is a technique for omitting the *ground* in favour of dealing
only with figures, a process which the Schoolmen and Descartes
handed on to the mathematical logicians of our time. There is a single
appetite to reduce all situations to more and more ethereal quality."[74]

Causes

McLuhan by the end of his life had long since become an iconic figure, in a world that knew little of his percept that the iconic merges
figure and ground. But the popular consciousness of McLuhan the icon
had earned him a limerick for his pronouncements on the merging of
effect and cause:

> Runs one of McLuhan's mad laws,
> The effect always precedes the cause.

Thus the baby's produced,
Ere the maid is seduced;
Is it impertinent to ask who the pa is?

If the question does not invite a serious answer, McLuhan nevertheless supplied one, naming a hardy reincarnation of efficient
causality as the offspring of print. And he pointed a finger at print for
obscuring the offspring's cousin — and child of earlier media — formal
causality: "Print gave great stress and access to all phases of efficient
causality."[75] To this McLuhan added a rare, plain statement of definition: "But I refer to formal cause not in the sense of classification of
forms, but to their operation upon us and upon one another."[76]

Aristotle might have protested such a wholesale revision of formal
causality, but he might also have been assuaged when McLuhan later
linked it to figure/ground. McLuhan had "gravitated toward the
center of formal causality," finding his media studies "forcing me to
re-invent it."[77] For two years, he buttonholed colleagues steeped in
the traditions of the medieval Schoolmen on the subject of formal
cause, "only to discover they had no use for it whatever," because the
danger of relativism lurked there.[78] They found the static universals
of Platonism safer. McLuhan replied in the words of Joyce, "how
cudious an epiphany."[79]

McLuhan's method remained linked, in his own accounts, for many
years to formal causality and *increasingly* to media effects. Responding
to an article about his work in *The Listener*, he noted: "My own writing
has been entirely in the world of formal causality, the study of *effects*,
rather than the assertion of values. This approach I owe to Harold
Innis and his *Bias of Communication*."[80] If McLuhan had followed at
first in Innis's footsteps, few could keep up with him once he began to
beat his own path. In correspondence, he looked to Etienne Gilson
for help in understanding "the causes for the non-interest in causes."[81]
The question eluded Gilson. McLuhan's attempt to engage Jacques
Maritain met with no success: "At no point does Maritain understand
formal causality in art and philosophy."[82]

At St. Michael's, in 1974, McLuhan tried to reopen the causality
dialogue nearly twenty years after his first efforts had been in vain.
(He had by now revised his definition of formal cause and was also

WEST DES MOINES PUBLIC LIBRARY

exploring efficient cause.) The results were only slightly more encouraging: "[Father Joseph Owens] conceded entirely, and at my insistence, that the formal cause of any philosophy is the public (either conscious or subliminal) amidst which the philosopher works. The implications of this he blithely ignores. I asked him especially which is the efficient cause in any writing or thinking, and he conceded at once that it was the user or reader, i.e., the cognitive agent."[83]

McLuhan was not about to concede the battle to articulate a large new percept, even if he was the only soldier.[84] In fact, he opened new fronts, summoning allies from Aquinas to Joyce, including that wheezy old colonel, Chesterton.[85] Casualties were registered on the other side and a glimpse of the final victory foreshadowed when McLuhan detected the inability of structuralists such as Claude Lévi-Strauss and Roman Jakobson to accommodate the distinction between acoustic and visual space.[86]

Cause and effect, efficient cause/formal cause . . . now came the tie-in to gestalt psychology and its foundational duality: "In gestalt terms, formal causality is *ground* as opposed to *figure*, and it is the interplay between these that releases insights. In Joyce this is partly accomplished by the use of a sub-plot. Since the phenomenologists have taken an increasing interest in language, they have also begun to pay more attention to the hidden *ground* in all structures, as witness Lévi-Strauss. Without knowing it, they are phasing themselves out of the Hegelian tradition."[87]

The subject could be broached in terms of environments, too: "Mass media in all their forms are necessarily environmental and therefore have the character of formal causality. In that sense all myth is the report of the operation of formal causality. Since environments change constantly, the formal causes of all the arts and sciences change too."[88]

For good measure, McLuhan added the linguistic perspective[89] (by now coming more and more to the forefront of his thought) and an implicit *ricorso* or return to media, via effects. This allowed him to equate formal cause, in linguistic terms, with a synchronic as opposed to a diachronic approach.[90]

The new equations here brought with them a turning point in the ideas now being worked out by the father-and-son team of Marshall and Eric McLuhan.[91] They realized, in developing their overview of media laws, that nature has only two parts and works as ground with no figures at all, there being no formal or final cause within nature.[92] This put a clear contrast in place between the two-part structure of natural phenomena and the four-part tetrads emerging as the new cornerstone of media analysis.

The McLuhans now identified the tetrads completely with formal causality and had a large new perspective: "Have discovered that every single artefact, verbal *and* non-verbal, has this four part structure, two figures and two grounds in interface, *which constitute metaphor*."[93] This was the justification for assimilating nonverbal artefacts to verbal ones and calling all human technologies, all extensions of the human body, linguistic *in structure*. To characterize the spectrum between "things of a tangible 'hardware' nature such as bowls and . . . computers" to "things of a 'software' nature such as theories or laws of science"[94] as *linguistic* is to add another ring to the statement in *Understanding Media* that "the spoken word was the first technology by which man was able to let go of his environment in order to grasp it in a new way."[95]

Structuralism

McLuhan's thinking in the 1970s, particularly in the middle years of the decade, was dominated by his own unique brand of structuralism. At first, it had little direct link to the complex and ramified school of thought deriving from the work of the Swiss linguistic genius Ferdinand de Saussure. In the early pages of *Understanding Media*, McLuhan had already outlined structuralism in the broadest terms: the trend of modern thought, in areas as diverse as physics, painting, and poetry, whereby "specialized segments of attention have shifted to total field."[96] It was a trend that supported his notion that the medium is the message; gave the phrase its full meaning; and illustrated effect preceding cause in twentieth-century intellectual history, and in the development of his own thought. It was also a trend that could accommodate the probes that he was still developing.

Shortly before *Understanding Media* appeared, McLuhan declared that structuralism was fundamental to his method of intellectual inquiry, linking it to "modern depth criticism," meaning Practical Criticism in the manner of I. A. Richards.[97] In McLuhan's own account, more than a decade later, when his overview of the subject had been reconfigured, he continued to acknowledge Richards as the principal source among those who had nourished his structuralist approach: "My structural approach began with I. A. Richards but developed very much through Sigfried Giedion, the Swiss art historian, and especially through my studies in classical rhetoric."[98] McLuhan also put Poe,[99] Lewis,[100] Innis, Joyce, Pound, and Eliot[101] under the heading of structuralists.

Structuralism appealed to McLuhan for its own merits *and* because it invited the type of interdisciplinary inquiry to which his own natural bent led him.[102] When McLuhan said he had "reached the structuralist stage where content is indifferent,"[103] he tied this directly to his media studies. He had learned structuralism as part of his literary apprenticeship at Cambridge, but it had also opened the way to him for media analysis, carrying him permanently beyond the precinct(s) of literary scholarship.

The flow of mail in response to *Understanding Media* brought McLuhan a letter from Montreal: "[Raymonde Dallaire of Montreal] claims there is a great affinity between linguistics and my sort of structural approach to media. She became interested in *Understanding Media* because she regards it as a suburb of linguistic study."[104] Though Dallaire's take on McLuhan's work sprang from the interdisciplinary impulse he never resisted, he paid little attention to it. It took a few more years, and a pointed suggestion to look to Saussure, to begin moving McLuhan toward a structuralism that was much less familiar to him than the legacy of Richards. It was a potent suggestion, combining the appeal of free play between media analysis and linguistics (itself a discipline at the crossroads of anthropology, psychology, and philosophy) with the prospect of sharpening the original McLuhan probe. Wrote Max Nanny: "By the way, I have found out that the difficulties concerning your insight 'The Medium is the Message' can elegantly be solved by a recourse to de Saussure's distinction between 'langue' and 'parole': the medium as 'langue' is the message; the medium as 'parole' is rather content oriented, or as you said, the user!"[105]

After Nanny made this suggestion, James M. Curtis published an article on McLuhan in relation to French structuralism to which

McLuhan reacted favorably: "Your piece on me and French Structuralism pleased me a good deal . . . The most controversial area of my structural approach concerns the factor known only to James Joyce, the greatest of all structuralists, namely the conflict and complementarity of audible and visible space."[106] To Curtis, McLuhan revealed his apprehensions and reservations about European structuralism: "So far as I can discover, the European structuralists work with a set of archetypes as paradigms. This ensures that there be a minimum of exploration and a maximum of mere matching in their activities."[107]

The situation was no better in North America, as far as McLuhan was concerned: "Apropos [D. E.] Berlyne, I agree that he is using the old visual systems approach but I think by pushing it as far as he does he has flipped into the non-visual world via structuralism. The same seems to me to be true of C. E. Osgood, with his semantic differential. By pushing the yes-no approach into the structural world, they get into territories which they don't understand for what they are."[108] The territories in question are those of linguistics and anthropology, already alluded to by McLuhan in writing to Curtis and repeated frequently in his correspondence, beginning in 1972.[109]

But there was a paradox in structuralism that appealed to McLuhan: "Paradoxically, what is called 'structuralism' in linguistics and in the arts is characterized by the disappearance of merely visual lay-out in favour of iconic and multi-sensuous structures."[110] And there was a further appeal. Not only could structuralism "solve the problem" of "the medium is the message," as Max Nanny had suggested, but it did so by fostering the integration of other McLuhan probes: "This approach is basically concerned with the *effects* of human artifacts, be they words or other signs or things . . . What I have used as an approach to the media was gathered from the symbolists. The structural linguists came out of the same symbolist world. Recall that Edgar Allen [*sic*] Poe started it all with his insistence that in order to make a poem, one must start with the effect and then look around for the means to such an effect."[111]

With respect to figure and ground, McLuhan wrote: "In Piaget's *Structuralism* he explains that with *figure-ground* there is no need for archetypes. They can be seen as existential results of the interplay of *figure* and *ground*. This was the work of Descartes in throwing aside rhetorical decorum and the public in favour of the pure ideas minus any *ground*."[112]

As McLuhan delved into Saussure and Piaget, a new brand of structuralism reconciling acoustic space and linear space became part of his working apparatus. "This matter is the theme of *Through the Vanishing Point* . . . But I push the matter a good deal further in *Take Today*, and this has been possible since discovering the nature of tactile space in quantum mechanics and modern physics."[113]

McLuhan was now citing Saussure and James A. Boon (*From Symbolism to Structuralism*) as supporting his own notion of media, inasmuch as "Saussure explains that a sign is an effect of a hidden process,"[114] though Saussure needed help that McLuhan was ready to give him: "[Saussure] regards all language as central to such hidden processes [ground for figures] and studies all language patterns as *effects*. He divides all structures into the *diachronic* or visual, and *synchronic* or acoustic. He doesn't happen to understand the difference between the visual and the acoustic, and so uses these terms only as classifications without fully understanding their structures."[115]

In so saying, McLuhan was also on his way to elaborating the interlocking laws of media and tetrads, and here too structuralism was exerting its influence. By 1976 he could say: "All of man's artifacts are *structurally* linguistic and metaphoric."[116] A year before the stroke that ended his research and writing, he could call the galaxy of ideas forming structuralism "the perfect fulfillment of my research."[117] In elaborating this idea, he reverted once more to his concern for the discarnate state of mankind under electronic technology.

15

Is McLuhan a Linguist?

They are far gone with linguistics, which has the same relation to literature as Dutch elm disease has to forestry!
            –*Marshall McLuhan to Eric McLuhan,*
                                    25 April 1977

Began to read Saussure's linguistics and found the sense that his followers failed to convey to me . . . Like the followers of Innis, they are unable to get with him.
                    –*Marshall McLuhan's diary,*
                                    20 April 1974

"Is it not significant that the Centre for Culture and Technology is *behind* the Medieval Centre?"[1] McLuhan asked in 1973. It was also behind the University of Toronto's Department of Linguistics, which was equally significant, in view of McLuhan's "linguistic turn" of the following year. But McLuhan was no stranger to linguistics when he made that turn. Twenty years before, in the earliest days of his interdisciplinary seminar, he had invited U.S. linguist W. Freeman Twadell to address the group on "temporal-spatial relations in current linguistic theory."[2]

McLuhan's major foray into linguistics belongs to the last decade of his career. The results of his linguistic studies are easily overlooked for various reasons. First, there is a temptation to confine assessment of McLuhan's work to *Understanding Media* and the flurry of other books he had published by 1970. Second, linguistic questions receive little attention in his posthumous works, despite the fact that they are clearly important and central. Third, the complexity and diversity of linguistics obscures its role in McLuhan's thought. But the effort to discover that role is well repaid.

Asking if McLuhan is a linguist is as much of a probe as any question he raised himself, and like his probes it is a valuable hermeneutic for providing insight into his explorations and discoveries. It also supplies a link for McLuhan's evolving thought, from the time of his graduate school training to the days of the interdisciplinary seminar at the University of Toronto to the preoccupations of his last year of scholarly activity, when he could say that structuralism was the perfect fulfillment of his research.

McLuhan's posthumously published *Laws of Media* states that the work puts "the modern study of technology and artefacts on a humanistic and linguistic basis for the first time."[3] In *The Global Village*, there is a similar claim: "In this book, we present a model for studying the structural impact of technologies on society. This model emerged from a discovery that all media and technologies have a fundamentally linguistic structure."[4] Because of the many directions linguistics has taken, because of the many directions McLuhan took, it is important to search out his exact sense in speaking of a linguistic basis for studying technology and a linguistic structure *in* technology. A clue begins to emerge from a look at the immediate sources for the late linguistic turn in McLuhan's intellectual investigations. It is also instructive to compare these sources with influences from his graduate school training in England.

McLuhan made reading notes and kept files on many topics related to linguistics, such as meaning, dictionary-making and semiotics (the study of any system that carries meaning). He also collected references to the works of many well-known linguists of the twentieth century, including Charles Hockett, Edward Sapir, Benjamin Lee Whorf, R. A. Wilson, and Noam Chomsky. There are references to Alfred Korzybski's study known as General Semantics (a language-based system for the training of the central nervous system) as early as 1943 in McLuhan's doctoral thesis. And he recorded notes on some of the very late writings of his former Cambridge teacher I. A. Richards, such as *Techniques in Language Control* (1974). McLuhan studied the great

Ferdinand de Saussure's *Course in General Linguistics* intensively and with great interest over a period of six months during 1974. By the time he had mined Saussure for every interesting idea, his copy of the book was awash with marginal annotations and reading notes. McLuhan's considerable linguistic industry was sustained over the entire period 1970 to 1975, when he was working with Eric on the material that would eventually form *Laws of Media*, the sequel to *Understanding Media*. (McLuhan's collaboration with Bruce Powers, who would eventually see *The Global Village* through the press after McLuhan's death, comes slightly later.)

McLuhan's eclectic reading in modern linguistic theory began in the same year that Jonathan Miller published *McLuhan*, in which the last and longest chapter ("Language, Literacy and the Media") is devoted to a criticism of McLuhan couched largely in terms of linguistic theory. Miller harks back constantly to the fundamental charge that McLuhan's work has no scientific basis. McLuhan turned to linguistics in order to arm himself for responding to Miller in future publications on the turf his critic had chosen. This is clear from the subtitle of *Laws of Media: The New Science*, with its careful echo of both Francis Bacon and Giambattista Vico.

Miller might not have proved to be a sufficient irritant to move McLuhan toward linguistics, if it were not that he was adding his voice to that of scholar Umberto Eco. Here was a critic of McLuhan's thought from an allied camp — that of semiotics. Unlike linguistics, the study of semiotics does not confine itself to human language but investigates all forms of communication. With such a wide scope, semiotics might be expected to prove compatible with the broad sweep of McLuhan's work, but Eco will admit no such accommodation. Understanding the criticisms of McLuhan put forward by Eco and Miller, understanding how misguided they are, is an important step to understanding McLuhan's work, and to appreciating the difficulties he faced in getting his message through — even to an intellectually sophisticated audience.

The medium is not the message. The starting point for this observation is Eco's reflection on a cartoon showing a cannibal chieftain wearing an alarm clock as a necklace. Eco disagrees with McLuhan's view that the invention of clocks universally fostered a concept of time as space divided into uniform chunks. He concedes that this happened for some persons but believes that the message of the clock could have a different meaning for others (as it did for the cannibal). Eco refers to this as the residual freedom of the individual to interpret in different ways. If we are willing to grant this point, Eco says, "it is still equally untrue that acting on the form and contents of the message can convert the person receiving it."[5]

As a criticism of the idea that the medium is the message, Eco's line of thought has strayed amazingly far from McLuhan in just a few sentences: (1) it does not deal with the unperceived effects of a technology at the sensory level, but conscious reflection on the technology; (2) it puts form and content together as if this were part of McLuhan's view, when in fact he always separates them.

McLuhan uses the term "media" broadly. This part of Eco's discussion starts by presenting the technical apparatus of semiotics and then charges that McLuhan does not respect the distinctions required by that apparatus: "To say that the alphabet and the street are 'media' is lumping a code together with a channel."[6] This is a bit like complaining that the cannibal (with the residual freedom Eco gave him) threatens the professional standards of the clock-makers' guild. Allowing McLuhan the freedom to define "media" broadly does not undermine the work of the semiotician.

But Eco continues, noting that electric light can be signal, message, or channel, whereas McLuhan is concerned only with the third of these when he says that electric light is a medium without a message. Now Eco's objection is too narrow a focus rather than too broad a definition. His examples of the cases where light is a signal (using light to flash a message in Morse code) or a message in itself (light left on in a window as an all-clear to a lover) do not have any impact on the scale, speed, or patterns of organization in society as a whole (McLuhan's definition of message) and do not, therefore, damage McLuhan's view. McLuhan is concerned with the effect of light, and this effect is produced whether light is signal, message (Eco's sense), or channel.

Just as McLuhan's broad definition of "media" does not jeopardize the semiotician's analysis, the semiotician's distinctions do not detract from the relevance of McLuhan's observations to his own purpose.

Eco concludes his comments on McLuhan's stretched sense of "media" by stating that "it is the code used that gives the light-signal its specific content."[7] This neither undermines nor is undermined by any of McLuhan's pronouncements on the subject. In fact, it has nothing to do with them.

All media are not active metaphors. Here Eco's argument is still that McLuhan ignores the semiotician's all-important concept of code: that although languages translate the form of an experience because they *are* codes, a metaphor is just a replacement *within* a code. On the one hand, Eco argues that the sense in which print is a medium should be distinguished from the sense in which language is a medium, and that this makes McLuhan's talk of media as metaphors too all-encompassing. On the other hand, he argues that McLuhan's analysis would be improved by replacing the notion of media as metaphors with that of code, as if there could be a unified code of media. He admits that "the press does not change the coding of experience with respect to the written language."[8] It would be of no use to McLuhan, therefore, to analyze in terms of codes, when it is precisely the changes brought about by new media that he wishes to study.

"The medium is the message" has three possible meanings. This is a far cry from saying, as Eco did earlier, that the medium is *not* the message. Now Eco is concerned that the potential meanings of McLuhan's phrase are contradictory. He gives them as (1) the form of the message is the real content of the message; (2) the code is the message; (3) the channel is the message. And while these are only potential meanings, they are somehow proof for Eco that "it is not true, as McLuhan states, that scholars of information have considered only the content of information without bothering about formal problems."[9]

Language is not a medium. This criticism comes not from Eco but from Jonathan Miller. He takes the view that McLuhan makes a "spurious assumption that one can consider language as a technical medium which exists independently of the mind which uses it."[10] The evidence for this view comes from a long ride on which Miller takes the reader, through the territory of linguistics to a destination that McLuhan never set for himself. At that point Miller no longer speaks of McLuhan's "spurious assumption" but "difficulties which arise when language is regarded as a medium."[11] Just as Eco condemns the absence of the semiotician's specialist viewpoint in McLuhan's work, Miller condemns the absence there of the distinction linguists make between knowing language and using it.

Miller writes as if making that distinction causes the collapse of McLuhan's claim that language is a medium. This simply could not be. The distinction made in linguistic theory between knowing language and using it does not even deal with words as expression of thought. But Miller continues to draw heavy artillery from the linguistic arsenal, and when he is finished, he rests and sniffs: "Any theory of human communication which does not take its implied differences into consideration has very little right to be taken seriously."[12]

In fact, McLuhan's objective is not to offer a theory of human communication, but to probe the effects of anything and everything we use in dealing with the world around us, including language. This purpose is not served by the specialized focus of linguistics, nor does linguistics discredit McLuhan's approach.

McLuhan takes metaphors literally. Jonathan Miller quotes the following passage from McLuhan: "The TV image is not a *still* shot. It is not photo in any sense, but a ceaselessly forming contour of things limned by the scanning-finger. The resulting plastic contour appears by light *through*, not light *on*, and the image so formed has the quality of sculpture and icon, rather than of picture."[13] Here Miller finds "a vivid example of a metaphor illicitly conjured into a concrete reality."[14] This charge is based on misinterpretation. McLuhan does not refer to the TV image as tactile because of the metaphorical finger scanning the screen, as Miller believes, but because the TV image requires of the eye a degree of involvement as intense as that of touch. McLuhan takes involvement and makes it tactile metaphorically; Miller takes a metaphorical term involving tactility and makes it into a mistake. It is his own, not McLuhan's. The proof that McLuhan does not give a concrete sense to the metaphors of tactility, sculpture, and iconicity is to be found in the same chapter that Miller quotes: "Iconographic art *uses the eye as we use our hand* to create an inclusive image, made up of many moments, phases, and aspects of the person and thing."[15]

Speech is as linear as print. With this claim, Miller presumes to undo a McLuhan percept. The crux of the argument is that sounds can be uttered only one at a time. Miller, believing himself to be clinching a point with the observation that speech can be recorded on a length of magnetic tape, triumphantly asks, "How linear can one get?"[16] This rather lame line of thinking ignores the very different qualities of the marginal linearity Miller describes and the much more powerful linearity of print, a linearity constantly forcing the eye to move from left to right, from top to bottom, over visible figures against visible ground.

Facing such irrelevant criticisms from Eco and Miller, McLuhan could have countered them easily by arguing from his own position. And so he did, in the case of Miller, in both private correspondence and the popular press.[17] But he also chose to delve into linguistics. If the initial impetus to move in this direction was the negative one provided by Eco and Miller, an equally important and positive influence came from a Brazilian anthropologist, Dr. Egon Schaden, a visiting scholar at the University of Toronto. He attended the media seminars at the Centre for Culture and Technology and provided an entry point to Saussure's linguistics for McLuhan by explaining a key concept from the work of the anthropologist Claude Lévi-Strauss. Saussure's distinction between synchronic analysis and diachronic analysis had found its way into Levi-Strauss's work.[18]

McLuhan immediately linked synchronic versus diachronic to a concept he had already been using for a long time (and which he had inherited from Harold Innis), that of the interplay of center and margin in dynamic structures. He noted that diachronic analysis is the chronological approach to language and society, whereas the synchronic is the structural approach, in which any moment, or aspect of culture, can be made to reveal the whole to which it belongs, and in which all past cultures survive as *resonance* (a central phenomenon in the McLuhan view). This was a breakthrough for McLuhan, who had tackled the study of structuralism (Saussure's legacy to twentieth-century thought both in and beyond linguistics) on his own the previous year, with little success. Nevertheless, he came back to it repeatedly, looking at treatments of the subject by William Wimsatt and Frederic Jameson, commenting in his diary on the "Saussure-Jakobson clique,"[19] and dismissing the whole enterprise as "sterile and in the visual mode of decadent scholastics."[20] But thanks to Schaden, structuralism was taking on a new look.

As soon as McLuhan began reading the *Course in General Linguistics*, he detected Saussure saying "the medium is the message."[21] He was also excited to find Saussure stating that language media are difficult to access, for this notion coincides with McLuhan's own teaching on visible figure versus invisible ground.[22] Saussure's discussion of perspective in painting, used to illustrate a point about synchronic versus diachronic analysis, appears to have started McLuhan thinking about the semiotician's notion of the sign — anything that stands for something other than itself.[23] In fact, Saussure's comments on perspective in painting are not linked to signs per se, but McLuhan quickly assimilates the drift of Saussure's teaching on signs to his own notion of sensory closure, noting that Saussure approaches all signs as *effects* — another key percept for McLuhan. A lesson on effects and closure is indeed implicit in the passage in which Saussure discusses perspective in painting. If it is left implicit, Saussure may perhaps be forgiven for insisting less strenuously on the matter than McLuhan, whose interests are elsewhere but whose reading of the *Course in General Linguistics* is entirely consistent with Saussure's principles.

By way of probing the limits of Saussure's view and its compatibility with his own thought, McLuhan puts zippers alongside Saussure's painting and treats them both as signs, or sensory closure. All of this is set in the context of the emerging law of media that every figure obscures a ground of hidden forces, which are the effects of the figure. The juxtaposition of painting and zipper, sign and sensory closure, tells us that when a painting is completed, alternative perspectives on space vanish, just as the surface concealed by a fastened zipper becomes a hidden ground, becomes space configured as a static entity by the zipper. Similarly, when the pure ground of thought and the pure ground of sound come together in the word (Saussure's sign), options are foreclosed. There is a further parallel to the way in which our physical senses are dulled to alternative input by the bias created by an ascendant medium.

McLuhan found much that was grist to his mill in Saussure: the notion of language as a medium including its effects and creating a service environment; vocal organs as hardware for the software of the language system; sound units as the sum of auditory impressions and movements of the speech organs, exemplifying the interplay of sensory input and sensory closure — all of these are hybrids of Saussurean concepts and McLuhanean formulation. The synchronic/diachronic contrast is related by McLuhan not only to that of center/margin but to those of figure/ground and eye/ear orientation. Saussure's description of how the grammatical structures of language interact with word-groups is assimilated to the interaction McLuhan describes between cliché and archetype.

But it is the sign as unperceived sensory closure, or media effect, that remains the keystone of Saussure's thought for McLuhan. It is surprising that Saussure's view of the sign functioning primarily as a link between thought processes and the continuum of sound is not taken further by McLuhan. In its full ramification, this idea corresponds closely to McLuhan's characterization of media working in pairs, one obscuring the operation of the other by creating the illusion of being its content. Indeed, McLuhan's description of thought as pure process, articulated in *Understanding Media* more than a decade before he read Saussure, completely parallels the latter's description of the formless domain of unverbalized thought.

BY THE TIME McLUHAN HAD given six months of study to the notions of system and sign in and beyond Saussure, he concluded that it was essentially a matter of Boolean algebra. For his purposes, there was no need to pursue the study further. But it had been enormously useful for McLuhan's emerging laws of media.[24] Saussure's views had provided a catalyst, thanks to which McLuhan was prepared to state that he saw a new pattern of all technology as organized ignorance.[25] He linked this pattern to four interlocking laws of media forming a *tetradic structure*, an idea central to his posthumous works of 1988 and 1989.[26]

The tetrad is characterized as a resonant structure and an update of "the ancient and medieval tradition of grammar-allied-to-rhetoric in a way that is consonant with the forms of awareness imposed on the twentieth century by electronic technology."[27] With the tetrad, the appropriation of ideas from linguistics reaches its full-blown form. It is McLuhan of late vintage. But it is also important to note in the tetrad a rich echo of his doctoral thesis tracing the trivium of grammar, dialectics, and rhetoric through from antiquity to the work of Thomas Nashe in the sixteenth century. Central in the whole tradition of the trivium and in Nashe is the concept of chiasmus — contrast by reverse parallelism — a notion that is fundamental to the McLuhan tetrad.

Looking back beyond the 1970s, beyond the influence of Saussure and the development of the tetrad, even beyond the Nashe thesis to McLuhan's earliest Cambridge years, one finds an equally powerful and in some respects even more fundamental influence. It is, once again, the influence of I. A. Richards, detectable in so many passages of McLuhan's writings: "All media are active metaphors in their power to translate experience into new forms. The spoken word was the first technology by which man was able to let go of his environment in order to grasp it in a new way."[28] From the approach to literary criticism pioneered by Richards, McLuhan absorbed and developed at least five key points:

1) The power of words. Richards deplored the "proper meaning superstition," the belief that word-meanings are fixed and independent of their use. He illustrated the power of words to control thought, urging that thought should bring words under *its* control by determining meaning from context. This was the theme of Richards's book (with C. K. Ogden) *The Meaning of Meaning.* The lesson stayed with McLuhan even through to his later writings. Here is an example from 1972's *Take Today* where the very first page, with its distinctively McLuhan chord, has an unmistakable Richards tone: "Nothing has its meaning alone. Every *figure* [consciously noted element of a structure or situation] must have its *ground* or environment [the rest of the structure or situation, which is not noticed]. A single word, divorced from its linguistic *ground* would be useless. A note in isolation is not music. Consciousness is corporate action involving *all* the senses (Latin *sensus communis* or 'common sense' is the translation of all the senses into each other). The 'meaning of meaning' is relationship."[29]

The "meaning of meaning" was a much used phrase in Cambridge circles before *The Meaning of Meaning* became a much read book. McLuhan makes one disparaging reference to the book as an example of "Tudor prose,"[30] but its title inspired his own best-known saying.

In an interview he gave in 1966, we read: "Back in the 1920s, there used to be much concern about 'the meaning of meaning.' At that time, the discovery that meaning was not statement so much as the simultaneous interaction of many things came as an exciting surprise. When I say that 'the medium is the message,' I am merely stating the fact that 'meaning' is a happening, the multitudinous interplay of events. I have found sometimes that it helps to say 'the medium is the message' [sic] because the medium is a complex set of events that roughly handles and works over entire populations."[31]

2) An eye for an ear. Richards was optimistic about avoiding the pitfalls of language and combating problems of communication. Part of the solution came from the human body itself: "The multiplicity of our channels is our best hope. The eye can check what the ear hears, and vice versa."[32] This is the basis of McLuhan's technological optimism. Neither he nor Richards was troubled by the paradox that intellectual power must be derived from the very source it needs to control.

3) Product versus process. Richards focuses on this contrast in connection with language: "Though a few students of primitive mentality or of the language of thought of the child have begun to give serious attention to the evolution of thinking, on the whole our historians of philosophy have been too much preoccupied with results. Their eye has been on the thoughts as products rather than on the thought-processes."[33] McLuhan uses Richards's notion in his own observations ranging over the environment, cultural contrasts, social history, and discourse: that environment is process, not container; the West speaks of space where the East speaks of spacing; historical descriptions of change are mere narratives that offer no insight into dynamics; debate packages knowledge for display, whereas dialogue organizes ignorance for discovery.

4) Understanding is a process of translation. Richards viewed any act of understanding or acquiring knowledge as a matter of interpreting and reinterpreting. He called this "translation." A key chapter in McLuhan's *Understanding Media*, entitled "Media as Translators," not only picks up this theme but links it to Richards's observations on the multiplicity of sensory channels: "Our very word 'grasp' or 'apprehension' points to the process of getting at one thing through another, of handling and sensing many facets at a time through more than one sense at a time. It begins to be evident that 'touch' is not skin but the interplay of the senses, and 'keeping in touch' or 'getting in touch' is a matter of a fruitful meeting of the senses, of sight translated into sound and sound into movement, and taste and smell."[34]

5) The probe. Many years after McLuhan had studied with Richards, he wrote to him to acknowledge that "I owe you an enormous debt since Cambridge days," adding that "your wonderful word 'feed-forward' suggests to me the principle of the probe . . . "[35] Throughout his writings, McLuhan uses the probe as an instrument for insight into media and their effects. It is akin to Richards's "speculative instruments," the set of key words whose meanings he stretched as means of investigating meaning. Though there were other sources of influence on McLuhan's thought, few came so early in his career or endured so long as that of I. A. Richards.

Linguistics is often said to be the most human of the sciences and the most scientific of the humanities. It is a saying that surely would have appealed to McLuhan, though it appears to be little help in answering the criticisms brought against him. What are the criteria of scientific theory that Jonathan Miller found lacking in McLuhan's work? It must be formal (i.e., formulated independently of language), testable, and have the power to predict, or show itself to be universally applicable. In *Laws of Media* the McLuhans follow the method implicit in this definition of scientific theory, but their discoveries ultimately challenge the first part of it, in that the laws of media prove not to require formulation independently of language: "Utterings are outering (extensions), so media are not *as* words, they actually *are* words."[36]

    There are four laws of media, and all four apply to all media. The McLuhan challenge to find a medium to which fewer than the four laws apply, or to find a fifth law, remains open. The laws are not given as statements but as questions, so as to invite their application to as wide a variety of humankind's endeavors as possible: "They apply to all human artefacts, whether hardware or software, whether bulldozers or buttons, or poetic styles or philosophical systems."[37] Here are the four questions that the McLuhans invite us to ask about any medium: What does it extend (amplify or enlarge)? What does it make obsolete? What does it retrieve? What does it reverse into?

For "extend," in the phrasing of the first law, we may also substitute "enhance," "intensify," "make possible," or "accelerate," depending on the case. A refrigerator enhances the availability of a wide range of foods. Perspective in painting intensifies a single point of view. A photocopier makes possible the reproduction of texts at the speed of the printing press. The computer accelerates the speed of calculations and retrieval of information.

Obsolescence is a consequence of extension. When a medium fulfills its function of extending the body, or replacing another medium, parts of the environment of whatever was extended become obsolete. When the car replaced the horse, it did away with stables, blacksmiths, saddlemakers, harness-menders, hitching posts, horse-troughs, carts, stagecoaches, etc.

Under the law of retrieval, older structures and environments, older forms of action, human organization, and thought are brought back by a new medium. They were part of the human environment that became obsolete at least two technologies ago. Feminism, in extremist form, retrieves the corporate identity of matriarchal society. A dinner table retrieves the picking and choosing options surrendered by early humans, who discovered in the lap a site for isolating, manipulating, and defending their food.

The principle of reversal comes into operation in cases when a technology is pushed to its limit: it will take on the complement of its original features or of its intended function. A dinner table, if very large, no longer offers the ease of reach for which tables were originally designed. If overcrowded, the dinner table can reverse from a place for sharing food into a site where table mates aggressively intrude on each other's space.

The laws of media interact. They reveal a dynamic pattern of interlocking effects typical of any technology or human construct. In the form of a tetrad, the four laws can be shown as follows:

EXTENSION	REVERSAL
RETRIEVAL	OBSOLESCENCE

Here extension and obsolescence are linked as action to reaction, which is not the case for retrieval and reversal. A medium does not reverse into its opposite because some older form has been retrieved; it reverses because it is pushed to its limit.

There are complementary qualities among the laws taken in pairs, *either horizontally or vertically.* This is clear from the effects noted in the following examples:

1) Alcohol enhances energy but reverses into depression.
2) The car enhances individual privacy but reverses into the corporate privacy of traffic jams.
3) Earth-orbiting satellites extend the planet and retrieve ecology.
4) Cubism makes visual space obsolete and reverses into the non-visual.
5) The microphone makes private space obsolete and reverses into collective space.

Here are some examples of complete tetrads:

WINE

extends	**reverses**
grape juice	via fermentation into vinegar
retrieves	**makes obsolete**
ritual observance	common flavors

DRUGS

tolerance of pain	addiction
foetal security	symptoms

STIRRUP

user's weight/power	tank
centaur	infantry

SYMBOLIST POETRY

image	imageless sound
multisensory awareness	logic

In the realm of language itself, *Laws of Media* offers, among others, tetrads for semiotics, written language, slang, cliché, the spoken word, symbolist poetry, hyperbole, rhetoric, dialectic, metaphor, irony, metonymy, and the word "is" as a copula. This profusion of tetrads may suggest that language is too complex to be described by a single tetrad, but both McLuhan's definition of language as mankind's first technology and the tetrad structure itself appear to be respected if it formulated as:

SELF-EXPRESSION THROUGH SPEECH

thought	feeling
gesture	grunts and groans

Given the consistently central place of language in McLuhan's work throughout his career, one is tempted to ask: Is McLuhan a linguist? The question would have made him laugh. It needs to be unasked, because it invites an answer that accepts assumptions, divisions, and categories. It was McLuhan's business to tear these down, not build them up, much less put himself within their confines. Those who taught McLuhan to think about language (Leavis, Forbes, Richards) did not call themselves linguists, nor did McLuhan develop their approaches to language along any lines that present-day linguists would claim as their own. And yet, if we are prepared to grant that psychoanalyst Jacques Lacan is a linguist because of his reconstruction of Saussure's concept of the sign, or that philosopher Jacques Derrida is a linguist because of his deconstruction of Saussure's analytical framework, then we must accord McLuhan the same honor. But Lacan, Derrida, and McLuhan all appropriate Saussure's notions to their own purposes outside linguistics. How far outside? In McLuhan's case, perhaps no further than the context that Saussure himself envisaged for linguistics, namely semiotics (*sémiologie*, in his terminology). In this respect McLuhan comes closer to realizing Saussure's ultimate objective than Lacan or Derrida or any other appropriator of Saussure's thought.

It is interesting to note that whereas Saussure imports metaphors (planets in the solar system, the chemistry of water, chess, music, natural species, patched cloth, plant life, photographs, tapestry, and life-belts) to describe language, McLuhan uses language itself as a metaphor for all media (all extension of our physical senses), all human artifacts. This suggests that McLuhan's approach offers the prospect of integrating linguistics and semiotics in a fashion bolder than any hinted at by Saussure himself and yet compatible with the foundations he laid. Moreover, McLuhan's metaphor *of* language *for* media is no metaphor at all, just as the body of Christ in the Roman Catholic faith, so important to McLuhan, is no metaphor but a real presence created by the mystery of transubstantiation in the Eucharist.

APPENDICES

APPENDIX ONE

Feedforward

McLUHAN'S WORK HAS recently enjoyed a renewed interest, suggesting that his teachings are better understood today than they were in an age when the evidence for them was less apparent. At the same time, it is still possible to come across the occasional piece in the press emblazoned with a heading such as "McLuhan wrong about TV."[1] It is also possible to open the newspaper as McLuhan did, as he counsels us to do, perceiving it as an environment. That environment bears out his discoveries of three decades ago, if we ask the questions McLuhan would ask today:

1) What is the tetrad for e-mail?
Answer: It *extends* writing, *renders obsolete* long-distance phone calls, *retrieves* the telegram (giving it a new and intensified form), and *reverses into* dialogue when the correspondents are on-line at the same time. (You don't believe the part about long-distance phone calls becoming obsolete? Of course you can still make long-distance phone calls, but nearly half the phone lines in use at any time in North America are being used for non-voice communication.)

2) At the end of "Newsnight" on BBC Television (BBC 2), the announcer shows viewers copies of the next day's papers. Is this what McLuhan calls "hybridization" of media?
Answer: Yes, because here the cool medium of television "contains" the hot medium of print when the announcer holds up the newspaper on camera. McLuhan comments on this tendency in *Understanding*

Media: "It is probably the print and book bias of the BBC and CBC that renders them so awkward and inhibited in radio and TV presentation."[2]

3) McLuhan often comments on popular language in relation to media and media effects. What do you think he would say about the expression "to split the scene" (meaning "to leave")?
Answer: *Split* is *tactile* and scene is visual. The expression suggests a desire for in-depth participation in an environment that does not offer that possibility. The solution is to react against the environment, to split the scene.

4) What is the role of environment in the street gang activity known as "swarming" (a group of attackers surrounding a victim)?
Answer: The activity articulates a reaction to an invisible, hostile environment by creating a Visible, hostile environment.

5) One of the signs of the Holy Spirit at Pentecost was the wind. How does wind relate to our physical senses?
Answer: Wind is primarily audio-tactile, but it also has an olfactory (sense of smell) dimension, capable of wrapping us in the environment of elsewhere. It is presence and absence together, coming to and intensifying all our senses except sight. Visually it reveals only its effects.

6) Look at the cover of Wired *magazine. What is the graphic design doing with the hot medium of the alphabet?*
Answer: Everything is working to turn it into a cool medium. Figure and ground are in constant play: where the color of the ground for a figure (letter) is different from that of the full page, the color of the alternate ground shades the figure (letter), and there is an interplay of backlit ground and backlit figures.

7) What is the effect of the fad for mounting fluorescent lighting on the underside of a car?
Answer: The car becomes iconic and sculptural, intensified as figure by a new intermediate ground of light. The illusion is created that the car is floating rather than rolling. Flashing or sequential lighting for

license plate frames is acceptable in conjunction with the hot medium of the letters and numbers so framed, but would not be for the cool medium of the car.

8) Glue, cement, nails, scotch tape, paper clips, and rubber bands are technologies for extending what?
Answer: All of them hold things together, making them extensions of fingers, hands, and arms.

9) What have been the effects of the car and the computer on police forces?
Answer: The car took the policeman off the beat and put him in his cruiser. The computer keeps him in the cruiser.

10) The "Late Night with David Letterman" Book of Top Ten Lists promotes itself with the caption "Like Watching TV in Convenient Book Form." Is this pure spoof or grain of truth?
Answer: It is a spoof on fatuous advertising and a probe of both television and book as media. The countdown sequence of items in each list is irrelevant, because they are interchangeable figures on the same ground. Even though they follow one another, they take on the mosaic quality of the image on a television screen. Like any good probe, the Letterman promo lets us get beyond the cliché it is spoofing.

11) What changes would Rush Limbaugh have to make in his appearance if he were a spokesman for the left wing?
Answer: He would need to be slimmer, with longer hair and a beard. These are iconic features of left-wing spokespersons.

12) What is made obsolete by the twinning of illustrated books and interactive CDs?
Answer: The integrity of the book. Unless the author has intended her work to be twinned, the interruptions created by the computer result in the loss of structure and effects of style intended by the author.

13) What effect would the computer have had on Shakespeare's writings?
Answer: It would depend on whether or not he used his style-checker.

When Hamlet's "to be or not to be" speech was run through a style-checker, it detected thirty-four errors and commented that the language was obsolete and overwritten, suggesting that the whole speech be concisely rephrased as "Is it better to live with bad luck or end it all and have nightmares?"

14) When it was discovered during the shooting of a movie that the real name of the actor playing John Lennon (up till then the filmmakers had known only his stage name) was the same as the real-life killer of Lennon, the actor was fired. Is there a lesson about technology here?
Answer: Yes, about what McLuhan called mankind's first technology: language. When language first emerged, mankind did not distinguish between word and thing. The word *was* the thing. It was dangerous to name a god or savage beast by its true name, because it might appear, so taboos and euphemisms came into use. In the late-twentieth century, this word magic still retains its power, because we remain unaware of media effects. The moviemakers acknowledged that it was just an extraordinary coincidence but felt that it was in the best interests of the project for another actor to be cast as John Lennon.

15) Remembering that McLuhan says that media contain or extend other media, what are the primary media contained by television?
Answer: Light (which contains no other medium) and speech (which extends thought).

16) The deciphering in the early 1980s of what was believed to be the earliest writing system indicated that the Sumerians kept extensive records relating to taxation, business contracts, agricultural and industrial output, bureaucratic titles, etc. Does this confirm any of McLuhan's observations?
Answer: It confirms his view that the effect of writing is to create fragmentation and specialization.

17) The technology has been in place since the early 1990s to put credit cards on line with electronic lotteries. What process does this intensify?
Answer: Annual global sales of lottery tickets already exceeded $25 billion before the development of this technology that makes money

more than ever a metaphor. McLuhan called money the poor man's credit card.

18) What are some consequences of computer commuting (working from home via computer)?
Answer: Environmental damage from overuse of cars is reduced, traffic accidents are reduced, child-care costs can be eliminated, expenses for dressing for the workplace and for eating away from home can be reduced, illness transmitted in the workplace can be reduced, relief from the aggravation of daily commuting is provided, time cost as well as monetary cost of commuting is eliminated, prejudicial practices are eliminated by the computer environment.

19) DNA testing of goatskin parchment may allow fragments from the Dead Sea Scrolls to be assembled and deciphered. Scholars will also be able to determine locations of goatherds relative to scribes, where and when scrolls were written, and whether Essenes wrote or simply collated the scrolls. What would McLuhan have to say about this?
Answer: The technology involved retrieves message as content in "the medium is the message."

20) What might explain the popularity of tattoos, body-piercing, etc., in the late-twentieth century?
Answer: The computer as an extension of the central nervous system and bioengineering have turned the body into a site for experimental art forms.

21) Among McLuhan's critics, a comment such as the following is typical: "McLuhan was wrong when he described the TV as creating a global village. Rather than bringing the world into our living rooms it has blinded us to the world of our living rooms as well as the greater community" (Jo/An Claytor, Globe and Mail, 14 October 1992). What is wrong with this comment?
Answer: McLuhan did not say that TV created the global village, he said that electronic interdependence (all electronic media together) restructured the world in the form of a global village. If TV has blinded us to the world of our living rooms, this is part of the restructuring that

McLuhan described without condoning it: "I don't approve of the global village. I say we live in it."[3]

22) Canadian poet and novelist David Helwig has described sound as the most concrete and imposing of perceptions, noting that you can turn your eyes away from an objectionable sight, but that you cannot turn your ears away. Is this related to a McLuhan percept?
Answer: Yes, the percept of acoustic space, which interested McLuhan because it is a sort of wraparound space, boundless and without horizon, unlike visual space, which is rational, linear, and sequential. One of McLuhan's observations, similar to Helwig's, is that you cannot see around a corner but you can hear around it.

23) Do pen-based computers, like the Apple Newton, that recognize the letters you print turn the alphabet into a cool medium?
Answer: No, these computers instantly translate what you write into high-definition typed text for transmission or printing. The *principle* of the alphabet is not affected by this technology, but the *future* of the alphabet is uncertain, because it is a high-definition medium now in constant use on low-definition computer screens.

24) What is the human reflex that goes with McLuhan's notion of closure as completing an image?
Answer: Squinting.

25) What is the human reflex that goes with McLuhan's notion of closure as the closing down of one of our physical senses?
Answer: The closing down *is* a reflex.

26)An advertisement promoting retirement savings plans for a bank gives a top-down view of stacks of coins arranged to spell out RSP. What lesson does this recall from McLuhan's teachings?
Answer: Money is a medium as much as the alphabet. In the advertisement, the two media are identified.

27) Does the advent of cable television support McLuhan's description of the global village?

Answer: Yes, he described the global village as "fission and fusion," "discontinuity, division and diversity."

28) *David Helwig has said that the Holocaust has been cheapened by being turned into a general phrase for evil. Is this related to a McLuhan concept?*
Answer: Yes, it is an example of an archetype turning into a cliché.

29) *"Morphing" is a film industry technique in which transformations of a primary image are computer-generated. It has been used in such films as* Terminator II, *where the evil humanoid turns to liquid, passes through iron bars, transforms body parts to weapons, etc. What is gained and lost in this process?*
Answer: Speed and technical efficiency are gained. Without the technique, illustrators must draw incremental changes in an image one by one. Morphing ensures uniformity of imagery, but pushed to the limit, it removes the illustrator from the craft altogether.

30) *A beer ad reads: "We take the time to brew it light." Is this a cliché?*
Answer: No, the cliché "take the time to do it right" is reworked here as a probe. This is what McLuhan means when he says that Madison Avenue has turned ads into art.

31) *Canadian artist Alan Flint shapes words out of wood, brick, cardboard, plastic, plaster, etc. In a field he dug out the word "WOUND" in giant letters to symbolize the effect of human systems on the earth. Is this an example of the medium being the message?*
Answer: Yes. Language is technology for McLuhan and words are artifacts. Flint's "WOUND" is part of the technology of language executed in a way that reminds us that the technology of digging wounds the earth. Flint weds his words to different technologies but in every case reminds us of the link between the word's meaning and the technology used in spelling it out. He also reminds us that words are artifacts and forces us to reflect on the medium and the message by forcing them together in new ways. (This is also another example of an artist making probes out of clichés.)

32) *What has been the effect of the wireless microphone on musical theater?*

Answer: Voices are mediated by backstage sound boards, the sound engineer's decisions as to appropriate volume level superseding performers' modulations and breaking the unity of the projected voice and the stage presence.

33) What techniques have newspapers like USA Today *borrowed from television?*
Answer: Heavy use of color, eye-catching graphics, news stories presented in concise texts. Compared to the page layouts of more traditional newspapers, those of *USA Today* approach what McLuhan called the tactility of the television screen. It is very much the newspaper of the TV generation.

34) Galvanic skin response (GSR) technology amplifies changes in the electrical conductivity of skin and transforms them into signals that can control a computer. What media does this technology potentially eliminate?
Answer: The skin responses are modulated forms of thought. All technologies from numbers to fingers that mediate between a user's thought and the operation of the computer are potentially eliminated by GSR.

35) One of the most memorable photographs taken when the Berlin Wall fell in 1989 showed East Germans and West Germans holding hands and dancing atop the Wall, with the Brandenburg Gate in the background. What made this image so arresting?
Answer: It is a powerful mix of iconic clichés for separation, union, celebration, and empire, never possible until that moment and never repeatable. (It was quickly appropriated by a telephone company as part of the reach-out-and-touch-someone advertising campaign.)

36) Is the international money market like a light bulb?
Answer: McLuhan calls the light bulb "pure information" — all medium and no message. On the money markets, media of exchange are exchanged for each other — not for commodities or services or anything else.

37) Illiteracy is inability to read and write; post-literacy is an environment

where reading habits (especially attention to detail from the age dominated by print) no longer prevail. What are some technological factors, other than the persuasiveness of TV, contributing to postliterate culture?
Answer: Word-processing at electric speed, the "authority" of style-checking software, books on tape and CD, low-density printing on PCs (designed for cursory rather than careful reading), formula books.

38) Is it correct to say that clichés are hot and archetypes are cool?
Answer: Yes, clichés are fixed, high-definition, and require no participation; archetypes are open-ended and invite participation.

39) What was the connection between weapon technology and environment in the Tokyo subway killings and the Oklahoma bombing?
Answer: In the Japanese case, the weapon technology (gas) was independent of the *immediate* environment of the attack (subway train) but enhanced in its effectiveness by the confined quarters of that environment. In the Oklahoma case, the weapon technology (fertilizer) was not independent of the *regional* environment (rural), in that it symbolized the environment the attacker believed to be threatened.

40) In his philosophical novel Lila, *Robert Pirsig says that "Dynamic Quality is not structured and yet is not chaotic. It is value that cannot be contained by static patterns" (p142). How does this relate to McLuhan's work?*
Answer: It is a description of both the media effects that McLuhan studies and the features of his own writing.

APPENDIX TWO

Recent Works on McLuhan

THE MCLUHAN OF POPULAR culture is still with us in the whimsical western-style musical tribute of Radio Free Vestibule to "Marshall" McLuhan; in the New York Theater Workshop production of *The Medium* that won actor Tom Nelis an Obie award in 1994 for his portrayal of McLuhan; in documentary comics;[1] and on the Internet.[2]

Also to be found is a McLuhan who is scarcely recognizable to anyone who has understood his work. Not content to continue paying lip service (or a tongue-in-cheek tribute) to a cliché McLuhan by simply leaving him on the masthead as "patron saint," *Wired* magazine spread its wings in the January 1996 issue with three feature articles on "the Holy Fool." Eric McLuhan remarked that the effort was good and original, but that unfortunately the parts that were good were not original, and the parts that were original were not good.[3]

Among the much more insightful and stimulating pieces that have also appeared recently are Judith Fitzgerald's "McLuhan! Not Atwood" (*Books in Canada*, December 1995) and Jeet Heer's "Marshall McLuhan and the Politics of Literary Reputation" (*The Literary Review of Canada*, April 1996). And the stamp of McLuhan's teaching is to be seen distinctly in works by his former students, such as Derrick de Kerckhove's *The Skin of Culture: Investigating the New Electronic Reality*[4] and B. W. Powe's *Outage: A Journey into Electric City*.[5] Another writer whose recent work shows the influence of McLuhan is Richard A. Lanham, whose *The Electronic Word: Democracy, Technology and the Arts* appeared in 1993.

It is not possible within the few pages remaining to the writer to comment on more than three works devoted in whole or in part to McLuhan.

When McLuhan's *Understanding Media* appeared in 1964, one reviewer obscurely titled his comments "Reverse Canadian."[6] Now a study has appeared titled *McLuhan, or Modernism in Reverse* (Toronto: University of Toronto Press, 1996). The claim that modernism flips into postmodernism is hardly controversial, but author Glen Willmott situates McLuhan at the rupture point,[7] a view that repelled McLuhan when one commentator tried it more than a quarter-century ago. "To say that [*Culture Is Our Business*] is 'the last of the modern movement that began with Eliot and Joyce' is meaningless, unless we are to think of abandoning the quest for forms altogether."[8] Since McLuhan offered this comment in private correspondence, it lacks the potential for satirical force required to buttress Willmott's argument. But Willmott rescues McLuhan from deconstruction by deconstructing himself, explaining that McLuhan is "that peculiar postmodern who sees in a totalizing consciousness of the break . . . the utopian conditions for a new world and a new being,"[9] and then dismissing as satirical[10] the most utopian of passages in McLuhan's writing.[11]

Or is it McLuhan himself who deconstructs his utopianism, his satire, and his Saussure-turned-Toynbee[12] formalism and rescues his historicism? Willmott casts his fear about a misguided rediscovery of "practical critical ideology"[13] as being of a piece with McLuhan's own fears about the popular audience for *Understanding Media*, but detaches that fear from the hope that McLuhan linked to it — a link Willmott himself has already pointed out.[14] It is a hope that allows discovery of a practical diacritical technique of intellectual investigation free of any ideology. Willmott concludes with a comment on McLuhan's style which "works to produce that one ecological message. For it is *not a message* at all, not a theory, but a medium, a formal or critical difference poised on the edge of enunciation . . . "[15] This is an important observation, illuminating the original McLuhan probe and anchoring McLuhan in the postmodern aesthetic.

But this is precisely the aesthetic from which McLuhan unwittingly dissociated himself by reading Saussure selectively, whereas much of deconstruction is arguably a radical misreading of Saussure.[16]

McLuhan's inattention to Saussure's use of the *coincidentia oppositorum/ coincidentia differentiarum* complementarity was a happy accident. It allowed him to build on Saussure when he might otherwise have dismissed him as a practitioner of sterile dialectics. McLuhan's Saussurean criticism misses Saussure's insight into the laws of information systems. It also misses Saussure's characterization of linguistics as operating in the borderland between sound and thought (their combination produces form and not substance), a notion that is wholly consistent with McLuhan's emphasis on resonant intervals. Saussure's criticism of nineteenth-century linguistics indicates that his orientation is to look for hidden ground. Noam Chomsky looks for hidden figure *as* ground in his early work, but McLuhan did not pick up on this either, observing simply: "I think [Lévi-Strauss and Chomsky] are working with *figure* minus ground in the Cartesian tradition."[17] McLuhan did not miss these points because he could not see them, but because he did not look, choosing instead to move on with what he regarded as a few rough diamonds from Saussure and Chomsky that could serve him elsewhere as drills.

S. D. Neill's *Clarifying McLuhan: An Assessment of Process and Product* (Westport, Connecticut: Greenwood Press, 1993) is a less playful work than Willmott's, though just as thoroughly deconstructive in its thrust. So, for example, in his chapter entitled "The McLuhan Approach to Evidence," Neill caps references to publications undermining the scientific credibility of brain hemisphere research with a reference to *Laws of Media*, where McLuhan and McLuhan appear to concede an exception to the universality of their own claim.[18] Being a partisan of the studies he cites, which dismiss left- and right-hemisphere cognitive styles as nothing more than metaphors, Neill is, of course, unwilling to accept the synesthesia McLuhan performed on Aristotelian logic, transforming the logical into the analogical. This is not to say that Neill does not recognize the place of metaphor *in* McLuhan's approach. In fact, he errs on the side of assuming that metaphor is a default mode in McLuhan's thought, whereas there is clear evidence for key McLuhanean notions where literal interpretation is demanded.[19]

Unlike Willmott, from whom he might have learned some valuable lessons on keeping things tentative and the technical requirements of deconstructive discourse, Neill's move toward self-deconstruction comes through recognizing that McLuhan would not have objected to Neill's objective of illustrating lack of rigor in McLuhan's thought.[20] A simple reference to lack of "rigor" would have been more helpful here. But Neill is helpful in his appendices, particularly Appendix II, "McLuhan's Media Charts Related to the Process of Communication," perhaps the only such discussion available in the literature on McLuhan's work.

There are various points where one might take issue with Judith Stamps's *Unthinking Modernity: Innis, McLuhan, and the Frankfurt School* (Montreal: McGill-Queen's University Press, 1995). The entire analysis seems strained to bring Innis, McLuhan, Theodor Adorno, and Walter Benjamin under its compass. McLuhan would have been surprised to learn from this book (1) that he had a theory of negative dialectics; (2) that he shared with the other principals a difficulty in coming to terms with reason and civilization in the post-World War II era (Benjamin died in 1940); (3) that he had a commitment to understand the relations between classifying and colonizing; (4) that he was a social scientist; and (5) that he wrote a work on the history of the West (*Understanding Media*). Stamps is suitably self-scrutinizing in the early pages ("Is it really possible to compare such ideas?") but quickly overcomes any hesitation about proceeding with the comparison, justifying the enterprise by its objective of gaining "a more holistic view of the issue if we can see it demonstrated or hear it described in more than one theoretical language."[21] The author acknowledges that she is developing what have only been "straws in the wind"[22] and that she reads McLuhan as he has "rarely been read,"[23] i.e., as a philosopher and neo-dialectician. This would be a splendid project if it began with a full discussion of McLuhan on dialectics (his 1943 Cambridge doctoral dissertation), but the topic receives only a few lines near the end of the one chapter devoted exclusively to McLuhan. In the thesis, McLuhan is an intellectual historian (and historiographer), but Stamp deals only with the later McLuhan, casting him as a social and cultural historian who "*in addition*, offered detailed discussions of the physical properties of media."[24]

Elsewhere, appearing to be on the verge of going in a more promising direction, Stamps disappoints. She speaks of challenging positive theory, reading history negatively, and developing new methods as all coming together in McLuhan. How exactly? "McLuhan wrote about marginal counter-environments as antidotes to rigid institutions and at the same time presented such antidotes."[25] If this is the synthesis McLuhan achieved, it does him little credit. Stamps's treatment of McLuhan's fusion of Aquinas's theory of perception with Gestalt theory (via I. A. Richards) in order to provide the historical perspective missing from Aquinas is at first more promising. But the matter of the tension between historicism and ahistoricism in the early McLuhan giving way to straight ahistoricism in the later McLuhan is much less convincing. Stamps says of her quadrumvirate that they "understood history as an open-ended series of qualitative changes that emerged at the margins of dominant institutions,"[26] but Stamps herself has not understood the history of McLuhan as an open-ended series of qualitative changes that emerged at the margins of his dominant metaphors. Moreover, her argument regarding the disappearance of the historicism/ahistoricism tension from McLuhan's work is rendered irrelevant by the recovery of the internal dynamics of the classical trivium, the element unifying all his writings from the Cambridge thesis to the posthumously published *Laws of Media* and *The Global Village*. Negative dialectics, the legacy of the Frankfurt school, works both toward and against McLuhan's notion that dialogue organizes ignorance for discovery, for it limits discovery to correctives rather than radical revision, replacement, assimilation, all of which McLuhan was prepared at any time to admit.

NOTES

Letters referred to throughout these notes are to be found in the Marshall McLuhan papers at the National Archives of Canada, abbreviated NAC, followed by volume and file numbers for documents other than alphabetically arranged correspondence. References to letters published in *Letters of Marshall McLuhan*, Matie Molinaro, Corinne McLuhan, William Toye, eds. (Toronto: Oxford University Press, 1987), are indicated by *Letters*. I have quoted from the latter, whenever possible, rather than their original counterparts in the NAC material, in order to remind interested readers of the opportunity to examine the fuller context of my quotations from a readily available source. Minor liberties have been taken with the punctuation of quotations from *Letters*, where it seemed anomalous, or to lessen the strain imposed on readers where McLuhan's sentences tend toward both the elliptical and the labyrinthine. References to *Understanding Media* are to the first edition (1964).

1 – The Fortunes of Family
1   With the exception of references given below, the sources of information for this chapter are private papers of the McLuhan family and interviews conducted by the author with Maurice McLuhan, Corinne McLuhan, and Eric McLuhan.
2   Two versions of the European origins of the McLuhans have circulated in the family. According to the first, they were Scots, who resided about twenty miles southwest of Inverness. The family operated a textile business and emigrated to Ireland about 1800, in order to take advantage of the higher grade of flax available there. In the second account, the McLuhans descended from Huguenots, who emigrated from France in the latter half of the sixteenth century, moving first to Scotland before settling in Ireland. At this time, the family name was spelled "McClughan," with "McLuhan" apparently coming into use only in the branch of the family that came to Canada. (In a letter of 2 June 1976 to

Marshall McLuhan, Mervyn McLuhan, of Atlanta, Georgia, notes: "It appears to me that the way we spell our name is more Irish than it is Scottish.")

William McClughan, the keeper of the castle in Belfast, is said to have been granted a coat of arms by King William in 1641. Dominated by a lion, it bore the motto *"Fortes et Fides"* — strong and faithful. Eventually, the family acquired a linen factory in Dromore, County Down. The house at the family farm was said to have been built with a tunnel connecting it to the village, a full mile away, to provide a means of escape in times of danger. The family business prospered and extended to include the Belfast Linen Company. As the family grew, some removed to Newtonards, County Down, where the family roll remains in the parish church.

In his discussion of the competing accounts of this family, Stuart Mackay of Edmonton points out that the only facts beyond doubt are that a family named McClughan or McLuhan did migrate from Scotland to Ireland and that they owned a linen business. The family produced a son William, father of the William McLuhan, Jr., who was shipped off to Canada in 1846.

Sheila Higgins, Newcastle, County Down, Ireland, wrote to Marshall McLuhan on 10 April 1978 to say that McClughan is certainly an old Dromore name. As variants, she gave McClune and McCluen. According to Ms. Higgins, it is likely that the first McClughan in Ireland came to Dromore with a plantation from Scotland in the seventeenth century. She noted that between 1609 and 1614, nearly ten thousand Scots left their homeland because of religious persecution and were given land in County Down. The McClunes, she added, were reputed for their humor.

3   "Before the introduction of the combine, prairie harvests required large numbers of labourers, for short periods of time. Harvest excursion trains, 1890-1930, brought workers west — about 14,000 in 1908. Railways offered harvest tickets from any station as far away as the Maritimes to Winnipeg for $15, and a return fare of $20 . . . A threshing crew of perhaps two dozen was paid $2-$3.25 each a day with board. Although the journey was rough and the work was gruelling, the excursions introduced Canadians and Britons to the Prairies. Many decided to return permanently to homestead. The collapse of the wheat economy in 1930 and changing farm technology ended the era of the harvest excursion." (*The Canadian Encyclopedia* [Edmonton: Hurtig Publishers, 1988], vol. 2, pp965-66.)

4   Acadia University calendar, 1907-08, p27.

5   Ibid., p42.

6   NAC, Herbert McLuhan to Marshall and Corinne McLuhan, 12 June 1961.

7   Isaiah 9:6.

8   Author's correspondence with Maurice McLuhan.

9   Red used one of Elsie's stories, "The Other Wise Man" by Dr. Henry van Dyke, to great effect in every pulpit he occupied during his career as a United Church minister.

10 The repertoire included "The Land of the Blue Flower" by Frances Hodgson Burnett, "The Man Among the Drums" by Beatrix Lloyd, "Ma'moiselle" by Florence L. Guertin, "The Part That Willie Gets," "Driving from the Rear Seat," "How Jimmie Learned to Swim," "Our Postman" (poem), "When Father Played Baseball" (poem), "Any School Morning," "Desperation" (poem), "Pilate's Soliloquy," selections from *101 Famous Poems* such as "The House by the Side of the Road" (Sam Walter Foss), "I Have a Rendezvous with Death" (Alan Seeger), "Miss Lily Mink Reads a Paper" (a parody of a talk to the Bean Valley Ladies' Literary Club), and "The Walrus and the Carpenter" (NAC, volume 2, file 2).

   Later in life, Marshall McLuhan recalled Elsie's stage career this way: "My mother, by the way, was a one woman theater. She travelled from coast to coast from year to year putting on plays and acts. Single. Yes, she put on whole plays single. Played all the parts, yes. With big audiences, yes" (Unpublished interview with Nina Sutton).

11 NAC, volume 7, file 17: *How to Build a Racer for $50* (reprinted from *The Rudder*, New York and London: Rudder Publishing, 1899). Marshall McLuhan's annotation reads: "I built and sailed this boat in Winnipeg in the late 1920s." It was a small cat-boat design called *The Lark*. Further annotations by McLuhan read: "The Lark is so planned that when sailing she settles down into the water . . . When resting at anchor with no one on board there is no more than 3 inches of the hull in the water. At the bow stem . . . the planking is exposed to the hot sun. When underway they settle under water and leaking is impossible to avoid. As long as they are dry 1/2 the time and wet the other 1/2 no corking or putty is going to solve this problem. I speak from bitter experience." He suggests canvassing the deck and hull and brass screws in the hull instead of nails to get a hull that will last fifty years.

12 See page 58.

13 NAC, Ed Robeneck to Marshall McLuhan, 29 April 1967.

14 *Sewanee Review*, October 1946, pp617-34.

15 *The Mechanical Bride*, pv.

16 Edgar Allan Poe, "A Descent into the Maelstrom," in *The Complete Tales and Poems of Edgar Allan Poe* (New York: The Modern Library, 1935), p135.

2 – Intellectual Seeds

1   His first-year program included English, History, Geology, Astronomy, Psychology, and Economics.

2   Diary, 6 March 1930.

3   "Conceived the idea that it might be possible to write a series of articles using Carlyle's observations of Signs of the Times as a peg on which to hang some 'modern signs'" (Diary, 2 January 1930); "Compared it with my own up to now and as it may be" (Diary, 7 January 1930); "These men have always been precocious or gifted, yet I wish that one day I may attain to their heights" (ibid.).

4   "If I ever wish to break into the world of letters I am going to use Macaulay's trick of starting out on a review of some book on a famous man or age" (Diary, 15 March 1930). McLuhan's first publication was to be an article on G. K. Chesterton, published in *The Dalhousie Review* 15 (1936).

5   Diary, 23 February 1930.

6   Diary, 8 March 1930.

7   Diary, 9 January 1930.

8   Diary, 31 January 1930.

9   Diary, 11 January 1930.

10   Diary, 31 March 1930; 7 April 1931.

11   Diary, 2 April 1930.

12   "My course as it now lies is to be the best that I can be, to follow my noblest inclinations, and if fame comes, to regard it as the least of my possessions" (Diary, 1 June 1930).

13   Diary, 7 April 1930; ibid.

14   Diary, 14 February 1930.

15   Diary, 5 January 1931.

16   "I wish my summer (5 months) would seem as short as my school term (7 months)" (Diary, 9 February 1930).

17   Diary, 9 May 1930.

18   Macaulay remains a subject of passionate interest for months: "I pray God for the boyish enthusiasm of Macaulay" (Diary, 1 October 1930); "What a mastery he had of our tongue" (Diary, 3 January 1931); "There is no such thing in Macaulay as a tedious page" (Diary, 4 January 1931); "The marvel of his work is the uninterrupted smoothness of narrative" (Diary, 12 January 1931).

19   Diary, 11 May 1930.

20   "Odd to say he uses a richer vocabulary than any man that I have yet come across. My little index of new words is an infallible guide for me, by which to pass judgements in such cases" (Diary, 28 May 1930).

21   Chesterton would later exert a great influence on McLuhan. At this early stage he reads Chesterton's preface to *Great Expectations* and says simply that he "found him somewhat tautological in his analogies" (Diary, 17 June 1930).

22   "We went out to St Vital and put in a fairly heavy day's work. Charlie Chataway and I put out two barrels and worked and loafed by ourselves all day" (Diary, 10 May 1930).

23 "I enjoyed it immensely, and it was the means of stimulating my thoughts so vigorously that the time and work during the rest of the day, in spite of the fact that the latter was the heaviest and messiest which we had yet undertaken, seemed mere trifles" (Diary, 12 May 1930).
24 Diary, 19 June 1930.
25 Diary, 24 September 1930. The entry continues: "By that I do not mean that I did not wish to learn any more or think that I knew it all."
26 Ibid.
27 Elsie and Herbert encouraged their son to continue in this habit by making him a Christmas gift of the *Oxford English Dictionary*. The edition was large enough to require its own table. (Interview with Maurice McLuhan.)
28 Diary, 7 January 1931.
29 Diary, 24 October 1930.
30 Diary, 2 January 1931.
31 Diary, 6 January 1931.
32 Diary, 5 October 1930.
33 Diary, 22 October 1930.
34 Diary, 30 October 1930; ibid.
35 Diary, 13 November 1930.
36 "I am one that needs continued and absolute quiet in order to get anything done" (Diary, 9 January 1930).
37 Diary, 1 April 1931.
38 Diary, 5 January 1930; 16 January 1930.
39 "Our domestic condition here is rather extreme as usual" (Diary, 6 February 1930); Diary, 15 March 1930; 10 March 1930.
40 Diary, 10 January 1930.
41 Diary, 6 April 1930.
42 "I believe Mother would have at least six more people down if she were given any encouragement. It takes all I can do to hold her within bounds" (Diary, 4 September 1931).
43 Diary, 26 August 1931.
44 "Mother is being praised extravagantly and wined and dined everywhere. Just her life alright" (Diary, 21 March 1930).
45 "Mother collared me, and we hammered away till midnight [but] got nowhere. It is good conversational practice, that's all" (Diary, 19 January 1930).
46 "Poor Mother, how seriously does she labor after righteousness and each effort increasing an already boundless egotism" (Diary, 2 December 1930).
47 Diary, 6 January 1931.
48 "I think my experience with Mother has given me an insight into the characters of women who are delightful companions for an evening but are veritable shrews and termagants as wives" (Diary, 17 January 1931).

49   "Had a lovely quiet day to ourselves. As I look back eight or 9 years or even less to a time when our holiday saw us on a streetcar headed for crowded parks or beaches I cannot say that I am delighted. It would be the same today if Mother had her way. It is impossible for her to relax a minute, to see anything worthwhile in quiet homely ways or peaceful meditation. I am very sorry for her and also for those with whom she is forced to live. I cannot say that in the last ten years there have been as many quiet peaceful days when she has been around. By some cruel trick of nature, each part of her character was so contrived as to make miserable the other parts" (Diary, 1 July 1931).

50   Diary, 1 July 1930.

51   Diary, 2 January 1931.

52   "Dad drew me into conversation on the subject of unemployment. He is working on a scheme with Prof. Jones and Frank Martin whereby our unemployed men will be absorbed into a socialistic arrangement . . . The idea presupposes that unemployment is the cause of the world's troubles. I spent two hours showing Dad that it is only a symptom, though like most symptoms it has aggravated the evil. The juggling with the unemployment question is pure politics. It presents no solution" (Diary, 22 May 1931).

53   Diary, 22 March 1930.

54   Author's correspondence with Maurice McLuhan.

55   "When I have had a bit more philosophy and psychology, which I shall augment with scripture study, I am going to work out some of the great 'laws' that govern the affairs of men, temporal and spiritual. Dozens of these laws are being used today unconsciously, by successful and happy people. I believe it will be the biggest step ever taken in philosophy if a hundred or so of these laws were to be carefully worked out and studied" (Diary, 26 October 1930). Cf. earlier: "I have not yet read more than a hundred pages [of the Bible] yet realize that they alone contain the laws that govern man and the universe. I am sure that God meant us to understand these and to exercise them. Dad put me on a trail that I shall shortly have traversed past his stopping point" (Diary, 15 June 1930).

56   Diary, 26 October 1930; ibid.; ibid.

57   "It merely goes to show that Macaulay was not quite so shallow, his ambitions not quite so worldly as many have claimed" (Diary, 28 January 1931).

58   Diary, 21 February 1931.

59   Diary, 8 March 1931.

60   Diary, 18 February 1931.

61   Diary, 1 April 1931.

62   Herbert McLuhan referred to his father-in-law, Henry Selden Hall, by the initials of his given names. (Interview with Maurice McLuhan.)

63   "Next to being great oneself, it would be the most satisfying to have a son

that threaded his way with ease among the perilous peaks of fame, or a brother or a close friend" (Diary, 27 March 1931).

64   Diary, 1 April 1931.
65   Diary, 4 January 1930.
66   Diary, 23 August 1931.
67   Diary, 16 March 1930.
68   "[He says that] what he learnt when he was younger is all wrong today, what I learn is all wrong tomorrow. He takes this attitude as shield for lack of knowledge on today's subjects" (Diary, 23 March 1930); 3 May 1931.
69   Diary, 13 April 1930.
70   Diary, 12 January 1930; ibid.
71   Diary, 16 February 1930.
72   Marshall McLuhan to Ezra Pound, *Letters*, p227.
73   Diary, 4 December 1930.
74   Ibid.
75   Ibid.
76   Diary, 15 June 1930.
77   Diary, 17 June 1930.
78   "Accordingly as a person proceeds in harmony and without friction with these [laws of the universe] he is happy, just, blest; and accordingly as he bumps against these timeless forces he is unhappy, unjust, and cursed. The latter conditions are merely degrees of the former and have no existence save as they are related to the positive aspects" (Diary, 22 November 1930).
79   Diary, 11 January 1931. Cf. 5 July 1931: "[The preacher] delivered himself of a quantity of balderdash and rigamarole that was nothing short of shameful."
80   Ibid.
81   Diary, 15 February 1931.
82   Diary, 14 February 1931.
83   Diary, 3 June 1931.
84   "The poor lonely people of the West are caught in the meshes of materialization. Salvation lies open to them but the intervening walls of wealth invest it with all the imaginary perils of that 'undiscovered country.' It is very plain that wealth is an almost insuperable barrier to this experience. It immeasurably strengthens all the conservative tendencies of our nature" (Diary, 3 June 1931).
85   Diary, 21 June 1931.
86   Diary, 10 April 1930; 19 March 1930; 18 January 1930; 19 June 1930; 18 January 1931; 20 March 1930.
87   Diary, 4 February 1931.
88   Diary, 24 January 1931.
89   Diary, 10 April 1930.

90 Diary, 14 January 1931.

91 Diary, 4 June 1931.

92 "She appeals to me by some means that I know not of. She is good looking, intelligent, etc., rather (in fact quite) a Yankee in her characteristics
as well as by birth" (Diary, 19 June 1930); 17 January 1931.

93 Diary, 6 January 1931.

94 Author's personal correspondence with Maurice McLuhan.

95 Diary, 17 January 1931.

96 Diary, 18 January 1931.

97 Diary, 22 January 1931.

98 Ibid.

99 Diary, 24 January 1931.

100 Diary, 13 February 1931.

101 Diary, 9 March 1930.

102 Diary, 14 January 1930.

103 Diary, 23 February 1930.

104 Diary, 27 March 1931.

105 Diary, 1 October 1930.

106 Diary, 23 June 1931.

107 Author's personal correspondence with Maurice McLuhan.

108 Diary, 12 September 1931; 14 September 1931.

109 Ibid. Though Marjorie had a steady boyfriend, she and Marshall saw each
other on various occasions, and their time together was already prompting his bouts of self-analysis: "Attended the first literary society that it has
been my lot to encounter. Marjorie Norris, who is a member of Professor
Philip's English Club, invited me to go with her. She was up for supper
and we proceeded thence ... . When I come in contact with true blue natural refinement, I always see myself in a disadvantageous light. I am
sarcastic, tactless, selfish and not by inclination or nature but largely due
to a miserable environment that has made it impossible to draw out anything but the disagreeable in me. I shall, I am determined to mend and
believe I am" (Diary, 12 November 1931).

110 Diary, 7 January 1931.

111 Diary, 5 February 1931.

112 Diary, 7 April 1931.

113 "At the Y an idea for an article struck me. I wrote it down, as I never get
the idea twice. Briefly it is 'The Evolution of Literary Society' Addison to
present time" (Diary, 11 January 1930). "It has occurred to me as a possible subject for a short paper to treat of the great reviews that blossomed
forth in the late eighteenth and early nineteenth centuries. That would
include a consideration of the circumstances that gave them birth and the
mighty pens that nourished them into maturity" (Diary, 23 May 1931).

114 Diary, 8 February 1930.

115   Diary, 26 March 1931.

116   Diary, 7 January 1931.

117   Diary, 31 July 1931.

118   He prized a history essay returned to him by "the fastidious Fieldhouse" with the comment: "This is that very very pure thing, a student's essay which I can finally say I enjoyed reading. Excellent work" (Diary, 26 March 1931).

119   Diary, 20 April 1931.

120   Diary, 27 April 1931.

121   Diary, 3 April 1931.

122   Diary, 8 May 1930.

123   Diary, 10 February 1931.

124   Interview with Corinne McLuhan.

125   Ibid.

126   Interview with Maurice McLuhan.

127   Diary, 9 April 1933.

128   Diary, 30 January 1933.

129   Ibid.

130   Ibid.

131   Ibid.

132   Ibid.

133   Ibid.

134   Ibid. Thinking, no doubt, of Elsie, he also wrote: "And, Oh God, what a world hast thou let thy mannikins make in which women must all have a profession, a business or a career?"

135   Ibid.

136   Ibid.

137   Diary, July 1933.

138   Marshall dominated the *Manitoban* that year with a dozen articles. In addition to the piece on Meredith (21 November), he wrote "German Character" (7 November), "Canada and Internationalism" (1 December), "Germany's Development" (3 November), "Germany and Internationalism" (27 October), "Public School Education" (17 October), "De Valera" (9 January 1934), "The Groupers" (23 January), "Not Spiritualism but Spiritism" (19 January), "Adult Education" (16 February), "Tomorrow and Tomorrow" (16 May), and "Morticians and Cosmeticians" (2 March). The last of these anticipates *The Mechanical Bride*: "Today when we lift up our eyes to the signboards whence cometh our help, we are apt to find 'help' in the most unexpected forms. It has been proven time and again that the foulest and most stinking of offenses against human dignity and decency can be committed with impunity in the name of trade . . . Simplicity and even harshness has always been the external characteristic of Christian burial, because it has always been the most

optimistic of burials. But simplicity does not mean big profits, and it has gradually given way to pagan pomp."

139 The two sides of the paradox identified here anticipate the complementarity of cliché and archetype articulated by McLuhan many years later.

140 Interview with Maurice McLuhan.

141 The thesis was organized under the following topics: Meredith's Education and Personality; Meredith's Art and Style in Poetry and Prose; Meredith's Attitude to Nature, Man and Society; Meredith as a Comic Writer; Meredith as the Romantic Writer.

142 Marshall McLuhan, "George Meredith as Poet and Dramatic Novelist" (M.A. thesis, University of Manitoba, April 1934), Preface.

143 Ibid.

3 – England's Green and Pleasant Land

1 Marshall McLuhan to Elsie, Herbert, and Maurice McLuhan, *Letters*, p18.

2 NAC, volume 7, file 7, 10 October 1934.

3 Marshall McLuhan to Elsie, Herbert, and Maurice McLuhan, *Letters*, p19.

4 Ibid., pp20-21.

5 Ibid., p21; ibid., p22; ibid., p23.

6 Marshall eventually became secretary of the Hesperides. (Interview with Eric McLuhan.)

7 Marshall McLuhan to Elsie, Herbert, and Maurice McLuhan, *Letters*, p23.

8 Ibid., p21.

9 Ibid.

10 Ibid., p24.

11 Ibid.

12 Ibid.

13 Ibid.

14 Ibid.

15 Ibid., p25.

16 Ibid.

17 Ibid., p34.

18 Ibid.

19 A report of Herbert from Winnipeg reached Marshall at Christmas: "We see your father occasionally. He seems quite lonely without his family" (NAC, Jennie Perry to Marshall McLuhan, 18 December 1934).

20 Marshall McLuhan to Elsie, Herbert, and Maurice McLuhan, *Letters*, p22.

21 "Had 1/2 a pound of beefsteak (exquisitely done) with a 3d. tin of peas, for supper," ibid., p27.

22 Ibid., p26.
23 Ibid.
24 Ibid., p28.
25 Ibid.
26 Ibid., p29.
27 Ibid., p39.
28 Ibid., p29.
29 Ibid., p31.
30 Ibid., p32.
31 Ibid.
32 Ibid.
33 In a 1937 article on The Cambridge English School, published under that title in *Fleur de Lis*, the undergraduate literary magazine of Saint Louis University, McLuhan sketched the beginnings and the aims of the School (a collective designation for the Cambridge University English faculty), together with a portrait of Quiller-Couch. The same article shows the influence of I. A. Richards on McLuhan as well as the orientations that link McLuhan and Ezra Pound. There had been opposition at Cambridge to the formation of an English faculty, to the appointment of a Professor of English Literature. "In 1910 Dr. Mayo said, 'It would be a Professorship of English fiction, and that of a light and comic character . . . A Professorship unworthy of this University.'" A more enlightened opinion soon prevailed. McLuhan wrote: "'Q' was not a don. He left Oxford in the early eighties for a career in journalism and literary craftsmanship. In middle life he was invited to take the Chair of English at Cambridge . . . 'Q' has never addressed his audiences as though they were receptacles, but always as though they were fellow craftsmen, fellow artists . . ." The appointment of I. A. Richards to the School was to become a turning point. "Dr. Richards improved the instruments of analysis, and has consolidated and generally made accessible the contribution of Coleridge — a contribution which had been obscured by a mass of academic criticism." McLuhan quotes Richards as saying, "The one and only goal of all critical endeavours . . . is improvement in communication," adding that "Dr. Richards has been a pioneer in the training of sensibility . . . Today, language, the indispensable mode of thought, is in danger from an organised cynicism which insists on exploiting the stupidity of the Many . . . modern advertising, in itself, presents an utterly irresponsible force exploiting language for the deception, or rather coercion, of the Many . . . And advertising is only one of the forces that are disintegrating [the poet's] medium of expression, and destroying the major means of effective communication among men. But it is not only poetry that is in danger." Here McLuhan is simultaneously anticipating the themes of *The Mechanical Bride*, *Culture Is Our Business*, and *From*

Cliché to Archetype. He continues, "Dr. Richards and others at the English School, in advocating a strenuous and practical criticism, have welcomed the warning of Mr. Pound in his vigorous book *How to Read*: 'Has literature a function in the State, in the aggregation of humans, in the republic, in the *res publica*?' . . . It has . . . It has to do with the clarity and vigour of 'any and every' thought and opinion. It has to do with the maintaining of the very cleanliness of the tools, the health of the very matter of thought itself . . ." In their separate fashions, Pound and McLuhan (as well as Joyce) joined Richards in promoting orthology — "A fundamental part of logic is the study of the right use of language, the clear definition, and, if needful, invention of terms" (Karl Pearson, *The Grammar of Science*, p454). References to "The Cambridge English School" in this note are to the draft version, NAC volume 128, file 65.

34 Writing later to E. K. Brown, then chairman of the English department at the University of Manitoba, Marshall noted that Meredith was "under severe anathema as 'bogus poet and prose writer' at Cambridge" (*Letters*, p80).

35 Interview with Maurice McLuhan. In the second term of his first year at Cambridge, Marshall took Quiller-Couch's course on the poetics of Aristotle. "There was just one other chap and so we were able to be a very chatty trio" (Marshall McLuhan to Elsie, Herbert, and Maurice McLuhan, *Letters*, p57).

36 Henry Latham, a former Master of Trinity Hall, had endowed this annual competition by written exam on a designated work of English literature. (*Letters*, p35.)

37 "[Peacock's work] is in reality much more pleasant but not as great in scope or as deeply conceived as Meredith's" (Marshall McLuhan to Elsie, Herbert, and Maurice McLuhan, *Letters*, p33).

38 McLuhan used his Latham Prize money to buy volumes of Keats, Jonson, Pound, Fowler, and Eliot. (Marshall McLuhan to Elsie McLuhan, *Letters*, p60.)

39 Marshall McLuhan to Elsie, Herbert, and Maurice McLuhan, ibid., p35.

40 Ibid.

41 Ibid.

42 Ibid., p37.

43 NAC, Alice E. McQuillen to Marshall McLuhan, 1 December 1934.

44 Marshall McLuhan to Elsie, Herbert, and Maurice McLuhan, *Letters*, p40.

45 Ibid., p41.

46 Ibid.

47 Ibid.

48 Ibid.

49 Ibid., p65.

50   Ibid., p42.

51   Ibid.

52   Ibid., p43.

53   Ibid.

54   Ibid.

55   This initiative came to nothing, and Elsie did not come to England.

56   Diary, 6 August 1935.

57   McLuhan was preparing himself for the French paper in the English tripos examination. "And I am a very sincere admirer of French literature and thought. Remy de Gourmont and Jacques Maritain are my principal contacts with 'recent' French thought. If only in view of the French stimulus behind Yeats and Joyce, James, Pound, [Edith] Whart[on], Eliot, I should agree that the French and English literatures cannot be studied profitably in isolation — not in their fullest intent" (Marshall McLuhan to E. K. Brown, *Letters*, p79).

58   Marshall McLuhan to Elsie, Herbert, and Maurice McLuhan, ibid., p44.

59   Ibid., p48.

60   Ibid.

61   Ibid.

62   Ibid., p52.

63   Ibid.

64   Marshall McLuhan to Maurice McLuhan, ibid., p45.

65   Ibid. Moving into Trinity Hall residence the following year, McLuhan must have relented at least a little in this view. In any case, with other students away over Christmas holidays, he confessed: "I have Bowen's radio and hear many good things" (*Letters*, p78).

66   The selection mixed masterpieces of English poetry with worthless verse, but readers' responses failed to reflect the distinction and displayed much misunderstanding. "Of all Richards' books, none united his diverse talents better than *Practical Criticism*. The documentation of hundreds of reader reports, or 'protocols,' on thirteen poems and the classification of errors made the book the most empirical and experimental of his studies. One hundred seventy-five pages of protocols constitute its first half . . . The second half is corrective, the method of 'close reading' . . . The protocols revealed that students at a prestigious university were misreading not especially 'cryptic' poems (not cryptic, said Richards, compared to Yeats's 'Byzantium'). The level of reading elsewhere could not be much different than at Cambridge and was probably worse. He ran the experiment at Harvard in 1931 and later at Bryn Mawr with similar results. Granted that reading poetry requires some training, the protocols were evidence that it was being given poorly" (John Paul Russo, *I. A. Richards: His Life and Work* [Baltimore: Johns Hopkins University Press, 1989], pp294-96).

67   Marshall McLuhan to Elsie McLuhan, *Letters*, p50.

68 Ibid.

69 Russo, p295.

70 NAC, volume 3, file 6 (Marshall McLuhan's notes on the lectures of I. A. Richards).

71 Richards had already touched on these questions as early as 1923, with C. K. Ogden, in the first edition of *The Meaning of Meaning*: "In some ways, the twentieth century suffers more grievously than any previous age from the ravages of such verbal superstitions. Owing, however, to developments in the methods of communication . . . the form of the disease has altered considerably; and . . . now takes more insidious forms than of yore . . . Influences making for its wide diffusion are the baffling complexity of the symbolic apparatus now at our disposal; . . . the extension of a knowledge of the cruder forms of symbolic extension (the three R's), combined with a widening of the gulf between the public and the scientific thought of the age; and finally the exploitation, for political and commercial purposes, of the printing press by the dissemination and reiteration of clichés" (W. T. Gordon, ed., *C. K. Ogden and Linguistics* [London: Routledge/Thoemmes, 1994), vol. 3, pp41-42]. Richards carried through on this theme in *Principles of Literary Criticism* (1924) and in *Practical Criticism*.

72 Marshall McLuhan to Elsie, Herbert, and Maurice McLuhan, *Letters*, pp58-59.

73 NAC, Marshall McLuhan to Professor John M. Dunsway, department of Modern Foreign Languages, Mercer University, Macon, Georgia. n.d.

74 Marshall McLuhan to Elsie, Herbert, and Maurice McLuhan, *Letters*, p40.

75 Ibid., p53. McLuhan sent a report of the mild English winter to Winnipeg and obtained the following response: "I went over to the university to mark papers this morning at 38 below zero Fahrenheit. Your careless talk of rowing on the Cam is, under the circumstances, rather provoking, but I bear you no malice" (Acadia University Archives, Watson Kirkconnell to Marshall McLuhan, 26 December 1934).

76 Marshall McLuhan to Elsie McLuhan, *Letters*, p61.

77 Marshall McLuhan to Elsie, Herbert, and Maurice McLuhan, *Letters*, p56.

78 Ibid., p66.

79 Ibid., p51.

80 Ibid.

81 Ibid.

82 Ibid.

83 Ibid., pp52-53. In his diary for 22 January 1935, McLuhan wrote: "Saw Potts about Ph.D. Expect to start it here in 1936 and finish in Canada 1937."

84   Marshall McLuhan to Elsie, Herbert, and Maurice McLuhan, *Letters*, p55.

85   Ibid., p58.

86   Ibid.

87   Ibid.

88   Ibid.

89   Ibid., p67.

90   Ibid.

91   Marshall McLuhan to Elsie McLuhan, ibid., p60.

92   Ibid., p64.

93   Marshall McLuhan to Elsie McLuhan, ibid., p53.

94   Marshall McLuhan to Elsie, Herbert, and Maurice McLuhan, ibid., p66.

95   "Last Sunday I was to the Willisons for dinner at 1. Then we listened to Elgar's First Symphony on their gramophone and chatted and read around their fire till after tea, after which we went to church. The first time I have been to *church* (outside of chapel) since I came. It was (evensong) [at] St. Clement's, which is 'Very High'" (*Letters*, p75).

96   Marshall McLuhan to Elsie McLuhan, ibid., p64.

97   The champions of Distributism advocated redistribution of property and the abolition of industrial production in favor of goods produced by local craftsmen. Chesterton wrote on the subject in *G.K.'s Weekly*, the official publication of the Distributist League.

98   Marshall McLuhan to Elsie, Herbert, and Maurice McLuhan, *Letters*, p68.

99   Ibid.

100   Ibid., pp68-69.

101   Ibid.

102   Interview with Eric McLuhan.

103   Marshall McLuhan to Elsie McLuhan, *Letters*, p73.

104   Ibid., p72. Elsie eventually engaged in some "religion-hunting" of her own that did her no good, as far as McLuhan was concerned: "I am deeply disturbed at your own deep unhappiness and self-inflicted misery. If you were to relax your bitter tension of will against yourself for half an hour. But even for this one must pray and pray. Not that the smug little prayers of Christian Science will do any good. They assume that everything is OK if one *wills* that it is. No knowledge ever comes from *outside* oneself in that sort of activity" (NAC, Marshall McLuhan to Elsie McLuhan, n.d.).

105   Marshall McLuhan to Elsie McLuhan, *Letters*, p72.

106   Ibid.

107   Ibid., p73.

108   Ibid.

109   Ibid.

110 Ibid.

111 Ibid., p74.

112 Ibid.

113 Ibid., p82. In the diary entry for the day of his reception into the Catholic Church (25 March 1937), McLuhan was to note that, in spite of the long period during which he investigated the faith before converting, he never had a vocation.

114 Marshall McLuhan to Elsie McLuhan, *Letters*, p83. In an earlier letter, he noted: "Such a choice unaccompanied by apostolic vows of chastity and poverty, becomes almost meaningless. This whole question can be decided by reasoning, provided one is not loath to employ reason" (ibid., p75).

115 Ibid., p69.

116 Ibid.

117 Ibid.

118 Ibid., p78.

119 Ibid., p70.

120 Ibid., p71.

121 Ibid.

122 Ibid., pp82-83.

123 Ibid., p78.

124 Marshall McLuhan, "G. K. Chesterton: A Practical Mystic," *The Dalhousie Review*, January 1936, p455; ibid.

125 Ibid.; ibid., p456; ibid.

126 Ibid. Here was an explanation for Mansfield Forbes's comment that Chesterton was not an adult, along with McLuhan's reply.

127 Ibid.; ibid.

128 Ibid.

129 Ibid. McLuhan links this observation to Chesterton's work with the Distributist League: "It is because he is concerned to maintain our endangered institutions that he earnestly seeks to re-establish agriculture and small property, the only basis of free culture" (ibid.). Though McLuhan was to complain in later years that Jonathan Miller's *McLuhan* ignored his early work, it is possible that Miller looked back precisely to the quotation above in deciding to cast McLuhan in the role of Agrarian Romantic.

130 Ibid., p457.

131 Ibid.

132 In his review of *The Gutenberg Galaxy*, Arthur Efron stated that "the admiration for the Middle Ages becomes embarrassing in a book otherwise so critical" (NAC, volume 8, file 52. "Making Peace with the Mechanical Bride").

133 "Chesterton," p457.

134 Ibid., p458; ibid.

135 Ibid., p461.

136 Ibid.

137 Ibid., p462.

138 Ibid.

139 Ibid.

140 Ibid.

141 Ibid.

142 Ibid., p463.

143 Ibid., p464.

144 Marshall McLuhan to Elsie McLuhan, *Letters*, p82.

145 Ibid.

146 Ibid., p79.

147 Ibid.

148 Interview with Eric McLuhan.

149 John Malcolm Brinnin, *The Third Rose* (Little Brown: Boston & Toronto, 1959), p334.

150 NAC, volume 16, files 1-2. Interview with Marshall McLuhan, *The Mike* (St. Michael's College student newspaper), 4 February 1971.

151 Diary, 9 March 1936.

152 Diary, 20 April 1936.

153 Diary, 21 April 1936.

154 Ibid.

155 Diary, 5 May 1936.

156 Diary, 9 May 1936.

157 Diary, 7 June 1936.

158 Diary, 20 June 1936.

159 Diary, 21 June 1936.

160 Diary, 22 June 1936.

161 "Let me congratulate you on your Second. I understand that Cambridge standards are practically as high as those at Oxford" (NAC, volume 7, file 7. Miss W. Gordon, National Educational Secretary, IODE, to Marshall McLuhan, 31 July 1936).

162 *Letters*, p85.

163 Ibid.

164 Ibid.

165 Ibid., p86.

166 Diary, 3 July 1936.

167 *Letters*, p85.

168 Diary, 5 July 1936.

169 Diary, 14 July 1936.

170 *Letters*, p85.

171 Diary, 27 July 1936.

172 Diary, 24 August 1936.

173 Elsie was, by now, head of the drama department at the Von Kunitz Academy. (*Letters*, p86.)

174 *Letters*, p79, p355.

175 NAC, Autobiographical note, 1977.

176 Ibid.

177 Ibid.

178 Ibid.

4 – *A Professor in Spite of Himself*

1 Marshall McLuhan to Elsie McLuhan, *Letters*, pp83-84.

2 Diary, 22 September 1936.

3 Ibid.

4 Diary, 23 September 1936.

5 Ibid.

6 Ibid.

7 Diary, 25 September 1936.

8 Diary, 2 October 1936.

9 Diary, 29 October 1936.

10 Diary, 29 September 1936.

11 *Letters*, p92.

12 Ibid.

13 Diary, 12 October 1936.

14 Diary, 7 October 1936.

15 Diary, 5 November 1936.

16 Diary, 22 January 1937.

17 Diary, 12 October 1936.

18 Diary, 11 February 1937.

19 Ibid.

20 Diary, 14 February 1937.

21 Ibid.

22 Diary, 23 March 1937.

23 NAC, Marshall McLuhan to Maurice McLuhan, "Thursday night," [1937].

24 Ibid.

25 Ibid.

26 Ibid.

27 Ibid.

28 Ibid.

29 Ibid.

30 NAC, volume 17, file 1. Quotation from Marshall McLuhan in Victor M. Parachin, "The Power of Prayer," *The Catholic Register*, n.d.

31 Interview with Eric McLuhan.

32 Diary, 25 March 1937.

33 Ibid.

34 NAC, volume 17, file 1. "McLuhan: Catholic Church Indestructible," *The Catholic Register*, 23 January 1977.

35 Ibid.

36 Marshall McLuhan to Martin Esslin, *Letters*, p440.

37 June Callwood, "The Informal Mr. McLuhan," *Globe and Mail*, 25 November 1974.

38 Jonathan Miller, *McLuhan* (London: Fontana/Collins, 1971), p21, p25.

39 NAC, Marshall McLuhan to Allen Maruyama, 27 August 1973. Cf. Marshall McLuhan to Joe Keogh, 6 July 1970: "Am enclosing Father Johnstone's piece. He's the first to notice that my approach to media is metaphysical rather than sociological or dialectical."

40 NAC, volume 18, file 61. Marshall McLuhan interview with Father Pierre Babin.

41 Other symbolic values of the number three include association with the right side, moral and spiritual dynamism, intellectual order, perfection, joyfulness, and hope. (Steven Olderr, *Symbolism: A Comprehensive Dictionary* [Jefferson, NC and London: McFarland, 1986].)

42 Diary, 10 May 1937.

43 Ibid.

44 Diary, 16 August 1937.

45 Diary, 19 August 1937.

46 Diary, 14 September 1937.

47 Diary, 18 September 1937.

48 Acadia University Archives, Kirkconnell Papers, Box 24, File P6-110. Marshall McLuhan to Watson Kirkconnell, 20 November 1937.

49 Diary, 1 October 1937.

50 Ibid.

51 Watson Kirkconnell (1895-1977), a scholar of enormous learning and a polyglot translator, with a towering record of productivity by the end of his distinguished career, was at this time teaching at Wesley College in Winnipeg. Though McLuhan never studied under Kirkconnell, he knew him well from Winnipeg days and began corresponding with him while at Cambridge.

52 Acadia University Archives, Kirkconnell Papers, Box 24, File P6-110. Marshall McLuhan to Watson Kirkconnell, 20 November 1937.

53 NAC, Walter Ong to Ronald A. Sarno, 1 June 1978.

54 Acadia University Archives, Kirkconnell Papers, Box 24, File P6-110. Marshall McLuhan to Watson Kirkconnell, 20 November 1937.

55 Diary, 13 October 1937.

56 Diary, 2 November 1937.

57 Diary, 28 October 1937.

58 NAC, Walter Ong to Ronald A. Sarno, 1 June 1978.

59   Ibid.
60   NAC, volume 216, file 9.
61   Ibid.
62   Ibid.
63   Diary, 18 May 1938.

5 – *California to Cambridge* Ricorso

1   Interview with Corinne McLuhan.
2   Diary, 10 July 1938.
3   Diary, 14 July 1938.
4   Diary, 21 July 1938.
5   Diary, 9 August 1939.
6   Diary, 15 August 1938.
7   Interview with Eric McLuhan.
8   Marshall offered a convenient explanation for the chary quality of his
      verbal ardor: "It's a pity you didn't know me before I went to Cambridge,
      before I was 'spoiled' as you say. *Then* you would have had at *least* one
      poem a day, celebrating your perfections, real, dubious and imaginary.
      You would have been showered with gorgeous epithets, and it would have
      served you right. Fatal fare, my fairly faerry fair!" (NAC, Marshall
      McLuhan to Corinne Lewis, 31 January 1939. An abbreviated version,
      without the passage cited above, appears in *Letters*, p105).
9   Diary, 1 November 1938.
10   Diary, 8 November 1938.
11   Diary, 24 September 1938; 9 November 1938; 21 November 1938.
12   Diary, 30 November 1938.
13   Diary, 19 December 1938.
14   Apart from her best beau, a number of other suitors with less serious claim
      to her hand had been "put on vacation." (Interview with Corinne
      McLuhan.)
15   Diary, 28 December 1938; interview with Corinne McLuhan.
16   Diary, 28 December 1938.
17   Interview with Corinne McLuhan.
18   Diary, 30 December 1938.
19   Interview with Corinne McLuhan.
20   Diary, 21 January 1939.
21   Interview with Corinne McLuhan.
22   Diary, 20 January 1939; 27 February 1939.
23   Diary, 17 March 1939. On this matter he took counsel with his friend and
      colleague Bernie Muller-Thym, who suggested that Marshall take a loan
      to finance his marriage. (Diary, 1 May 1939.)
24   Marshall McLuhan to Elsie McLuhan, *Letters*, p104.
25   Marshall McLuhan to Corinne Lewis, *Letters*, p105.

26   Diary, 13 March 1939.

27   Interview with Corinne McLuhan.

28   Ibid.

29   Diary, 10 June 1939.

30   Diary, 16 June 1939.

31   Interview with Corinne McLuhan. Marshall had addressed an extremely long letter to her on the subject of the Catholic faith on 21 January 1939. It ranges over the Incarnation, the difference between Catholic and Protestant attitudes, orthodoxy, and the Reformation, but ends on an intensely personal note: "I don't think it is unfair of me to talk about these things to you. But I must say, that I am anything but eager to do so. For I am more than a little afraid that you may become discouraged. And, since our free will is the most fundamental character we possess (it being inseparable from the rational nature) I feel the utmost repugnance to influencing another person, except where readiness to inquire, examine, or consider, is obvious. However, you should know that, in the event of a 'mixed marriage,' the non-Catholic is obliged to receive a certain mini-mum of instruction about the Church . . . Having been a Protestant most of my life, the idea of marrying one seems much more natural to me than it does to a 'cradle Catholic.' And obviously, the most ideal marriage for a convert is with a convert . . . You and I are faced with one of those sit-uations (which fortunately are not very numerous in one life-time) which cannot possibly be *adequately* judged beforehand. It strikes me as a colossal gamble, or rather, a very great adventure. And personally I am consider-ably exhilarated by the risk! This exhilaration may compensate for the absence of romance!" (*Letters*, pp101-2).

32   Diary, 17 June 1939.

33   Diary, 18 June 1939.

34   Interview with Corinne McLuhan.

35   Diary, 17 July 1939.

36   Interview with Corinne McLuhan.

37   Diary, 21 July 1939.

38   Diary, 22 July 1939.

39   Diary, 23 July 1939.

40   Interview with Corinne McLuhan.

41   Diary, 2 August 1939.

42   Interview with Corinne McLuhan.

43   "I was planning to leave last Thursday for home — on the point of pack-ing — and suddenly I just *couldn't* go. It was a huge bewildering sudden shock of realization of how much Marshall really meant to me; the next thing I knew we were married" (Corinne McLuhan to Herbert McLuhan, *Letters*, p113).

44   Interview with Corinne McLuhan.

45   Ibid.

46   Ibid.

47   Ibid.

48   Ibid.

49   NAC, Elsie McLuhan to Marshall and Corinne McLuhan, 9 August 1939. Corinne, who had not yet met Herbert McLuhan, addressed a note to him as she and Marshall were en route to New York: "Dear Mr. 'Mac' — I do appreciate so very much your sweet letter which greeted us this morning in St. Louis. I regret more than I can say that I shan't be able to know you until we return. I had been looking forward to our meeting, for Marshall has said so many lovely things about you. I shall probably be writing you frantic S.O.S.'s for advice in managing this handsome husband I've just acquired" (*Letters*, p115).

50   Diary, 12 August 1939.

51   Interview with Corinne McLuhan.

52   Diary, 16 August 1939.

53   Diary, 21 August 1939.

54   Diary, 24 August 1939.

55   Interview with Corinne McLuhan.

56   Marshall McLuhan to Elsie McLuhan, *Letters*, p116.

57   Diary, 28 August 1939.

58   Interview with Corinne McLuhan.

59   Marshall McLuhan to Elsie McLuhan, *Letters*, p116.

60   Diary, 1 September 1939.

61   Interview with Corinne McLuhan.

62   Ibid.

63   Diary, 3 September 1939.

64   Marshall McLuhan to Elsie McLuhan, *Letters*, p117.

65   NAC, volume 7, file 123.

66   Interview with Corinne McLuhan.

67   Marshall McLuhan to Charles W. Lewis, *Letters*, p118.

68   Interview with Corinne McLuhan.

69   Marshall McLuhan to Elsie McLuhan, *Letters*, p117.

70   NAC, Marshall McLuhan to Muz Lewis (Corinne's grandmother), n.d. Meals were seldom occasions for guests, he added, except among undergraduates.

71   Diary, 15, 17, 21 September, 11 November, 23 December 1939.

72   NAC, Marshall McLuhan to Muz Lewis, n.d.

73   Diary, 9, 10 October 1939.

74   Diary, 21 October 1938 (*sic*).

75   Marshall McLuhan to Elsie McLuhan, *Letters*, p118. Wilson, later of Oxford, but professor of English at Bedford College, University of London, when the McLuhans arrived in England, was evacuated to

Cambridge with the outbreak of war and acted as Marshall's research supervisor.

76   Ibid., p120.
77   Ibid., p121.
78   Ibid., p122.
79   Ibid., pp124-25.
80   Ibid.
81   Ibid., p110.
82   Marshall McLuhan interview with Nina Sutton. His resource file on the soft American male ego began growing substantially soon after he and Corinne arrived in England.
83   Marshall McLuhan to Maurice McLuhan, *Letters*, p124.
84   NAC, Marshall McLuhan to Elsie McLuhan, 16 April 1940.
85   Marshall McLuhan to Elsie McLuhan, *Letters*, p127.
86   Ibid.

6 – Breaching and Bridging

1   Marshall McLuhan to Corinne Lewis, *Letters*, p108.
2   Ibid., p107.
3   Ibid. The references are to V. I. Pudovkin and Sergei Eisenstein.
4   Marshall McLuhan to Corinne Lewis, *Letters*, p107. In the preface to an early draft of *The Mechanical Bride*, dating from approximately the same time, McLuhan wrote: "Until the education which is carried on by press, radio and movies is actually brought into the classroom for intellectual observation and discussion, the main business of the classroom can't even begin. That is what this book does" (NAC, volume 64, file 1). In another draft of the same text, reprising the theme of the opening quotation for the current chapter, he said: "After looking at the things which are made to entertain and to occupy adolescents today, the reader may feel a certain sympathy for the school-teacher who is expected to raise goose-bumps of esthetic joy by introducing a jive-hound to Wordsworth's 'Daffodils'" (ibid.).
5   Marshall McLuhan to Corinne Lewis, *Letters*, p107.
6   NAC, Walter Ong to Marshall McLuhan, 3 July 1978.
7   Interview with Corinne McLuhan.
8   Interview with Eric McLuhan.
9   Ira B. Nadel, *Joyce and the Jews* (Iowa City: University of Iowa Press, 1989), p106.
10   NAC, volume 128, file 67.
11   Interview with Eric McLuhan.
12   Preface to early draft of *The Mechanical Bride*.
13   Interview with Corinne McLuhan.
14   NAC, Elsie McLuhan to Marshall McLuhan, 20 January 1942.

15   NAC, Marshall McLuhan to Felix Giovanelli, n.d. [1942].

16   NAC, *Thomas Nashe and the Learning of His Time*, Microfilm copy, (henceforth Nashe), p*ii*.

17   Ibid.

18   John Lyly. *Euphues*. London: Routledge, 1916. Euphuism, named after Euphues, a character created by sixteenth century dramatist and novelist John Lyly, is an artificially elegant style of speech and writing — associated especially with Lyly's imitators — and characterized in particular by ornate paraphrases and strained similes.

19   Ronald B. McKerrow, ed., *The Works of Thomas Nashe* (London: Sidgwick and Jackson, 1910).

20   Nashe, p*iv*.

21   Ibid., p*vi*.

22   Ibid., p*ix*.

23   Ibid., p2.

24   Ibid., p78. McLuhan later notes that "'writing in aphorism' was part of the Stoic technique of dialectics and rhetoric which deeply interested Hippocratics from a scientific point of view" (p177).

25   Also characterized by McLuhan as the counterpart in the ancient world to the Trinity. (Ibid., p291.)

26   Ibid., p2.

27   Ibid., p12.

28   Ibid., pp19-20.

29   Ibid., p20. McLuhan's acknowledgments of Gilson further on show great admiration for the medievalist's work: "Had these [1939] lectures [by Gilson of which McLuhan had seen a report] been published before now, I should have been able to reduce the extent of this and the next section on grammar, and have had more space to devote to the sixteenth century itself. Moreover, the authority of Professor Gilson's great scholarship would have been available to support many of my own interpretations. If, therefore, this and the next section on grammar have some merit undetectable in the rest of this study, I wish that all credit for it should go to Professor Gilson" (ibid., p116).

30   Ibid., pp40-41.

31   Ibid., p41.

32   Ibid., p49: "The essential opposition between the arts of the trivium being such, then, as frequently to pit the one against the other, with results of the greatest importance, it is useful to recognize that the present exposition of the history of the trivium is being made from a grammatical point of view."

33   See especially *Laws of Media*.

34   Laurentius Valla (c. 1405-57), Italian humanist, author of *De Elegantia Latinae Linguae*; Juan Luis Vives (1492-1540), Spanish philosopher and

humanist, editor of St. Augustine's *Civitas Dei*; Petrus Ramus (1515-72), French humanist and author of the fiercely assailed *Dialectic*, 1543. Walter Ong, who first learned of Ramus while studying under McLuhan at St. Louis University, would later become the acknowledged authority on the work of Ramus.

35   Nashe, p84.

36   Ibid., p100.

37   Still in connection with the Ciceronian tradition, McLuhan notes (ibid., p187) that the rhetoricians of the Middle Ages opposed any effort to particularize or narrow their art, a comment that applies equally to his own intellectual procedures.

38   Ibid., p159.

39   Ibid., pp185-86.

40   Ibid., p212.

41   Ibid., pp216-17.

42   Ibid., p278. Watson's book was published in Cambridge in 1908.

43   Ibid., p279.

44   Gilson is later cited on classicism as the spirit of scholasticism misapplied. (Ibid., p313.)

45   Ibid., p291. In this context, McLuhan notes that St. Thomas alone reconciled grammar and dialectics.

46   Ibid.

47   Ibid., p358.

48   Ibid., p363.

49   Ibid., p393.

50   Ibid., pp393-94.

51   Ibid., p396.

52   This insight is pursued: "Sophistry was recognized as an art necessary for all good men to master in order that they might detect and refute it. Just as sophistry serves to heighten horror in *Christs Teares*, it serves to heighten comedy in *Have With You*, and it is also a means of scoffing at Harvey's reputedly insufficient training in logic" (ibid., p400).

53   Ibid., p415.

54   Ibid., p447.

7 – *Duelogue*

1   NAC, Marshall McLuhan to Walter H. Johns, chairman on Grants in Aid to Research, n.d.

2   Marshall McLuhan to Wyndham Lewis, *Letters*, p134.

3   NAC, John Crowe Ransom to Marshall McLuhan, 5 April 1943. The essay was accepted and published by *The Sewanee Review* in 1944.

4   NAC, John Crowe Ransom to Marshall McLuhan, 25 September 1943. The essay was accepted and published by *The Sewanee Review* in 1944.

5   "I can't quite feel that Leavis is the answer to Richards and Empson; the best answer; the perfect complement. I believe we need re-examinations of the aesthetic problem more radical than that" (NAC, John Crowe Ransom to Marshall McLuhan, 25 September 1943).

6   See bibliography.

7   NAC, Donald C. Bryant to Marshall McLuhan, n.d.

8   NAC, volume 129, file 3. "Medieval Grammar as the Basis of Bacon's *Novum Organum*." The manuscript is of particular interest for its concluding paragraph: "Anthropology and psychology together have also revindicated the traditional 'magical' view of language, fusing the seemingly distinct activities of the brothers Grimm, on the one hand, as philologists, and on the other, as students of folk-lore, so that we are once more in a position to adopt a sympathetic view of the divine *Logos* of late antiquity. Quite incidental to the radical readjustments in awareness we can relax where Francis Bacon is concerned. We can take him in our stride, as it were, nodding at him as a useful landmark in a great literary tradition whose representatives today are Jung and Count Korzybski."

9   Ibid.

10 NAC, Marshall McLuhan to John H. Randall, 22 May 1944.

11 Ibid.

12 Ibid.

13 Ibid.

14 Ibid.

15 Marshall McLuhan, *Lewisletter* (The Wyndham Lewis Society, Glasgow) #5, October 1976. In front of his students, Lewis played out the caricature of the eccentric professor. McLuhan speaks of his "classroom habits, the donning of large, heavy sweaters, and his manifestations of terror when anyone sneezed . . ." (NAC, Marshall McLuhan to George Woodcock, 30 March 1967).

16 NAC, Anne Wyndham Lewis to Corinne McLuhan, 16 June 1976.

17 Robert Fulford, "It's time to remember why Wyndham Lewis blasted Toronto's cold," *Toronto Daily Star*, 16 October 1982.

18 *Toronto Daily Star*, 15 February 1943, p7.

19 Marshall McLuhan, *Lewisletter* (The Wyndham Lewis Society, Glasgow) #5, October 1976.

20 *Letters*, p129.

21 McLuhan believed that Lewis drew much of the inspiration for his fiction from Flaubert and noted that Lewis's friend, Thomas W. Earp, had translated Flaubert into English. (NAC, Marshall McLuhan to Felix Giovanelli, 2 January 1945.) Lewis told McLuhan that he considered most of his novels nothing more than "potboilers." (Interview with Corinne McLuhan.)

22 Pound used the term "vortex" to capture the dynamic spirit of the

pre-World War II London art world. For Lewis, too, "Vorticism" described the surging concentration of energy in the emerging forms of modern art. His own paintings, and those of other Vorticists, were typically marked by bold and dramatic geometric forms. Though their canvases were often abstract and nonrepresentational, the Vorticists also depicted highly stylized machinery and cityscapes dominated by sprawling industry. "Vorticism, [Lewis] recalled in *Wyndham Lewis and the Artist*, had accepted the machine world and had 'identified itself with that brutality in a stoical embrace.' The difference which separated the Vorticist from the Futurist was never clear to those who thought of Lewis as a Futurist. In *Blast* 1, Lewis made the distinction. The Vorticist, he said, is 'not the Slave of Commotion but its Master.' At the same time, Pound defined Futurism as 'the disgorging spray of a vortex with no drive behind it. DISPERSAL.' Just as the sculptor Hildebrand had seen in Symbolism not a counter-movement to naturalism but an attempt to escape its consequences, so Lewis saw in Futurism not a counter-movement, but a surrender, as Pound saw in it an uncontrolled dissolution" (Sheila Watson, "Wyndham Lewis and Expressionism," Ph.D. dissertation, University of Toronto, 1964, under the direction of Marshall McLuhan, pp119–20). Long after Vorticism had ceased to absorb even Lewis's painterly energies, he was asked to define it and replied: "There is no such thing. For years I thought I had discovered a form that was not in nature; then one day I discovered it in looking through a catalogue of deep-sea fish" (Reported in Marshall McLuhan to Sheila Watson, *Letters*, p481).

23 NAC, volume 30, file 7.

24 The format adopted by McLuhan in his *Counterblast*.

25 Sheila Watson, "Wyndham Lewis and Expressionism," p*i*.

26 Ibid., p*vi*.

27 *Time and Western Man*, p*xii*.

28 NAC, Marshall McLuhan to George Woodcock, 30 March 1967.

29 Marshall McLuhan, *Lewisletter* (The Wyndham Lewis Society, Glasgow) #5, October 1976. Hemingway's recommendation was nothing short of an amazing gesture, given the rage that he had expressed when "The Dumb Ox" essay, with its harsh criticism of his work, appeared in Lewis's *Men Without Art* in 1934.

30 Interview with Corinne McLuhan.

31 *Letters*, p147. McLuhan added: "It will be easy to be nice to these people once you have some of their money in your pocket and some of their whiskey where it will do the most good!" (ibid.).

32 NAC, volume 169, file 7.

33 Lewis remained in St. Louis from February to July 1944. He was obliged to return to Canada every month to renew his visitor's visa to the United States.

34   Interview with Corinne McLuhan.

35   Ibid.

36   Ibid. Having celebrated his second birthday, Eric was matching wits with his father: "Last night I had locked Eric in the nursery and was preparing my retreat by saying 'Daddy tired. Daddy lie down.' He said: 'Rug, rug.' Got his dog-rug for me. Made me lie down. Then got a blanket to put over me. Then he lay on it" (Marshall McLuhan to Elsie McLuhan, *Letters*, p151).

37   *Letters*, p160.

38   This refers to Lewis returning to St. Louis to complete his portrait commissions at the same time that McLuhan took up his new teaching position in Windsor.

39   NAC, Wyndham Lewis to Marshall McLuhan, 4 February 1945. McLuhan later referred to Lewis's similar treatment of his friend John Reid as "the great and inexplicable goring" (Marshall McLuhan to Dorothy Shakespear Pound, *Letters*, p195).

40   NAC, Wyndham Lewis to Marshall McLuhan, 31 March 1953. The explanation for Lewis's fit of pique remains a matter of conjecture. It is possible that he came to view the motives for McLuhan's elaborate and highly visible stage-managing of Lewis's sojourn in St. Louis as self-serving rather than altruistic.

41   "In *Blasting and Bombardiering*, Lewis himself explained the futility of sallying forth on a duck-board walk in a world in which revolutionary technology had provided unequal and unexpected extensions and amputations of power" (Sheila Watson, "Wyndham Lewis and Expressionism," p*viii*).

42   Ibid., p16.

43   ". . . Lewis's call for a reunion of the great Trinity of the plastic arts: Sculpture, Painting, and Architecture" (ibid., p81).

44   See footnote 22 on vortex above.

45   "More than any other instrument the camera symbolized for Lewis the instrument which destroyed man's sense of organic unity by the separation of sight and touch. The result of such separation, he said, results in an exasperated subjectivity and a sense of estrangement and disunity" (Sheila Watson, "Wyndham Lewis and Expressionism, p128).

46   "As Lewis examined and constructed space he articulated a myth of men torn between visions of a closed and an expanding world" (ibid., p356).

47   "The very name [Passchendaele] with its suggestion of *splashiness* and of *passion* at once was subtly appropriate. This nonsense could not have come to its full flower at any other place but *Passchendaele*. It was preordained" (quoted from Lewis, ibid., p357).

48   "Had Lewis not begun as an expressionist, he would not have understood the problems of expressionism, nor perhaps their relationship to technology" (ibid., p382).

49 NAC, volume 30, file 7.

50 Ibid.

51 Ibid.

52 "Enjoyed Sheila [Watson's] essay on Wyndham Lewis in *White Pelican*. Reminds me how much of my media approach comes from him" (Diary, 3 August 1974).

53 NAC, volume 166, file 23. Marshall McLuhan to James M. Curtis, 27 September 1972.

54 *Letters*, p137-38.

55 Ibid., p138.

56 Older comic-strip afficionados will recall that before her marriage to Dagwood Bumstead, his wife was the showgirl Blondie Boopadoop.

57 *Letters*, p150.

58 NAC, volume 129, file 8.

59 Marshall McLuhan to Wyndham and Anne Lewis, *Letters*, p131.

60 "A Dialogue: Marshall McLuhan and Gerald E. Stearn," in Gerald Emanuel Stearn, ed., *McLuhan: Hot and Cool* (New York: New American Library, 1967), p263.

61 Marshall McLuhan to Wyndham Lewis, *Letters*, p146.

62 Ibid., p147.

63 Ibid.

64 Lewis took McLuhan's letter of application to Assumption, adding his endorsement.

65 In his letter of application to Father Stan Murphy, McLuhan explained his position with respect to the military draft: "As a Canadian who hasn't taken out first papers, I can return to Canada without embarrassment. However, were I to be drafted here, I could not return to Canada, save to serve in the Canadian army — supposing, at least, I wish to be *persona grata* in the U.S.A. after the war" (*Letters*, p156). He explained that he hoped to avoid army service so that he could support his family and continue with his research and writing. (At age thirty-three, an academic, and the father of a young child, McLuhan was not called up.) He suggested feature courses he could teach on practical criticism of prose and poetry, culture and environment, and the dichotomy of European and American culture. He also outlined the manuscript he was then working on, dealing with culture and neurosis from Machiavelli to Marx.

66 Marshall McLuhan to Wyndham Lewis, *Letters*, p165.

8 – *Conversations with Congenial Minds*

1 *Letters*, p135.

2 Ibid., p147.

3 Ibid.

4 Ibid.

5 Marshall McLuhan to J. Stanley Murphy, ibid., p158.

6 NAC, volume 23, file 79. Marshall Fishwick to Marshall McLuhan, 16 September 1972. (A copy of an essay about McLuhan by James Curtis — see bibliography — had been sent by the author to Fishwick for comments.)

7 "I have not wandered as far from literature as might appear. In so far as literature is the study and training of perception, the electric age has complicated the literary lot a great deal" (Marshall McLuhan to Michael Wolff, *Letters*, p304).

8 ". . . trying to achieve a readiness to act in some unforeseeable way when that way should define itself" (Marshall McLuhan to Wyndham Lewis, *Letters*, p147).

9 Approaching a publisher with the manuscript for his first book two years later, McLuhan said: "Most of these materials I have on slides and in that form I have presented them to school kids, to women's clubs, to pedagogues, to graduate students, to ecclesiastics, and to business men" (NAC, Marshall McLuhan to Mr. Erskine, Reynall and Hitchcock, Publishers, New York, 16 April 1946).

10 Marshall McLuhan to J. Stanley Murphy, *Letters*, p158.

11 Interview with Corinne McLuhan.

12 Ibid.

13 *Letters*, p165.

14 Ibid.

15 Ibid., p166.

16 Ibid.

17 Acadia University Archives, Kirkconnell Papers, Watson Kirkconnell to Marshall McLuhan, 7 November 1944. The paper in question was an early version of the article McLuhan published under the same title in *The Classical Journal* in 1946. McLuhan recast the debate on education between Robert Maynard Hutchins's clutch of supporters and John Dewey's disciples in terms of the confrontation between grammarians and rhetoricians vs. dialecticians. The article is reprinted in Eugene McNamara, ed., *The Literary Criticism of Marshall McLuhan* (New York: McGraw-Hill, 1969), pp223-34.

18 Marshall McLuhan to Walter Ong and Clement McNaspy, *Letters*, p165.

19 NAC, Marshall McLuhan to Elsie McLuhan, 18 June [1945].

20 Ibid.

21 NAC, Joseph W. Beach, chair, English department, University of Minnesota, to Marshall McLuhan, 1 August 1945.

22 Interview with Corinne McLuhan.

23 Ibid.

24 NAC, Marshall McLuhan to Elsie McLuhan, n.d.

25 Ibid.

26 Teresa in honor of the saint, Carolyn for Corinne's sister, aunt, and

grandmother; Mary in honor of the Blessed Virgin, Corinne for mother and grandmother.

27   Marshall McLuhan to Elsie McLuhan, *Letters*, p167.

28   Marshall McLuhan to Felix Giovanelli, *Letters*, p183.

29   In an early chapter of *Understanding Media*, McLuhan links the lesson on perception he has presented through the Greek myth of Narcissus first to the concept of "idol" in the Psalms, then to technology, and his key concept of "closure," before identifying all of these in the theory of communication and social change developed by Blake, citing the lines from his "Jerusalem" announcing the theme of the organs of perception: "If Perceptive Organs vary, Objects of Perception seem to vary:/If Perceptive Organs close, their objects seem to close also" (*Understanding Media*, p46).

30   "Should you accept this book, I could come to New York for consultations at any time. Having done oral analyses of every sort of current published material for ten years, I have developed a certain facility so that I can turn out 15 or 20 written commentaries a day without any trouble. So I could recast or expand the job on the spot. The thing which takes me most time is the deciding what to leave out" (NAC, Marshall McLuhan to Mr. Erskine, Reynall and Hitchcock, Publishers, New York, 16 April 1946). In ancient mythology, the giant Typhon was the brother of Osiris. Typhon laid snares for Osiris while he was on an expedition and murdered him when he returned. Horus, the son of Osiris, avenged his father's murder, and Typhon was put to death. In Greek mythology, Typhon was usually represented as a hundred-headed monster. For the Egyptians, Typhon symbolized the source of all evils and was generally depicted as a wolf or a crocodile. "After making his study of the nursery rhyme 'Where are you going my pretty maid?' the anthropologist C. B. Lewis pointed out that 'the folk has neither part nor lot in the making of folklore.' That is also true of the folklore of industrial man, so much of which stems from the laboratory, the studio, and the advertising agencies" (*The Mechanical Bride*, pv).

31   NAC, Marshall McLuhan to Felix Giovanelli, n.d.

32   Marshall McLuhan to Clement McNaspy, *Letters*, p180.

33   Ibid.

34   NAC, volume 64.

35   Ibid.

36   Ibid.

37   "Like all simple men of single mind (and success is certainly not to be had or desired in a technological world by complex men with varied outlooks) Mr. Luce understands what he is doing only in a small degree" (ibid.).

38   *The Mechanical Bride*, pp9-11.

39   NAC, volume 64.

40   Ibid.

41   Ibid.

42   Ibid.

43   Marshall McLuhan to Felix Giovanelli, *Letters*, p182.

44   NAC, Marshall McLuhan to Elsie McLuhan, n.d.

45   Marshall McLuhan to Felix Giovanelli, *Letters*, p182.

46   Ibid., p181.

47   Ibid., NAC, Marshall McLuhan to Elsie McLuhan, n.d.

48   NAC, volume 152, file 2. On the question of Joyce, Hugh Kenner wrote to McLuhan to say that "Frye denies that Joyce remained in spite of himself a Catholic, denies that he left the Church through pride, denies even that the he was proud. You must take him in hand" (NAC, Hugh Kenner to Marshall McLuhan, 24 June 1946). There is no available record of any discussion between McLuhan and Frye on the matter Kenner raises. McLuhan's own view of Joyce remains an interesting one in view of such observations as the following: "From Judaism, Joyce accepted the Rabbinic doctrine that language was not divided from being; conversely, he rejected the Catholic or Patristic view that the letter represented only the spirit and not the thing itself" (Ira B. Nadel, *Joyce and the Jews* [Iowa City: Iowa University Press, 1989], p123).

49   "We haven't had anything of yours for a long time and I hope it won't be much longer before we can see something. I talked with Cleanth Brooks a short while ago; he is an admirer of yours, and told me of some smart things you had talked with him [*sic*]" (NAC, John Crowe Ransom to Marshall McLuhan, 12 January 1946). When McLuhan submitted an essay the following year, he found Ransom once again unreceptive to (and uninformed about) ideas carefully developed around the topic of McLuhan's Cambridge doctoral dissertation: "I wish you didn't rely on ambiguous terms like *dialectic*, *rhetoric*, and *grammar*" (NAC, John Crowe Ransom to Marshall McLuhan, 31 Aug 1947).

50   Marshall McLuhan to Felix Giovanelli, *Letters*, p183.

51   Marshall McLuhan to Walter J. Ong, ibid., p186.

52   Ibid.

53   Ibid.

54   Interview with Corinne McLuhan.

55   McLuhan had met Kenner in Toronto in June 1946 and had suggested to him that he apply for the vacancy at Assumption (*Letters*, p189).

56   NAC, Marshall McLuhan to Elsie McLuhan, n.d.

57   Interview with Eric McLuhan.

58   NAC, Marshall McLuhan to Elsie McLuhan, n.d.

59   Marshall McLuhan to Walter J. Ong, *Letters*, p186.

60   Jacques Maritain (1882-1973), a French philosopher, was, like McLuhan, a convert to Catholicism and profoundly influenced by Thomism.

Maritain gave a lecture series at the Pontifical Institute every year from 1932 to 1945. "Frazer" is a reference to Sir James George Frazer (1854-1941), the British social anthropologist and folklorist, perhaps best known as the author of *The Golden Bough*. "Malinowski" is a reference to Bronislaw Malinowski (1884-1942), a Polish-born, British anthropologist, perhaps best known as the author of *Argonauts of the Western Pacific*.

61 Marshall McLuhan to Walter J. Ong, *Letters*, pp186-87.
62 Ibid.; ibid.
63 Ibid.
64 NAC, Notebook, 27 November 1946.
65 Ibid.
66 Ibid.
67 Interview with Jack and Mary Wilson.
68 Ibid.
69 NAC, volume 64, file 1.
70 At an annual salary of $4,000, 20 percent of which reverted to St. Michael's for the rent of the St. Joseph Street house, and income tax at ten times the rate McLuhan had paid in St. Louis, the family was short of money. At the end of one year in Toronto, the McLuhans were unable to afford to send Eric to summer camp. Elsie sent them money for this purpose, but they returned it to her (NAC, volume 3, file 1).
71 NAC, Marshall McLuhan to Felix Giovanelli, n.d.
72 Ibid. McLuhan also makes the analogy here with visual art: "It would not be entirely misleading to say that the method of the book is 'cubist' in that it employs the 'circulating point of view.'"
73 Ibid.
74 NAC, Marshall McLuhan to Mr. Erskine, Reynall and Hitchcock, Publishers, New York, 16 April 1946.
75 NAC, volume 64, file 1.
76 Ibid.
77 Ibid.
78 Ibid. Elsewhere, McLuhan had emphasized another aspect of the book's purpose in these terms: "to present a cross-section of major social pressures and interests of the moment" (NAC, Marshall McLuhan to Mr. Erskine, Reynall and Hitchcock, Publishers, New York, 16 April 1946).
79 NAC, volume 64, file 1.
80 Ibid.
81 Interview with Jack and Mary Wilson.
82 In announcing this hope to Walter Ong, McLuhan referred to the work as his "book of exhibits with commentary on popular culture" (*Letters*, p188).
83 NAC, volume 129, file 25 ("Time, Life and Fortune," 1947).
84 *Letters*, p190.

85   NAC, volume 129, file 29. The draft version of this publication (see also bibliography) includes the following observations: (1) "Unlike Vico and Joyce, but like Freud, Blake mistook a psychology for metaphysics and theology. His rigorous monism had no place for 'the many' save as modes of primal, divine energy"; (2) "Professor Frye's inside view of Blake in which every part of the bard's thought is seen to have a strict etiolation and coherence, is perhaps in need of some further development from the outside. Blake is psychologically in the tradition of patristic allegory, unbroken from Philo of Alexandria to the Cambridge Platonists, and he needs to be closely compared and contrasted with Vico"; (3) [re: obsession with mechanistic abstraction] "The Ford Motor Company has in its museum working models of all locomotives and all motor cars ever made. But it has no records of production methods employed in the manufacture of its early cars — a fact which rightly shocked Sigfried Giedion."

86   Marshall McLuhan to Walter J. Ong, *Letters*, p191.

87   Ibid.

88   Ibid., p190.

89   Ibid., pp190-91.

90   "But how well you have entered this problem of wit — writing in the middle ages. Are you not the very first to enter that world with comprehension in a century or more?. . . Notice that your own discussion on 'tension' as the mode of Christian being is specifically psychological — the basic approach of present day esthetic analysis. What is now needed is a great revival of patristic study in light of these things . . . How grand if *you*, Walter, could do a series of selections from the fathers . . . Even fifty pages of this sort of thing done well would possibly start things moving" (*Letters*, pp190-91).

91   Ibid., p191.

92   Ibid.

93   Ibid.

94   Interview with Corinne McLuhan.

95   Marshall McLuhan to David Sohn, *Letters*, p456.

96   Interview with Eric McLuhan.

97   NAC, Dorothy Pound to Marshall McLuhan, 21 June 1948.

98   Marshall McLuhan to Ezra Pound, *Letters*, p194.

99   Ibid., p193.

100 NAC, Ezra Pound to Marshall McLuhan, 18 June 1948.

101 Marshall McLuhan to Ezra Pound, *Letters*, p193; p194; p195.

102 Ibid., p197.

103 "A propos of your valuable comment (in G. to K.) anent Francis Picabia and the technique for getting rid of rubbish by transposition of terms, inversion of clichés, etc., I have thought of *Finnegans Wake* as a gigantic experiment in that mode" (ibid., p200).

104 Ibid., p201.

105 Ibid.

106 "All [Pound's] strategies depend on the prior condition of alertness and eager appetite for truth. W. Lewis: 'I write from the standpoint of genius.' E.P.: 'I write for those who are top flight inventors and creators in the arts.' T. S. Eliot: 'I croon to those who are living and partly living a song of their remote but better selves.' Therefore Lewis and Pound are ignored and Eliot is *widely* misunderstood" (ibid., p203). McLuhan's comments on Pound dating from much later also involve comparison with Eliot: "Pound has a horror of popular culture which was the occasion of his blue-pencilling a good deal of 'The Waste Land.' Much of what he threw out of 'The Waste Land' was from the music hall world that Eliot loved. Pound took culture very seriously and phonetically and moralistically" (NAC, Marshall McLuhan to Joe Keogh, 6 July 1970).

107 Marshall McLuhan to Dorothy Shakespear Pound, *Letters*, p205.

108 Ibid. (emphasis added)

109 Marshall McLuhan to Ezra Pound, ibid., p207.

110 Sidney Earle Smith (1897-1959) was president of the University of Toronto from 1945 to 1957.

111 NAC, Marshall McLuhan to Elsie McLuhan, n.d.

112 *Letters*, p194.

113 Ibid., footnote 2.

114 Ibid., p205.

115 NAC, Marshall McLuhan to Pete Buckner, 2 January 1974.

116 *Letters*, p205.

117 Ibid.

118 Ibid., p211.

119 Ibid., p241.

120 "The idea of a book on Al Capp I like very much. It would be extremely fast work — possibly the quickest of our many projects" (NAC, volume 168, file 20. Hugh Kenner to Marshall McLuhan, 23 April 1948).

121 "At the top of page 160 you have taken over my Hopkins-Joyce hook-up (inscape-epiphany). Now that could have become a useful little article of 10-16 pages. Your not tagging me with the discovery makes it impossible for me to write that article at any future time without accrediting *you* with the discovery . . . the question remains, is the firm to be Kenner and McLuhan or Kenner operating on his own with the combined assets?" (NAC, Marshall McLuhan to Hugh Kenner, 7 January 1949).

122 NAC, Hugh Kenner to Marshall McLuhan, 19 January 1949.

123 Marshall McLuhan to Felix Giovanelli, *Letters*, p215.

124 Ibid., p214.

125 Interview with Jack and Mary Wilson.

126 Interview with Corinne McLuhan.

127   Edmund Carpenter, "The Inner Trip." Address to the Cigar Institute of America, 8 December 1967. (NAC, volume 179, file 39.)

128   Not long after Innis's death in 1952, McLuhan made contact with a former Innis associate, J. Bartlet Brebner, who provided him with interesting and insightful comments on Innis. "[Innis] was like a man with a popcorn shaker, whose shape and strength he never ascertained. Had he lived longer, he would have been forced into philosophy, at least to the degree of optimism or pessimism instead of skepticism about man. [In Arthur Kroker's *Technology and the Canadian Mind: Innis, McLuhan, Grant*, Innis is identified with technological realism and McLuhan with technological optimism.] . . . I think that the war, at least by 1940, had robbed him of the comfort of skepticism, but thereafter he too became a prisoner of time. As you perhaps know, I have been curious about his possible relationships with the Bergsonians and anti-Bergsonians, especially Pound, Eliot, and Wyndham Lewis . . . I was struck by the coincidence of Lewis's presence in Toronto, his articles in *Saturday Night*, and the publication of one of his books by Ryerson [Press], for whom Innis acted in an editorial capacity . . . His humour and his amazing courage carried him through ten or twelve years that would have broken most men or sharply distorted them" (NAC, volume 145, file 41. J. Bartlet Brebner to Marshall McLuhan, 2 December 1953).

129   NAC, Marshall McLuhan to Peter Drucker, 26 April 1960.

130   Marshall McLuhan, "Harold Innis," *Explorations* 25 (June 1969). This is an edited version of McLuhan's introduction to the 1964 paperback edition of Innis's *The Bias of Communication*, published originally in 1951.

131   Ibid.

132   Marshall McLuhan to William Kuhns, *Letters*, p448.

133   NAC, Marshall McLuhan to Fritz Wilhelmsen, department of Philosophy, University of Dallas, 18 January 1971.

134   NAC, volume 166, file 25. Marshall McLuhan to *The Listener*, 22 October 1975.

135   Marshall McLuhan to William Kuhns, *Letters*, p448.

136   Marshall McLuhan to Harold Adams Innis, ibid., p220.

137   Marshall McLuhan, "Harold Innis," *Explorations* 25 (June 1969).

138   NAC, Marshall McLuhan to Chuck Bayley, Vancouver Board of School Trustees, 16 December 1964.

139   NAC, Marshall McLuhan to Father Lawrence Shook, 20 June 1972.

140   NAC, volume 203, file 22. Marshall McLuhan to Michael Fox, editor, *Queen's Quarterly*, 23 February 1976.

141   NAC, Marshall McLuhan to Mark Slade, 9 February 1972.

142   "More and more I see the Innis approach as a gestalt *figure-ground* approach. Innis was one of the very few people to recognize the ground or environment created by technologies as the area of change" (NAC, Marshall McLuhan to Joel Persky, 27 February 1973).

143   NAC, Marshall McLuhan to Chuck Bayley, 16 December 1964.

144   Max Weber (1864-1920), a German economist who delineated the rela-
       tionship between capitalism and Protestant ethics.

145   NAC, Marshall McLuhan to Chuck Bayley, 16 December 1964.

146   NAC, volume 149, file 20. Marshall McLuhan to Hans Selye, 25 July
       1974.

147   "The mosaic structure of insights employed in the work of the later Innis
       is never far removed from the comic irony of an Abraham Lincoln"
       (Marshall McLuhan, "Harold Innis," *Explorations* 25 (June 1969); "One
       can say of Innis what Bertrand Russell said of Einstein . . . 'Many of the
       ideas can be expressed in non-mathematical language, but they are none
       the less difficult on that account. What is demanded is a change in our
       imaginative picture of the world" (ibid.); "Have been struck by the
       numerous Harold Innis qualities of [Henry] David Thoreau. Thoreau
       had the same ecological concerns as Innis. As with Innis, his ecological
       vision had been classified as picturesque, or romantic, etc." (NAC,
       Marshall McLuhan to Hugo McPherson, 12 June 1970).

148   "In effect, Coleridge is saying that the area of assimilation and cultural
       environment creates a vast ignorance in each of us. Once this area is spot-
       ted, it is easy to fill in the conditions and assimilations that create it.
       Symbolism initiated the technique of separating effects from causes,
       studying the effects in order to learn the causes. It is the technique of
       Ovid's *Metamorphoses*, and necessarily the technique of Darwin's origins
       [*sic*] of species. Darwin seems to have used the same number of books as
       Ovid [=15] and probably was as conscious of using Ovid as Joyce was in
       his *Dubliners*. Inevitably, Darwin, in starting with species, was dealing
       with effects. The causes were infinitely remote and only to be guessed at
       from the effects. Such is the technique of the symbolist poem which
       creates reader participation by this method. Harold Innis was never
       understood simply because he worked with causality at all times . . . "
       (NAC, Marshall McLuhan to Fritz Wilhelmsen, Department of
       Philosophy, University of Dallas, 18 January 1971).

149   Marshall McLuhan, "Harold Innis," *Explorations* 25 (June 1969).

150   NAC, Evelyn Schrifte to Marshall McLuhan, 23 March 1950.

151   "Part III of Lewis's *The Doom of Youth* (1932) contains 'A Gallery of
       Exhibits' made up of newspaper headlines and extracts, with comments
       by Lewis — illustrating what Lewis saw as the 'class-war of "Young and
       Old"' — that prefigures McLuhan's treatment of advertisements and
       other examples of popular culture in *The Mechanical Bride*. Lewis dis-
       cusses advertising — 'The spirit of advertisement and boost lives and has
       its feverish being in the world of hyperbolic suggestion' — in Book I,
       Chapter II of *Time and Western Man* (1928)" (*Letters*, p217).

152   NAC, Marshall McLuhan to Felix Giovanelli, n.d.

153   Marshall McLuhan to Ezra Pound, *Letters*, p218.

154   Ibid.

155   In the 1970s, when figure/ground analysis came to dominate McLuhan's thinking, he said: "If you study symbolism you will discover that it is a technique of rip-off by which *figures* are deliberately deprived of their *ground*" (Marshall McLuhan to William Kuhns, *Letters*, p448).

156   "Work done in last three years on techniques of Flaubert, Rimbaud, Laforgue has opened my eyes for the first time to the ways in which you, Joyce, Eliot have used 'landscapes' to achieve many of your effects" (NAC, Marshall McLuhan to Ezra Pound, 2 August 1951). McLuhan's literary essays from 1943 to 1962 were collected under the title *The Interior Landscape* by Eugene McNamara, who provides no explanation for the phrase. I am indebted to my colleague Michael Bishop for the succinct summary of Arthur Rimbaud's *paysage intérieur*, or *inner landscape*, as the domain "where reference, referentiality, becomes esoteric, strictly and manifestly subjective, though intuitable and completely appreciable as private, visionary meaning or figuration — a radically new 'descriptive'/ representative mode that, say, the paintings of Redon, Moreau, and Puvis de Chavannes may differently emblematize" (personal communication).

157   Marshall McLuhan to Ezra Pound, *Letters*, p218.

158   Ibid.

159   Marshall McLuhan to Harold Adams Innis, ibid., p221.

160   Ibid., p222.

161   NAC, Marshall McLuhan to Elsie McLuhan, n.d.

162   *Letters*, p229.

163   NAC, Marshall McLuhan to Warren Brodie, 29 July 1969. The theme of sex and technology intertwined with a third figure, that of Death, was to be explored years after the publication of *The Mechanical Bride* by McLuhan's associate Wilson Bryan ("Bill") Key in his *Subliminal Seduction* and other publications.

164   "Today when we lift up our eyes to the signboards whence cometh our help we are apt to find 'help' in the most unexpected forms . . . It has been proven time and again that the foulest and most stinking of offenses against human dignity and decency can be committed with impunity in the name of trade . . . Simplicity and even harshness has always been the external characteristic of Christian burial because it has always been the most optimistic of burials. But simplicity does not mean . . . profits, and it has gradually given way to pagan pomp."

165   Dennis Duffy, *McLuhan*, p. 12. Though without the benefit of contrast among McLuhan's publications, some early commentators had offered the same opinion as Duffy: "Mr. McLuhan may well be as detached as can humanly be expected, but despite his sophistication, his wide range of reading, his perceptive power, and his wit, he is a thoroughly disgusted

man" (Thomas H. Carter, "The Totem with No Face," [Review of *The Mechanical Bride*] *Shenandoah* 4, 2-3 (1953), 118-21).

166   "My approach to the media begins with the effects and moves backward to causes. The rest of the media people start with what they think are the causes and ignore the effects. Starting with the 'causes' means taking a strong moral stance, usually of disapproval" (NAC, Marshall McLuhan to John Bassett, 19 March 1971).

167   Marshall McLuhan to Harold Adams Innis, *Letters*, p222.

168   *The Mechanical Bride*, p104.

169   Ibid., p68.

170   NAC, volume 64, file 1.

171   Ibid.

172   Ibid.

173   Robert Martin, "Scientific Angle on Our Culture Is Revealing," *Daily Times Herald* (Dallas), 4 November 1951.

174   Craig M. Pearson, "Courting Numb Minds," *Hartford Courant*, n.d.

175   *New York Times*, 21 October 1951.

176   J. V. McAree writing in *Globe and Mail*, 19 March 1952.

177   Gerald W. Johnson, "Our Culture on a Griddle," *New York Herald Tribune*, 10 February 1952.

178   *The New Republic*, 26 November 1951.

179   *Advertising and Selling*, November 1951.

180   *Letters*, p234. Ong's review appeared in *Social Order*, 2, 2 (1952).

181   NAC, Marshall McLuhan to Elsie McLuhan, n.d.

182   Ibid.

183   NAC, Marshall McLuhan to Geoffrey Cannon (*Radio Times*, London), 22 September 1970.

184   *Letters*, p227.

185   NAC, Ezra Pound to Marshall McLuhan, 5 July 1952.

186   Ibid.

187   McLuhan listed the main sections of the projected book as The Invention of Writing-Alphabet; Invention of Printing; Telegraph [as the] ultimate stage of mechanization of writing; Radio-telephone; Cinema-TV. (*Letters*, p232.) To Walter Ong, McLuhan offered this synopsis: "Tracing impact of print, and now, the switch to media which represents not the mechanization of writing but of word and gesture (radio, movies, TV). Necessarily a much greater change than from script to print" (*Letters*, p234).

188   *Letters*, p246.

189   Ibid., p235.

190   Ibid., 231.

191   Ibid. McLuhan was beginning to embroider on a theme developed by Wyndham Lewis in *Time and Western Man*.

192   Only his use of quotation marks in a letter from McLuhan to Walter Ong

hint that he may have been speaking metaphorically and not literally: "I don't see how it is possible to teach English literature, or any European literature, without full knowledge of the 'secret doctrine' for which the arts are the sole means of grace. I realize now that my own rejection of philosophy as a study in my pre-Catholic days was owing to the sense that it was a meaningless truncation [meaningless (without connection) because it is a truncation (disconnected)]. Not that my present interest is due to any conviction of truth in the secret doctrine. Quite the contrary. It is rather to a sense of it as the fecund source of lies and misconceptions, e.g. Puritan Inner Light. Can you think of any reason why Catholic students of philosophy and literature today should not be given the facts about these 'secrets'? I can find nobody here who can or will discuss the question" (*Letters*, p244).

193   McLuhan included gnostics in the cavalcade of cabals, and in this respect implicated Northrop Frye: "Frye's *Blake* is [the] best exposition of contemporary gnosticism I know" (*Letters*, p237). Years later, knowing of his father's views on the Masons and the Rosicrucians, Eric McLuhan introduced a healthy perspective on the matter: "Trouble is, of course, there's heaps of accusation and innuendo, and few discern[i]ble facts — and the fact that it has a McCarthy-ish flavour doesn't help. Too many of the sources for facts (such as they are) suffer from being too partisan and conservative (e.g. the mag[azine] *The Remnant*)" (NAC, Eric McLuhan to Marshall and Corinne McLuhan, 22 September 1976). The basis of McLuhan's opposition to gnosticism lay in its tenet of an "uncreated divine spark hidden in our corrupt clay" (Marshall McLuhan to Walter J. Ong, *Letters*, p244).

194   *Letters*, p233. Pound encouraged McLuhan not to remain passive in the face of perceived opposition to his work. (NAC, Ezra Pound to Marshall McLuhan, 6 December 1952.)

195   Ibid., p234.

196   Interview with Corinne McLuhan.

197   "Yes," McLuhan said, "our six children make a complex life for us, in a way which 25 years ago they would not. The disappearance of servants and large houses (not unplanned) is linked to the Manichean hatred of the family, and the Church has been most culpable in allowing this concerted campaign to be met only by sporadic individual initiative and resistance" (Marshall McLuhan to Walter J. Ong, *Letters*, p238).

9 – A Beachhead in Toronto

1   Marshall McLuhan to Walter Ong, *Letters*, ibid., p236.

2   Ibid., p238.

3   "Under the Interdisciplinary Research and Study Program approved by the Board of Trustees of the Ford Foundation we are glad to make a grant

of $44,250 to the University for the proposal submitted by Prof. E. S. Carpenter and others on 'Changing Patterns of Language and Behavior and the New Media of Communication'" (NAC, volume 204, file 22. H. Rowen Gaitler, Jr., director, Ford Foundation, to Sidney Smith, president of the University of Toronto, 19 May 1953).

4   NAC, 204, file 22. Sidney Smith to Marshall McLuhan, 29 May 1953.

5   NAC, volume 204, file 4.

6   *Letters*, p233.

7   NAC, volume 145, file 41.

8   NAC, Report of the Ford Seminar at Toronto University 1953-55. "In our [interdisciplinary] group the doctrinaires are much disturbed by Acoustic or non-Euclidian space. It gives too complete and simple a physiological account of their metaphysics" (*Letters*, pp245-46). *Too complete*. This reaction among his colleagues must have confirmed for McLuhan just how far-reaching and powerful the fragmenting effect of the Gutenberg era had become.

9   "Under these conditions it is also easy to observe how free is the human mind from any taint of either objectivity or receptivity. The ordinary conditions of university life seem framed to protect rather than to soften the action of the blinkered mind. In fact, the least expected result of our inter-action was the quite obvious anxiety and resentment that grew in proportion as understanding of one another's fields began to develop. It was as though we began to view each [other] as hostile code-crackers. It would seem that 'specialism' within the university has fostered a coding system as a basis for the easy and rapid achievement of 'professional' or 'expert' status. Any attempt to hand on the codes or to pool them for group benefits breeds involuntary panic and dismay. And this state of mind depends in turn on failure to perceive the fact that the culture of any time has an operative cohesion which can only become the greater as it is recognized and understood. The anxiety of the specialist to separate himself leads to the impoverishment of his own field as well as to a general confusion of tongues" (ibid.).

10 Ibid.

11 A decade later, in *Against Interpretation*, Susan Sontag ascribed the partitioning of form and content to the ancient Greeks.

12 NAC, Report of the Ford Seminar at Toronto University 1953-55.

13 Ibid.

14 Ibid.

15 Ibid.

16 Ibid.

17 "I remember well our discussion of the Contemporary Institute in July. If you should care to work out any further details of its operations and organizations, I know that whatever you would present would be regarded

with interest here" (NAC volume 204, file 26. Richard C. Sheldon, Ford Foundation, to Marshall McLuhan, 30 September 1955).

18   "On the basis of our discussion I think it quite unlikely that the Foundation could be able to support a proposal of this sort" (NAC, volume 204, file 26. Bernard Berelson, director, Ford Foundation, to Marshall McLuhan, 17 September 1956).

19   *Letters*, p236.

20   McLuhan family papers. Jack Birt to Marshall McLuhan, 18 July 1980.

21   Ibid.

22   Ibid.

23   Ibid.

24   Lewis had published a novel under this title in 1951.

25   *Letters*, p242.

26   Ibid., p235.

27   *The Mechanical Bride*, pv.

28   *Counterblast*, p5. McLuhan blasts the sports page of the newspaper and the comics that uphold "Homeric culture," the Canadian beaver as a symbol of dammed-up creativity, satellites for surrounding the earth with a manmade environment, art galleries for pigeonholing the works of the human spirit, and the printed page for locking humankind into a visual bias. (The book, like Lewis's *Blast*, is a riot of typographical dislocation.) But McLuhan blesses too: the Beatles, for challenging the world to discover new sensory modes; Glenn Gould, for making audiences obsolete; culture shock, for dislocating mind into meaning; and Madison Avenue, for raising advertising to an art form. (This comes as a surprise, unless one remembers the quotation from *The Mechanical Bride* (pv) above.)

29   See page 117.

30   NAC, Jack Bell to Marshall McLuhan, 10 March 1977.

31   NAC, volume 148, file 30.

32   Ibid. The Commission was not accepting any more briefs by the time the communication from Idea Consultants reached them.

33   NAC, volume 148, file 31.

34   Ibid.

35   NAC, volume 148, file 31.

36   NAC, Bernie Muller-Thym to Marshall McLuhan, 18 April 1956.

37   NAC, volume 148, file 31.

38   NAC, volume 148, file 32.

39   Ibid.

40   Ibid.

41   Ibid.

42   NAC, Ezra Pound to Ted Carpenter, 18 January 1957.

43   *Letters*, p251. The whimsical name is a good-natured swipe at "Pontifical

Institute of Medieval Studies" as well as a reminder that the ideal in McLuhan's program for educational reform revolved around the classical trivium.

44 NAC, volume 148, volume 7. Marshall McLuhan and Louis Forsdale, "Global Capers," 28 May 1958.

45 Ibid.

46 NAC, Marshall McLuhan to Eric McLuhan, 1 December 1975.

47 Marshall McLuhan to Edward S. Morgan, *Letters*, p253.

48 NAC, volume 6, file 5, 1 June 1973.

49 NAC, volume 8, file 14. He told Corinne he had thought up the expression on the plane, while traveling to the conference.

50 Samuel L. Becker, "Viewpoint: McLuhan as Rorschach," *Journal of Broadcasting* 19, 2 (1975), pp235-40.

51 In *Understanding Media* we read: "closure or equilibrium-seeking" (p44); "closure or displacement of perception" (p46); "closure or psychic consequence" (p67); and "closure or completion of image" (p331).

52 Christie McCormick, "The Undiluted Wisdom of Marshall McLuhan," *Montreal Gazette*, 16 May 1975.

53 Harold Innis, *The Bias of Communication* (Toronto: University of Toronto Press, 1951 [repr. 1971]), p33. McLuhan acknowledged this debt to Innis throughout his career: "When I say 'the medium is the message,' I am using the insight of Harold Innis in *The Bias of Communication*. What is implied in this phrase is that the medium consists of all the services evoked or provoked by any innovation. When the Chinese shifted their writing from bamboo to paper, they developed new centralized political forms. For literate and visually oriented people, it is always a shock to learn that many of the dominant attitudes of their daily lives have been structured by subliminal factors and the psychic effects of seemingly inert or neutral forms" ("English Literature as Control Tower in Communication Study," *English Quarterly* 7, 1 (1974), p4).

54 NAC, Marshall McLuhan to Barry Day, 11 June 1970. (italics added)

55 McLuhan marginalized at least one other thinker in this elect company: "I suddenly realized that the entire moral discussion of [Aldous Huxley's] *Ends and Means* is a garbled attempt to say the medium is the message" (NAC, Marshall McLuhan to William Jovanovich, 2 February 1966).

56 NAC, Marshall McLuhan to Jim Davey, 7 May 1971.

57 NAC, Marshall McLuhan to James M. Curtis, 12 September 1972.

58 NAC, Marshall McLuhan to Pete Buckner, 5 January 1971.

59 NAC, Marshall McLuhan to Jacques Maritain, 28 May 1969.

60 NAC, Marshall McLuhan to Jerome Agel, 27 March 1973.

61 NAC, Marshall McLuhan to Jitendra Kumar, 17 November 1972.

62 NAC, Marshall McLuhan to Chuck Bayley, 16 December 1964.

63 NAC, Marshall McLuhan to *Time*, 6 July 1964.

64 NAC, Marshall McLuhan to Charles Schultz, Educational Broadcasting Corporation, 15 October 1964.

65 McLuhan extended the same image to media other than language, transforming it slightly: "In practice, any medium surrounds not only the users but all the earlier media as well. What results is an interface of resonance and metamorphosis" (NAC, Marshall McLuhan to Herbert E. Krugman, 13 January 1971).

66 NAC, Joe Keogh to Marshall McLuhan, 6 September 1969.

67 Marshall McLuhan to *The Listener*, *Letters*, p443.

68 Applying the rule to "the medium is the message," the rule gives (1) "the [contained] medium is the message [of the containing medium]." Here the sense of "message" given by the expansion is McLuhan's sense, and it defines the relationship between media. The expansion can also run (2) "the [effect of a containing] medium is [more powerful than] the [effect of the] message [of the contained medium]." Now the sense of "message" is both McLuhan's defining relationship for media *and* the more conventional sense of message, covering facts, data, information, viewpoints, meaning, exhortation, etc. Another result of applying Richards's rule is (3) "the [effect of a containing] medium is [so powerful that it supersedes the effect of] the message [of the contained medium]." Both the McLuhan sense and the conventional sense of "message" obtain here.

69 C. K. Ogden and I. A. Richards, *The Meaning of Meaning* (in W. T. Gordon, ed., *C. K. Ogden and Linguistics* [London: Routledge/ Thoemmes, 1994], v3, p181ff).

70 Marshall McLuhan to Eric McLuhan, *Letters*, p418.

71 Ibid.

72 Marshall McLuhan to Edward T. Hall, *Letters*, p422. (italics added)

73 NAC, Charles Reich to Marshall McLuhan, 22 January 1971.

74 NAC, Marshall McLuhan to Peter Newman, 5 February 1971.

75 NAC, volume 32, file 45. Max Nanny to Marshall McLuhan, 3 June 1971.

76 NAC, Marshall McLuhan to Robert Manning, 21 July 1971.

77 "The content can be no better than the user, ergo the need to improve the quality of perception in the user" (NAC, Marshall McLuhan to Lou Forsdale, 9 September 1971).

78 NAC, Marshall McLuhan to Barbara Rowes, 8 November 1976.

79 "I am bringing out a new book on *The Laws of the Media* in which the structure of every human artifact, whether it's tv or a safety pin, a bulldozer or a wire-tap, is shown to be linguistic in character . . . In the course of doing this work, I discovered what was wrong with the Shannon-Weaver model of communication. What they call 'NOISE,' I call the medium — that is all the side effects, all the unintended patterns and

changes . . . The S/W model of communication is merely a transportation model which has no place for the side-effects of the service
environments, or the transformational factors. For example, the motor
car is not a medium but a *figure* in a *ground* of services, i.e. highways,
factories, oil companies, etc. It is always the service environment that is
the medium, and this is usually 'hidden' in the sense of being unnoticed"
(NAC, Marshall McLuhan to Jerome Agel, 26 March 1976).

80   Ibid.
81   NAC, Marshall McLuhan to Gertrude LeMoyne (*La Presse*, Montreal), 3
      August 1976.
82   Norman Mailer, "Of a Small and Modest Malignancy, Wicked and
      Bristling with Dots," *Esquire*, November 1977, pp125-48, (p128).
83   *Letters*, p264.
84   NAC, volume 72, file 6.
85   Ibid.
86   Ibid.
87   Ibid.
88   Ibid.
89   Ibid.
90   Ibid.
91   Ibid.
92   Ibid.
93   Ibid.
94   *Letters*, p258.
95   Ibid., p261.
96   Ibid., p259.
97   "A road is at first in Low Definition, coming into existence to fetch rural
      produce to town areas (before road, of course, the pedestrian and the
      mounted man). As it goes into High Definition, it fetches the town to the
      country. It next becomes a substitute for the country and then destroys the
      country. As it continues to improve, or be more of a road, it destroys the
      city and is at that stage metamorphosed into a new kind of city" (*Letters*,
      p262).
98   The Engineering department at the University of Toronto told
      McLuhan: "Yes, we have a lot of models and systems that would take that
      kind of information flow. We have found, strangely, a lot of examples of
      reversal of flow in various saturation situations" (NAC, Marshall
      McLuhan to Harry Skornia, 11 March 1960). The fourth of the inte-
      grated laws of media that eventually capped McLuhan's work
      corresponds to this phenomenon.
99   "The last few days have seen a major breakthrough in media study.
      Working with the fact that each medium embodies one or more of the
      human senses, [this had been a topic in the Ford Seminar and was to

become a major project for the Centre for Culture and Technology] it struck me that we are impelled in perceiving each medium to complete the scale or spectrum of our sensorium. So that, radio impels us to provide a visual world moment by moment, and photography, which is so adequate in visual terms, compels us to complete the tactual and kinesthetic part of the sensorium. Thus the degree of sensuous completion is one way in which the lines of force in any medium are structured" (NAC, Marshall McLuhan to Harry Skornia, 25 January 1960).

100   Marshall McLuhan to Peter Drucker, *Letters*, p269.
101   Ibid., p270.
102   Ibid., p272.
103   Ibid., p256.
104   NAC, volume 72, file 6. *Report on Understanding New Media*, p2.
105   Ibid., p6.
106   Ibid., n.p.
107   Ibid.
108   Ibid.
109   Ibid.
110   "Wells Foshay and I spent Sunday afternoon together, and he is so excited about the present development (the dynamics of media as related to the charts) that he wants me at once as a visiting professor, but failing that, on any basis at all, to carry on this work" (NAC, Marshall McLuhan to Harry Skornia, 15 March 1960).
111   Ibid.
112   NAC, Marshall McLuhan to Harry Skornia, 7 April 1960.
113   In print, the manuscript produced a text of 279 pages.
114   NAC, Walter Ong to Ronald A. Sarno, 1 June 1978. In response to Sarno's query to Ong about his influence on McLuhan, Ong replied: "In *The Gutenberg Galaxy* (1962) Marshall McLuhan quotes extensively and at critical points from my *Ramus, Method and the Decay of Dialogue* and from two other studies of mine on Ramus . . . I can go through *The Gutenberg Galaxy* and underline scores of passages that echo our talk — the St. Louis *topoi* or *loci communes* [McLuhan, Ong, Bernie Muller-Thym, the young Jesuits George Klubertanz, William A. Van Roo, and Charles Leo Sweeney]."
115   *The Gutenberg Galaxy*, p50.
116   *The Mechanical Bride*, p4.
117   McLuhan pursued and developed the core ideas from *The Gutenberg Galaxy* for many years afterward, calling the alphabet "the supreme streamlining which gets rid of the spoken word" (NAC, Marshall McLuhan to Sister St. John O'Malley, 9 February 1978); dubbing the alphabet's primary effect "spliteracy" (NAC, Marshall McLuhan to Mary Jane Schultz, 20 November 1973); glossing Joyce's *allforabit* — "the

alphabet throws everything away and retains a fragment of the experience, the private point of view" (NAC, Marshall McLuhan to Pat O'Neill,
21 August 1969). Work on the alphabet remained among McLuhan's active
projects: "The work I am doing with Bob Logan on the alphabet and
ancient science will provide a beach-head for exploring the effects of the
alphabet in giving priority to efficient cause over others" (NAC, Marshall
McLuhan to Reverend Gerald Pocock, 7 May 1976).

118 NAC, Harry Skornia to Arthur Efron, 6 November 1962.
119 Ibid.
120 Ibid.
121 NAC, volume 8, file 52.
122 Ibid.
123 *Letters*, pp280-81.
124 Interview with Corinne McLuhan.
125 *Letters*, p285.
126 John Ayre, *Northrop Frye* (Toronto: Random House, 1989), p275.

10 – From the Centre Out

1 "He and I discussed it candidly, and the position amounts to this: that,
after this year, the decision will be up to his successor, but now it lies with
him" (NAC, volume 204, file 4. Ernest Sirluck to Marshall McLuhan, 3
October 1963).

2 NAC, volume 204, file 4. D. S. Claringbold to Marshall McLuhan, 25
October 1963. During its seventeen years of operation, the Centre
received grants from IBM, the John Culkin Trust Fund, the Lindsley
Foundation, the Ken Foundation, and the Social Sciences and
Humanities Research Council of Canada, totaling nearly one hundred
thousand dollars.

3 NAC, Marshall McLuhan to J. H. Sword, 22 November 1963.

4 "Having established such sensory ratios in an entire culture it becomes
practical to predict the precise shift in sensory ratios that would occur
with any new technology, since all technologies are extensions of the
body, or the senses. The 'content' of any medium or technology has
scarcely any effect on the sensory ratios. That is why 'the medium is the
message.' However the content of any medium is always another medium.
To that extent content has some slight effect on a culture. The content of
American movies for example, is very much more literary than the
content of Russian movies. On the other hand, the Russian movies could
not survive the impact of the sound-track" (NAC, volume 204, file 27.
Marshall McLuhan to Peter Drucker, 25 March 1964).

5 NAC, volume 205, file 5. Marshall McLuhan to J. H. Sword, 21 April
1964.

6 *From Cliché to Archetype*, p21.

7   "New Centre 'with a meaning,'" *Toronto Star*, 24 August 1964.

8   Ibid.

9   Ibid.

10   "We have been spending a good deal of time lately on an Innis College building. There is a User's Committee and it is at the point of submitting a report to PACAF. But the situation remains pretty vague — there is no definite site, nor any definite target date for completion. Logic suggests that the site will be small and therefore the building itself will be high-rise. I have come to the conclusion that it is not practical to pursue the idea of providing in an Innis College building space for the Centre. If the building were to be spread out as New [College] is, this could be attempted, but in a high-rise it seems unlikely that a scheme could be worked out that would give the Centre the kind of separate identity it doubtless requires" (NAC, volume 203, file 16. Robin Harris, principal, Innis College, to Marshall McLuhan, 2 February 1965).

11   NAC, volume 203, file 16. Marshall McLuhan to Robin Harris, 5 February 1965.

12   NAC, volume 204, file 1.

13   NAC, Arthur Porter to W. J. Flinn, 2 April 1968.

14   NAC, volume 77, file 6. Ted Carpenter to Marshall McLuhan, n.d.

15   Wyndham Lewis's *The Childermass*, McLuhan observed, deals with accelerated media change as a type of massacre of innocents.

16   NAC, volume 77, file 9.

17   Ibid., Leon Wilson to Marshall McLuhan, 25 October 1962.

18   Ibid.

19   Ibid.

20   Ibid.

21   Ibid.

22   Ibid., Leon Wilson to Marshall McLuhan, 30 October 1962.

23   In lighter moments, McLuhan compared his message on media to that of a person interrupting neighbors at dinner and alerting them to a fire in their roof, only to find that they are annoyed at the interruption. He summarized the absurdity of the situation by asking: "How can one have a moral point of view about a burning house unless one has a special devotion to roast pig?" (NAC, Marshall McLuhan to John Rowan, 17 December 1969). Charles Lamb had written, "You want roast pig? Burn your house down." McLuhan loved the coincidence of Lamb and pig, as well as the sentiment. (Interview with Eric McLuhan.)

24   NAC, volume 77, file 9. Leon Wilson to Marshall McLuhan, 28 June 1963.

25   Interview with Eric McLuhan.

26   NAC, volume 77, file 9. David Segal to Marshall McLuhan, 12 July 1963.

27   Ibid., David Segal to Marshall McLuhan, 26 July 1963.

28 Ibid., David Segal to Marshall McLuhan, 23 August 1963.

29 *Understanding Media*, p329.

30 NAC, volume 77, file 9. David Segal to Marshall McLuhan, 11 September 1963.

31 NAC, Marshall McLuhan to Richard Berg, 16 November 1964.

32 NAC, volume 76, file 32.

33 Ibid.

34 Ibid.

35 Ibid. McLuhan's point was that the development of the balance wheel as a part of a clock mechanism transformed the wheel into a linear form for measuring time.

36 Ibid.

37 NAC, volume 77, file 9. Leon Wilson to Marshall McLuhan, 25 October 1962. Wilson reminds McLuhan of the offer in this letter. Basic English is an 850-word system designed for use as both an international auxiliary language and a means of clarifying thought. It was developed by Charles Kay Ogden, I. A. Richards's collaborator on *The Meaning of Meaning*. McLuhan learned of Basic English through Richards, who went on to develop the 500-word system of Every Man's English.

38 NAC, volume 77, file 9. Marshall McLuhan to David Segal, 8 September 1964.

39 Chapter two of *Understanding Media* is titled "Media Hot and Cold," but McLuhan usually prefers to make the contrast in terms of *hot* and *cool*. In a letter to Claude Bissell (NAC, 28 January 1966), McLuhan defines a cool medium as one in which the user shares in a creative process without any real merging in it.

40 Christopher Ricks, "Electronic Man," *New Statesman*, 11 December 1964.

41 Ibid. "And there is, too, a heady market for prophecies, especially those which skilfully and at the last moment substitute a sermon for a prophecy. Like Jacques Barzun, Mr. McLuhan has the suspenseful air of being about to lift the veil."

42 C. J. Fox, "Our Mass Communications," *Commonweal Review*, 16 October 1964.

43 Ronald Bates, "The Medium Is the Message," *The Tamarack Review* 33 (1964), pp79-86.

44 Arnold Rockman, "A rich, sprawling book," *Toronto Star*, 13 June 1964.

45 Lister Sinclair, "Understanding Media hard to understand," *The Globe Magazine*, 11 July 1964.

46 Alan Thomas, "Misunderstanding Media," *Toronto Telegram*, 22 August 1964.

47 Ibid.

48 Joseph B. Ford, "Letters to the Editor," *Time*, 10 July 1964.

49   Douglas Parker, "Reverse Canadian," *Riverside (California) Press-Enterprise*, 24 May 1964. This view arose out of passages from *Understanding Media* such as the following: "The achievements of the Western world, it is obvious, are testimony to the tremendous values of literacy. But many people are also disposed to object that we have purchased our structure of specialist technology and values at too high a price" (p84). In his public pronouncements and in correspondence, McLuhan reworked this theme in various forms such as the following: "In so far as print bias renders us helpless and ineffectual in the new electronic age, I am strongly inclined to cultivate the kinds of perception that are relevant to our state" (*Letters*, p302). From such statements commentators construed his stance as "anti-book." Yet in the same context, McLuhan noted: "Not that I am an anti-book person, or an anti-lineal thinker. If I have any normal and natural preferences, they are for the values of the literate world" (ibid.).

50   Feigen articulated his message through the medium of his dummy and achieved remarkable success in working with autistic children. An interesting echo of Feigen's work is to be found in McLuhan's comment on the ventriloquism of Edgar Bergen in *The Mechanical Bride*: "The big planning and executive agency — Bergen — appears to be mindless and unfeeling. The supposedly mindless robot — Charlie [McCarthy] appears to be acutely sensitive and conscious. It is in the unannounced interplay of perceptions like these that the power and appeal of this show consist" (*The Mechanical Bride*, p18).

51   Barrington Nevitt and Maurice McLuhan, eds., *Who Was Marshall McLuhan?* (Toronto: Stoddart Publishing, 1995), p198.

52   Gerald M. Feigen, "The McLuhan Festival," in George Sanderson and Frank Macdonald, eds., *Marshall McLuhan: The Man and His Message* (Golden, Colorado: Fulcrum, 1989), pp65-69, (p65).

53   Ibid., p66.

54   Ibid.

55   Ibid., p68.

56   Howard Luck Gossage, "You Can See Why the Mighty Would Be Curious," in Gerald Emanuel Stearn, ed., *McLuhan: Hot and Cool* (New York: Signet Books, 1969), pp20-30, (p25).

57   Feigen in Sanderson and Macdonald, p69.

58   Tom Wolfe, "Suppose he is what he sounds like . . .," in Gerald Emanuel Stearn, ed., *McLuhan: Hot and Cool* (New York: Signet Books, 1969), pp31-48, (p47).

59   Feigen in Sanderson and Macdonald, p69.

60   NAC, Marshall McLuhan to Lou Forsdale, 28 January 1965.

61   NAC, Marshall McLuhan to Peter Drucker, 2 February 1965.

62   NAC, Jonathan Miller to Marshall McLuhan, 28 April 1965.

63   NAC, Marshall McLuhan to Barbara Rowes, 9 August 1977.

64   NAC, Marshall McLuhan to Nils Treving, 12 November 1975.

65   *Understanding Media*, p314.

66   Ibid., p329.

67   Ibid.

68   NAC, Marshall McLuhan to Eric McLuhan, 15 March 1976.

69   NAC, Marshall McLuhan to Mitchell Sharp, 4 November 1964. Sharp replied: "It took politics and television to show me the value of my 'craggy unconventional countenance.'" (NAC, 16 November 1964).

70   *Understanding Media*, p332.

71   Ibid., p335.

72   NAC, Jonathan Miller to Marshall McLuhan, 28 April 1965. (emphasis added)

73   Marshall McLuhan to Hugo McPherson, *Letters*, p409.

74   NAC, Jonathan Miller to Marshall McLuhan, 28 April 1965. McLuhan never maintained that the scanning process is imposed on the TV viewer.

75   Ibid.

76   NAC, Marshall McLuhan to Jonathan Miller, 4 May 1965.

77   "Alan Williams was telling me that you reacted very favourably to the news that Jonathan Miller was writing a book about you for my series" (NAC, Frank Kermode to Marshall McLuhan, 25 June 1969).

78   *Letters*, p375.

79   NAC, Marshall McLuhan to Frank Kermode, 4 March 1971.

80   *Letters*, p440.

81   "Jonathan Miller has been continuing his anti-McLuhan crusade in the July 15th *Listener*. Having at last taken time to read his *McLuhan* book, I can honestly say I am amazed that he would take so much trouble to accomplish such a pitiable objective. He doesn't know what I am talking about because he has never taken a step outside the boundaries of visual space so dear to the positivist and the quantifier in these recent centuries. It all ended with Lewis Carroll and the new science of nuclear physics, to say nothing of poetry and the arts in this century. These things Miller has no inkling about, except as mysterious, irrational mythologies that he finds extremely repugnant. In the name of 19th century rationalism he mounts an anti-Catholic crusade against McLuhan in the spirit of the Rev. Paisley of Belfast . . . He belongs to the same vintage as Lewis Mumford who, likewise, cannot understand us at all" (NAC, Marshall McLuhan to Dave Dooley, 12 August 1971).

82   NAC, volume 23, file 79. Marshall McLuhan to Marshall Fishwick, 30 November 1972.

83   NAC, Marshall McLuhan to Barbara Rowes, 29 April 1976.

84   NAC, "Electroencephalographic aspects of low involvement: Implications for the McLuhan hypothesis," by Herbert E. Krugman,

21-23 May 1970. Krugman's report was published in *The Journal of Advertising Research*, volume 11, 1 February 1971.

85 Ibid.

86 Ibid.

87 "Herbert Krugman of General Electric Research Laboratories recently provided ample proof of the validity of the hypothesis, using encephalographic and head camera means of testing responses to various media. Being an ordinary run-of-the-mill psychologist, he was flabbergasted to discover that there was no brain-wave response to the content of these media, but a very large and diversified response to the diverse media themselves" (NAC, Marshall McLuhan to Frank Kermode, 4 March 1971).

88 NAC, Marshall McLuhan to Herbert Krugman, 25 June 1970.

89 Ibid.

90 Ibid.

91 York University, Canadian Speakers' and Writers' Service Archives (henceforth CSWS), file 229.

92 Ibid., file 230.

93 *Christian Science Monitor*, 20 March 1967.

94 NAC, Marshall McLuhan to Max Nanny, 8 April 1971.

95 NAC, Marshall McLuhan to Herbert Krugman, 13 January 1971.

96 York University, CSWS, file 244.

97 NAC, Marshall McLuhan to Bill Jovanovich, 26 October 1965. (emphasis added)

98 Ibid., n.d.

99 Norman Mailer, "Of a Small and Modest Malignancy, Wicked and Bristling with Dots," *Esquire*, November 1977, pp125-48, (p126).

11 – The Good Ground

1 NAC, Marshall McLuhan to Bonnie Brennan, executive director, National Catholic Communications Center, 28 October 1966.

2 NAC, Marshall McLuhan to Ruth Nanda Anshen, 26 January 1972.

3 Diary, 25 July 1967. Compare: "Apropos Pop Theology, the God who is dead, of course, is the Newtonian God, the visual image of a visually organized cosmos. With the dethronement of the visual sense by the audible-tactile media of radio and TV, religion, or the relating to the divine, can no longer have a primarily visual bias. The present irrelevance of our political and educational establishments stems from the same situation. God, of course, is not involved in any of this" (NAC, Marshall McLuhan to Marshall Fishwick, 5 January 1973).

4 NAC, Marshall McLuhan to Kristin L. Popik, 28 May 1971.

5 NAC, Allen Maruyama, "Conversation with Marshall McLuhan." To this McLuhan added "resistance to learning" and man being "threatened by understanding."

6   *Finnegans Wake*, page 81, line 1.

7   *Letters*, p450.

8   Marshall McLuhan to Bruce P. Tracy, ibid., p452.

9   Marshall McLuhan to Margaret Atwood, ibid., p457. Cf. Judith Fitzgerald, "McLuhan, not Atwood!" *Books in Canada*, vol. 24, no. 9 (December 1995), pp3-5.

10 NAC, Marshall McLuhan to Bill Kuhns, 5 January 1970.

11 "Somewhat amazed at the conversation you report in Appendix I. 'The user is the content' — always — so that the hearer who has ears to hear is able to respond to the revealed word because of the content of his own being. There is a good deal of this sort of observation in the Acts, chapters 16-17. The message is the effect on the general society, whereas the meaning is the effect on the individual, but don't say that I think 'the medium has no content'! All media are mythical in the strict sense of being artificial fictions, and forms designed to enhance or speed human transactions. [re: resistance to learning] [You] seem to have forgotten your own contribution here! After we had discussed phonetically literate man as the only private individual in human history, you mentioned that the reluctance (of this type) of Western man to consider the effects of his own technologies upon his psyche and society was his simple resistance to any invasion of privacy. Let us recall how violently people resisted and resented Jung and Freud when they invaded our privacy. I see no reason, however, to suppose that the Christian is more inclined to study these matters than the non-Christian" (NAC, Marshall McLuhan to Allen Maruyama, 11 January 1972).

12 Marshall McLuhan to Robert J. Leuver, *Letters*, pp386-87.

13 NAC, Marshall McLuhan to Walter Ong, 18 December 1969.

14 NAC, Marshall McLuhan to Allen Maruyama, 31 December 1971.

15 NAC, Marshall McLuhan to Alexis de Beauregard, 11 May 1972.

16 Ibid.

17 Diary, 21 May 1972.

18 NAC, Etienne Gilson to L. K. Shook, 8 June 1972.

19 NAC, Marshall McLuhan to L. K. Shook, 20 June 1972.

20 NAC, Marshall McLuhan to William Wimsatt, 22 January 1973. Compare: "'Antichrist' in Nietzsche seems to mean that when the bureaucratic mode of the Catholic church is pushed to its limit, it flips into Antichrist. This seems to have been the view of James Joyce in *Dubliners*" (NAC, Marshall McLuhan to David Staines, 2 June 1977).

21 NAC, Marshall McLuhan to Larry Henderson (*The Catholic Register*), 20 October 1975.

22 NAC, Marshall McLuhan to Clare Boothe Luce, 7 January 1976.

23 This discovery was in *Understanding Media*, but at a lower level of integration with McLuhan's other discoveries twelve years earlier.

24 NAC, Marshall McLuhan to Barbara Rowes, 29 April 1976.

25 Interview with Eric McLuhan.

26 York University, CSWS Archive.

27 *The Mechanical Bride*, p11.

28 NAC, volume 64.

29 NAC, volume 38, file 81. "Candor in Canada" (*Time*, n.d.).

30 York University, CSWS Archive, Bob Ellis to Marshall McLuhan, 22 February 1966.

31 Ibid.

32 NAC, Ralph Baldwin to Marshall and Corinne McLuhan, 21 June 1966.

33 *Letters*, p175.

34 "Visually, the hour was almost as exciting as the ideas it showcased. In a remarkable blend of techniques, even his most theoretical ideas were given apt visual expression. Film clips of McLuhan talking, his face lit from odd angles in strange shifting colors, were interspersed with narration behind montage effects and a kaleidoscopic use of patterns . . ." (Chris Condon, "McLuhan the Magnificent," *The National Catholic Reporter*, 29 March 1967).

35 Diary, 19 July 1967.

36 Marshall McLuhan to Wilfred and Sheila Watson, *Letters*, p347.

37 John Culkin, "Marshall's New York Adventure," in George Sanderson and Frank Macdonald, eds., *Marshall McLuhan: The Man and His Message* (Golden, Colorado: Fulcrum, 1989), pp99-110, (p99).

38 Diary, 31 August 1967.

39 John Culkin, in Sanderson & Macdonald, p107.

40 Ibid., p108.

41 Diary, 25 November 1967.

42 Interview with Corinne McLuhan.

43 "During my year at Fordham I had very little contact with New York University, as a result of my low noise level tolerance since the operation" (NAC, Marshall McLuhan to Neil Postman, 24 October 1968).

44 "Each [thunder] is an index to the human and institutional changes which occur with each technological innovation" (NAC, Marshall McLuhan to Tim Bost, 28 January 1974).

45 *Letters*, p346.

46 Ibid., p347.

47 NAC, Marshall McLuhan to Harry Skornia, 14 December 1967.

48 *Letters*, p346.

49 Diary, 25 December 1967.

50 John Culkin, in Sanderson & Macdonald, p107.

51 Interview with Corinne McLuhan.

52 John Culkin in Sanderson & Macdonald, p107.

53 Michael Horowitz, "McLuhan among the Catholics," *Westside News and Free Press*, 14 December 1967.

54 There were notable exceptions. The *Globe and Mail*'s Kay Kritzwiser wrote: "The internationally known communications authority and author of *The Gutenberg Galaxy* is winning a wider audience for his revolutionary views on the concept of language in the electronic age" (*The Globe Magazine*, 4 January 1964). Most reports did not pick up on this dimension of McLuhan's work, much less emphasize it.

55 Ron Poulton, "Joys of Wychwood," *Toronto Sun Magazine*, 23 May 1976.

56 NAC, Marshall McLuhan to Claire Smith, Harold Ober Associates, New York, 30 October 1968.

57 *Letters*, p375.

58 NAC, Marshall McLuhan to Vince Lackner, 8 November 1974.

59 Diary, 2 July 1973.

60 NAC, volume 7, file 23. 3 November 1977.

61 NAC, Marshall McLuhan to Maurice McLuhan, 12 December 1968.

62 Ibid.

63 University of Toronto president Claude Bissell feared that McLuhan would stay in the United States after his year at Fordham. Bissell made McLuhan a verbal offer of the presidency of a college within the University of Toronto's system of federated colleges, but McLuhan turned this down, knowing that he would detest administrative duties. Corinne had told Bissell of the offers McLuhan had received from a number of U.S. colleges and universities. (Interview with Corinne McLuhan.)

64 NAC, Arthur Porter to W. J. Flinn, 2 May 1968.

65 Editorial, *Maclean's*, 17 March 1980.

65 NAC, volume 203, file 16. Margaret Stewart to Office of Chief Accountant, University of Toronto, 29 May 1969.

67 NAC, volume 203, file 16. 2 May 1969.

68 NAC, Tom Hedley to Marshall McLuhan, 8 April 1968.

69 NAC, "The Man in the Mask: Pierre Trudeau," 1968.

70 28 October 1968.

71 Kildare Dobbs, "The McLuhan view of Pierre Trudeau," *Toronto Daily Star*, 19 November 1968.

72 *Letters*, p352.

73 Ibid., p354.

74 Ibid.

75 Ibid., p357.

76 Ibid.

77 "The method of presentation you have used is, I think, your most effective. These sharp, pithy utterances, disposed around a group of concrete examples, whether poems or pictures, do compel the reader to attend to some of the possibilities that you are so constantly putting before him, and, if I may say so, affront his prejudices and fling him back upon his

reservations to the minimum extent" (NAC, Cleanth Brooks to Marshall McLuhan, 11 September 1968).

78 Marshall McLuhan to George Steiner, *Letters*, p361.

79 NAC, volume 6, file 8. 4 June 1969.

80 NAC, Marshall McLuhan to Richard Berg, 1 Aug 1969.

81 *Letters*, p362.

82 Ibid., p368-69.

83 Ibid., p384.

84 Richard Brown to *Globe and Mail* (NAC, draft of letter, 23 June 1980).

85 French-born architect, painter, and designer René Cera was chief architect for the T. Eaton Company. McLuhan met Cera through a Winnipeg friend, Betty Trott, who became Cera's wife.

86 He learned quickly, and Marshall was pleased: "Red is a great resource man here at the Centre and enables me to get on with writing with Mrs. Stewart while he encounters the public and pursues media studies" (NAC, Marshall McLuhan to Teri McLuhan, 11 September 1969).

87 NAC, volume 204, file 8. Maurice started at the Centre on 18 August 1969 and left on 30 April 1972.

88 "That's what Marshall did for me. He enabled me to come to grips with ideas that were quite different and quite innovative, as far as any other approach had been. And I stumbled onto one or two leads in this and began to see the worthwhileness of his whole approach. You could understand any civilization, any age at any particular time, and understand the technologies that were directing their activity" (Interview with Maurice McLuhan.)

89 Author's personal communication with Professor Henry Schogt.

90 Marshall McLuhan to Robert J. Leuver, *Letters*, p386.

12 – To the Four Corners of the Global Village

1 Interview with Eric McLuhan.

2 "Commercials become villains at communications conference," *Globe and Mail*, 25 August 1973.

3 *Culture Is Our Business*, p7.

4 The front *and* back covers of the book were executed as a parody of the "Man in the Hathaway Shirt" ads.

5 NAC, Marshall McLuhan to Bill Jovanovich, 23 July 1970.

6 Marshall McLuhan and Joseph Keogh, "Salt and scandal in the Gospels," *Explorations* 26 (December 1969), pp82-85.

7 NAC, volume 28, file 12.

8 Ibid.

9 "What your review seems to assume is that I do have a personal feeling about these things and about my public . . . My metaphysical approach is not moral. That is why I get such very great joy from contemplating these forms of culture. Your review overlooks this side of my work and teaching.

The language of forms is a source of perpetual joy and discovery that is quite inexhaustible . . . To say that [*Culture Is Our Business*] is 'the last of the modern movement that began with Eliot and Joyce' is meaningless unless we are to think of abandoning the quest for forms altogether . . . I am a metaphysician, interested in the life of the forms and their surprising modalities. That is why I have no interest at all in the academic world and its attempts at tidying up experience . . . By the way, it is not flattering to say 'his observations on the current political scene seem straight out of George Orwell.' I have always regarded Orwell as a complete ass, lacking all perception and understanding. The political scene on which he comments is something that was going on 100 years ago. Apropos my 'outrageous puns' have you never considered that the pun is itself a metaphysical technique for 'swarming over' the diversity of perception that is in any part of language?" (NAC, Marshall McLuhan to Joe Keogh, volume 28, file 12).

10   NAC, Joe Keogh to Marshall McLuhan, 11 July 1970.

11   NAC, Wilfred Watson to Marshall McLuhan, 29 June 1960.

12   "I found I was completely swallowed up by the cliché archetype book when I started to work on it in May. I seemed to be probing into mysteries so deep that I wondered if the book mightn't demand a total sacrifice if I went further. So I halted. I followed out the atomic fission/fusion analogy [already in *Understanding Media*, page 50] with most illuminating results, especially re: archetype and atomic fusion. Thus Frye's ironic mode appears to be a grate or oven in which to disintegrate the archetype into cliché . . ." (NAC, Wilfred Watson to Marshall McLuhan, 3 September, n.y).

13   Interview with Corinne McLuhan.

14   "Collaboration is very difficult. I'm not sure *From Cliché to Archetype* was very successful. I didn't understand much of what we were saying, and I'm not sure he did. We spent most of the time 'dialoguing' and took very little time to write it. He thought that all we would have to do was to dialogue in front of a secretary, who could record it, and of course that couldn't work . . . You have to think to write, of course, but thinking and writing are not the same thing" (H. J. Kirchhoff, "Poetry and drama: it all adds up." *Globe and Mail*, 9 February 1989, page A13. Includes interview with Wilfred Watson where the quotation appears).

15   "[*From Cliché to Archetype*] is a paradox from beginning to end. It is the clichés that are alive, and the archetypes that are dead" (NAC, Marshall McLuhan to Ted Carpenter, 9 April 1969).

16   NAC, Marshall McLuhan to Pete Buckner, 19 June 1974.

17   *From Cliché to Archetype*, p21.

18   *Letters*, p375.

19   McLuhan felt that *From Cliché to Archetype* dealt with the theme that

Hegel had missed. "Hegel, in his famous triad of thesis, antithesis and synthesis, missed [media law] number three, namely that there is an unforeseeable retrieval of some previously discarded human mode of action or awareness when innovation occurs, e.g. in the age of electricity we retrieve the occult, just as in the Gutenberg time, while they were pursuing primitive Christianity, there was a huge retrieval of pagan antiquity. The failure of Hegel and Marx to notice this unavoidable dynamic of backwash and retrieval was fatal to the Russian revolution of 1917. With the innovation of Western specialism and organization came (in Russia) a great nostalgic wave for an earlier form of feudalism" (NAC, Marshall McLuhan to A. Richard Barber, 19 December 1973).

20 NAC, Marshall McLuhan to Alex Brazynetz, 21 October 1974. *From Cliché to Archetype* was translated into French as *Du cliché à l'archétype* by Derrick de Kerckhove. It also appeared in an Italian translation by Francesca Valente and Carla Pezzini under the title *Dal cliché all'archetipo: l'uomo tecnològico nel villaggio globale*.

21 Diary, 19 May 1974.

22 "Asking Jacqueline Ridley a translation for figure/ground, suddenly realized whole of cliché/archetype is figure/ground" (Diary, 26 May 1974). McLuhan also made a connection between figure/ground analysis and Northrop Frye's archetypes: "[The] Frye literary strategy is to elevate C-M oral cult *ground* into C/M *figures*, e.g., the sea, or the seasons, or the womb become literary figures of rhetorical, mental postures" (NAC, volume 172, file 7).

23 "So far as I can discover, the European structuralists work with a set of archetypes as paradigms. This ensures that there be a minimum of exploration and a maximum of mere matching in their activities" (NAC, Marshall McLuhan to James M. Curtis, 27 September 1972).

24 Pages 7ff., 15, 85ff., 118, 128-29.

25 P7ff.

26 Pp128-29.

27 "Surely the problem with the phenomenologists, including Frye, is that they present only figure minus ground, in the strictly 'left hemisphere' tradition. In Piaget's *Structuralism* he explains that with figure-ground there is no need for archetypes. They can be seen as the existential results of the interplay of figure and ground. This was the work of Descartes in throwing aside rhetorical decorum and the public in favour of the pure ideas minus any ground. It is the hang-up of Hegel and all that followed from him, including Lévi-Strauss" (NAC, Marshall McLuhan to Cleanth Brooks, 16 May 1977).

28 Marshall McLuhan to D. Carlton Williams, *Letters*, p417.

29 NAC, Marshall McLuhan to Yves Doré, 13 December 1976.

30 As opposed to *data*. The distinction is maintained by G. Spencer Brown

in *Laws of Form* (Toronto: Bantam Books, 1973, p*xxi*) following R. D. Laing's suggestion: "Laing suggests that what in empirical science are called *data*, being in a real sense *arbitrarily* chosen by the nature of the hypothesis already formed, could more honestly be called *capta*."

31 NAC, Marshall McLuhan to Herbert Krugman, 13 January 1971.
32 NAC, Marshall McLuhan to David Sohn, 3 February 1971.
33 *New York Times Review of Books*, 13 December 1970.
34 *Understanding Media*, p66.
35 *Toronto Daily Star*, 30 December 1970.
36 *Letters*, p414.
37 NAC, Marshall McLuhan to Donald Theall, 6 August 1970.
38 NAC, Marshall McLuhan to McGill-Queen's University Press, 11 August 1970.
39 NAC, Marshall McLuhan to Susan Stewart, promotion manager, McGill-Queen's University Press, 7 April 1971.
40 NAC, Joe Keogh to Marshall McLuhan, 1 April 1969.
41 "Vos idées sont trop importantes et trop vitalement intéressantes pour qu'on en débatte à la TV, surtout avec un sorbonnard, aveugle volontaire. Je ne sais si l'humour de vos interventions a été compris . . . Une lecture des pénétrantes réflexions de Philarete Chasles (1798-1873) sur les 25 signes phonétiques de l'alphabet, lecture faite par hasard dans les années trente, m'avait sensibilisé sur vos problèmes et je subodorais ces choses qui font l'intérêt passionnant de la *Galaxie*" (NAC, volume 148, file 23, René Giard, 11 July 1972).
42 NAC, Sam Sorbara to Marshall McLuhan, 3 October 1969.
43 Cy Jameson, "Now We Know: McLuhan Was Right," *The Reporter*, June 1976, pp12-13.
44 NAC, volume 10, file 33. Raymer B. Matson, "The Christian and McLuhan," 1968.
45 It sent the other half into hysterics, scoffing at McLuhan's naiveté. Samuel L. Becker, "Viewpoint: McLuhan as Rorschach," *Journal of Broadcasting* 19: 2 (1975), p237.
46 Ibid.
47 Ibid.
48 "closure *or* equilibrium-seeking" (*Understanding Media*, p44, emphasis added); "closure *or* completion of image" (*Understanding Media*, p331, emphasis added).
49 NAC, volume 10, file 16.
50 Ibid.
51 "Except for light, all other media come in pairs, with one acting as the 'content' of the other, obscuring the operation of both" (*Understanding Media*, p52).
52 "Conversation with Marshall McLuhan," *Videography*, October 1977.

53   *Understanding Media*, p329.

54   Bob Cohen, "Marshall McLuhan Is Alive and Well," *Windsor Star*, 25 October 1975.

55   *Marshall McLuhan*, Santa Susana Press (California State University: Northridge, CA), 1975.

56   Diary, 5 July 1972.

57   D. A. N. Jones, "The Media in Sunderland," *The Listener*, 26 October 1967.

58   Ibid.

59   Ibid.

60   NAC, volume 10, file 17.

61   Ibid.

62   NAC, volume 8, file 37.

63   M. P. Scott, "McLuhan Brilliance just too blinding," Letter to *Montreal Star*, 7 December 1974.

64   James Lincoln Collier, "Sex and the Western World: McLuhan's Misunderstanding," *Village Voice*, 7 September 1967.

65   NAC, volume 12, file 73. Henry Venable to Melvin Krausberg.

66   "Asst. Prof. M. McLuhan," "I Predict," *National Lampoon*, July 1973.

67   NAC, volume 2, files 1-38.

68   Ibid.

69   Ibid.

70   Only a summer trip to Japan was canceled when the doctors cautioned of the effect that intense heat could have on McLuhan's condition. (NAC, Marshall McLuhan to Robert B. Shea, 9 July 1971.)

71   NAC, Marshall McLuhan to Richard Berg, 10 March 1971.

72   NAC, Marshall McLuhan to Sam D. Neill, 12 September 1972.

73   Interview with Corinne McLuhan.

74   "Barry Nevitt and I have really got the remainder of the book written. In fact, we have about 1000 pages of book. We plan to keep it down to about 200, for final form . . . This is going to be a real shaker of a book . . . The fact that we really have discovered all the basic patterns and problems and answers for every kind of organization, regardless of ideology or geography, inspires levity rather than gravity" (NAC, Marshall McLuhan to Bill Jovanovich, 14 February 1970).

75   NAC, Marshall McLuhan to Charles Silberman, 23 August 1972.

76   NAC, Marshall McLuhan to Bill Jovanovich, 12 September 1972.

77   Interview with Eric McLuhan.

78   NAC, Marshall McLuhan to Claire Smith, 4 May 1971.

79   NAC, Marshall McLuhan to Pete Buckner, 7 December 1970.

80   NAC, Bill Jovanovich to Matie Molinaro, 29 November 1972.

81   NAC, Eric McLuhan to Barrington Nevitt, 21 June 1971.

82   NAC, Barrington Nevitt to Eric McLuhan, 9 July 1971.

83   NAC, Marshall McLuhan to Sam D. Neill, 12 September 1972.
84   NAC, Marshall McLuhan to Don and Louise Cowan, 13 May 1975.
85   Ibid.
86   Mavor Moore, "The prophet as performer," *Globe and Mail*, 3 June 1972.
87   Diary, 3 June 1972.
88   NAC, Marshall McLuhan to Sam Neill, 12 September 1972.
89   "I certainly did not get a clear message about a shift to 'full understanding.' This came across in *Counterblast*. It may be hidden in discussion of the figure-ground interplay. It may also be hidden in references to human scale, but the idea of comprehensivity is not made, it seems to me" (NAC, Sam D. Neill to Marshall McLuhan, 15 September 1972).
90   NAC, Kamala Bhatia to Marshall McLuhan, 18 November 1972. For Bhatia, who addressed McLuhan as "Dr. McLuhan Gurujee," these discoveries offset the factual inaccuracy in his account of Buddhism, the sort of error his critics were more often likely to seize on as evidence of sloppy scholarship: "[Re: correction to *Take Today*, p198] Buddhism did not enter India with the Moslems in the 16th century; historically Buddhism came with the Buddha in 653 B.C., while the Moslem religion was born in 700 A.D. and did not reach India till 1000 A.D." (NAC, Kamala Bhatia to Marshall McLuhan, 1 December 1974).
91   NAC, Marshall McLuhan to Bill Jovanovich, 9 November 1973.
92   NAC, Marshall McLuhan to John Eberhard, 16 November 1973.
93   NAC, Marshall McLuhan to Bill Jovanovich, 31 October 1973.
94   NAC, Bill Jovanovich to Marshall McLuhan, 6 November 1973.
95   NAC, Marshall McLuhan to Bill Jovanovich, 9 November 1973.
96   NAC, Marshall McLuhan to Bill Jovanovich, 6 August 1976.
97   NAC, Marshall McLuhan to Jerome Agel, 27 March 1978.
98   NAC, Marshall McLuhan to M. C. Schumiatcher, 5 May 1972.
99   Diary, 25 May 1972.
100   Diary, 2 August 1972.
101   Marshall McLuhan to the Editor, *Toronto Daily Star*, 24 July 1974.
102   Ibid. (emphasis added)
103   Ibid.
104   Ibid.
105   Ibid.
106   Ibid.
107   Ibid.
108   "There is panic in abortion thinking: McLuhan," *Toronto Daily Star*, 31 July 1974.
109   *Toronto Daily Star*, 30 September 1976.
110   Diary, 29 September 1976; *Toronto Daily Star*, 30 September 1976.
111   NAC, Marshall McLuhan to Ruth Nanda Anshen, 5 February 1971.
112   NAC, Marshall McLuhan to Ted Carpenter, 4 January 1972.

113   NAC, Marshall McLuhan to Ruth Nanda Anshen, 26 January 1972.

114   "Long ago I thought of it as a series of 1,000 word essays on key figures. The 1,000 words would provide ample space in which to interweave the influences and patterns which they shared and created" (ibid.).

115   Ibid. (emphasis added)

116   NAC, Marshall McLuhan to T. C. Clark, 26 July 1974.

117   NAC, Marshall McLuhan to Ruth Nanda Anshen, 1 November 1973.

118   NAC, Marshall McLuhan to Pete Buckner, 2 January 1974.

119   NAC, Marshall McLuhan to Pete Buckner, 19 June 1974.

120   Ibid.

121   Interview with Corinne McLuhan.

122   NAC, Sister Jeanne Louise Parish to Marshall McLuhan, 4 May 1972.

123   NAC, Marshall McLuhan to Sister Jeanne Louise Parish, 19 April 1972.

124   Ibid.

125   On April 14, before the McLuhans left Hawaii, Clare Boothe Luce hosted a luncheon in McLuhan's honor. This stimulating occasion dispelled some of his disappointment from the previous day, as did a dinner with Leon Edel and his wife. Edel told McLuhan that his observations on Henry James and the typewriter were "right on."

126   Diary, 26 July 1972.

127   NAC, Marshall McLuhan to Frank Taylor, McGraw-Hill editor in chief, 15 November 1968.

128   Ibid.

129   "Another book of mine which is due out in the Summer or Fall is my doctoral dissertation (Cambridge) which I am planning to title 'Cicero to Joyce.' It is the study of the tradition of eloquence achieved by encyclopedism, which I refer to in the essay 'James Joyce Trivial and Quadrivial'" (NAC, Marshall McLuhan to Barry Day, McCann-Erickson Advertising, London, 4 February 1970).

130   NAC, R. I. K. Davidson, editor, University of Toronto Press, to Marshall McLuhan, 8 May 1974.

131   Ibid.

132   Diary, 14 May 1974.

133   Eric McLuhan to Marshall McLuhan, 22 February 1976.

134   "I propose therefore that you scrap any idea of junking the thesis — it's really a VERY useable piece of work, even AS IT STANDS!. . . I will today begin on this: i.e., will start up the set of folders (subject to revision by you) and begin poking notes and bibliographic items in them" (NAC, Eric McLuhan to Marshall McLuhan, 17 September 1976).

135   NAC, volume 62, file 24. Here McLuhan is contrasting the "centre *minus* margin" (C-M) approach, as part of the grammatical component of the trivium, an approach that assumes acoustic space and multiple centers without defined peripheries, and which is, therefore an *integral* approach,

to the "centre with margin" (C/M) approach, which is *fragmentary*. C/A is an abbreviation for the cliché/archetype process and may be read here as "retrieval." "Nature Linnaeus" refers to the concept of nature *as in* the works of Linnaeus or Carl Linné (1707-78), a Swedish scholar who was the founder of modern botany. McLuhan's formulaic note may be paraphrased with appropriate expansions as follows: "The Scholastics of the Middle Ages had declared war against grammar, traditional grammar, patristic grammar . . . Ramus and his crowd were driving their panzers, as it were, into that territory to reduce the amount of territory held by those old guys. They wanted to introduce their own kind of grammar, dialectical grammar. [But] with Gutenberg this flips into a retrieval of pagan antiquity and the disappearance of Scholasticism . . ." (Interview with Eric McLuhan).

136 NAC, Ian Montagnes to Marshall McLuhan, 21 September 1978.
137 Bret and his wife Jane, a teacher and writer from Texas, became friends of the McLuhans when an article she had written on the Catholic liturgy and media attracted McLuhan's attention.
138 Marshall McLuhan to Tom and Dorothy Easterbrook, *Letters*, p454.
139 Ibid., p455.
140 Ibid., p432.
141 NAC, volume 148, file 6.
142 Interview with Bob Logan.
143 Diary, 27 March 1972.
144 Interview with Kathy Hutchon Kawasaki.
145 NAC, Marshall McLuhan to Izzy Abrahami, 16 November 1972.
146 Bella Stumbo, "McLuhan Delivers His Media Message," *Los Angeles Times*, 28 February 1972.
147 NAC, Marshall McLuhan to Jitendra Kumar, 17 November 1972.
148 Diary, 26 September 1972.
149 Diary, 27 September 1972.
150 NAC, Marshall McLuhan to Father John Kelly, 12 November 1973.
151 NAC, Father John Kelly to Marshall McLuhan, 13 November 1973.
152 "Marshall was resented by people at the University of Toronto because he enjoyed his work and used techniques they could not touch. He was not a threat to anyone" (Interview with Bob Logan). One colleague, in a moment of pique and unusual candor, exclaimed, "You know why we hate you Marshall? It's because you're getting all this fame when so many bet-ter-qualified men are not" (Interview with Eric McLuhan).
153 Diary, 4 October 1973.
154 Diary, 23 March 1973; "All that Toffler is trying to say about future shock is that breakthrough is breakdown. For years I have been explaining that every breakdown is a breakthrough. Toffler prefers the ordinary journal-istic line of moral dismay instead of intellectual grasp" (NAC, Marshall McLuhan to Tom Hedley, 7 October 1970). "My own students, like

Hugh Kenner and Walter Ong (not to mention Alvin Toffler) write popular books using my material by the simple expedient of eliminating the hidden *ground* of effects" (NAC, Marshall McLuhan to Kaj Spencer, 8 November 1977); Diary, 8 April 1973; ibid.

155 McLuhan wrote to Bell Canada in December 1977 to complain about delays of three to six seconds between the end of dialing a number and receiving a ring signal. He received a reply noting that no such complaint had ever been registered by any other subscriber. The company also sent him technical information about control switching systems, to which he replied that "the people involved in the study have never paid any attention to the effects of any medium whatever," adding that "the telephone is the most prominent of these discarnate instruments" (NAC, Marshall McLuhan to J. E. Skinner, 31 January 1978). By contrast, he wrote to British writer John Wain: "God bless the telephone . . ." (*Letters*, p407).

156 Interview with Tom and Jeannine Langan.

157 "I always open a book on page 69 or 96. Your equation on page 96 applies to me 100%. I am 'self-looped,' but good!" (NAC, Marshall McLuhan to Arthur Porter, 24 July 1970); "I want to get down a few words about why I found *The Winter in the Hills* a great delight. I have opened at page 127 at random . . . (Marshall McLuhan to John Wain, *Letters*, p407).

158 Interview with Eric McLuhan.

159 Marshall McLuhan to Jerome Agel, 15 June 1973.

160 NAC, Marshall McLuhan to Louise Cowan, 20 December 1974. Eric had been reading Sterne with a view to writing his Ph.D. thesis on *Tristram Shandy*. Eric and his father made the discovery of the five divisions of rhetoric in Sterne together.

161 Diary, 13 April 1974.

162 NAC, Marshall McLuhan to Christine Breech, 9 November 1976.

163 NAC, Marshall McLuhan to Ralph Cohen, 18 March 1975. Compare: "I think that the reason why awareness of the five divisions [of rhetoric] tended to get submerged in the later 18th century was owing to the steady pressure of Gutenberg lineality. The parts of the rhetoric are sequential, but the divisions are simultaneous; and whatever is simultaneous tends to be contrary to the Gutenberg pressure" (Marshall McLuhan to Ralph and Libby Cohen, 15 September 1978).

164 NAC, volume 62, file 24.

165 "It seems to me that this structure [of the epyllion or little epic] is quite conscious and deliberate in the sonnet as aetiological epic. The epyllion [which] has the form of *The Rape of the Lock*, as well as Tennyson's *Idylls*, seems to interest nobody. I came across the matter in Marjorie Crump's *The Epyllion from Theocritus to Ovid*. It seems to me that it is used by Eliot, Pound, and Joyce, everywhere. Why has Ovid been banished structurally?" (NAC, Marshall McLuhan to M. C. (Muriel) Bradbrook, 21 May 1974).

166   NAC, Marshall McLuhan to Ralph and Libby Cohen, 15 September 1978.

167   Diary, 22 April 1975.

168   NAC, Gene Bier to Marshall McLuhan, 10 September 1976.

169   Diary, 23 March 1974; NAC, volume 6, file 8; Diary, 19 April 1974; Eric, Liz, and Michael; Diary, 19 February 1974.

170   Diary, 30 May 1974.

171   Ibid.

172   Interview with Eric McLuhan.

173   NAC, Marshall McLuhan to Lou Forsdale, 21 June 1974.

174   Interview with Eric McLuhan.

175   Diary, 31 December 1974.

176   Diary, 28 January 1975.

177   Diary, 4 February 1975.

178   "The christening went off triumphantly, and Emily made a suitable operatic sound as Satan was being expelled from her forever!" (NAC, Marshall McLuhan to Patricia and Norman Ellis, 17 June 1975).

179   NAC, Marshall McLuhan to Pete Buckner, 14 May 1975. McLuhan was at the University of Dallas from 10 April to 10 May and returned briefly to lecture again at the end of October. The added incentive to making these trips was the chance to visit with Eric, now enrolled in a Ph.D. program at the University of Dallas.

180   Diary, 20 April 1975.

181   Diary, 1 July 1975.

182   Diary, 5 December 1975.

183   Diary, 5 January 1976.

184   Marshall McLuhan to Sheila Watson, *Letters*, p516.

185   "People who criticize McLuhan don't understand that science is about failure. McLuhan was never afraid to be wrong" (Interview with Bob Logan).

186   Marshall McLuhan and R. K. Logan, "Alphabet, Mother of Invention," *Et Cetera*, December 1977, pp373-83; Robert K. Logan and Marshall McLuhan, "The double bind of communication and the world problematique," *Human Futures*, Summer 1979, pp1-3. McLuhan and Logan were collaborating on a book when McLuhan died. The research they completed together is summarized by Logan in a chapter entitled "Axiomatics of the Innis-McLuhan Approach" in his book *The Alphabet Effect* (New York: Morrow, 1986).

187   "Yesterday I was told by the Dean of Graduate Studies that because I was born on July 21, I would have an extra year before retirement, so I shall retire officially in 1977. However, I am to be allowed three additional years in charge of the Centre" (NAC, Marshall McLuhan to Pete Buckner, 17 June 1976).

188   NAC, Marshall McLuhan to Eric McLuhan, 14 May 1976.

189   Diary, 10 May 1976.

190   Ibid.

191   Unknown to Allen, this was the name of one of the aunts of Elsie McLuhan.

192   Interview with Matie Molinaro.

193   *Letters*, p520; NAC, Woody Allen to Marshall McLuhan, 2 September 1976; NAC, Jerome Agel to Marshall and Corinne McLuhan, 31 December 1976; NAC, Mark Adams to Marshall McLuhan, 8 October 1978; NAC, Marshall McLuhan to Jerome Agel, 5 January 1977; Diary, 24 May 1977.

194   Interview with Eric McLuhan.

195   Interview with Kathy Hutchon Kawasaki.

196   28 November 1977.

197   Interview with Eric McLuhan.

198   Interview with Bob Logan.

199   Trudeau drew the line at McLuhan's suggestions on humor: "I have my doubts about the sort of jokes you mention [for defusing English-French tensions in Canada]. I am thinking of the 'Polish' jokes which I do not believe have helped the Western view of people of Polish extraction, nor have the 'Newfie' jokes helped the image of the people of our tenth province. Perhaps jokes about the situation and not about the cultural differences would help; however, I do not envision hiring gag-writers in the near future" (NAC, Pierre Trudeau to Marshall McLuhan, 14 August 1978).

200   NAC, Marshall McLuhan to Fritz Wilhelmsen, 5 November 1976.

201   Interview with Eric McLuhan.

202   NAC, Marshall McLuhan to Don and Louise Cowan, 25 November 1976.

203   NAC, Marshall McLuhan to Eric McLuhan, 15 September 1976.

204   NAC, Marshall McLuhan to Eric McLuhan, 8 March 1977.

205   NAC, volume 160, file 19. Stevan R. Harnad to Marshall McLuhan, 12 March 1973.

206   NAC, Marshall McLuhan to Stevan R. Harnad, 4 July 1978.

207   NAC, Marshall McLuhan to Kaj Spencer, 8 November 1977.

208   Ibid.

209   Interview with Eric McLuhan.

210   ". . . only to discover that it is not *connected* in the sense of any visual or lineal relationship. The syllogism, as the word *copula* declares, is actually a form of intercourse minus connection. It is an interface, as the word *supposition* indicates, but not a connection, i.e. 'logical connection' is only a metaphor" (Marshall McLuhan to Roger Poole, 27 February 1978).

211   The term *myth* is found in McLuhan's writings in its classical and literary sense of a reconciliation of opposites and in the commoner sense: "All

media are mythical in the sense of being artificial fictions and forms designed to enhance or speed human transactions" (NAC, Marshall McLuhan to Allen Maruyama, 11 January 1972; cf. *Letters*, p292). Both senses apply in McLuhan's description of his Myth and Media course: "It is from the field of English itself that most of the coordinating is done. It approaches media as environmental services which, in the twentieth century, provide the *ground* for politics, business, entertainment and education alike [hence McLuhan's own forays into each of these domains]. To study the effects of this 'hidden' ground [in quotation marks because McLuhan insisted it is visible to anyone who will abandon the concept approach for the percept approach] on all other activities of our time is the somewhat unique program of this course. All other courses in communication study not the *ground* but the 'inputs' of content of the conventional media. They ignore the transforming action of the hidden ground as it interplays with the visible technologies and their programs. Myth and Media is concerned with the archetypal structures that emerge with electric speeds of environmental service and information."

212   NAC, Marshall McLuhan to Clare Boothe Luce, 7 January 1976; Marshall McLuhan to Joe Foyle, 18 July 1979.
213   Diary, 13 August 1978.
214   NAC, volume 171, file 20.
215   For all his travels, McLuhan turned down over three hundred invitations to speak between 1970 and 1976. (Interview with Eric McLuhan.)
216   Diary, 20 January 1978.
217   Diary, 3 March 1978.
218   Diary, 17 October 1978.
219   Diary, 8 December 1978. "They were left hemisphere people and simply frozen by prospect of right hemisphere dominance."
220   Diary, 18 December 1978.
221   Diary, 19 December 1978.

13 – The Final Vortex

1   NAC, Marshall McLuhan to Muriel Bradbrook, 18 April 1979. McLuhan's "Figures and Grounds in Linguistic Criticism," a review of Mario J. Valdes and Owen J. Miller, *Interpretation of Narrative* (Toronto: University of Toronto Press, 1978), appeared in *Et Cetera* 36, 3 (1979), pp289-94.
2   Interview with Eric McLuhan.
3   Poole stayed with the McLuhans in November 1978, while attending a conference at York University: "I shall never, ever forget looking out of the windows of St. Clair subway station in the midst of that blizzard on 27th November and seeing you both draw up in your car cool as cucumbers, as if nothing had happened . . . Sitting there, drawing diagrams about Ricoeur on metaphor and Derrida on figure and ground, as the snow fell

and fell. Wonderful. Corinne providing drinks and cheer and encouragement. And the Distant Early Warning cards [a deck of playing cards
imprinted with McLuhan aphorisms and probes] as we stood over the
kitchen table and wondered if your next book could be a re-arrangeable
format, Marshall" (NAC, Roger Poole to Marshall and Corinne
McLuhan, 9 January 1979); NAC, Roger Poole to Marshall McLuhan, 8
April 1979.

4   NAC, Marshall McLuhan to Roger Poole, 2 May 1979.
5   Ibid.
6   NAC, James Maroosis to Marshall McLuhan, 9 April 1979.
7   Interview with Eric McLuhan.
8   Ibid.
9   Ibid.
10   Interview with Corinne McLuhan. Compare NAC, volume 10, file 33,
     Raymer B. Matson, "The Christian and McLuhan," 1968: "How was
     Jesus cool? The Father was in him, yet he emptied himself. God was
     veiled, hidden. His glory was anything but explicit; for the most part it
     was implicit, cool. Whether or not Jesus knew he was the Christ of God
     . . . he saw no need to shout it from the house-tops . . . Jesus taught in
     aphorism, parable, story, parallel, pun, word-play . . . all cool techniques
     . . . In Christ, Medium becomes message. Christ came to demonstrate
     God's love for man and to call all men to Him through himself as Mediator,
     as Medium. And in so doing he became the proclamation of his Church,
     the message of God to man. God's medium became God's message."
11   Interview with Tom and Jeannine Langan.
12   Interview with Eric McLuhan.
13   Diary, 1 January 1978.
14   Interview with Corinne McLuhan.
15   Interview with Eric McLuhan.
16   "I do not think that you should have tried to mislead an old friend and
     colleague of your father's into thinking that his condition is not serious.
     Since talking to you, I have found out that he did indeed have a left
     hemoplegia, accompanied by some paralysis and by aphasia, and also
     involving a near-total blockage of the carotid artery" ("Tom," department
     of English, St. Michael's College, to Eric McLuhan, 18 October 1979).
17   Interview with Eric McLuhan.
18   Ibid.
19   Interview with Corinne McLuhan.
20   NAC, volume 203, file 24. Report of Committee, page 8.
21   Author's personal communication with Rubin L. Gorewitz.
22   NAC, volume 203, file 29. Gerald M. Goldhaber, chairman, dept. of
     Communications, State University of New York, Buffalo, to James Ham, 10
     June 1980; NAC, volume 203, file 29. Gerald Feigen to James Ham, n.d.

23   NAC, volume 203, file 29. Neil Postman to James Ham, 25 March 1980.

24   NAC, volume 203, file 29. d'Arcy Hayman to James Ham, 29 February 1980.

25   NAC, volume 203, file 29. Frank Taylor to James Ham, 14 April 1980.

26   NAC, volume 203, file 29. Tony Schwartz, Environmental Media Consul-tants, New York, to James Ham, 9 April 1980.

27   NAC, volume 203, file 29. John Cage to James Ham, 11 March 1980.

28   York University, CSWS Archives, Ivar Blackberg to James Ham, 18 April 1980.

29   Ibid., William Lee to Marshall McLuhan, 27 March 1980.

30   Harry Boyle, "Metro Morning" broadcast, CBC Radio, Toronto, 18 March 1980.

31   Editorial, *Maclean's*, 17 March 1980.

32   NAC, volume 203, file 24. Lorna Marsden, associate dean, to Mr. Whistler, 8 February 1980.

33   *Globe and Mail*, 26 March 1980.

34   "Robert Logan, a University of Toronto physics professor who said he has worked with McLuhan for six years, is attempting to get the Centre's activities under the wing of another center at the University. But Mr. Leyerle said, 'I don't want to discuss Logan. He's stirring in something which is none of his business'" (ibid.). The feisty Logan had galled Leyerle by giving the press a blistering comment: "The crime of North American society is that we destroy our history to balance our budget."

35   NAC, volume 203, file 24. Report of Assistant Dean McCulloch on the review of the Centre for Culture and Technology, 19 February 1980.

36   Ibid.

37   Ibid.

38   NAC, volume 203, file 24. Claude Bissell to Assistant Dean McCulloch, 30 April 1980.

39   NAC, volume 203, file 24. E. A. McCulloch, assistant dean, to Marshall McLuhan, 19 June, 1980.

40   A long-standing interest McLuhan developed from his reading of Jacques Lusseyran's *And There Was Light*, an account of how Lusseyran's sensory life was enriched when he became blind as the result of an accident at age eight.

41   NAC, volume 203, file 24.

42   NAC, appointment book 1980.

43   "Every time I get up before a large audience I think of you Dad and think to myself This One's For You [Barry Manilow song], Dad — so I better do a good job — and guess what, it's a standing ovation. Soon you'll be standing up there with me and we'll really do a job together. But Dad, understand that what you've been through takes time. You're doing beau-tifully, but be patient. I know for sure you will be completely fine in a

matter of months. I realize how frustrating it is for you right now — but know I'm covering for you out here on the West Coast (with all your ideas) and soon on the East Coast. By the time my energy runs out, you'll be taking over. I love you so much" (NAC, Mary McLuhan to Marshall McLuhan, 24 November 1979).

44   Interview with Jane Jacobs.

45   An ecclesiastical regulation of the Church states that mass cannot be validly performed by silent reading. The words must be formed at least with the lips. The aphasic McLuhan was thus able to "say" mass.

46   Interview with Eric McLuhan.

47   "Liz would arrive to relieve Teri; they had worked out over the months a routine of relief. Michael popped in and cracked a few jokes. Teri had pointed out to me that the bewildering well of silence her father was obliged to live in opened the door for some of his children to begin *real* communication with him for the first time in their lives. Marshall, on the other hand, she noted, was compelled to listen for the first time in his life. Opportunities for everyone, and a precarious time to make up for lost time." (Author's personal communication with Father Stroud.)

14 – *Understanding McLuhan*

1   McLuhan made occasional (and occasionally reluctant) but unequivocal (and well received) statements about the solution to the problem of television (cf. introductory quotation to this chapter): "I suggest that on survival grounds we might consider the need to turn off TV for good" (*Canadian Forum*, May 1981, p6). On the serious side, such statements from McLuhan influenced Jerry Mander's *Four Arguments for the Elimination of Television*; in a whimsical vein, he may have provided the idea for *The Day Television Died*, a zany satirical novel by Don MacGuire.

2   He even managed to exasperate those whom he naively believed to be interested in teaching the same lessons he was:

"McLuhan: In your own work, Mr. Auden, you have spent much time exploring the ways in which our new culture in this century destroyed the unconscious or rather pushed the unconscious up out of the private psyche, destroying private identity.

"W. H. Auden: I don't think so.

"McLuhan: The simple process by which the unconscious was pushed up into consciousness with the help of electricity, Freud, and Jung is one of the big dramas of our time. And it's true that the private identity, the private individual, has been swept away by this huge surge of the unconscious up into consciousness.

"W. H. Auden: It's not how I feel about things . . . I'm rooted in the nineteenth century" (Marshall McLuhan/W. H. Auden, "Duel or Duet," edited by Robert O'Driscoll, *Canadian Forum*, May 1981).

This was precisely what McLuhan wished to uproot through the provocation of his probes. As the mariner of the millennial vortex, McLuhan was trying to bring the twentieth century into the twentieth-first *and* the nineteenth century into the twentieth.

3   John Fekete, *The Critical Twilight: Exploration in the Ideology of Anglo-American Literary Theory from Eliot to McLuhan* (London: Routledge, 1977), p135.

4   Ibid., p138; p139.

5   In Gerald E. Stearn, ed., *McLuhan: Hot and Cool*, p238.

6   Ibid., p285.

7   *The Critical Twilight*, p214.

8   "The new electronic interdependence recreates the world in the image of a global village" (*The Medium Is the Massage*, p67). Less well known are McLuhan's references to the "global city" as early as *The Mechanical Bride*: "It has already been suggested that the overall effect of the press today has been to develop the image of the world as a single city" (p10); and his explicit drawing together of the two terms: "Today with electronics we have discovered that we live in a global village, and the job is to create a global *city*, as center for the village margins" (*Letters*, p278). The letter continues: "The problem of urban planning today in the field of nuclei that *is* the global village is assuming more and more the character of language itself, in which all words at all times comprise all the senses, but in evershifting ratios which permit ever new light to come through" (ibid.). This is McLuhan, more than a decade before he discovered Saussure and linguistics, assimilating the global village to language. He is not only applying the center/margin probe from economic theory to urban/suburban dynamics (his letter is addressed to town planner Jacqueline Tyrwhitt), but making the link between physical senses and word senses by way of the economy of the sensorium, evoking finally the pure medium of light, and allowing us but a glimpse of the global city, like an evanescent television image — the television screen itself being invisible ground par excellence, and here both ground and emerging figure for McLuhan's multiple metaphors.

9   "A Dialogue: Q & A," in Gerald E. Stearn, ed., *McLuhan: Hot and Cool*, p272.

10 Derrick de Kerckhove, "Understanding McLuhan"; John O'Neill, "McLuhan's Loss of Innis-Sense"; Wilfred Watson, "McLuhan's Wordplay" appeared in *Canadian Forum*, May 1981; Bruce E. Gronbeck, "McLuhan as Rhetorical Theorist"; Walter J. Ong, "McLuhan as Teacher: The Future Is a Thing of the Past"; David R. Olson, "McLuhan: Preface to Literacy"; Thomas W. Cooper, "McLuhan and Innis: The Canadian Theme of Boundless Exploration"; James W. Carey, "McLuhan and Mumford: The Roots of Modern Media Analysis"; (cf. NAC, Marshall

McLuhan's diary, 31 May 1972: "At work on Mumford who galls and bores"); Paul Levinson, "McLuhan and Rationality"; James M. Curtis, "McLuhan: The Aesthete as Historian" appeared as the symposium "The Living McLuhan" in *Journal of Communication* 31, 3 (1981).

11   Robert K. Logan published *The Alphabet Effect* (New York: Morrow, 1986) as a sequel to his collaboration with McLuhan. In 1985, a Ph.D. thesis entitled "The Social and Neurophysiological Effects of Television and Their Implications for Marketing Practice" was submitted to the University of New South Wales by Merrelyn Emery. Much in the work is a vindication of McLuhan's pronouncements on television: "A check of literature on V[isual] D[isplay] U[nits] confirms that the maladaptive agent is indeed the C[athode] R[ay] T[ube] rather than any other dimension of television viewing" (Abstract); "Conversation is by far the more powerful medium for genuine learning" (p757); "Television in the service of well-informed democracies has failed" (ibid.); "Medium, not content, is dominant and the industry has learnt to shape the content to fit the demands of the medium" (p762). As for McLuhan's posthumous work, *The Global Village: Transformations in World Life and the Media in the 21st Century* (Marshall McLuhan and Bruce R. Powers) appeared shortly after *Laws of Media* (see chapter 15 for discussion). *The Global Village* covers material that is familiar from McLuhan's other writings but with important additions and in an illuminating manner of presentation. At the outset, broadened definitions of figure/ground are presented (p5) along with their insightful and useful consequences: "The tetrads for print in the United States, China, or Africa would have three different grounds" (p11). Coincidentally or not, *The Global Village* addresses questions that some of McLuhan's correspondents put to him. Thus, William Wimsatt wrote: "Though I have wept and fasted, wept and prayed, I remain stubborn in one central question about this discourse of yours. If I understand you, you use 'interface' and 'interval' interchangeably, and I do not see why" (NAC, William Wimsatt to Marshall McLuhan, 12 December 1973). McLuhan replied, ascribing "Resonant Interval" to Werner Heisenberg and Linus Pauling and explaining that this interval is acoustic rather than visual, but without directly answering Wimsatt's question, though implying that his acoustic/visual distinction makes the question irrelevant. The substance of this question is reprised in *The Global Village*, where McLuhan and Powers emphasize the tetrad of media laws as a resonant structure, and as an update of the "ancient and medieval tradition of grammar-allied-to-rhetoric in a way that is consonant with the forms of awareness imposed on the twentieth century by electronic technology" (p7). The echo of McLuhan's dissertation on Nashe is clear here. The authors also emphasize throughout the notion of all of mankind's artifacts being structurally linguistic and metaphoric.

12   *Understanding Media*, p57.
13   Among the projects coming out of the Centre for Culture and Technology
     was a short film titled "The Horse That's Known By Touch Alone," in
     which McLuhan and Harley Parker added sound and commentary to
     children's drawings of horses to illustrate the difference between visual and
     tactile space. (NAC, Marshall McLuhan to Lou Forsdale, 29 September
     1970); NAC, Marshall McLuhan to Prof. Roger J. Broughton, dept. of
     Neurology and Neurosurgery, McGill University, 15 May 1968.
14   "When you go 'through the vanishing point' you are suddenly in a world
     of 360 degrees [the world of acoustic space]" (Marshall McLuhan to Bill
     Jovanovich, 3 September, n.y.).
15   McLuhan borrowed the terminology used here from economic theory
     and turned it into one of his favored probes. It occurs prominently in
     Understanding Media: "Speed-up creates what some economists refer to
     as a *center-margin* [abbreviated C/M] structure. When this becomes too
     extensive for the generating and control center, pieces begin to detach
     themselves and to set up new center-margin systems of their own . . .
     Land powers can more easily attain a more unified center-margin pat-
     tern than sea powers. It is the relative slowness of sea travel that inspires
     sea powers to foster multiple centers by a kind of seeding process. Sea
     powers thus tend to create centers without margins [abbreviated C-M],
     and land empires favor the center-margin structure. Electric speeds
     create centers everywhere. Margins cease to exist on this planet"
     (*Understanding Media*, p91).
16   NAC, Marshall McLuhan to Jacques Maritain, 28 May 1969.
17   Marshall McLuhan to J. G. Keogh, *Letters*, p361.
18   Marshall McLuhan to Robert J. Leuver, ibid., p386; ibid.; ibid.
19   Ibid.
20   NAC, Marshall McLuhan to Neil Postman, 28 August 1979.
21   NAC, Richard Berg to Marshall McLuhan, 21 November 1976.
22   *Understanding Media*, p27. Two years earlier, in *The Gutenberg Galaxy*
     (p63), McLuhan had already introduced the term with his references to
     "the *unified field* of electric all-at-onceness" and the "acoustic field
     approach" of Charles Seltman's *Approach to Greek Art*.
23   *Understanding Media*, p225.
24   There are scattered references to "gestalt" (pattern) in *Understanding Media*
     (*inter alia* p54, p201) without specific mention of gestalt psychology.
25   Ed Wachtel, "McLuhan in the Classroom: The Method is the Message,"
     Et Cetera: A Review of General Semantics 35 (1978), pp195-98. "The figure
     /ground approach is not new. The terms 'figure' and 'ground' were intro-
     duced about 1915 by a Danish psychologist named Edgar Rubin."
26   Compare: "The medium of the motor car is all of the service environ-
     ment it creates in the process of being used. The highways and the

factories and the oil companies, etc., are the medium of the car. The car is merely a *figure* in this great *ground* of services" (NAC, Marshall McLuhan to Vlada Petric, 14 January 1976).

27 "The enclosed represents a new direction of study here. It is related to the old Figure and Ground studies of the gestalt people. The medium, as such, is ground and is scarcely perceived. We are getting ready for our push into the sensory typology study. It is a direct follow-up on my NAEB study of the sensory modalities. Without the modalities, however, the typologies are meaningless" (NAC, Marshall McLuhan to Harry Skornia, 1 April 1965).

28 NAC, Marshall McLuhan to Charles Silberman, 23 August 1972.

29 NAC, Marshall McLuhan to Jamie Shalleck, editor, *AND/OR Press*, 27 February 1970.

30 NAC, Marshall McLuhan to Prof. O. Rudzik, University of Toronto, 23 November 1972.

31 NAC, Marshall McLuhan to David Parsons, 11 February 1972.

32 NAC, Marshall McLuhan to Joel Persky, 27 February 1973.

33 NAC, Marshall McLuhan to Reverend Gerald Pocock, 7 May 1976.

34 NAC, Marshall McLuhan to Bill Key, 26 September 1973.

35 NAC, Marshall McLuhan to William Wimsatt, 17 April 1973.

36 NAC, Marshall McLuhan to Max Nanny, 27 July 1973.

37 NAC, Marshall McLuhan to Richard Berg, 9 March 1973.

38 Marshall McLuhan to Jane Bret, *Letters*, pp459-60.

39 NAC, Marshall McLuhan to Joe Foyle, 11 March 1974.

40 NAC, Marshall McLuhan to Geoffrey Cannon (*Radio Times*, London), 22 September 1970.

41 NAC, volume 172, file 7.

42 NAC, Marshall McLuhan to Hans Selye, director, Institute of Experimental Medicine and Surgery, University of Montreal, 12 August 1974.

43 NAC, Marshall McLuhan to Yousuf Karsh, 8 November 1976.

44 NAC, Marshall McLuhan to Pete Buckner, 12 September 1972.

45 NAC, Marshall McLuhan to Eric McLuhan, 9 February 1977.

46 Diary, 1 August 1973.

47 Diary, 26 May 1974.

48 NAC, Marshall McLuhan to Jerome Agel, 27 March 1973.

49 NAC, Marshall McLuhan to Fritz Wilhelmsen, 28 June 1974. Compare: "It took me some while to discover why my writings interest the French and the Latin world generally, until I came across the work of Ferdinand de Saussure. I think that the reason that Saussure was so long in demanding attention is owing to the misunderstandings of the linguists generally concerning him. His celebrated distinction between 'diachronic' and 'synchronic' are quite basically the contrast between the world of the eye and the world of the ear, between the sequential and the simultaneous. *La*

langue is natural, simultaneous, total and hidden [like ground], while *la parole* is obvious and conscious. Lévi-Strauss has built his structures on these distinctions which are alien to the pragmatic and empirical British tradition" (NAC, Marshall McLuhan to Ralph Cohen, 11 July 1974).

50   NAC, Marshall McLuhan to Hans Selye, director, Institute of Experimental Medicine and Surgery, University of Montreal, 12 August 1974.

51   Marshall McLuhan to Clare Westcott, *Letters*, p514.

52   NAC, Marshall McLuhan to Bill Davis, 28 August 1973.

53   NAC, Kamala Bhatia to Marshall McLuhan, 8 June 1978.

54   McLuhan had written to Poole: "Currently Fred Jameson is here, one of the more confused of the formalists. In one of his lectures, was able to derive the idea that the 'text' was really the hidden *ground* of effects, rather than the written or printed form. If so, this throws some light on their interest in my phrase 'the medium is the message' since the medium is always the *ground* and not the *figure* in my usage. One universal assumption of these formalist critics is that they study *figure* and not the *ground*, being Hegelian in this respect. The Hegelian dialectic is entirely *figure* without *ground*, and thus compelled to use other figures in place of *ground*" (NAC, Marshall McLuhan to Roger Poole, 24 November 1977).

55   NAC, Roger Poole to Marshall McLuhan, 31 March 1978.

56   NAC, Marshall McLuhan to Roger Poole, 24 July 1978.

57   Ibid. (emphasis added)

58   NAC, Marshall McLuhan to Lou Forsdale, 6 April 1977.

59   NAC, volume 3, file 6; ibid.

60   NAC, Marshall McLuhan to Bernie Muller-Thym, 19 February 1960.

61   York University, CSWS Archive, file 287.

62   Marshall McLuhan to Frank Kermode, *Letters*, p426.

63   Marshall McLuhan to Harry Skornia, ibid., p305.

64   NAC, Marshall McLuhan to Bonnie Brennan, executive director, National Catholic Communications Center, 28 October 1966.

65   Ibid.

66   William Wimsatt agreed: "When Cleanth [Brooks] and I wrote our history [*Literary Criticism: A Short History*] a few years later [after reading McLuhan's thesis on Thomas Nashe around 1948] we tried to register the debt to you by some sizable quotations from your published essays. About the effects of forms (media) you find yourself in the very good company, as I guess you know, of Samuel Johnson in *Rambler* 125 . . ." (NAC, William Wimsatt to Marshall McLuhan, 19 November 1971).

67   "Symbolism initiated the technique of separating effects from causes, studying the effects in order to learn the causes. It is the technique of Ovid's *Metamorphoses*, and necessarily the technique of Darwin's origins [*sic*] of species. Darwin seems to have used the same number of books as

Ovid [=15] and probably was as conscious of using Ovid as Joyce was in his *Dubliners*. Inevitably, Darwin, in starting with species, was dealing with effects. The causes were infinitely remote and only to be guessed at from the effects. Such is the technique of the symbolist poem which creates reader participation by this method. Harold Innis was never understood simply because he worked with causality at all times . . ." (NAC, Marshall McLuhan to Fritz Wilhelmsen, dept. of Philosophy, University of Dallas, 18 January 1971).

68   NAC, Marshall McLuhan to Muriel Bradbrook, 5 November 1971.

69   Even below the speed of light, McLuhan found, the reversal occurred: "In *Scientific American* recently, an item on the bicycle explained that 'the bicycle literally paved the way for the motor car.' That is, the *effects* of the car came first, namely, hard surfaced highways, and so it is with anti-gravitation?" (NAC, Marshall McLuhan to Melvin Kranzberg, 10 July 1973); *Letters*, p492.

70   NAC, Marshall McLuhan to Bonnie Brennan, 12 September 1973.

71   NAC, Marshall McLuhan to Pete Buckner, 19 June 1974.

72   NAC, Marshall McLuhan to Barbara Rowes, 15 April 1976.

73   NAC, Marshall McLuhan to Sister St. John O'Malley, 9 February 1978.

74   Ibid.

75   Marshall McLuhan to Peter Drucker, *Letters*, p259.

76   Ibid.

77   Ibid.; ibid.

78   Ibid.

79   Ibid.

80   NAC, volume 166, file 25.

81   *Letters*, p421.

82   NAC, Marshall McLuhan to Fritz Wilhelmsen, 17 June 1975.

83   NAC, Marshall McLuhan to Fritz Wilhelmsen, 19 September 1975.

84   McLuhan had succeeded in raising the interest of various correspondents, among them one who noted that "the bias still clung to by many thinkers [is] that language is not a technology at all. [He cites Suzanne Langer, *Philosophy in a New Key*] "when she distinguishes between *sign* and *symbol*, between the functional and symbolic aspects of language," inquiring: "Might this correspond to the distinction you draw between *efficient* and *formal* causality?" (NAC, volume 127, file 19. Elio Flatto to Marshall McLuhan, 2 July 1975).

85   "Have been meditating steadily on the formal causality bit and how it disappeared with dialectics in the later Middle Ages. It is inseparable from the disappearance of rhetoric as a discipline . . . Have a look at St. Thomas' objections as a manifestation of his rhetorical awareness. Chesterton, by the same token, never writes a sentence without keeping in mind the divergent opinions of a diverse group, which is to say he does

not have a point of view" (NAC, volume 166, file 25. Marshall McLuhan to Fritz Wilhelmsen, 31 July 1975).

86 Diary, 16 August 1974.

87 NAC, volume 166, file 25. Marshall McLuhan to Fritz Wilhelmsen, 31 July 1975.

88 NAC, Marshall McLuhan to Ruth Nanda Anshen, 2 July 1975.

89 McLuhan had discovered in Aristotle's *Categories* a treatise on media. (Marshall McLuhan to Joe Keogh, 24 July 1970.) The importance of this work for the origins of the philosophy of language resonates with McLuhan's emerging view of media as linguistic in structure.

90 NAC, Marshall McLuhan to Barbara Rowes, 29 April 1976. To this he added darkly that "it could very well be that there are big, fraternal society interests that take a stand against formal cause. After all, formal causality is closely related to the acoustic and to the Oriental, and to the Third World in general. Since, however, the electric world is simultaneous and acoustic in structure, survival requires that we understand this" (ibid.).

91 McLuhan had piqued his son's interest in the subject in their exchange of letters during his year in Dallas: "If the user, i.e., the content, is efficient causality, we have some new things to think about" (NAC, Marshall McLuhan to Eric McLuhan, 24 September 1975) and "Re-reading Sherlock Holmes' *Short Stories* I have been making notes about the detective use of formal cause and *figure-ground*" (NAC, Marshall McLuhan to Eric McLuhan, 14 October 1975).

92 Interview with Eric McLuhan.

93 NAC, Marshall McLuhan to Mark Slade, 19 April 1979. (emphasis added)

94 *Laws of Media*, p3.

95 *Understanding Media*, p57.

96 Ibid., p13.

97 "As for the lenses with which I examine the world, they are certainly transferable. They can be acquired. Basically I use a structural approach, a large number derived from modern depth criticism" (NAC, Marshall McLuhan to Philip E. Slater, dept. of Sociology, Brandeis University, 12 December 1963).

98 NAC, Marshall McLuhan to Marshall Fishwick, 17 December 1975.

99 "My own approach to change is to start with the effects, an approach which I picked up from Edgar Allen [*sic*] Poe and the symbolist poets. More recently, I have learned that the philosophical term for the study of effects is *formal* causality. It is the structural approach familiar to linguistics and literary criticism" (NAC, Marshall McLuhan to Elio Flatto, 12 June 1975).

100 "Another person to whom I owe a good deal in terms of structural

awareness is Wyndham Lewis" (NAC, Marshall McLuhan to James M. Curtis, 27 September 1972).

101 "Structuralism in all its forms is necessarily acoustic, i.e. simultaneous and multi-levelled. The followers of Ferdinand de Saussure divided the acoustic into *diachrony* and *synchrony*. Diachrony is the conventional historical form of scholarship and synchrony is structural analysis based on the fact that all acoustic structures have every part of them in any part at all. Personally, I acquired this synchrony through Joyce, Pound, Eliot, and the new criticism, and in turn applied it to the new media" (NAC, Marshall McLuhan to Ray di Lorenzo, 5 April 1974).

102 "This method is really shared in many fields and can be bolstered by interplay among fields" (NAC, Marshall McLuhan to Philip E. Slater, 12 December 1963).

103 Marshall McLuhan to Peter Drucker, *Letters*, p270.

104 NAC, Marshall McLuhan to Bill Jovanovich, 14 December 1965.

105 Max Nanny to Marshall McLuhan, 3 June 1971.

106 NAC, Marshall McLuhan to James M. Curtis, 12 September 1972.

107 NAC, volume 173, file 23. Marshall McLuhan to James M. Curtis, 27 September 1972.

108 NAC, Marshall McLuhan to Mark Slade, 3 May 1973.

109 "One basic discovery, however, I have made, Fritz, that wherever you see the word 'structural' you can read 'audile-tactile'" (NAC, Marshall McLuhan to Fritz Wilhelmsen, 28 January 1974).

110 NAC, Marshall McLuhan to D. S. Berlyne, 23 November 1972.

111 NAC, Marshall McLuhan to William Massee, 13 June 1974.

112 NAC, Marshall McLuhan to Cleanth Brooks, 16 May 1977.

113 NAC, Marshall McLuhan to James M. Curtis, 12 September 1972.

114 James A. Boon, *From Symbolism to Structuralism* (New York: Harper and Row, 1972); NAC, Marshall McLuhan to Fritz Wilhelmsen, 28 June 1974.

115 NAC, Marshall McLuhan to Joe Foyle, 12 June 1974.

116 NAC, Marshall McLuhan to Barbara Rowes, 29 April 1976.

117 "I have found [Jean-Marie Benoist's *The Structural Revolution*] a perfect fulfillment of my research about the effect of electricity on French philosophy, i.e. structuralism is the light-through that is X-ray and is also the pattern perceived by the TV viewer . . . It becomes quite obvious that Sartre, as well as the entire symbolist revolution, relates to the X-ray characteristics of electric experience, i.e., to the discarnate condition and its resulting violence" (NAC, Marshall McLuhan to Claude de Beauregard, 19 December 1978).

15 – *Is McLuhan a Linguist?*

1 NAC, Marshall McLuhan to John Leyerle, 23 November 1973. McLuhan subsequently characterized his integrated laws of media as

both linguistic in structure and a modern counterpart to the the ancient and medieval traditions of grammar allied to rhetoric.

2   NAC, Marshall McLuhan to W. Freeman Twadell, 2 February 1954.
3   McLuhan & McLuhan, 1988: 128.
4   McLuhan and Powers, 1989: p*x*.
5   *Travels in Hyperreality*, p138.
6   Ibid.
7   Ibid., p139.
8   Ibid., pp233-34.
9   Ibid, p235.
10 *McLuhan*, p108.
11 Ibid., p111.
12 Ibid, p110.
13 *Understanding Media*, p313.
14 *McLuhan*, p121.
15 *Understanding Media*, p334. (emphasis added)
16 McLuhan, p113.
17 McLuhan's reply to Miller's piece on McLuhan in *The Listener*, 15 July 1971, was published in the magazine on 26 August 1971 and is reprinted in *Letters of Marshall McLuhan*, pp435-38.
18 Diary, 6 March 1974. For a discussion of Saussure's influence outside linguistics, see W. T. Gordon, *Saussure for Beginners* (New York and London: Writers & Readers Publishing, 1996).
19 Diary, 4 March 1974. Here Saussure's name is linked to that of another linguist, Roman Jakobson, who carried on and developed his ideas.
20 Diary, 21 February 1974.
21 Diary, 20 April 1974.
22 Diary, 19 June 1974.
23 Diary, 11 June 1974.
24 Diary, 15 June 1974.
25 Diary, 11 June 1974.
26 Saussure was sufficiently important to McLuhan to deserve prominent mention in the trial-balloon version of the laws of media published in the journal *Technology and Culture* in January 1975.
27 *Global Village*, p7.
28 *Understanding Media*, p57.
29 *Take Today*, p3.
30 Diary, 9 February 1937.
31 *Vogue*, vol. 123, August 1966, pp70-73, p111.
32 Ann Berthoff, *Richards on Rhetoric* (New York: Oxford University Press, 1991), p19.
33 Ibid., p50.
34 *Understanding Media*, p60.

35 *Letters*, p355.
36 *Laws of Media*, pix.
37 Ibid., p98.

Notes to Appendix 1: Feedforward

1 Peter March, "McLuhan wrong about TV: This 'cool' medium carries plenty of information," *Daily News* (Halifax, Nova Scotia), 8 April 1996. Occasionally, an intrepid soul will respond to such misrepresentations of McLuhan's thought: "Letters: Misunderstanding McLuhan," *Daily News*, 11 April 1996.
2 *Understanding Media*, p307.
3 See page 304.

Notes to Appendix 2: Recent Works on McLuhan

1 W. T. Gordon, *McLuhan for Beginners* (New York & London: Writers & Readers Publishing, 1997).
2 http://www.icgc.com/mcluhan_studies
3 Personal communication. (After Samuel Johnson.)
4 Reviewed in *Globe and Mail*, 8 July 1995. (C7)
5 Reviewed in *Globe and Mail*, 15 April 1995.
6 Douglas Parker, "Reverse Canadian," *Riverside (California) Press-Enterprise*, 24 May 1964.
7 Willmott not only situates McLuhan at the point of maximal resonance between obsolescence and reversal but makes him responsible for it, speaking of a "historical-epistemological formalism inaugurated by McLuhan" (p136).
8 NAC, volume 28, file 12.
9 Glen Willmott, *McLuhan, or Modernism in Reverse* (Toronto: University of Toronto Press, 1996), p166.
10 Ibid., p172.
11 "Today computers hold out the promise of a means of instant translation of any code or language into any other code or language. The computer, in short, promises by technology a Pentecostal condition of universal understanding and unity. The next logical step would seem to be, not to translate, but to by-pass languages in favor of a general cosmic consciousness which might be very like the collective unconscious dreamt of by Bergson. The condition of 'weightlessness' that biologists say promises a physical immortality, may be paralleled by the condition of speechlessness that could confer a perpetuity of collective harmony and peace" (*Understanding Media*, p80). The passage is quoted in A. S. Byatt's *Babel Tower* (New York: Random House, 1996), p150.
12 "[Electronic man] is transmitted instantly everywhere and has become a disembodied angel. What [Arnold] Toynbee calls the 'etherealization'

trend of history goes all the way with telephone and TV . . ." (NAC, Marshall McLuhan to David Sohn, 3 February 1971).

13   Willmott, p207.

14   Ibid., p173.

15   Ibid., p205.

16   See Raymond Tallis, *Not Saussure* (London: Macmillan, 1988).

17   *Letters*, p472.

18   Neill, p26.

19   On the subject of discarnate mankind under electronic technology, McLuhan said: "By the way, when you are on the air, you are literally disembodied. Out of the air, they can pull you in by an arial [*sic*] and put you in a room. This is complete angelism. This is disembodied. This is the Cartesian angel, the pure subjective being. Which is everywhere at the same moment. The angels that the middle ages talked about could only be in one place at a time. The radio angel is everywhere at once. The electric angel is much more potent than the old philosophical angels" (Unpublished interview).

20   Neill, p37.

21   Stamps, p*xii*.

22   Ibid., p*xiii*.

23   Ibid., p*xii*.

24   Ibid., p15, emphasis added.

25   Ibid., p21.

26   Ibid., p20.

BIBLIOGRAPHY

Books by Marshall McLuhan

The Mechanical Bride: Folklore of Industrial Man. New York: Vanguard Press, 1951; London: Routledge & Kegan Paul, 1967.

Selected Poetry of Tennyson. Edited by Marshall McLuhan. New York: Rinehart, 1954.

Report on Project in Understanding New Media. Washington, D.C.: U.S. Office of Education, 1960.

Explorations in Communication: An Anthology. Edited by Edmund Carpenter and Marshall McLuhan. Boston: Beacon Press, 1960.

The Gutenberg Galaxy: The Making of Typographic Man. Toronto: University of Toronto Press, 1962. Translated into French by Jean Paré and published as *La Galaxie Gutenberg: la genèse de l'homme typographique.* Montreal: Hurtubise HMH, 1967; Paris: Gallimard, 1977, 2 vols.

Understanding Media: The Extensions of Man. New York: McGraw-Hill, 1964; second edition 1965; first MIT Press edition, Cambridge, Mass.: MIT Press, 1994, with an introduction by Lewis Lapham. 1964 edition translated into French by Jean Paré and published as *Pour comprendre les média: les prolongements technologiques de l'homme.* Montreal: Hurtubise HMH, 1968. Reissued in a new edition (Bibliothèque Québécoise, #36) in 1993. Translations of *Understanding Media* have appeared in more than twenty languages.

Voices of Literature. (2 vols.) Edited by Marshall McLuhan and Richard J. Schoeck. New York: Holt, Rinehart and Winston, 1964, 1965.

McLuhan: Hot & Cool. A Primer for the Understanding of and a Critical Symposium with a Rebuttal by McLuhan. Edited by Gerald Emanuel Stearn. New York: Dial Press, 1967. New York: The New American Library, 1969. Thirty-one selections include reprinted essays (in whole or in part) from Howard Luck Gossage, Tom Wolfe, John Culkin, Walter Ong, Dell Hymes, Frank Kermode, George Steiner, Susan Sontag, and five selections from McLuhan's writings. The book concludes with the transcript of a dialogue between the editor and McLuhan, originally published in *Encounter* in June 1967, wherein McLuhan responds to commentaries on his work from some of the other contributors to the volume.

The Medium Is the Massage: An Inventory of Effects. With Quentin Fiore and Jerome Agel. New York: Bantam, 1967. Translated into French and published as *Message et massage*. Montreal: Hurtubise HMH, 1968.

Verbi-Voco-Visual Explorations. New York: Something Else Press, 1967. (Reprint of *Explorations*, no. 8.)

Through the Vanishing Point: Space in Poetry and Painting. With Harley Parker. New York: Harper & Row, 1968.

War and Peace in the Global Village: an inventory of some of the current spastic situations that could be eliminated by more feedforward. With Quentin Fiore and Jerome Agel. New York: Bantam, 1968. Reprinted, New York: Touchstone Books, 1989. Translated into French as *Guerre et paix dans le village planétaire: un inventaire de quelques situations spasmodiques courantes qui pourraient être supprimées par le feedforward*. Montreal: Hurtubise HMH, 1970; Paris: Laffont, 1970.

Counterblast. With Harley Parker. New York: Harcourt, Brace and World, 1969. Translated into French by Jean Paré. (Montreal: Hurtubise, 1972; Paris: Mame, 1972.)

The Interior Landscape: The Literary Criticism of Marshall McLuhan 1943-1962. Edited by Eugene McNamara. New York: McGraw-Hill, 1969.

Mutations 1990. Translation by François Chesneau of *The Future of Sex* (see Other Works below). Montreal: Hurtubise HMH, 1969.

From Cliché to Archetype. With Wilfred Watson. New York: Viking, 1970. Translated into French by Derrick de Kerckhove and published as *Du cliché à l'archétype: la foire du sens*. Montreal: Hurtubise HMH, 1973; Paris: Mame, 1973. Translated into Italian by Francesca Valente and Carla Pezzini and published as *Dal cliché all'archetipo: l'uomo tecnològico nel villaggio globale*.

Culture Is Our Business. New York: McGraw-Hill, 1970.

Take Today. With Barrington Nevitt. Toronto: Longman, 1972.

Autre homme autre chrétien à l'âge électronique. With Pierre Babin. Lyon: Éditions du Chalet, 1977.

City as Classroom: Understanding Language and Media. With Eric McLuhan and Kathryn Hutchon. Toronto: Book Society of Canada Limited, 1977.

D'Oeil à oreille. Translation by Derrick de Kerckhove of articles by and interviews with McLuhan. Montreal: Hurtubise, 1977.

The Possum and the Midwife. [Text of McLuhan lecture on Ezra Pound.] Moscow: University of Idaho Press, 1978.

Letters of Marshall McLuhan. Selected and edited by Matie Molinaro, Corinne McLuhan, and William Toye. Toronto: Oxford University Press, 1987.

Images from the Film Spiral. Selected by Sorel Etrog with text by Marshall McLuhan. Toronto: Exile Editions, 1987.

Laws of Media: The New Science. With Eric McLuhan. Toronto: University of Toronto Press, 1988.

The Global Village: transformations in world life and media in the 21st century. With Bruce R. Powers. New York: Oxford University Press, 1989.

Essential McLuhan. Edited by Eric McLuhan and Frank Zingrone. Toronto: Anansi, 1995.

Other Works by Marshall McLuhan

Macaulay: What a Man! *The Manitoban* (University of Manitoba student newspaper), 28 October 1930.

Public School Education. *The Manitoban*, 17 October 1933.

Germany and Internationalism. *The Manitoban*, 27 October 1933.

Germany's Development. *The Manitoban*, 3 November 1933.

German Character. *The Manitoban*, 7 November 1933.

George Meredith. *The Manitoban*, 21 November 1933.

Canada and Internationalism. *The Manitoban*, 1 December 1933.

De Valera. *The Manitoban*, 9 January 1934.

Not Spiritualism but Spiritism. *The Manitoban*, 19 January 1934.

The Groupers. *The Manitoban*, 23 January 1934.

Adult Education. *The Manitoban*, 16 February 1934.

Morticians and Cosmeticians. *The Manitoban*, 2 March 1934.

Tomorrow and Tomorrow. *The Manitoban*, 16 May 1934.

George Meredith as a Poet and Dramatic Novelist. M.A. thesis, University of
    Manitoba, 1934.

G. K. Chesterton: A Practical Mystic. *The Dalhousie Review* 15 (1936), 455-64.

The Cambridge English School. *Fleur de Lis* (Saint Louis University student lit-
    erary magazine), 1937, 21-25.

Peter or Peter Pan. *Fleur de Lis*, May 1938, 7-9.

Review of *The Culture of Cities* by Lewis Mumford. *Fleur de Lis*, December 1938,
    38-39.

Apes and Angles. *Fleur de Lis*, December 1940, 7-9.

Review of *Art and Prudence* by Mortimer J. Adler. *Fleur de Lis*, October 1940.

Review of *Poetry and the Modern World* by David Daiches. *Fleur de Lis*, March 1941.

Review of *American Renaissance* by F. O. Matthiessen. *Fleur de Lis*, October 1941.

Aesthetic Pattern in Keats' Odes. *University of Toronto Quarterly* 12, 2 (1943),
    167-79. Reprinted in Eugene McNamara, ed., *The Literary Criticism of
    Marshall McLuhan 1943-1962*, 99-113.

Education of Free Men in Democracy: The Liberal Arts. *St. Louis Studies in
    Honor of St. Thomas Aquinas*, 1943, 47-50.

Herbert's *Virtue. The Explicator* 2, 1 (1943), 4. Reprinted in L. G. Locke, W. M. Gibson, and G. Arms, eds., *Readings for Liberal Education* (New York: Rinehart, 1948).

The Place of Thomas Nashe in the Learning of His Time. Ph.D. dissertation, Cambridge University, April 1943.

Dagwood's America. *Columbia*, January 1944, 3, 22.

Edgar Poe's Tradition. *Sewanee Review* 52, 1 (1944), 24-33. Reprinted in Eugene McNamara, ed., *The Literary Criticism of Marshall McLuhan 1943-1962*, 211-21.

Eliot's *The Hippopotamus. The Explicator* 2, 7 (1944), 50.

Henley's *Invictus. The Explicator* 3, 3 (1944), 22.

Kipling and Forster. *Sewanee Review* 52, 3 (1944), 332-43.

Poetic vs. Rhetorical Exegesis. The Case for Leavis against Richards and Empson. *Sewanee Review* 52, 2 (1944), 266-76.

Wyndham Lewis: Lemuel in Lilliput. *Saint Louis Studies in Honor of St. Thomas Aquinas*, 1944, 58-72.

The Analogical Mirrors. In *Gerard Manley Hopkins: The Kenyon Critics Edition*. Norfolk, CT: New Directions Books, 1945, 15-27. Reprinted in Eugene McNamara, ed., *The Literary Criticism of Marshall McLuhan 1943-1962*, 63-73.

Another Aesthetic Peep-Show. Review of *The Aesthetic Adventure* by William Gaunt. *Sewanee Review* 53 (1945), 674-77.

The New York Wits. *Kenyon Review* 7 (1945), 12-28.

An Ancient Quarrel in Modern America (Sophists vs. Grammarians). *The Classical Journal*, January 1946, 156-62. Reprinted in Eugene McNamara, ed., *The Literary Criticism of Marshall McLuhan 1943-1962*, 223-34.

Footprints in the Sands of Crime. *Sewanee Review* 54 (1946), 617-34.

Out of the Castle into the Counting-House. *Politics*, September 1946, 277-79.

Review of *William Ernest Henley* by Jerome Hamilton Buckley. *Modern Language Quarterly* 7 (1946), 368-70.

Mr. Connolly and Mr. Hook. Review of *The Condemned Playground. Essays 1927-1944* by Cyril Connolly and *Education for Modern Man* by Sidney Hook. *Sewanee Review* 55 (1947), 167-72.

American Advertising. *Horizon* 93, 4 (October 1947), 132-41. Reprinted in Eric McLuhan and Frank Zingrone, eds., *Essential McLuhan* (Toronto: Anansi, 1995), 13-20.

Inside Blake and Hollywood. *Sewanee Review* 55 (1947), 710-15.

Introduction to *Paradox in Chesterton* by Hugh Kenner. New York: Sheed and Ward, 1947.

The Southern Quality. *Sewanee Review* 55 (1947), 357-83. Reprinted in Eugene McNamara, ed., *The Literary Criticism of Marshall McLuhan 1943-1962*, 185-209.

Henry IV, a Mirror for Magistrates. *University of Toronto Quarterly* 17, 2 (1948), 152-60.

The 'Colour-Bar' of BBC English. *Canadian Forum*, April 1949, 9-10.

Mr. Eliot's Historical Decorum. *Renascence* 2, 1 (1949), 9-15. Reprinted in *Renascence* 25, 4 (1972-73), 183-89.

Pound's Critical Prose. In Peter Russell, ed., *Examination of Ezra Pound: A Collection of Essays* (London: Peter Nevill, 1950), 165-71. Reprinted in Eugene McNamara, ed., *The Literary Criticism of Marshall McLuhan 1943-1962*, 75-81.

T. S. Eliot [Review of eleven books about Eliot]. *Renascence* 3, 1 (1950), 43-48.

John Dos Passos: Technique vs. Sensibility. In Charles Gardiner, ed., *Fifty Years of the American Novel: A Christian Appraisal* (New York: Charles Scribner's Sons, 1951), 151-64. Reprinted in Eugene McNamara, ed., *The Literary Criticism of Marshall McLuhan 1943-1962*, 49-62.

Joyce, Aquinas and the Poetic Process. *Renascence* 4, 1 (1951), 3-11.

Review of three books on Ezra Pound. *Renascence* 3, 2 (1951), 200-2.

A Survey of Joyce Criticism. *Renascence* 4, 1 (1951), 12-18.

Tennyson and Picturesque Poetry. *Essays in Criticism* 1, 3 (1951), 262-82. Reprinted in Eugene McNamara, ed., *The Literary Criticism of Marshall McLuhan 1943-1962*, 135-55.

Advertising as a Magical Institution. *Commerce Journal*, January 1952, 25-29.

The Aesthetic Moment in Landscape Poetry. In Alan Downe, ed., *English Institute Essays* (New York: Columbia University Press, 1952), 168-81. Reprinted in Eugene McNamara, ed., *The Literary Criticism of Marshall McLuhan 1943-1962*, 157-67.

Defrosting Canadian Culture. *American Mercury*, March 1952, 91-97.

Review of *Auden: An Introductory Essay* by Richard Hoggart. *Renascence* 4, 2 (1952), 220-21.

Review of *The Poetry of Ezra Pound* by Hugh Kenner. *Renascence*, 4, 2 (1952), 215-17.

Review of *Word Index to James Joyce's Ulysses* by Miles L. Hanley. *Renascence* 4, 2 (1952), 186-87.

Technology and Political Change. *International Journal* 7, 3 (Summer 1952), 189-95.

The Age of Advertising. *Commonweal*, 11 September 1953, 555-57.

Comics and Culture. *Saturday Night*, February 1953, 1, 19-20.

Culture Without Literacy. *Explorations: Studies in Culture and Communications,* no. 1, December 1953, 117-27. Reprinted in Eric McLuhan and Frank Zingrone, eds., *Essential McLuhan* (Toronto: Anansi, 1995), 302-13.

From Eliot to Seneca. *University of Toronto Quarterly* 22, 2 (1953), 199-202.

James Joyce: Trivial and Quadrivial. *Thought*, Spring 1953, 75-98. Reprinted in Eugene McNamara, ed., *The Literary Criticism of Marshall McLuhan 1943-1962*, 23-47.

The Later Innis. *Queen's Quarterly* 60, 3 (1953), 385-94.

Maritain on Art. *Renascence* 6, 1 (1953), 40-44.

The Poetry of George Herbert and Symbolist Communication. *Thought*, Autumn 1953.

Review of *Light on a Dark Horse: An Autobiography 1901-1935* by Roy Campbell. *Renascence* 5, 2 (1953), 157-59.

Wyndham Lewis: His Theory of Art and Communication. *Shenandoah*, Autumn 1953, 77-88. Reprinted in Eugene McNamara, ed., *The Literary Criticism of Marshall McLuhan 1943-1962*, 83-94.

Catholic Humanism and Modern Letters. In *Christian Humanism in Letters: The McAuley Lectures, Series 2*, 1954 (West Hartford, CT: St. Joseph College, 1954), 49-67.

Joyce, Mallarmé, and the Press. *Sewanee Review* 62 (1954), 38-55. Reprinted in Eugene McNamara, ed., *The Literary Criticism of Marshall McLuhan 1943-1962*, 5-21. Reprinted in Eric McLuhan and Frank Zingrone, eds., *Essential McLuhan* (Toronto: Anansi, 1995), 60-71.

Media as Art Forms. *Explorations*, no. 2, April 1954, 6-13.

New Media as Political Forms. *Explorations*, no. 3, August 1954, 120-26.

Poetry and Society. Review of *Dream and Responsibility* by Peter Viereck. *Poetry* 84, 2 (May 1954), 93-95.

Through Emerald Eyes. Review of *Three Great Irishmen: Shaw, Yeats, Joyce* by Aarland Ussher. *Renascence* 6, 2 (1954), 157-58.

Five Sovereign Fingers Taxed the Breath. *Explorations*, no. 4, February 1955. Reprinted in *Shenandoah*, Autumn 1955, 50-52.

Nihilism Exposed. Review of *Wyndham Lewis* by Hugh Kenner. *Renascence* 8, 2 (1955), 97-99.

Paganism on Tip-toe. Review of *The Poetry of T. S. Eliot* by D. E. S. Maxwell. *Renascence* 7, 3 (1955), 158.

Radio and Television vs. The ABCED-Minded. *Explorations*, no. 5, June 1955, 12-18.

Space, Time, and Poetry. *Explorations*, no. 4, February 1955, 56-62.

Educational Effects of Mass Media of Communication. *Teachers College Record*, March 1956, 400-3.

The Media Fit the Battle of Jericho. *Explorations*, no. 6 (July 1956), 15-19. Reprinted in Eric McLuhan and Frank Zingrone, eds., *Essential McLuhan* (Toronto: Anansi, 1995), 298-302.

Music and Silence. Review of two books on Joyce. *Renascence* 8, 3 (1956), 152-53.

'Stylistic.' Review of *Mimesis: The Representation of Reality in Western Literature* by Erich Auerbach. *Renascence* 9, 2 (1956), 99-100.

Brain Storming (and other essays). *Explorations*, no. 8, October 1957 (unpaginated).

Characterization in Western Art, 1600-1900. *Explorations*, no. 8, October 1957, unpaginated.

Classical Treatment. Review of *Eliot's Poetry and Plays* by Grover Smith. *Renascence*, 10, 2 (1957), 102-3.

Classrooms Without Walls. *Explorations*, no. 7, March 1957, 22-26.

Coleridge as Artist. In Clarence D. Thorpe, Carlos Baker, and Bennett Weaver, eds., *The Major English Romantic Poets: A Symposium in Reappraisal* (Carbondale: Southern Illinois University Press, 1957), 83-99. Reprinted in Eugene McNamara, ed., *The Literary Criticism of Marshall McLuhan 1943-1962*, 115-33.

Compliment Accepted [Review of six books on James Joyce]. *Renascence* 10, 2 (1957), 106-8.

David Riesman and the Avant-Garde. *Explorations*, no. 7, March 1957, 112-16.

Eternal Ones of the Dream. (with Edmund Carpenter). *Explorations*, no. 7, March 1957, unpaginated.

Jazz and Modern Letters. *Explorations*, no. 7, March 1957, 74-76.

Manifestos. *Explorations*, no. 8 (October 1957), unpaginated.

Third Program in the Human Age. *Explorations*, no. 8, October 1957, 16-18.

The Organization Man. *Explorations*, no. 8, October 1957, unpaginated.

People of the Word. *Explorations*, no. 8, October 1957, unpaginated.

Sight, Sound, and the Fury. In Bernard Rosenberg and David Manning White, eds., *Mass Culture: The Popular Arts in America* (London: Collier-Macmillan, 1957), 489-95.

Soviet Novels. (with Edmund Carpenter). *Explorations*, no. 7, (March 1957), 123-24.

One Wheel, All Square [Review of five books on James Joyce]. *Renascence* 10, 4 (1958), 196-200.

Our New Electronic Culture: The Role of Mass Communications in Meeting Today's Problems. *National Association of Educational Broadcasters Journal*, October 1958, 19-20, 24-26.

Joyce or No Joyce. Review of *Joyce among the Jesuits* by Kevin Sullivan. *Renascence* 12, 1 (1959), 53-54.

Myth and Mass Media. *Daedalus*, Spring 1959, 339-48.

Virgil, Yeats, and 13,000 Friends. Review of *On Poetry and Poets* by T. S. Eliot. *Renascence* 11, 2 (1959), 94-95.

Yeats and Zane Grey. Review of *The Letters of William Butler Yeats*, edited by Allan Wade. *Renascence*, 11, 3 (1959), 166-68.

Acoustic Space. (with Edmund Carpenter). In Edmund Carpenter and Marshall McLuhan, eds., *Explorations in Communication: An Anthology* (Boston: Beacon Press, 1960), 65-70.

A Critical Discipline. Review of *Wyndham Lewis: A Portrait of the Artist as the Enemy* by Geoffrey Wagner. *Renascence* 12, 2 (1960), 93-95.

Another Eliot Party. Review of *T. S. Eliot: A Symposium for His Seventieth Birthday* edited by Neville Braybrooke. *Renascence* 12, 3 (1960), 156-57.

Around the World, Around the Clock. Review of *The Image Industries* by William Lynch. *Renascence* 12, 4 (1960), 204-5.

Flirting with Shadows. Review of *The Invisible Poet* by Hugh Kenner. *Renascence* 12, 4 (1960), 212-14.

Joyce as Critic. Review of *The Critical Writings of James Joyce* edited by Ellsworth Mason and Richard Ellmann. *Renascence* 12, 4 (1960), 202-3.

Melodic and Scribal. Review of *Song in the Works of James Joyce* by J. C. Hodgart and Mabel P. Worthington. *Renascence* 13, 1 (1960), 51.

The Personal Approach. Review of *Shakespeare and Company* by Sylvia Beach. *Renascence* 13, 1 (1960), 42-43.

Romanticism Reviewed. Review of *Romantic Image* by Frank Kermode. *Renascence* 12, 4 (1960), 207-9.

The Electric Culture. The Books at the Wake. *Renascence* 13, 4 (1961), 219-20.

The Humanities in the Electronic Age. *Humanities*, Fall 1961, 3-11.

Inside the Five Sense Sensorium. *Canadian Architect*, June 1961, 49-51.

The New Media and the New Education. *Basilian Teacher*, December 1961, 93-100.

Producers and Consumers. Review of *James Joyce* by Richard Ellmann. *Renascence* 13, 4 (1961), 217-19.

The Chaplin Bloom. Review of *James Joyce: The Poetry of Conscience* by Mary Parr. *Renascence* 14, 4 (1962), 216-17.

A Fresh Perspective on Dialogue. *The Superior Student* 4, 7 (1962), 2-6.

Joyce, Aquinas, and the Poetic Process. In Thomas E. Connolly, ed., *Joyce's Portrait: Criticisms and Critiques* (New York: Appleton-Century-Crofts, 1962), 249-56.

Phase Two. Review of *The Art of James Joyce* by A. Walton Litz. *Renascence* 14, 3 (1962), 166-67.

Prospect of America. *University of Toronto Quarterly* 32, 1 (1962), 107-8.

Empson, Milton, and God. Review of *Milton's God* by William Empson. *Renascence* 15, 2 (1963), 112.

Printing and the Mind. *The Times Literary Supplement*, 19 July 1963.

Introduction to *The Bias of Communication* by Harold A. Innis. Reprint edition. Toronto: University of Toronto Press, 1964. Also appears in *Explorations* 25 (June 1969).

Murder by Television. *Canadian Forum*, January 1964, 222-23.

Notes on Burroughs [Review of *Naked Lunch* and *Nova Express* by William Burroughs]. *Nation*, 28 December 1964, 517-19.

Art as Anti-Environment. *Art News Annual* 31 (1965).

T. S. Eliot. *The Canadian Forum*, February 1965, 243-44.

Wordfowling in Blunderland. *Saturday Night*, August 1965, 23-27.

Address at Vision 65. *American Scholar* 35 (1965-66), 196-205. Reprinted in Eric McLuhan and Frank Zingrone, eds., *Essential McLuhan* (Toronto: Anansi, 1995), 219-32.

The All-at-Once World of Marshall McLuhan. *Vogue* 123 (August 1966), 70-73, 111.

Cybernation and Culture. In Charles Dechert, ed., *The Social Impact of Cybernetics* (South Bend, IN: University of Notre Dame Press, 1966), 95-108.

The Emperor's Old Clothes. In Gyorgy Kepes, ed., *The Man-Made Object* (New York: G. Braziller, 1966), 90-95.

Electronics and the Psychic Drop-Out. *This Magazine Is About Schools* 1, 1 (April 1966), 37-42.

The Invisible Environment. *Canadian Architect*, May 1966, 71-74.

Questions and Answers with Marshall McLuhan. *Take One*, November/December 1966, 7-10.

Television in a New Light. In Stanley T. Donner, ed., *The Meaning of Commercial Television* (Austin: University of Texas Press, 1966), 87-107.

The Future of Education. (with George B. Leonard). *Look*, 21 February 1967, 23-25.

The Future of Sex. (with George B. Leonard). *Look*, 25 July 1967, 56-63.

Love. *Saturday Night*, February 1967, 25-28.

Marshall McLuhan Massages the Medium. *Nation's Schools*, June 1967, 36-37.

The Relation of Environment to Anti-Environment. In Floyd W. Matson and Ashley Montagu, eds., *The Human Dialogue: Perspectives on Communication* (New York: Free Press, 1967), 39-47.

Adopt a University. *This Magazine Is about Schools* 2, 4 (Autumn 1968), 50-55.

All the Candidates Are Asleep. *Saturday Evening Post*, August 1968, 34-36.

Guaranteed Income in the Electric Age. In Richard Kostelanetz, ed., *Beyond Left and Right: Radical Thought for Our Times* (New York: William Morrow, 1968), 72-83.

The Reversal of the Overheated Image. *Playboy*, December 1968.

Review of *Federalism and the French Canadians* by Pierre Trudeau. *New York Times Book Review*, 17 November 1968.

Playboy Interview: Marshall McLuhan — A Candid Conversation with the High Priest of Popcult and Metaphysician of Media. *Playboy*, March 1969, 53-54, 59-62, 64-66, 68, 70, 72, 74, 158. Reprinted in Eric McLuhan and Frank Zingrone, eds., *Essential McLuhan* (Toronto: Anansi, 1995), 233-69.

Salt and Scandal in the Gospels. (with Joe Keogh). *Explorations* 26 (December 1969), 82-85.

Wyndham Lewis. *Atlantic Monthly*, December 1969, 93-98.

Cicero and the Renaissance Training for Prince and Poet. *Renaissance and Reformation* (Victoria, B.C.) 6, 3 (1970). Reprinted in Eric McLuhan and Frank Zingrone, eds., *Essential McLuhan* (Toronto: Anansi, 1995), 313-18.

The Man Who Came to Listen. (with Barrington Nevitt). In Tony Bonaparte and John Flaherty, eds., *Peter Drucker: Contributions to Business Enterprise* (New York: New York University Press, 1970), 35-55.

Foreword to A. J. Kirshner, *Training That Makes Sense* (San Rafael, CA: Academic Therapy Publications, 1972), 5-7.

The Popular Hero and Anti-Hero. In Ray B. Browne et al., eds., *Heroes of Popular Culture* (Bowling Green, OH: Bowling Green University Popular Press, 1972).

The Argument: Causality in the Electric World. (with Barrington Nevitt). *Technology and Culture* 14, 1 (1973), 1-18.

Do Americans Go to Church to Be Alone? *The Critic*, January/February 1973, 14-23.

The Medium Is the Message. In C. David Mortensen, ed., *Basic Readings in Communication Theory* (New York: Harper and Row, 1973), 139-52.

Mr. Nixon and the Dropout Strategy. *New York Times*, 29 July 1973.

Understanding McLuhan — and Fie on Any Who Don't. *The Globe and Mail*, 10 September 1973.

Watergate as Theatre. *Performing Arts in Canada*, Winter 1973, 14-15.

Mr. Eliot and the Saint Louis Blues. *The Antigonish Review*, 18 (Summer 1974), 23-27.

English Literature as Control Tower in Communication Study. *English Quarterly* (University of Waterloo), Spring 1974, 3-7.

Medium Meaning Message. (with Barrington Nevitt). *Communication* (UK) 1 (1974), 27-33. Reprinted in Barrington Nevitt, *The Communication Ecology: Re-presentation versus Replica* (Toronto: Butterworths, 1982), 140-44.

A Media Approach to Inflation. *New York Times*, 21 September 1974.

There Is Panic in Abortion Thinking: McLuhan. *Toronto Daily Star*, 31 July 1974.

Letter to *The Listener*, 22 October 1975.

McLuhan's Laws of the Media. *Technology and Culture*, January 1975, 74-78.

The Debates. *New York Times*, 23 September 1976.

The Violence of the Media. *Canadian Forum*, September 1976, 9-12.

Laws of the Media. *Et Cetera: A Review of General Semantics*, June 1977, 173-78.

Alphabet, Mother of Invention. (with R. K. Logan). *Et Cetera: A Review of General Semantics*, December 1977, 373-83.

Canada: The Borderline Case. In David Staines, ed., *The Canadian Imagination: Dimensions of a Literary Culture* (Cambridge, MA: Harvard University Press, 1977), 226-48.

The Rise and Fall of Nature. *Journal of Communication* 27, 4 (1977), 80-81.

The Brain and the Media: The "Western" Hemisphere. *Journal of Communication* 28, 4 (1978), 54-60.

A Last Look at the Tube. *New York*, 3 April 1978, 45.

Figures and Grounds in Linguistic Criticism. Review of Mario J. Valdes and Owen J. Miller, *Interpretation of Narrative* (Toronto: University of Toronto Press, 1978). *Et Cetera: A Review of General Semantics* 36, 3 (1979), 289-94.

The Double Bind of Communication and the World Problematique. (with Robert K. Logan). *Human Futures*, Summer 1979, 1-3.

Pound, Eliot, and the Rhetoric of *The Waste Land*. *New Literary History* 10, 3 (1979), 557-80.

Foreword to Karl Appel, *Karl Appel: Works on Paper*. (New York: Abbeville Press, 1980).

Electronic Banking and the Death of Privacy. (with Bruce Powers). *Journal of Communication* 31, 1 (1981), 164-69.

Other References

Ayre, John. *Northrop Frye*. Toronto: Random House, 1989.

Becker, Samuel L. Viewpoint: McLuhan as Rorschach. *Journal of Broadcasting* 19, 2 (1975), 235-40.

Berthoff, Ann E., ed. *Richards on Rhetoric. I. A. Richards: Selected Essays (1929-1974)*. New York: Oxford University Press, 1991.

Boon, James A. *From Symbolism to Structuralism*. New York: Harper and Row, 1972.

Brinnin, John Malcolm. *The Third Rose*. Little Brown: Boston & Toronto, 1959.

Brown, G. Spencer. *Laws of Form*. Toronto: Bantam Books, 1973.

Carey, James W. McLuhan and Mumford: The Roots of Modern Media Analysis. *Journal of Communication* 31, 3 (1981).

Cooper, Thomas W. McLuhan and Innis: The Canadian Theme of Boundless Exploration. *Journal of Communication* 31, 3 (1981).

Curtis, James M. Marshall McLuhan and French Structuralism. *Boundary Two* 1, 1 (1972), 134-46.

Curtis, James M. McLuhan: The Aesthete as Historian. *Journal of Communication* 31, 3 (1981).

De Kerckhove, Derrick. *The Skin of Culture: Investigating the New Electronic Reality*. Toronto: Somerville House, 1995.

De Kerckhove, Derrick. Understanding McLuhan. *Canadian Forum*, May 1981.

Dobbs, Kildare. The McLuhan View of Pierre Trudeau. *Toronto Daily Star*, 19 November 1968.

Duffy, Dennis. *Marshall McLuhan*. Toronto: McClelland and Stewart, 1969.

Eco, Umberto. *Travels in Hyperreality*. San Diego: Harcourt Brace Jovanovich, 1986.

Elliott, George P. Marshall McLuhan: Double Agent. *The Public Interest* 4 (1966), 116-22. [On McLuhan as a "double agent" for civilization and barbarism.]

Emery, Merrelyn. The Social and Neurophysiological Effects of Television and Their Implications for Marketing Practice. University of New South Wales, doctoral dissertation, 1985.

Fekete, John. *The Critical Twilight: Explorations in the Ideology of Anglo-American Literary Theory from Eliot to McLuhan*. London: Routledge, 1977.

Fitzgerald, Judith. McLuhan, Not Atwood! *Books in Canada* 24, 9 (December 1995), 3-5.

Gordon, W. Terrence, ed., *C. K. Ogden and Linguistics*. London: Routledge/Thoemmes, 1994. 5 vols.

Gordon, W. Terrence. *Saussure for Beginners*. New York and London: Writers & Readers Publishing, 1996.

Gordon, W. Terrence. *McLuhan for Beginners*. New York and London: Writers & Readers Publishing, 1997.

Gronbeck, Bruce E. McLuhan as Rhetorical Theorist. *Journal of Communication* 31, 3 (1981).

Heer, Jeet. Marshall McLuhan and the Politics of Literary Reputation. *The Literary Review of Canada*, April 1996, 23.

Kirchhoff, H. J. Poetry and Drama: It All Adds Up. *The Globe and Mail*, 9 February 1989.

Kroker, Arthur. *Technology and the Canadian Mind: Innis, McLuhan, Grant*. Montreal: New World Perspectives, 1984.

Krugman, Herbert E. Electroencephalographic Aspects of Low Involvement: Implications for the McLuhan Hypothesis. *The Journal of Advertising Research* 11, 1 (February 1971).

Lanham, Richard A. *The Electronic Word: Democracy, Technology and the Arts*. Chicago: University of Chicago Press, 1993.

Legman, Gershon. Folklore of Industrial Man. *Neurotica* 8 (Spring 1951). [An abstract of the then forthcoming *Mechanical Bride*.]

Levinson, Paul. McLuhan and Rationality. *Journal of Communication* 31, 3 (1981).

Logan, Robert K. *The Alphabet Effect*. New York: Morrow, 1986.

McKerrow, Ronald B., ed. *The Works of Thomas Nashe* (London: Sidgwick and Jackson, 1910).

Mailer, Norman. Of a Small and Modest Malignancy, Wicked and Bristling with Dots. *Esquire*, November 1977, 125-48.

Miller, Jonathan. *McLuhan*. London: Fontana/Collins, 1971.

Nadel, Ira B. *Joyce and the Jews*. Iowa City: University of Iowa Press, 1989.

National Broadcasting Corporation. Sunday Showcase. McLuhan on McLuhanism. NBC [between 1959 and 1960].

Neill, S. D. *Clarifying McLuhan: An Assessment of Process and Product*. Westport, CT: Greenwood Press, 1993.

Nevitt, Barrington, and Maurice McLuhan, eds. *Who Was Marshall McLuhan?* Toronto: Stoddart, 1995.

O'Driscoll, Robert, ed. Marshall McLuhan/W. H. Auden, Duel or Duet. *Canadian Forum*, May 1981.

Olson, David R. McLuhan: Preface to Literacy. *Journal of Communication* 31, 3 (1981).

O'Neill, John. McLuhan's Loss of Innis-Sense. *Canadian Forum*, May 1981.

Ong, Walter J. McLuhan as Teacher: The Future Is a Thing of the Past. *Journal of Communication* 31, 3 (1981).

Patterson, Graeme. *History and Communications: Harold Innis, Marshall McLuhan, the Interpretation of History*. Toronto: University of Toronto Press, 1990.

Powe, B. W. *Outage. A Journey into Electric City*. Toronto: Random House, 1995.

Rosen, Jay. The Messages of "The Medium Is the Message." *Et Cetera: A Review of General Semantics* 47, 1 (1990), 45-51.

Russo, John Paul. *I. A. Richards: His Life and Work*. Baltimore: Johns Hopkins University Press, 1989.

Sanderson, George, and Frank Macdonald, eds., *Marshall McLuhan: The Man and His Message*. Golden, Colorado: Fulcrum, 1989.

Stamps, Judith. *Unthinking Modernity: Innis, McLuhan, and the Frankfurt School*. Montreal: McGill-Queen's University Press, 1995.

Theall, Donald F. *Understanding McLuhan: The Medium Is the Rear View Mirror*. Montreal: McGill-Queen's University Press, 1971.

Venable, William Henry. Flaws in McLuhan's Laws. *Technology and Culture* 17 (1976), 256-62.

Wachtel, Ed. McLuhan in the Classroom: The Method Is the Message. *Et Cetera: A Review of General Semantics* 35 (1978), 195-98.

Watson, Sheila. Wyndham Lewis and Expressionism. University of Toronto, doctoral dissertation, 1964 (directed by Marshall McLuhan).

Watson, Wilfred. McLuhan's Wordplay. *Canadian Forum*, May 1981.

Willmott, Glen. *McLuhan, or Modernism in Reverse*. Toronto: University of Toronto Press, 1996.

Wolfe, Tom. The Video McLuhan. Written and narrated by Tom Wolfe. Toronto: McLuhan Productions, 1996.

INDEX